Sport Psychology

Sport Psychology

Contemporary Themes

2nd Edition

David Lavallee
Professor and Head of the School of Sport, University of Stirling, UK

John Kremer
Reader in Applied Social Psychology, Queen's University Belfast, UK

Aidan Moran
Professor of Cognitive Psychology, University College, Dublin, Ireland

Mark Williams
Professor of Motor Behaviour, Liverpool John Moores University, UK

First edition 2004
Second edition 2012
Published by
PALGRAVE MACMILLAN

Palgrave Macmillan in the UK is an imprint of Macmillan Publishers Limited, registered in England, company number 785998, of Houndmills, Basingstoke, Hampshire RG21 6XS.

Palgrave Macmillan in the US is a division of St Martin's Press LLC, 175 Fifth Avenue, New York, NY 10010.

Palgrave Macmillan is the global academic imprint of the above companies and has companies and representatives throughout the world.

Palgrave® and Macmillan® are registered trademarks in the United States, the United Kingdom, Europe and other countries.

ISBN 978–0–230–23174–0

This book is printed on paper suitable for recycling and made from fully managed and sustained forest sources. Logging, pulping and manufacturing processes are expected to conform to the environmental regulations of the country of origin.

A catalogue record for this book is available from the British Library.

A catalog record for this book is available from the Library of Congress.

10 9 8 7 6 5 4 3 2 1
21 20 19 18 17 16 15 14 13 12

Printed in China

To our families, for all their support

Contents

List of Figures and Tables

Figures

Tables

Preface

Sport psychology continues to attract considerable attention, in both psychology and the sport sciences where an increasing number of students encounter the subject as part of their programme of study. Sport psychologists have also tended to concentrate their efforts on a limited number of themes, and it is the aim of this second edition of *Sport Psychology: Contemporary Themes* to draw together in one text the contemporary literature around these themes in an accessible and up-to-date manner. Each of the 11 chapters follows a consistent format with subheadings to assist the reader: Introduction, History and Development; Theories and Models; Methods and Measures; and Practical Issues and Interventions. Case Studies, Further Readings and Study Questions are also included with each chapter.

Principally the book is targeted towards psychology, sport science and sport studies students who are taking advanced undergraduate and graduate modules in sport and exercise psychology. The book has been written in a way that is suitable for recommendation either as a main text or as a supplementary reading, and can be used in association with projects and tutorial work dealing with applied topics such as sport and exercise. Beyond this primary audience, the text will be of interest to a wider readership across the sport sciences, social sciences and humanities, as it provides a concise overview of current research and debate on each topic. It is not expected that the book will necessarily be read from cover to cover. For this reason, each chapter has been written so that it may stand alone, but we have made every effort to ensure that the book as a whole is consistent and addresses all major theoretical perspectives and applied concerns in the field. For those who do read the entire book, it is hoped that they will have developed an appreciation of important advances, dialogues and debates in contemporary sport psychology, and the sort of issues that are raised when applying theories and methods in this field.

The book's introductory chapter describes the genesis and history of sport psychology, charting the development of professional structures, the ongoing tensions between pure and applied work and the distinctions between sport and exercise psychology as revealed over recent years. In Chapter 2 a brief history of the applied aspects of the field is provided, followed by a review of different models of practice within sport psychology. Practical issues associated with confidentiality, ethics, counselling, consultancy, competence and testing are also outlined.

Chapter 3 focuses on the topic of imagery, and examines how it is used by athletes, how effective it is in improving athletic performance and what theoretical and practical issues are raised by the study of imagery in action. In Chapter 4, Motivation, the antecedents, correlates and consequences of participation in physical activity are explored. The relationship between intrinsic and extrinsic factors is highlighted in this review of the contemporary literature, along with techniques for enhancing long-term motivation. Chapters 5 and 6, which focus on Concentration and Anxiety respectively, explore how each of these topics can be measured effectively, examine what research reveals about the relationship between these topics and sporting performance and reviews what strategies are most effective in competitive situations.

In Chapter 7, the essential attributes that distinguish experts from novices are reviewed and provide a principled basis for determining the types of practice that are most likely to be beneficial for enhancing the development of expertise. Chapter 8 reviews the extant literature on acquiring skill in sport and focuses on the emerging themes within this area. Chapter 9 considers the relationship between team dynamics and performance, in particular dealing with factors such as maturity, playing position, type of sport (interactive/co-active) and venue. Techniques for measuring team cohesion are also outlined, along with practical guidance on the development of appropriate team atmosphere. The athlete's career is the focus of Chapter 10, with a focus on the different transitions that they are presented with throughout their career. Finally, Chapter 11 deals with the relationship between physical activity and psychological well-being, and focuses on the particular circumstances in which exercise may or may not improve mental health.

1 Introduction

INTRODUCTION, HISTORY AND DEVELOPMENT

To begin at the beginning, what do we mean by the term 'sport and exercise psychology'? Sounds straightforward but the term can mean many different things to different people. To a coach or athlete it may mean the actions of a 'Mr Motivator' who is brought in to help the team or individual 'psych up' for an important game. To a sport scientist it may describe that branch of the discipline that focuses on the brain and central nervous system and their influence on sports' performance. To a health psychologist it may be defined as the psychology of physical activity in general. To a clinical psychologist it may mean particular therapeutic interventions associated with physical activity. To a sport and exercise psychologist the term may describe a subdiscipline of psychology that applies psychological theories and methods to an understanding of physical exercise in general and competitive sport in particular. Each working definition is appropriate for its own target audience. Some focus on practical application, some highlight professional concerns while others consider the subdiscipline in its entirety. At the very least the diversity of interpretations should immediately alert us to an appreciation of the disparate sources of influence and the broad church which is now known as sport and exercise psychology.

A related question which then springs to mind is who is it for? Again, the answer you find will depend entirely on whom you ask. According to some, its primary audience should be those who actually take part in sport. To others, sport and exercise psychology should feed the disciplines and professions associated with sport and exercise science or perhaps applied psychology. Others would argue it should not be 'for' anyone in particular but should aim to advance scientific knowledge as a noble end in itself. Once more, there is no simple answer to the question posed, but to restrict ownership to any single constituency is not likely to help the subdiscipline develop. Instead there may be a need to adopt a more flexible and pragmatic approach, arguing that work, whether applied or academic, can be tailored to meet the needs of a variety of potential users both inside and outside the world of sport.

As to where this enterprise first began, it is often said that there is nothing new under the sun and undoubtedly this sentiment can be applied to sport and

1

exercise psychology. From the earliest descriptions of sport we encounter discussion of associations between the physical and the psychological, whether in terms of competitive sport itself ('the psychology of sport') or physical activity and psychological functioning ('the psychology of exercise'). In this respect, this book represents a culmination of a long and noble history, stretching back over many centuries. In another respect, it is the case that the history of sport psychology as a distinct and defined entity or subdiscipline is regrettably brief, spanning only a few decades. In succeeding chapters the spotlight will fall on the more recent history of research but it is always worthwhile revisiting the past to see what lessons can be learnt and what pitfalls can be avoided in the future as this exciting field of scientific endeavour continues to unfold and evolve.

The story of sport psychology began in earnest with the writings of the ancient Greeks, a civilisation which vigorously extolled the virtues of physical prowess, celebrated male and female athleticism and had no hesitation in associating the ongoing health of the nation state with the personal health of its citizens. From Homer onwards, Greek literature is peppered with references not only to the significance of sport but also to the psychology of sport. Greek historians vividly illustrate how training methods of ancient Greek athletes owed as much to psychology as to any other science, and indeed how organised and professional that training became over time (see Gardiner, 1930; Sweet, 1987). Even as early as the fourth century BC, Aristotle was able to write, in his work *Nicomachean Ethics*: 'We argue more about the navigation of ships than about the training of athletes, because it has been less well organised as a science.' Six hundred years later, in his book *Gymnastic*, Philostratus challenges this 'traditional' science, railing against the rigidity of what had become the gold standard of athletic training, known as the 'tetrad' or four-day system, a system guided by psychological as well as physiological principles (day one, preparation; day two, concentration; day three, moderation; day four, relaxation). From these writings it is clear that trainers were acting as sport psychologists as well as physiologists, dieticians and life coaches and, what is more, nothing was left to chance in terms of 'total preparation' for the Greek games.

At the present time, as sport becomes increasingly professional in every sense of the word, it is worthwhile reflecting on the history of these games and in particular the reason for their ultimate demise. According to Harris (1964), the root of the problem lay with professionalism that spawned the 'stiltifying aim, "At all costs avoid losing"' (p. 190). The deleterious effects of extrinsic rewards on motivation will be explored in greater detail in Chapter 4, but for now it is interesting to reflect on Harris's analysis of how things started to go awry:

> It was in the heavyweight events of the Greek athletic programme that the professional's desire to avoid taking risks and to avoid defeat at all costs showed its deadly results. We have seen the great increase in the number of drawn matches in these events as time went on, and the situation reached

the height of absurdity in the ability of the boxer Melancomas to go on skipping round his opponent for two days without exchanging a blow.

The world of professional sport should take note – we skip history at our cost!

In a more positive vein, to the ancient Greek and also the later Roman civilisations, sport and physical prowess occupied a pivotal role. Their games were not only a source of community entertainment, but also represented a celebration and confirmation of the vitality of their cultures and burgeoning empires. Of all the ancient Mediterranean city states, the one that elevated the celebration of physical prowess to its ultimate pitch was the Spartan. In the seventh century BC, and following a brutal war with Messenia which left the Spartans victorious (but outnumbered ten to one by those they had vanquished), Sparta set about developing a city state which was as harsh as it was efficient. From the moment of birth, boys and girls faced tests of physical endurance literally designed to cull the weakest so as to ensure a fit and healthy population. For example, the state demanded that young children should be left exposed on an open hillside for several days to determine who was physically capable of survival. The Duke of Wellington is said to have remarked that the Battle of Waterloo was won on the playing fields of Eton. More than two thousand years earlier, Sparta had in place an education system which the Iron Duke doubtless would have envied. By the age of seven, every Spartan boy was sent to military and athletic boarding school to be taught toughness, discipline, endurance of severe pain and survival skills. At the age of twenty, Spartan men then moved to the army barracks where they continued to live out their 'Spartan' existence, away from unmanly distractions including their wives and families.

Leaving aside the brutal excesses of this particular regime, it is interesting that many of the early beliefs concerning sport and exercise psychology continue to stand the test of time so well. For example, today's exercise psychologists constantly extol the motto, *Mens sana in corpore sano* [A healthy mind in a healthy body]. The phrase actually derives from the Roman author Juvenal and his 10th Satire, written in the first century AD. This satire ponders a number of topics and especially the onset of old age, which was the focus of the original quotation, *Orandum est ut mens sana in corpore sano* [Your prayer must be that you may have a sound mind in a sound body].

While the lessons of history are powerful, we must not become slaves to history. As Chapter 11 hopes to demonstrate, contemporary research highlights that the relationship between health, physical exercise and psychological well-being is far from straightforward, but praying for a sound mind and body in old age is no bad thing.

From these early days of sport and exercise psychology, charting a history of work through to the beginning of the twentieth century is well nigh impossible. Instead, it is fair to say that sport in its many guises has always provided fertile opportunities for both participants and spectators to reflect on psychological

RESEARCH BOX

Unlike the other studies highlighted in the Research Boxes throughout this book, the study selected for this chapter is the oldest experimental paradigm in social psychology and the first to look at what we now perceive as a sport psychology phenomenon. The research by Norman Triplett (1898) attempted to explain the subject of pacemaking and competition. A keen amateur cyclist himself, Triplett initially gained access to the official records of the *Racing Board of the League of American Wheelmen* at the end of the 1887 season. These data included the times of three types of professional races; actual race times (against either other paced or timed competitors), paced races against time and unpaced races. Consistently Triplett found that times in the unpaced races were slower and this archival research provided the impetus for a follow-up study involving an experiment in which children wound a length of silk on to a reel, either working alongside a co-actor performing an identical task or alone. Those winding line while sitting alongside another who was also reeling recorded significantly faster times than those reeling alone. This led Triplett to conclude that the presence of others in competition served as a stimulus to arouse the competitive instinct and this, in turn, led to the release of energy stores ('dynamogism') that could not be released when competing alone.

This pioneering study paved the way for later social psychological research on social facilitation. What is more, and predating the extensive literature on competitive anxiety in sport (see Chapter 6), Triplett acknowledged that individuals, whether professional cyclists or children, often responded very differently to the rigours of competition. Some rose to the challenge and performed better ('the arousal of their competitive instincts and the idea of a faster movement') while others were overstimulated by the prospect and actually performed worse in the presence of others ('going to pieces'). Trying to untangle the complex relationship between arousal and performance remains a problem which sport psychologists wrestle with over one hundred years later, and a recent replication of Triplett's work (Strube, 2005) employing contemporary analyses critiques the original conclusions. However, Davis, Huss and Becker (2009) acknowledge that regardless of the results, Triplett made a perceptive observation of a real-world phenomenon.

issues. However, despite this long-standing preoccupation with the psychology of sport, it was only in the 1960s that people began to describe themselves as sport psychologists. Before that time there were a number of significant pioneers who legitimately could be labelled as sport psychologists but whose endeavours were rarely supported by the normal dedicated infrastructures associated with academia and scientific discovery. For example, from the 1890s, various psychology departments included staff with an interest in the psychology of sport but these individuals rarely fostered structures which withstood the test of time. The one exception to this rule relates to work on motor skills and motor development (see Chapter 7) which has long featured as a significant component of most psychology degrees and from the 1890s onwards has often based analyses of motor skills on sport-related activities (Wiggins, 1984).

Across the discipline as a whole, psychological research with a sporting dimension began to appear around the turn of the nineteenth century. The most famous early example of a systematic research programme was Norman Triplett's archival and experimental work on 'dynamogenic factors' (1898) in the United States.

Other writers in this period were offering less systematic and empirical appraisals of sporting behaviour than Triplett's. For example, at roughly the same time as LeBon and Freud were describing the psychodynamics of crowd behaviour in general, articles dealing with spectator psychology were beginning to appear. These included papers by Patrick (1903) on the psychology of American football and Howard (1912) on the cathartic effects associated with watching sport. However, calls for further spectator research (Howard, 1912) went unheeded, at least until the 1950s (Hastorf and Cantril, 1954).

Leaving these early contributions to one side, almost without exception sport psychologists identify the mid-1920s as the watershed in the development of sport psychology and this is due almost entirely to the work of one man, Dr Coleman Roberts Griffith. Griffith's interest in sport psychology began informally during his time as a PhD student at the University of Illinois but continued in earnest following his appointment to the teaching staff at the same university under the watchful eye of Professor George Huff, head of the department of physical education and director of physical welfare for men. An educational psychologist by training, Griffith taught within both the psychology department and the department of physical welfare. In 1923 he introduced a course titled 'Psychology and athletics', and two years later, in 1925 was instrumental, along with Huff, in establishing and subsequently directing the Athletic Research Laboratory. His research interests were wide-ranging and included work dealing with motor skills, motor learning, perception, personality and individual differences, but always with a primary emphasis on practical application. This orientation is reflected in the content of Griffith's two celebrated texts, The Psychology of Coaching (1926) and Psychology and Athletics (1928), especially the former which outlines guiding principles for successful coaching.

It would be reassuring to describe Griffith's work as marking the launching pad for sport psychology, particularly as the University of Illinois continues to be regarded as a centre of excellence in this field; a great many eminent sport psychologists having completed postgraduate study there, including Schmidt, Martens, Gould, Roberts and Duda. Sadly the truth is more depressing. In 1932, through economic necessity, the Athletic Association was forced to withdraw funding from the laboratory. Griffith subsequently resigned his post and the Athletic Research Laboratory closed. Disillusioned, Griffith then turned his considerable energies back towards his original area of interest, educational psychology, publishing four texts in this area while making only occasional forays back into the world of sport psychology (Green, 2009). This included a chapter on psychology and athletics in his *Introduction to Applied Psychology*, published in 1941, and his work as a consultant sport psychologist with the Chicago Cubs baseball team in 1938.

In North America, the 1940s and 1950s are now characterised as a period of stagnation, with the exception of motor learning research that flourished in the post-war years through the work of John Lawther (Pennsylvania State University), Franklin Henry (University of California) and Arthur Slater-Hammel (Indiana University) (see Chapter 9). According to Salmela (1981), in Eastern Europe this period was also relatively quiet, although as early as 1926 Coleman Griffith had visited two newly established sport psychology laboratories in Berlin, run under the auspices of Sippel and Schulte, while other European universities, including Leipzig, had at least some sport psychology on their curricula. In addition, there is evidence, dating back to the early part of the twentieth century, of Soviet sport scientists looking at the psychological benefits of physical activity.

Although historical evidence is incomplete, it would appear that these initiatives survived in some form through World War II, but it was the period between 1945 and 1957 that marked the true emergence of sport psychology in the former Soviet Union, under the guidance, in particular, of Peter Roudik and A. C. Puni (Hanin and Martens, 1978). Some of this work ran in parallel with the Soviet space programme, for example yoga techniques were used to train cosmonauts and these same self-regulation skills were later employed with Eastern bloc athletes during preparation for the 1976 Olympics (Garfield and Bennett, 1984).

By the time of the 1956 Olympics in Melbourne, sport psychologists were accompanying Eastern European teams, although at that time, it is more likely that they were passive observers rather than active consultants. From the 1970s onwards Olympic competitors from East Germany and the Soviet Union were using sport psychologists as a matter of routine (Roberts and Kiiecik, 1989) and Eastern bloc countries in general had come to accept the benefits to be gained from psychological interventions, for example in relation to self-regulation, mental practice and imagery. Even as early as the 1968 Mexico Olympics, Dr Miroslav Vanek had put in place a large-scale psychological and psychomotor screening and interview programme involving the 124 Czechoslovakian athletes at the games, a programme which subsequently met with mixed success (Vanek and Cratty, 1970). Indeed it was Vanek who became the driving force behind the establishment of the International Society of Sport Psychology (ISSP) that met for the first time in Rome in 1965.

The long-standing relationship between sport and 'psychology' in Eastern European countries revealed itself from behind the Iron Curtain, albeit bizarrely, during the course of the World Chess Championships in the Philippines in 1978 (Patmore, 1986, pp. 231–2), at the same time maybe debunking some of the aura which had come to surround Soviet sport psychology. In an early round of the championship, when playing a fellow Soviet player Boris Spassky, Korchnoi had become paranoid over Spassky gaining access to his biorhythm chart. He went on to accuse Spassky of deliberately directing 'psi' waves against him during games, waves that he then employed a team of Swiss parapsychologists to intercept. In the grand final, his opponent Anatoly Karpov was accompanied by the renowned Soviet parapsychologist Dr Vladimir Zukhar, who sat pointedly in the front row of the stalls 'psyching out' Korchnoi. In desperation, Korchnoi retaliated by hiring two Americans to help him meditate and 'psych out' Zukhar. The story then moves from the sublime to the ridiculous as the American meditators were exposed as alleged criminals who were actually out on bail for attempted murder! Their banishment from the hall was followed swiftly by Korchnoi's resignation in game 32.

Returning closer to home, without doubt the mid-1960s marked the genesis of organised sport psychology in the Western world (although it was not until 1988 that a sport psychologist actually accompanied the US Olympic team in an official capacity). The late 1960s witnessed a rapid growth of the subject within physical education departments in the United States, reflected in terms of both the size of teaching classes and the volume of published research. On some occasions the subject evolved with support from previous links with psychology and motor learning, but more often the impetus for growth came from sport scientists whose background was primarily in physical education but whose interests lay in the field of psychology. It was at this time that the broad themes which still concern many sport psychologists to this day were defined, namely motivation, competitive anxiety, individual differences, motor skills, motor learning, aggression, psychological skills training/interventions, social cognition and team dynamics.

The stage was now set for the subdiscipline to develop the structures normally associated with any academic discipline. As mentioned above, the First International Congress of Sport Psychology was organised in Rome by the newly formed ISSP in 1965, and in the same year preliminary meetings were held which by 1968 had led to the development of the European Federation of Sport Psychology (FEPSAC) as well as the official recognition of the North American Society for the Psychology of Sport and Physical Activity (NASPSPA), as distinct from its parent body, the American Association of Health, Physical Education and Recreation (AAHPER). Over time the NASPSPA has gone on to form three divisions, namely motor learning/control, motor development and sport psychology. Throughout the early stages of growth, the parent discipline of psychology maintained a discreet distance. It was not until 1986, a further twenty years later, that the American Psychological Association (APA) finally took official cognisance of sport psychology with the formation of a new section, Division 47, concerned with exercise and sport psychology.

The 1970s saw a consolidation of the subject, with the launching of the *International Journal of Sport Psychology* in 1970 and the *Journal of Sport Psychology* in 1979. Since then numerous other journals have also come to provide outlets for sport psychology research, including *Journal of Applied Sport Psychology, Journal of Sport & Exercise Psychology, Journal of Sport Behavior, Journal of Sport Sciences, Psychology of Sport and Exercise, Journal of Clinical Sport Psychology* and *The Sport Psychologist*.

Developments in other Western countries have followed the lead taken by the United States. For example, the Canadian Society for Psychomotor Learning and Sport Psychology (CSPLSP) became independent from its parent body, the Canadian Association for Health, Physical Education and Recreation, in 1977. Elsewhere documented evidence is less easy to find, although it is interesting to note that the Brazilian soccer team that won the World Cup in Sweden in 1958 brought a sport psychologist to help foster team spirit and cohesiveness through post-hypnotic suggestion – much to the amusement of the assembled soccer pundits (Patmore, 1986, p. 229).

In comparison with North America, the road to recognition and respectability in the United Kingdom has been considerably longer. The players involved have also been far fewer in number but the basic storyline is remarkably similar. The story begins with the formation of the British Association of Sports Sciences (BASS), which held its inaugural meeting in 1984. This general forum for sports scientists soon divided into different sections, namely biomechanics, physiology and psychology, together with an open section, and changed its title to the British Association of Sport and Exercise Sciences (BASES) during the 1990s. In 1988 BASS (later BASES) took the first step towards implementing a register of sport psychologists, a final draft of which became available in 1992. Only those members who are accredited by BASES are eligible to be recommended as professional sport psychologists by the Sports Council, or to be employed by sports' governing bodies under the auspices of the National Coaching Foundation. To gain accreditation, BASES members must normally have either a primary degree in sport science together with a postgraduate degree (by course or research) in sport psychology or a primary degree in psychology plus a postgraduate degree (by course or research) in sport science. In addition applicants must have gained at least three years of supervised experience in the field.

The British Psychological Society (BPS), the representative body for psychology and psychologists in the United Kingdom, has mirrored the caution of the APA in taking its time to become professionally acquainted with sport psychology. In 1992 the Scientific Affairs Committee of the BPS agreed in principle to the establishment of a sport and exercise psychology interest group in the BPS, a decision endorsed by the formation of a separate BPS Sport and Exercise Psychology Section at the annual conference in April 1993. A Division of Sport and Exercise Psychology was subsequently formed in 2004 in response to the increase in academic status and public recognition of sport and exercise psychology and ensures that members who practise and offer services within sport and exercise psychology are qualified and trained according to the Charter, Statutes and Rules of the BPS.

These professional developments may at first glance appear relatively trivial but they will be vital in determining the direction in which sport and exercise psychology heads over coming years, the priorities which will occupy centre stage and the degree of regulation over those who operate as sport and exercise psychologists. For example, recent years have witnessed ever clearer lines of demarcation being drawn between sport psychology and exercise psychology, the former focusing on 'healthy' athletes and their engagement with competitive sport, the latter dealing with the psychological effects of physical exercise in both clinical and non-clinical settings. Many exercise psychologists would see themselves as being more closely aligned with health and clinical psychology than sport psychology, and it will be interesting to see how relationships continue to develop over time, and whether existing structures will be able to accommodate their different priorities. Furthermore, the necessary tensions between pure and applied sport psychology will continue to provide a dynamic which may be common to applied psychology in general but which nevertheless requires constant attention. Certainly, the history of sport and exercise psychology has been intriguing and its future looks no less interesting.

THEORIES AND MODELS

The contemporary theories and models associated with particular sport and exercise domains will be elaborated in subsequent chapters. At a more general level, the early years of sport psychology tended to be characterised by the adoption and subsequent application of theories, which had originated elsewhere in psychology. The pioneers of sport psychology in the 1960s and 1970s, normally coming from an academic background in physical education and the sport sciences, drew heavily on existing psychological theories and models which appeared to them to be relevant to the topic in question. By way of example, Hull's 'drive theory of motivation' and Yerkes and Dodson's law (known as the 'inverted-U hypothesis') became the mainstays for explaining competitive anxiety in sport, Atkinson's 'achievement motivation theory' dominated discussion of participation motivation and Zajonc's 'drive theory' was used to interpret the effects of social influence on sport performance (see Martens, 1975).

Very often these adopted theories had been developed to consider personal and social phenomena in specific contexts including educational, occupational and clinical settings, and the justification for generalising to other contexts, including sport and exercise, was not always obvious. One prime example is Locke and Latham's work on goal setting, which was developed to consider motivation at work but was then commonly applied to the world of sport, despite the obvious dissimilarities between the two contexts (Burton, 1992).

While traditional perspectives served as valuable catalysts for research activity, it was not long before sport-specific theories and models began to emerge, as the difficulties associated with the wholesale 'borrowing' of theories became increasingly apparent. As a consequence, from the end of the 1970s an increasing number of theories emerged which were dedicated to understanding sport and exercise behaviour (Feltz, 1987). This trend has continued over time, with ever more sophisticated models being developed to understand complex phenomena, including, for example, competitive anxiety, attentional styles and concentration, participation motivation and team dynamics, as the following chapters will demonstrate.

During the 1970s and 1980s the tendency had been to cherry-pick from the rich crop of available psychological theories. One consequence of this process of selectivity may have been a somewhat blinkered view of the discipline as a whole and its accumulated knowledge, and a tendency to develop sophisticated levels of expertise but only within narrowly defined domains. This tendency may have limited the potential for cross-fertilisation of ideas from other psychological subdisciplines as well as increasing the response time to new developments outside sport psychology. However, it is noteworthy how far more broadminded contemporary sport and exercise psychology has become. One illustration of this trend is revealed by considering the respective contents lists of the two editions of one of the most popular sport psychology texts, *Psychological Dynamics of Sport* (1986) by Diane Gill (significantly renamed *Psychological Dynamics of Sport and Exercise* for the third edition, published in 2008). The third edition is able to draw on a far more diverse literature and generally gives an impression of a greater breadth of coverage across the discipline that was not always true of earlier sport psychology texts. It is also noteworthy that exercise psychology warrants special attention, again in contrast with most earlier works.

1986	2008
Introduction to Sport Psychology	The Scope of Sport and Exercise
History and Current Status of Sport	Psychology
Psychology	History of Sport and Exercise
Personality	Psychology
Individual Differences in Cognitive	Approaches to Understanding and
Styles and Abilities	Using Sport and Exercise Psychology
Competitiveness and Competitive	Personality
Anxiety	Attention and Cognitive Styles
Gender Roles and Sport Behaviour	Self Perceptions
Attitudes and Sport Behaviour	Behavioral Approaches
Arousal and Sport Performance	Motivational Orientations:
Behaviour Modification in Sport	Achievement and Competitiveness
Cognitive Approaches: Intrinsic	Cognitive Approaches to
Motivation in Sport	Motivation
Social Influence and Motor	Participation Motivation
Performance	Emotion Models and Research
Aggression in Sport	Emotional Control and Stress
Individual and Group Performance	Management
in Sport	Social Influence
Interpersonal Relationships in Sport	Aggression and Character
Groups	Development
	Group Dynamics and Interpersonal
	Relationships
	Gender, Diversity, and Cultural
	Competence

Diane Gill's text represents one of a burgeoning collection of dedicated sport and exercise psychology texts. For those who are unfamiliar with the sport psychology literature, it is important to recognise that you will encounter two literatures. Gill's text falls into the category of texts prepared for students and researchers of sport psychology. The second category includes the interesting array of books written with the more lucrative applied sport psychology market in mind. Typically, there is little overlap between the two lists; a vivid demon- stration of the two faces of sport psychology. One strives for academic credibility while the other is driven by market forces; one aspires to scientific principles in terms of theories and methods, the other operates according to a more pragmatic maxim – if it works, use it. While many applied sport psychologists do have a sound grounding in the disciplines of either sport science or psychology, there are those whose background owes more to the 'university of life', and as a con- sequence the issue of registration/certification of sport psychologists continues to be significant across the globe. The respected applied social psychologist Kurt

Lewin once remarked, 'No research without action, no action without research' (Ash, 1992). This is a sentiment that should continue to inform these discussions. To gain a full appreciation of the depth of this divide, it is suggested that you spend some time looking through examples of books from both camps, so that you will at least be able to categorise appropriately in the future.

Often there has been friction between those who are reluctant to practise or offer professional advice before developing a sounder research base, and those who are attracted by the practical results that they are able to achieve through immediate action or intervention. This is not a new problem for sport psychology. Coleman Griffith combined his research with consultancy work, for example with the Chicago Cubs baseball team and the University of Illinois football team. Apparently, the former intervention was far from successful. Philip P. Wrigley, the Cubs' president, hired Griffith to find the psychological profile of a champion baseball player but, with hindsight, predictably he failed, much to the chagrin of Wrigley and the considerable amusement of the players themselves who apparently found the whole exercise highly amusing (Furlong, 1976).

The more recent seeds of this conflict between theory and practice can be traced back to the mid-1960s, a watershed being the publication of *Problem Athletes and How to Handle Them* by Bruce Ogilvie, a clinical psychologist from San Jose State University, and Thomas Tutko (1966). Despite the criticism and hostility that the book provoked from within academic sport psychology, their work quickly gained popularity within the world of sport. The Athletic Motivation Inventory (AMI) became established as the most commonly used inventory for measuring personality dimensions which were believed to be associated with sporting success, and Bruce Ogilvie duly took on the somewhat controversial mantle of the father of applied sport psychology.

It should not be thought that the conflict between the pure and the applied is confined to sport psychology alone. Similar debates have raged and continue to smoulder within almost all professional or applied areas of psychology, and are almost certainly a necessary tension within any applied science. However, this particular conflict did lead to a rift within sport psychology in the United States in the mid-1980s, when a group of applied sport psychologists broke from NASPSPA to form the Association for the Advancement of Applied Sport Psychology (AAASP; later renamed the Association for Applied Sport Psychology, AASP), an organisation specifically for sport psychologists working in applied settings. This association now includes three sections, dealing with health psychology, social psychology and intervention/performance enhancement, and since 1987 has been supported by its own journal, *The Sport Psychologist*.

METHODS AND MEASURES

Psychology as a whole, probably more than any other scientific discipline, is characterised by methodological pluralism. This involves the use of a wide range of techniques for understanding, predicting and interpreting human behaviour and experience. Empirical methods (based on systematic observations) can include the quantitative ('how much/many?' or quantity) and the qualitative ('why?' or quality), and furthermore can involve numerous techniques including experimental (e.g., laboratory, field or natural) and non-experimental methods (e.g., archival research, case studies, surveys, discourse analysis, content analysis, grounded analysis, interviews, focus groups). Some of these techniques endeavour to provide general laws as to how people in general will behave (nomothetic approaches), some focus on determining individual responses and interpretations in particular contexts (idiographic approaches), while others consider not behaviour but the meanings associated with our actions (hermeneutic approaches). It is important to recognise that none of these methods or perspectives is intrinsically better than any other; it is the judicious use of a combination of appropriate methodologies that generally characterises good research. Increasingly psychology has become more open-minded about the utility of a range of alternative methods, with less and less reliance on simple and sovereign techniques, most especially controlled laboratory experiments.

The approach to research methods currently being adopted by sport and exercise psychologists follows that which has characterised psychology as a whole over the last fifty years. In the same way that only selected psychological theories and models were adopted by sport psychology, so the tendency in the past has been to rely on a restricted range of methods and afford primacy to traditional, quantitative procedures. On a positive note, the adherence to traditional methods, and a preoccupation with measurement, has ensured a degree of rigour and the establishment of a set of high standards that maintain the quality of published work. On the downside, historically there has been intolerance for alternative approaches and this may have stifled innovation and creativity. The primary reliance on experimental procedures may also have encouraged reductionism, where a small number of variables are teased out for analysis but in the process the bigger picture is lost from view. Multivariate statistical procedures, including structural equation modelling (SEM), have the potential to redress the balance by allowing consideration of many interacting influences and factors, wary that clarity rather than confusion (or statistical sophistication versus multivariate obfuscation) does not become the undesired consequence of this trend (Gill, 1997).

Historically, the preoccupation with measurement is revealed both in the huge number of published studies that have attempted to quantify the personality of the athlete (Ruffer, 1976) and, more generally, in the number of sport-specific psychological measures actually available for use. *The Directory of Psychological Tests in the Sport and Exercise Sciences* (Ostrow, 1996) lists several hundred, dealing with topics including motivation, attitudes, confidence, anxiety, body image and aggression. Whatever test is used, it is important to determine a number of issues prior to testing.

First, is there a sound rationale for using this particular test with this particular population? Early research tended not to dwell too long on this question and instead a number of standard psychological tests, including most notably Cattell's 16PF (16 Personality Factors), Eysenck's EPI (Eysenck Personality Inventory), the MMPI (Minnesota Multiphasic Personality Inventory) and more recently the MBTI (Myers–Briggs Type Indicator), have been used. Hindsight has revealed these endeavours to be generally disappointing, and recent years have seen a steady decline in this particular type of work. There is a strong consensus that, for whatever research purpose tests are used, it is not appropriate to rely on psychological tests to select participants, and this was one of a number of concerns associated with the use of the AMI as developed by Tutko, Ogilvie and colleagues in the early 1970s. The scale purported to measure traits associated with high athletic achievement (i.e., drive, aggression, determination, responsibility, leadership, self-confidence, emotional control, mental toughness, coachability, conscience development and trust) was made available to coaches who returned completed questionnaires to the authors for scoring and interpretation. How this information was then used was not controlled and, despite the poor reported association between scores and actual performance (e.g., Davis, 1991), there was concern that players' profiles could have been influential in subsequent selection decisions.

One reason for the general decline in use of psychological tests could relate to the second issue, which should precede testing – what is the theoretical perspective that underpins the research? The majority of early research using tests, although seemingly atheoretical, implicitly subscribed to a trait approach to personality, which posits that we are defined psychologically by our scores on a finite number of personality traits and that these traits and their significance remain relatively constant over time. This perception of the static nature of personality has been challenged within psychology and replaced by more dynamic, interactionist and idiographic approaches including, for example, personal construct theory. By 1980, a challenge was beginning to emerge in sport psychology itself. Morgan (1980) summarised this debate in his article 'Sport Personology: The Credulous-Skeptical Argument in Perspective'. While debate did continue for many years, gradually the pendulum has swung towards the sceptical who duly acknowledge some individual psychological differences between athletes and non-athletes, between athletes in different sports and in different positions on teams and between winners and losers, but question the capacity of psychological tests to capture these differences or changes over time and context.

The third issue that must be addressed prior to testing is – what test to use? Initially it is important to determine the psychometric robustness of the instrument. Normally this is defined in terms of reliability (are test scores consistent over time and context?), validity (does the test measure what it purports to measure?) and standardisation (is the test able to be administered uniformly, and are established norm tables of scores available for different populations?).

Next it is important to decide whether to use a general or sport-specific test. Increasingly the trend has been away from general measures and towards tailored instruments designed to measure specific, sport-related characteristics. There are a considerable number of sport-specific scales available (see Ostrow, 1996), but issues associated with the reliability and validity of these scales have yet to be resolved. Certainly the use of more focused measures of specific, sport-related skills would appear to be a move in the right direction but caution must be exercised.

The final issue concerns who to test and when? Traits are typically regarded as stable characteristics and yet there is increasing evidence to suggest that an involvement in sport and exercise may have an effect on psychological functioning and health (see Chapter 11), and hence personality characteristics may change over time. It is interesting that one of the most common tests used by sport psychologists was originally designed to consider mood states, which fluctuate over time and place, but has often been employed to define the psychological profile of a successful athlete. The Profile of Mood States (POMS) (see LeUnes and Burger, 1998) measures six mood states, with a positive 'iceberg profile' associated with elevated scores on vigour and depressed scores on tension, depression, anger, fatigue and confusion. The accumulated evidence from over twenty years of research is not surprisingly mixed (Beedie *et al.*, 2000). For example, there is little to show that POMS can discriminate between successful and unsuccessful athletes, although athletes in general do appear to have a more positive profile than non-athletes and there is some support for the suggestion that an iceberg profile is associated with above-average performance for an individual athlete and especially in open-skills (i.e., open to the environment) sports. However, the use of a measure of mood state to determine a personality profile has to remain questionable, and exemplifies the difficulties associated with attempting to measure psychological determinants of physical performance.

In recent years there is evidence to indicate that the exclusive reliance on quantitative methods may be less strong, and at long last appeals for a more eclectic approach to data gathering (e.g., Martens, 1979a) may be having an effect. We are still some way from embracing alternative and mixed methodologies, however, and qualitative techniques have yet to make significant inroads into the literature. Nevertheless, with an ever-growing appreciation of these legitimate alternatives and the launch of the journal *Qualitative Research in Sport and Exercise* in 2009, the future looks interesting.

PRACTICAL ISSUES AND INTERVENTIONS

By its subject matter, sport and exercise psychology cannot avoid being defined as an applied, practical science and consequently, as the previous discussions reveal, there has been an almost constant dialogue about how best to translate theory into practice and at what price. In 1979, Rainer Martens of the University of Illinois and more recently the publishing company Human Kinetics published a paper in the *Journal of Sport Psychology* titled 'From Smocks to Jocks' (1979b). It was a clarion call for sport psychology to become more relevant to those engaged with sport, along with an acknowledgement that traditional approaches may not have helped to make the subdiscipline more accessible to sportspeople or progress our common stock of knowledge. The earlier discussion of the schism between pure and applied sport psychology reveals how difficult the process of translating theory into practice can be but there are encouraging signs that the gap may be narrowing, with a growing acceptance of the legitimacy of alternative roles for different types of sport psychologist, along with appropriate structures for ensuring the regulation of core professional competencies.

Recognition of these different roles for sport psychologists is not new. In 1984, Robert Singer, then president of the ISSP, outlined three roles which he felt could be played by sport psychologists. The first role was as basic researchers, second as educational sport psychologists (who use their background in physical education to teach and educate athletes and coaches) and third as clinical sport psychologists (who draw on their training to counsel or help sportspeople). To this list we could easily add a fourth, occupational psychology, as those with training in industrial and organisational psychology also have much to offer to the world of sport, especially professional sport.

Each division of psychology brings with it certain skills and experience of different types of intervention. Educational psychologists are adept at identifying behavioural and emotional problems among young people in particular, and developing programmes to resolve these difficulties. It is also significant that all educational psychologists must have spent time teaching prior to their professional training, and can bring these skills to coach and athlete education programmes. Clinical psychologists normally provide therapy in either individual or group settings, very often using cognitive-behavioural techniques to effect change. It has long been recognised that their counselling skills can easily transfer into sports settings (Lavallee and Cockerill, 2002) where intervention programmes can make the difference between average and above-average performance for athletes. The role of clinical psychology is acknowledged in the accreditation procedures that operate in North America and the United Kingdom. A unique category has been established for clinical sport psychologists, with qualification depending not only on the common criteria for all sport psychologists but also an appropriate qualification in clinical psychology. Increasingly clinical psychologists have recognised the positive relationship between exercise and mental health and a considerable number now operate as exercise psychologists, either advocating exercise as a form of therapy for clinical disorders or identifying the role of exercise in relation to other psychological and physical problems (e.g., body shape and weight control).

Undoubtedly we are living in very interesting and exciting times for sport and exercise psychology. There is now a more confident sense of identity and purpose that at any time in the past, and there is a growing corpus of knowledge which genuinely has sport and exercise as its primary focus. The number of significant 'players' in the world of sport and exercise psychology also continues to grow apace and this is starting to bring a fresh vitality to a field that could stand accused of having remained too exclusive for too long. With this influx of new blood have come new ideas and new perspectives, and the parent discipline of psychology is no longer far removed from proceedings. At the same time, as sport and exercise psychology has matured, so there has been less desire unceremoniously to borrow packaged ideas from psychology in order to endeavour to provide simple answers to complex phenomena. Now the mood is shifting and, in common with other psychological subdisciplines, sport psychology is becoming more critical and self-reflective in recognition of the complexity of the world with which it deals. Sport psychologists are recognising the need to develop programmes of research and theoretical frameworks that can cope with a higher level of sophistication, and are using a richer variety of research methods than at any time in the past. Against this backdrop, this book aims to consider those areas of work that have generated the most significant interest over recent years.

STUDY QUESTIONS

1. Discuss the early history of sport and exercise psychology.
2. Provide some examples of how different countries around the world have contributed to the professional development of sport psychology as a field.
3. With regard to the application of theories and models within the field, contrast the development in the 1960s and 70s with that of the present day.
4. List and explain some of the issues that are important to understand prior to using psychological tests in sport contexts.
5. List and describe the different roles of sport and exercise psychologists.

FURTHER READING

Gill, D. L. (1997) 'Sport and Exercise Psychology', in J. Massengale and R. Swanson (eds), *History of Exercise and Sport Science* (Champaign, IL: Human Kinetics), 293–320.

Lavallee, D., Jones, M. V. and Williams, J. M. (2008) *Key Studies in Sport and Exercise Psychology* (Columbus, OH: McGraw-Hill).

Lidor, R., Morris, T., Bardaxoglou, N. and Becker, B. (eds) (2001) *The World Sport Psychology Sourcebook* (Morgantown, WV: Fitness Information Technology).

Tenenbaum, G. and Eklund, R. C. (eds) (2007) *Handbook of Sport Psychology*, 3rd edn (New York: John Wiley & Sons).

Williams, J. M. (ed.) (2010) *Applied Sport Psychology*, 6th edn (Columbus, OH: McGraw-Hill).

2 Practising Sport Psychology

INTRODUCTION, HISTORY AND DEVELOPMENT

Interest in the practice of sport psychology is not new. Ever since Norman Triplett's (1898) ground-breaking publication on social influence on cycling performance, mainstream psychologists have taken an interest in sport. For example, as outlined in Chapter 1, Coleman Griffith was an educational psychologist who worked as a consultant for collegiate and professional sports teams in America in the 1930s. Several prominent psychologists around the world also applied their theories and research in sport contexts following Griffith, but this work was conducted sporadically and did not begin to have a noteworthy impact until the 1960s. It was the foundation of the International Society of Sport Psychology (ISSP) in 1965, as well as the official incorporation of both the North American Society for the Psychology of Sport and Physical Activity (NASPSPA) and European Federation of Sport Psychology (FEPSAC) in 1968, which provided the platform for applied sport psychology to influence the parent discipline.

Following the development of these professional organisations, several sport psychology journals also began publications that welcomed articles of an applied nature, including the *International Journal of Sport Psychology* in 1970, *Journal of Sport Behavior* in 1978 and *Journal of Sport Psychology* in 1979 (renamed the *Journal of Sport & Exercise Psychology* in 1987). Sport psychology classes started to be taught through physical education programmes (cf. Cratty, 1968; Lawther, 1972; Morgan, 1970) and scholarly conferences organised specifically for applied sport psychology were initiated. Consequently, applied sport psychologists were able to begin to make significant contributions in the dissemination of information in the quickly developing field.

It was during the 1980s and 90s that applied issues began to move towards the forefront of sport psychology (Gill, 1997). The knowledge base in the area was beginning to develop more of a focus on professional practice, and this led sport psychologists to further develop their own particular subdiscipline. This was accomplished with the start of specialised training programmes in applied sport psychology (Andersen, Raalte and Brewer, 2001), as well as the establishment of professional organisations devoted more to applied issues, including the Association for the Advancement of Applied Sport Psychology (AAASP) in 1986 (later renamed the Association for Applied Sport Psychology; AASP). It was also during this time that publications focusing predominantly on applied work were launched, including *The Sport Psychologist* journal in 1987, the *Journal of Applied Sport Psychology* in 1989 and several key textbooks (e.g., Murphy, 1995a; Van Raalte and Brewer, 1996). As a result of these developments, applied sport psychology came to be considered part of the larger subdiscipline, which focuses on identifying and understanding psychological theories and techniques that can be applied in sport settings to enhance the performance and personal growth of athletes as well as in exercise contexts with physical activity participants (Williams, 1998).

Contemporary sport psychology is incredibly diverse, and this is reflected in the continued expansion of professional organisations and journals (e.g., *Journal of Clinical Sport Psychology*), each with their own orientation. There has been a dramatic increase in the number of practising sport psychologists world-wide in recent years as well as the establishment of more than 100 postgraduate degree programmes in applied sport psychology in over 50 countries (Burke *et al.*, 2008). Slowly at first and then ever more rapidly, the field has gained a position of influence in the world of sport. The role of the sport psychologist is now widely valued and accepted by athletes, coaches, administrators and others involved in sport and exercise (Morris and Terry, in press). Practising sport psychologists are also beginning to recognise the needs of others outside these areas, particularly groups that can benefit from different kinds of psychological support to help them to compete at the highest levels (e.g., business professionals, military personnel, medical professionals). Such advances have led the field to become more accessible within, and accountable to, mainstream psychology.

THEORIES AND MODELS

The theories and models employed in the practice of sport psychology are numerous, and have developed in a somewhat piecemeal fashion as the field has progressed. As a result of there not being a clear focus or agreement as to an appropriate knowledge base in this area during the 1960s and 70s, research topics were widespread and targeted towards many different populations. These ranged from theory development in the area of personality to experimental testing of motor learning and performance theories (Gill, 1997). Sport psychology later started to develop a cognitive focus, with attention being directed to athletes' thoughts and images, and this led to an increase in field research and the ensuing development of specific models of practice in the 1980s and 90s. Applied sport psychologists today rely on these models to work across the broad areas of performance enhancement, psychological testing and counselling interventions (Moran, 2010). While the theories and models proposed to explain the performance enhancement process will be described in this section of the chapter, those associated with psychological testing and counselling interventions are outlined in the Methods and Measures section.

The development of psychological skills to enhance performance has historically served as the foundation for sport psychology practice (Andersen, Van Raalte and Brewer, 2001), and is based for the most part on the classic cognitive and behavioural therapy literature. The models in which they are used, however, are not ones based on cognitive-behavioural therapy but rather models in which the sport psychologist is viewed primarily as an educator who teaches psychological skills to athletes, teams and coaches. As will be outlined later in this chapter, the reason for this may be due to the places that sport psychology is often practised, such as during training and at competitions (Andersen, 2000).

Boutcher and Rotella (1987) initially developed a four-stage model of practice, which includes an analysis of the skills needed in a particular sport from a number of disciplinary perspectives, assessment to determine the individuals strengths and weaknesses, conceptualisation through a goal-setting strategy and development of general skills which can then be applied to performance situations. Martens (1987) also proposed a model that focused on educating athletes about psychological skills and how they influence performance, training athletes on the appropriate psychological skills and having the athletes practise these skills until they can be integrated into competition. Vealey (1988) later outlined a three-stage model, and this approach focused on the attainment of psychological skills, development of these skills in training and competition and the development of coping strategies to manage situations where the skills prove inadequate or lose their effectiveness.

Drawing on each of these models, Morris and Thomas (1995) formulated a seven-phase model of performance enhancement. The first stage in this model is orientation, where the purpose is clarified, objectives identified and commitment determined in relation to performance enhancement. Once the task is identified, the psychologist conducts an analysis of the particular sport, and this is followed by an individual/team assessment that is completed to develop a profile of strengths and weaknesses. This profile is often based on the results of selected psychological tests and inventories, interviews, observations of the athlete performing (via videos, diaries and/ or performance statistics) and talking to coaches and significant others of the athlete. The fourth stage in this model of performance enhancement is conceptualisation through a profile analysis, where the psychologist needs to consider the personal characteristics of the athlete in conjunction with their sport. The fifth stage is psychological skills training, and the main techniques currently being used to enhance performance include imagery, goal setting, cognitive techniques, attention/concentration and confidence

(Andersen, 2000). These skills are first practised in the sixth stage before they are implemented within competition. The seventh and final stage in this process is evaluation, and this considers evidence of performance enhancement, improved personal adjustment and adherence to the psychological skills training programme.

While each of these models of practice has been widely recognised and employed by applied sport psychologists, they are all somewhat limited, in that they implicitly suggest that performance enhancement through psychological skills training is accomplished through a single, sequential set of procedures. It should also be noted that the models that have been proposed to explain psychological skills training within sport may not adequately represent the performance enhancement process in some sports and not be appropriate for all levels of participation (Morris and Thomas, 2003).

METHODS AND MEASURES

Sport psychology is practised in a variety of settings and with a range of different populations. Thus, as one might expect, the roles, responsibilities and goals of the sport psychologist vary across these settings and populations (Andersen, Raalte and Brewer, 2001). As highlighted in the previous section, the development of psychological skills to enhance performance is a principal area for applied sport psychologists. For others, however, the delivery of psychological care and the development of athletes above and beyond efforts for enhancing performance is the focus. In this model, the development of life skills, coping resources, and care and attention to counselling issues often seen in the sporting domain is the focus (e.g., Jones, Lavallee and Tod, in press). Indeed, the emerging literature in the field suggests that counselling approaches are becoming more prevalent than ever before.

The use of counselling interventions by practising sport psychologists involves working therapeutically with athletes with a variety of problems, difficulties and life issues and crises. These issues can be remedial in nature and require intervention by a counsellor (Andersen, 2005). Practitioners who employ counselling interventions also need to be prepared to help athletes who experience emotional problems associated with such things as depression, drug and alcohol dependence, pathology/personality disorders, anger and aggression control, eating disorders and interpersonal conflict (Gardner and Moore, 2006; Lesyk, 1998). Although this list is far from comprehensive, it does provide an idea of which client issues have the potential to become problematic, especially for those without specialist training in counselling, psychotherapy or clinical psychology.

In terms of effective counselling practice, the sport psychology community has continually highlighted the importance of establishing and

RESEARCH BOX

During a speech in 2004, the President of the International Olympic Committee, Jacques Rogge, stated, 'The world of sport is not separate from the rest of the world. Sport breaks down barriers, promotes self-esteem, and can teach life skills and healthy behavior.' This quote demonstrates a widely held belief that sport has the ability to teach people positive life skills. Despite this belief, studies investigating the development of life skills through of sport are limited. Jones, Lavallee and Tod (in press) recently designed a study to evaluate a life-skills intervention (entitled ELITE; Enhancement of Leadership Intercommunication Teamwork and Excellence) among a sample of British university athletes. The researchers, who hypothesised the participants would increase their perceived use of communication and organisation skills, employed a multiple baseline design where the same treatment was sequentially applied to the separate and independent target behaviours. Results revealed that the intervention led to improvements in the targeted life skills, and the participants valued both communication and organisation skills.

What implications can be drawn from such a study? Sport psychologists can help coaches create a climate where athletes are encouraged to demonstrate life skills such as communication and organisation in day-to-day training and competition activities. For example, athletes could be encouraged to talk to one another during scheduled breaks to find a solution to a performance problem. Similarly, responsibility for warm ups could be delegated to athletes so they have to both organise the other athletes and communicate the warm up procedures. Other life skills (e.g., respect, initiative, discipline, mastery motivation) could be encouraged so that athletes are required to demonstrate these skills in order to be part of the team or training group.

developing a trusting relationship with the athlete. Anderson and Clarke (2002) agree with this to the extent that establishing such a relationship is critical, but highlight that this does not constitute counselling per se. Rather it constitutes the use of counselling skills, and their key point is that the purpose of developing the relationship can vary when you are working as an educational sport psychologist and when you are counselling. While some authors in the past have attested to the difficulty and inappropriateness of performing both roles simultaneously (e.g., Nideffer, 1981; Suinn, 1980), Anderson and Clarke (2002) argue that it is not possible for the two roles to intertwine and that one psychologist cannot adopt both roles with one athlete. Understanding the limitations and restrictions of one's role as a sport psychologist, and therefore knowing when to refer clients appropriately, is of particular importance.

As discussed in the Methods and Measures section in Chapter 1, historically psychological testing has been given a considerable amount of attention by sport psychologists. While there has been a continual decline in the actual use of tests over the years, there has been something of a renewal in interest in this area among practising sport psychologists recently. This can be attributed partly to the publication of the *Directory of Psychological Tests in the Sport and Exercise Sciences* (Ostrow, 1996), which summarises information on more than 300 psychological scales, questionnaires and inventories, as well as *Assessment in Sport Psychology* (Nideffer and Sagal, 2001) and *Advances in Sport and Exercise Psychology Measurement* (Duda, 1998). However, despite continued recognition of the importance of psychometrically sound measures within the field, no consensus has emerged with regards to the benefits of this type of quantitative approach (Andersen, 2005).

Due to the fact that some of the classic questionnaires used in psychology are unhelpful and inappropriate when used in a sports context (Wolfson, 2002), and laypeople also often place undue credence on results obtained from psychological tests, practising sport psychologists more than ever need to understand psychological testing and use tests sensibly and sensitively. Where psychological tests are employed, it is imperative that the measures are appropriate, their psychometric properties (especially in relation to validity and reliability) are known, they are used for the purpose and population for which they were designed and they are not used to inform selection procedures (Kremer, 2002). Interpretation of the results and subsequent feedback must also be appropriate and written consent should be obtained for the release of data. However, those interested in applying interventions, whether they come from a sport or psychology background, need to understand the research process to evaluate the effectiveness of their intervention(s) (Andersen, 2005).

Psychologists in many subdisciplines are trained as both practitioners and researchers, with psychological assessment providing the bridge between the research and practice. As researchers they are sensitive to applied issues, while as practitioners they are sensitive to research. As suggested in Nideffer and Sagal (2001), however, training in sport psychology has historically tended to be either research- or applied-focused (as has the focus of professional associations in the field). An applied psychologist wanting to help an athlete cope with stress needs sufficient (research-based) knowledge about coping behaviours and sources of stress as well as relevant data about the particular sport he or she is dealing with. Likewise, a sport psychologist researching coping processes needs to understand and help to impart the practical applications of the knowledge generated.

PRACTICAL ISSUES AND INTERVENTIONS

Across the globe, the demand for sport psychology continues to grow. As teams and individuals constantly strive to find the winning edge, it becomes increasingly likely that a sport psychologist will be involved to help find that edge. However, these powerful market forces can be dangerous, especially when demand has the potential to outstrip supply. In these circumstances caution must be exercised in both promoting and developing the subject, with appropriate regulation of those who describe themselves as sport psychologists and due regard to the subject's limitations and weaknesses alongside its strengths.

To many athletes and coaches, professional sport psychologists may already be viewed with a degree of suspicion because of previous negative experiences or stereotypical images (Brewer et al., 1998; Patmore, 1986). For example, consultants may have failed to deliver the goods which they over-optimistically promised, or have packaged their services in such a way that clients had been turned off. Certainly, sport psychologists have often been regarded with suspicion by the media, at worst characterised as Svengali-like puppet-masters who attempt to pull the athlete's strings with one goal in mind, performance enhancement, at whatever price and with little regard to the sensitivities or wishes of the individual or team concerned.

The day-to-day reality of applied sport psychology is somewhat different, however. Increasingly practising sport psychologists will work hand in glove with athletes, coaches, administrators, dieticians, physiotherapists, physiologists, biomechanists and other technical specialists as part of a team devising packages and programmes which the coach and/or athlete feels will be of benefit to him or her. There is little cloak and dagger or behind-the-scenes manoeuvring, and it is to be hoped that the continuance of this open and 'upfront' approach will effectively sweep away any remaining worries and apprehensions that may linger on. Undoubtedly, lurking on the fringes of the subject there will be those whose professional conduct leaves a great deal to be desired but as sport becomes increasingly systematic, and athletes become increasingly sophisticated and knowledgeable, then the scope for sharp or poor practice becomes that much more limited. Equally, there are professional codes of conduct that govern conduct and these cannot and should not be ignored. In the United States, the American Psychological Association's (APA's) revised ethical standards (2002) have been adopted by the two organisations that oversee the work of sport psychologists, the NASPSPA and the AASP. The APA ethical guidelines make reference to the following nine principles likely to be relevant to the work of an applied sport psychologist:

- Responsibility
- Competence
- Moral and legal standards

- Public statements
- Confidentiality
- Welfare of the consumer
- Professional relationships
- Assessment techniques
- Research with human subjects

The legal status of these guidelines is not absolutely clear, although, as Sachs previously suggested (1993), the APA states that the principles should apply to psychologists, students of psychology and to others who do work of a psychological nature under the supervision of a 'psychologist', and are 'intended' for the guidance of non-members of the association who are engaged in psychological research or practice.

Within the United Kingdom, the British Association of Sport and Exercise Sciences (BASES) took the lead in 1988 by developing a code of conduct for sport psychologists (Biddle, Bull, and Seheult, 1992). This code was introduced in conjunction with the development of a register of accredited sport psychologists and contains 29 statements under five headings: competence, consent and confidentiality, psychological testing, research ethics and personal conduct. In parallel, the British Psychological Society (BPS) also maintains a code of conduct that applies to all its members and the practice of psychology generally across the United Kingdom. The latest version of the BPS Code of Ethics and Conduct (British Psychological Society, 2009) includes a code of conduct for UK psychologists under four headings: general competence, obtaining consent, confidentiality and personal conduct.

While applied sport psychologists engage in the same range of activities and services as professionals in other areas of applied psychology, there are numerous practical issues and interventions unique to practitioners in the field (Moran, 2012). But are the services of sport psychologists so unique that they require unique standards for ethical conduct? In 1987, Zeigler put forward the case that a code of ethics designed specifically for applied sport psychologists was a vital aspect of the overall professionalisation of the field. Since then, others have suggested that the application of psychology ethical codes often leads to conflicts among practitioners, involving boundaries of practice and title usages (e.g., Whelan, Meyers, and Elkin, 1996). It is fair to say that the creation of unique codes of ethics within the field has given sport psychologists some autonomy. It is still the case, however, that sport psychology professionals frequently (and unfortunately) find themselves in ethical dilemmas for which no clear rules are present to guide their behaviours.

This is accentuated in survey conducted by the AAASP with their members on ethical beliefs and behaviours specific to the practise of applied sport psychology (Petitpas *et al.*, 1993; later replicated by Etzel, Watson and Zizzi., 2003). Respondents in the study by Petitpas *et al.* were provided with 47 ethical situations and asked to report their own behaviour and ethical belief about the choices. They also were asked to provide a description of difficult ethical situations they encountered in an open-ended format. Although there were few differences found as a function of the respondents' gender, professional status and academic discipline, eight of the ethical situations provided were found to be difficult ethical judgements, while 24 situations were identified as controversial behaviours (defined as those found to be significantly diverse based on the opinions of respondents). The ethical situations identified by the respondents in this survey as controversial are listed in Table 2.1. Interestingly, further analyses of the open-ended responses revealed that most questionable practices cited by the participants corresponded to violations of APA ethical standards, and such results led the researchers to recommend that all applied sport psychologists be routinely trained in ethical considerations. Etzel *et al.* (2004) later found that there appeared to be less controversy a decade later as a result of the adoption of the AASP ethics code, the ease of access to the code on the Internet, increased exposure to ethical issues in the AASP Newsletter, regular ethics workshops at the AASP annual conference and more frequent inclusion of ethics into education and training.

Just as in all other applied disciplines, sport psychologists are responsible for abiding by codes of practice and modes of professional training. As a rule of thumb, practising sport psychologists should be guided by the code of ethical conduct of the professional bodies to which they belong. It is unlikely that the guidance offered in different codes of conduct will be in direct conflict, but where there are differences then the more rigorous code should be adhered to (Kremer, 2002).

While general ethical principles have been routinely cited in the sport psychology literature over the last few decades, it is only recently that the specific concerns unique to the role of practising sport psychologists are being addressed. For example, there are potential dilemmas about confidentiality and especially when the intervention has been established not by the athlete but by his or her coach. This dilemma is described succinctly by Sachs (1993) as follows:

The duty of psychologists is towards their client first and foremost. However, in some sports settings the 'client' is not necessarily an individual. It is one thing to be in private practice and have Jane Athlete present with a problem about performance anxiety or an eating disorder, for example. It is another thing to be employed by the New York Knickerbockers and have Joe Athlete come in and discuss some basketball related or other concerns. In the latter case, under what conditions does the practitioner have an obligation to share some/all of the information with the coach/management of the team?

(p. 923)

Table 2.1   *Behaviours identified as controversial in the AAASP Ethics Survey*

1. Conflict with confidentiality
   - reporting recruiting violations to appropriate officials*
   - reporting an athlete's gambling activity*
   - reporting an athlete who uses cocaine
   - reporting an athlete who uses steroids
   - reporting abusive coaching practices
   - reporting an athlete who committed burglary
   - reporting an athlete who acknowledged committing rape in the past*

2. Conflict between personal values and professional ethics
   - consulting with athletes in a sport that you find morally objectionable (e.g., boxing)*
   - working with an athlete who uses performance-enhancing drugs*
   - refusing to continue working with a client after you discover that he or she is involved in illegal activity*
   - working with an athlete whose sexual or religious practices you oppose

3. Conflict with dual relationships
   - accepting goods or services in exchange for sport psychology consultation
   - serving concurrently as coach and sport psychologist for a team
   - serving concurrently as college instructor and psychologist for a student-athlete
   - being sexually attracted to a client
   - becoming sexually involved with a client after discontinuing a professional relationship
   - entering into a business relationship with a client

4. Conflict with self-presentation or advertising
   - publicly claiming to be sport psychologist
   - advertising sport psychology services
   - including client testimonials in advertising
   - using institutional affiliation to recruit private clients

Source: (Petitpas *et al.*, 1993)
Note: * indicates that the behaviour was also identified as a difficult judgement by the respondents. 'Socialising with clients' and 'Allowing out-of-town clients to reside in your home while services are being provided' were also behaviours identified as difficult judgements.

As in other contractual or consultative contexts, there also is an ethical dilemma of disclosure if hired by an organisation to work with individuals who are members of the team. The resolution of such dilemmas is not easy but should be discussed and clarified, possibly in writing, as to how this and other issues will be handled before the formal consultation begins and not with hindsight (Kremer, 2002).

Under what conditions does the practitioner have an obligation to share some/all of the information with the coach/management of the team? This dilemma will be familiar to many applied sport psychologists and, if not handled carefully, has the potential to destroy the personal relationship with the athlete. In reality, the solution is not unproblematic but can be managed. In relation to confidentiality, psychologists should convey personally identifiable information obtained in the course of professional work to others, only with the express permission of those who would be identified (British Psychological Society, 2009). To prevent any problems arising, there must be a recognition of the issue from the outset, followed by an open and honest discussion of the nature of the relationship, including the bounds of confidentiality, with all those involved.

Confidentiality issues can also arise as a function of the entrepreneurial nature of sport psychology and the high public visibility of some clients. For example, there is a marketing dilemma in the use of client endorsements and the public identification of those clients. It is recommended to err on the side of caution and respect for privacy; even if the clients waive their rights to confidentiality, such decisions may reflect the power differentials between sport psychologists and their clients rather than a freely accepted agreement (Kremer, 2002).

Because sport psychology service delivery is sometimes provided in public, practitioners can find themselves in situations in which conversations with athletes at practice or competitions move into somewhat sensitive issues (Andersen, 2005). Some refer athletes to someone less public in these instances, but unfortunately there are difficulties in referral. The loose boundaries that accompany the profession can also sometimes create circumstances when the psychologist travels with the team and stays in the same hotel, and such identification can pose a threat to service delivery. Moreover, if a psychologist becomes overly associated with a coach (e.g., is always near the coach at games), then the athletes may be less likely to feel comfortable confiding sensitive material that they would not share with the coach. Indeed, the questions of where and when one engages in sport psychology services depends on the practitioner's model of service delivery and boundaries, and is perhaps more different and varied than most other applied psychological services (Andersen, 2000). Like some community and organisational psychologists, the boundaries of practice for sport psychologists are different from those of the majority of applied psychologists that often do not extend beyond the consulting room and constitute a standard psychologist–client, 50-minute in-office session (Gardner and Moore, 2006). Practising sport psychologists therefore need to ensure that they set out the rules of engagement from the very beginning with informed consent, and with all parties knowing who the client is and what confidentiality means.

A further concern relates to the sport psychologist's competency, whether in terms of knowledge of other sport sciences, psychology or the sport itself. In relation to psychological expertise, there is a serious danger that a sport psychologist may find him or herself unwittingly crossing the boundaries of professional competency. An applied psychologist must always recognise where the boundaries of professional competence lie. To overstep that mark may not only be harmful to the client, but it may also make the practitioner vulnerable to a challenge of professional negligence.

The question of who is qualified to practise sport psychology has been an issue of debate ever since the field started to provide professional services to athletes and coaches. Numerous position statements have been written on this topic, including the United States Olympic Committee guidelines (1983) which was perhaps the first systematic attempt to provide credentials for sport psychologists. The issue of certification, which is the attempt to codify a common standard of preparation and practice (Zaichkowsky and Perna, 1996), has also started to be addressed by the field. The primary objective of certification is to provide a standard by which the public may accept as reliable evidence that an individual has attained specified professional competencies and a means by which certified and non-certified individuals can be compared. Credentials, on the other hand, are related to a title or claim of competence, and include statutory designations (such as those enacted by a legislative body) which are protected by law and non-statutory (such as recognition by professional organisations) designations which are not protected by law. Certification is not based on laws per se, but is generally established by academic or professional organisations (Zaichkowsky and Perna, 1996). The AASP developed a rigorous certification programme in 1989 (see Table 2.2) and has encouraged individual countries to follow its lead.

While the list of client issues which have the potential to become problematic are considerable, some also have the potential to lead to the necessity for interventions beyond the scope of those without specialist training in other areas of psychology (e.g., clinical). Heyman and Andersen (1998) suggest that three issues should typically trigger a referral process through to professionals with more specialist skills:

- The length of time a problem has existed, its severity and relationship with other life events
- Unusual emotional reactions (e.g., depression and anger)
- Lack of efficacy of traditional performance enhancement interventions

Without doubt there will be occasions where 'the listening ear' of the sport psychologist will have a positive therapeutic value. However, in terms of an active intervention strategy, it may be best to consider the sport psychologist as but one small part of a wider referral process. As a result, it is the duty of practising

Table 2.2   *Criteria for standard AAASP certification*

Certification by AAASP requires current membership in the Association at the time of application and having attended at least two AAASP conferences, while continuing certification is contingent upon maintaining active membership status in AAASP. Completion of a doctoral degree from an institution of higher education is required. Sport psychology is a unique discipline which requires specialised education and training in both the exercise and sport sciences and in psychology. The (12) necessary but sufficient areas of training and knowledge are outlined below. Certification by AAASP does require documentation of necessary levels of training and expertise in each area as specified on the application form. Applicants must also have completed 400 hours of supervised experience with a qualified person (i.e., one who has an appropriate background in applied sport psychology) during which the individual receives training in the use of sport psychology principles and techniques (e.g., supervised practica in applied sport psychology, in which the focus of the assessments and interventions are participants in physical activity, exercise or sport).

1. Knowledge of professional ethics and standards. This requirement can be met by taking one course on these topics or by taking several courses in which these topics comprise parts of the courses or by completing other comparable experiences.
2. Knowledge of the sport psychology subdisciplines of intervention/ performance enhancement, health/exercise psychology and social psychology as evidenced by three courses or two courses and one independent study in sport psychology (two of these courses must be taken at the graduate level).
3. Knowledge of the biomechanical and/or physiological bases of sport (e.g., kinesiology, biomechanics, exercise physiology).
4. Knowledge of the historical, philosophical, social or motor behaviour bases of sport (e.g., motor learning/control, motor development, issues in sport/physical education, sociology of sport history and philosophy of sport/physical education).
5. Knowledge of psychopathology and its assessment (e.g., abnormal psychology, psychopathology).
6. Training designed to foster basic skills in counselling (e.g., graduate coursework on basic intervention techniques in counselling, supervised practica in counselling, clinical or industrial/organisational psychology).
7. Knowledge of skills and techniques within sport or exercise (e.g., skills and techniques courses, clinics, formal coaching experiences or organised participation in sport or exercise).
8. Knowledge and skills in research design, statistics and psychological assessment. At least two of the following four criteria must be met through educational experiences that focus on general psychological principles (rather than sport-specific ones).

(continued)

Table 2.2   Continued

9. Knowledge of the biological bases of behaviour (e.g., biomechanics/
    kinesiology, comparative psychology, exercise physiology, neuropsychology,
    physiological psychology, psychopharmacology, sensation).
10. Knowledge of the cognitive-affective bases of behaviour (e.g., cognition,
    emotion, learning, memory, motivation, motor development, motor learning/
    control, perception, thinking).
11. Knowledge of the social bases of behaviour (e.g., cultural/ethnic and group
    processes, gender roles in sport, organisation and system theory, social
    psychology, sociology of sport).
12. Knowledge of individual behaviour (e.g., developmental psychology, exercise
    behaviour, health psychology, individual differences, personality theory).

sport psychologists to develop an established network of contacts which can be
accessed when the need arises.

The sport psychologist–client relationship has the potential to be problematic, especially where the client comes to depend overly on the person providing him or her with specialist or expert knowledge. Kremer (2002) suggests
that the fundamental goal of the intervention must be reflected on with the
following concern in mind: should the sport psychologist be endeavouring to
foster a long-term dependency, or should she or he aim to empower the athlete to a position where the psychologist naturally and intentionally becomes
superfluous? A powerful argument can be advanced that the latter represents a
healthier long-term aspiration. These matters aside, where a relationship begins
to become 'dysfunctional', then the onus falls on the psychologist to take whatever steps are necessary to put matters right.

A final practical concern is one which an increasing number of sport psychologists are likely to encounter – the use of banned drugs or other illegal means
to enhance performance. It is very unlikely that a sport psychologist should
continue to work with an athlete once this type of behaviour is suspected, not
only because it may implicate the practitioner in an unlawful conspiracy but
also because such actions fly directly in the face of what the sport psychologist
is trying to achieve – the fostering of self-control and self-determination, and
an attempt to maximise the athlete's 'true' potential.

With all these caveats in mind, working as a practising sport psychologist is
potentially very rewarding (professionally if not always financially), as it is possible to see theory in action, to identify which procedures work in practice and
which do not stand the acid test of application. For any professional this type of
work can be challenging, while for the discipline it is a challenge which is not
only useful, it is crucial as the ultimate reality check.

CASE STUDY

Tim is a 19-year-old cyclist who has built a good national reputation as an amateur time trialist. He is seen as having the potential to turn professional in the near future should he choose. He is completely dedicated to his sport; Tim left school at 16 with no educational qualifications and since that time has not worked, choosing instead to train and compete on a full-time basis. Over the last two years Tim has seen a sport psychologist on a regular basis, usually once a month (although because of his financial circumstances the sport psychologist hasn't charged for all the sessions). The sport psychologist working with Tim has always found him very receptive to advice and has helped him with a number of areas including stress management, imagery and concentration. Recently the sport psychologist has become concerned with changes in Tim's behaviour. His performance on the track had plateaued and he has become more anxious about his prospects of turning professional. He also appears to be more agitated in the sport psychologist's presence and is unwilling to engage in eye contact, whereas previously he had been very open and honest. While it is unclear as to why this is happening, the sport psychologist has become concerned that Tim may have turned to performance-enhancing drugs and certainly this is a topic of conversation with which he is most reluctant to engage.

1. With reference to the Theories and Models section in the chapter, how would you interpret what is happening in this case study?
2. With reference to Methods and Measures, what techniques would you employ to help to understand and quantify the issues?
3. With reference to Practical Issues and Interventions, how would you deal with this situation?

STUDY QUESTIONS

1. Discuss how applied sport psychology has developed into the field that it is today, and provide examples of what makes sport psychology unique from other disciplines of psychology.
2. Describe the three areas that applied sport psychologists work in – namely, performance enhancement, psychological testing and counselling interventions.

3. With reference to competency among sport psychologists, contrast certification with credentials.
4. Describe at least three issues that should trigger a referral process through to professionals with more specialist skills.
5. With reference to confidentiality, consider some of the special concerns faced by practising sport psychologists.

FURTHER READING

Andersen, M. B. (ed.) (2005) *Sport Psychology in Practice* (Champaign, IL: Human Kinetics).

Etzel, E. F. (2009) *Counseling and Psychological Services for College Student-Athletes* (Morgantown, WV: Fitness Information Technology).

Gardner, F. and Moore, Z. (2006) *Clinical Sport Psychology* (Champaign, IL: Human Kinetics).

Hemmings, B. and Holder, T. (2009) *Applied Sport Psychology: A Case-Based Approach* (Oxford: Wiley-Blackwell).

Williams, J. M. (ed.) (2010) *Applied Sport Psychology: Personal Growth to Peak Performance*, 6th edn (Mountain View, CA: Mayfield).

3 Imagery

INTRODUCTION, HISTORY AND DEVELOPMENT

One of the remarkable features of the human mind is its capacity to 'represent' (literally 're-present') experiences of stimuli, which are not physically present at that time. For example, if you close your eyes, you should be able to imagine the sight and sound of a jet plane leaving a trail of white smoke across a blue expanse of sky. Interestingly, this ability to use one's imagination is crucial to success in sport. To explain, anecdotal and descriptive evidence suggests that mental imagery (also known as 'visualisation'), or the ability to represent in the mind information that is not currently being perceived by the sense organs, is widely used by sport performers in an effort to enhance athletic performance. For example, consider the remarkable kinaesthetic imagery skills of Michael Phelps, the 14-times Olympic gold medallist in swimming, when he revealed that 'swimmers like to say that they can 'feel' the water ... I didn't have to fight the water. Instead, I could feel how I moved in it. How to be balanced. What might make me go faster or slower' (Phelp, 2008, p 10). In a similar vein, Mike Atherton, the former cricket batsman and England captain, highlighted the value of mental rehearsal for test matches. In particular, he said: 'I do the visualisation stuff – what's going to come, who's going to bowl, how they are going to bowl, what tactics they will use ... so that nothing can come as a surprise' (quoted in Selvey, 1998, p. 2). Complementing such anecdotal evidence, surveys indicate that elite athletes (e.g., US Olympic performers; Ungerleider and Golding, 1991) use mental imagery extensively while training for competition. Indeed, Taylor, Gould and Rolo (2008) found that imagery usage was one of the strongest predictors of athletic success for a sample of US Olympians. Interestingly, athletes are not the only ones who use 'visualisation' training in sport. Therefore, sport psychologists use imagery interventions in an effort to improve such mental skills in athletes as self-confidence, motivation, physical rehabilitation and the ability to control competitive anxiety (see Murphy, Nordin and Cumming, 2008; Weinberg, 2008). For this reason, imagery has been acclaimed as a 'central pillar of applied sport psychology' (Perry and Morris, 1995, p. 339). Furthermore, outside the domain of sport, mental imagery has been shown to enhance skilled performance in laparoscopic surgery (Arora *et al.*, 2010). But from a psychological perspective, what exactly is 'mental imagery'? How can it be measured? Does it actually improve skill learning and performance in sport? If so, why? The purpose of this chapter is to answer these and other questions concerning the role of mental imagery in sport.

After you have read this sentence, close your eyes for 10 seconds, imagine standing in front of where you live and try to count the number of windows that you can 'see' in your 'mind's eye'. In answering this question, most people use their imagination to create a mental picture of their house and then 'zoom in' on the windows while counting them.

This simple example illustrates the fact that imagery involves perception without sensation. To explain, you were not actually looking at the front of your house when you counted the windows that were 'visible'. But your mind was able to simulate the experience of 'seeing' the house and its windows because you relied on your memory of what your house looks like. Therefore, unlike perception (where information flows from the senses into your mind), forming a mental image of something is a bit like running perception backwards in your head (because you have to go from memory to sensation; see Behrmann, 2000).

In general, psychologists use the term mental imagery to describe the process by which we represent things (e.g., people, places, experiences, situations) in our minds in the absence of appropriate sensory input (Moran, 2002). For example, if you close your eyes, you should be able to imagine what your bedroom would look like if it were painted a different colour (a visual image). You could also use imagery to create other experiences such as the 'sound' of your friend's voice (an auditory image) or the tight muscular feeling that occurs when you cycle up a steep hill (a kinaesthetic image). This exercise reveals two important characteristics of the construct of imagery. First, it is a multisensory experience – people can form images in each of the different sensory modalities. Thus you can 'see' your favourite actor, 'hear' a familiar song, 'smell' the aroma of freshly brewed coffee, 'feel' the weight of a heavy book and 'taste' a glass of cold water. In addition, the more senses that we use when forming an image, the more 'vivid' it seems.

Of the various senses contributing to imagery experiences in daily life, vision is by far the most popular. To illustrate, Kosslyn *et al.* (1990) showed that about two-thirds of people's mental images in everyday life are visual in nature. Interestingly, neuroscientific studies from the 1990s corroborate the primacy of visual imagery over that generated from other sensory modalities. For example, Kosslyn Ganis and Thompson (2001) concluded that visual images rely on about two-thirds of the same brain areas that are used in visual perception, especially areas 17 ('V1') and 18 ('V2') in the occipital lobe (at the back of our heads). Visual images are not the only ones that are important to athletes, however. Recall from the beginning of this chapter that Michael Phelps attached great significance to *kinaesthetic* or 'feeling-oriented' imagery – that which involves the 'sensation of how it feels to perform an action, including the force and effort involved in movement and balance, and spatial location' (Callow and Waters, 2005, pp. 444–5). Over the past decade, a great deal of research has accumulated on 'motor imagery' or the ability to imagine actions without engaging in the actual physical movements involved (Guillot and Collet, 2010; Moran, 2009b). For example, Moran and MacIntyre (1998) investigated kinaesthetic imagery or the mental simulation of sensations associated with bodily movements using a sample of elite canoe-slalom athletes participating in World Cup competitions. These athletes were firstly interviewed about their understanding and use of 'feeling-oriented' imagery in their sport. Then, they were assessed using a battery of measures that included specially devised Likert rating scales and the Movement Imagery Questionnaire – Revised (Hall and Martin, 1997). Next, in an effort to validate their subjective reports on their imagery experiences, the canoe-slalom competitors were timed as they engaged in a 'mental travel' procedure, during which they had to visualise a recent race in their imagination and execute it as if they were paddling physically. The time taken to complete these mental races was then compared with actual race times. As expected, there was a significant positive correlation between mental and physical race times ($r = .078$, $p < 0.05$). Finally, a content analysis of the canoeists' accounts of their kinaesthetic imagery experiences revealed the importance that these performers attached to sensations of 'force' and 'effort'.

Apart from representing different types of content, how else do imagery dimensions differ from each other? According to Richardson (1995), they vary in two ways – 'vividness' (i.e., the number of senses involved in generating the experience) and 'controllability' (i.e., the ease with which mental images can be manipulated by the person who creates them). To illustrate the latter, try to imagine your bedroom door. Can you 'see' whether the handle is on the left or right side of this door? If you can perform this task easily and accurately, then your imagery control skills are probably quite good.

In summary, mental imagery has three important characteristics. First, it is a multisensory construct that enables us to bring to mind experiences of absent objects, events and/or experiences. To illustrate, Hardy, Jones, and Gould (1996) defined it as 'a symbolic sensory experience that may occur in any sensory mode' (p. 28). Second, mental images vary in their vividness and controllability – two dimensions which facilitate their measurement (see the Methods and Measures section of this chapter). Finally, imagery is believed to be functionally equivalent to perception, in the sense that it shares a great deal of the same brain 'machinery' (or neural substrates) and psychological mechanisms with that cognitive activity (Moran, 2009b).

In sport psychology, 'mental practice' (MP) refers to a systematic form of covert rehearsal, in which people imagine themselves performing an action without engaging in the actual physical movements involved (Driskell, Copper and Moran, 1994). It is also known as 'motor imagery' (Decety and Michel, 1989) or 'symbolic rehearsal', 'covert rehearsal' or 'imaginary practice' (Kremer *et al.*, in press). Also, because it relies on simulated movements (Decety and Ingvar, 1990), MP is sometimes known as 'visuo-motor behavioural rehearsal' (VMBR) (Suinn, 1994).

Psychological interest in MP is as old as psychology itself. For example, James (1890) observed that, through imaginative anticipation, people can learn to skate in the summer and swim in winter. During the 1890s, various expressions of the 'ideo-motor principle' were proposed. This principle suggested that people's thoughts have muscular concomitants. Indeed, in 1899 Beaunis (cited in Washburn, 1916) proposed that 'it is well known that the idea of a movement suffices to produce the movement or make it tend to be produced' (p. 138). Similarly, Carpenter (1894) claimed that low-level neural impulses are produced during imagined movement and that these impulse are identical in nature (but lower in amplitude) to those emitted in actual movement. Clearly, these references show that MP was well established as a research topic in the early years of experimental psychology. Unfortunately, as a result of the behaviourist manifesto (Watson, 1913), which attacked 'mentalistic' constructs such as imagery, interest in mental practice declined around the 1920s. This lull in imagery research continued until the advent of the cognitive revolution in psychology in the 1960s. It was during this decade that the first comprehensive reviews of mental practice began to emerge (Richardson, 1967a, 1967b). Since then, partly as a result of the development of objective measures of imagery processes (e.g., the mental rotation task devised by Shepard and Metzler, 1971), the topic of visualisation has attracted a resurgence of interest from theoretical and applied sport psychologists. Interestingly, research on mental practice is not confined solely to the world of sport. For example, the potential utility of mental rehearsal has been recognised in the domain of stroke rehabilitation (Braun *et al.*, 2006), music performance (Meister *et al.*, 2004) and medical surgery (Arora *et al.*, 2010).

Unfortunately, despite its venerable status, research on mental practice has encountered many criticisms over the years. For example, consider the term 'mental practice' itself. Specifically, it conveys a dualistic distinction between the 'physical' and 'mental' domains that is incompatible with current neuroscientific understanding of how the brain works. To explain, the fact that 'visualising' something in the mind's eye usually elicits measurable brain activity in the visual cortical areas (Kosslyn, Ganis and Thompson, 2001) suggests that mind and body are not really separate processes but function as an integrated unit. In addition, it is wrong to assume that mental practice refers to a standardised, homogeneous intervention. To illustrate, visualising a perfect golf drive could mean either 'seeing' yourself swinging a club or else 'seeing' someone else (e.g., Tiger Woods) performing the same action. Clearly, instructions in mental practice studies should indicate explicitly whether participants should visualise key skills from a *first person* perspective (as if one were executing the action concerned) or from a *third person* perspective (as if one were watching someone else execute the action). This issue of the importance of imagery *perspective* in imagery research is addressed in more detail by Morris, Spittle and Watt (2005).

THEORIES AND MODELS

Although many theories have been proposed since the 1930s to explain MP effects (see Kremer *et al.*, in press; Moran, 2012), the precise psychological mechanisms underlying symbolic rehearsal remain unclear. Perhaps the main reason for this tentative situation is that most MP studies are parametric variations of a standard experimental method (described above) rather than *theoretically* driven studies testing theoretically derived hypotheses. Nevertheless, four main theories of mental practice have dominated sport psychology in recent years – the 'neuromuscular model' (e.g., Jacobson, 1932), the 'cognitive (or "symbolic") account' (e.g., Denis, 1985), the 'bio-informational theory' (e.g., Lang, 1979) and most recently, the PETTLEP approach (Holmes and Collins, 2001, 2002). As outlined in more detail below, the neuromuscular approach postulates that mental practice effects are caused mainly by faint activity in the peripheral musculature, whereas the cognitive model suggests that central representations (i.e., brain structures) are the key mechanisms underlying MP effects. The bio-informational theory postulates that MP effects are the product of an interaction between three different factors – the environment in which the skill in question is being rehearsed ('stimulus' information), what is felt by the performer as the movement occurs ('response' information) and the perceived importance of this skill to the person involved ('meaning' information). Finally, the PETTLEP approach postulates that in order to produce optimal 'functional equivalence' between motor imagery and motor production, imagery interventions should replicate athletes' sporting environments as well as the emotions that they experience when performing their skills.

Neuromuscular theories of mental practice

Neuromuscular theories of MP may be traced back to Carpenter's (1894) 'ideo-motor' principle (see also Washburn, 1916). These theories shared two main assumptions. First, they suggested that the imagination of any physical action tends to elicit a pattern of faint and localised muscle movements. In addition, they claimed that such muscular activity could provide kinaesthetic feedback to the performer that enables him or her to make adjustments to this skill on future occasions. Support for this version of neuromuscular theory was received from Jacobson (1932), who speculated that visualisation causes tiny 'innervations' to occur in the muscles that are actually used in the physical performance of the skill being rehearsed covertly. Such minute 'subliminal' muscular activity was held to be similar to, but of a lower magnitude than, that produced by the actual physical execution of the movements involved. Another term for this theory is the 'inflow explanation' approach (Kohl and Roenker, 1983), which proposed that the covert efferent activity patterns elicited by imagery 'facilitate appropriate conceptualising for future imagery trials' (p. 180).

How valid is this neuromuscular account of mental practice? Conclusive support for it would require evidence of a strong positive relationship between the muscular activity elicited by imagery of a given skill and that detected during the actual performance of this skill. Unfortunately, such evidence has been conspicuously lacking in relevant research literature to date. Indeed, there is no reliable evidence that the faint muscular activity which occurs during imagery of a given skill or movement resembles that recorded during its actual physical performance. Interestingly, Shaw (1938) found that increased electromyographic (EMG) activity during motor imagery was distributed across a variety of muscle groups in the body – including some which were not directly related to the imagined action. Therefore, it seems that the muscular innervations that are typically elicited by imagery probably reflect generalised arousal processes of the body. Additional research casts further doubts on the type of muscular activity elicited by imagery. For example, despite using nuclear magnetic resonance (NMR) spectroscopy to monitor what happens in people's muscles during the imaginary performance of a specific skill, Decety *et al.* (1993) could not detect any change in relevant muscular metabolic indices. In summary, there is relatively little evidence to support a relationship between the muscular activity elicited by MP and the subsequent performance of sport skills.

Cognitive theories of mental practice

Cognitive (or 'symbolic') accounts of visualisation propose that mental practice facilitates both the coding and rehearsal of key elements of the task. One of the earliest proponents of this approach was Sackett (1934), who discovered that people's performance on a finger-maze task improved following mental rehearsal of the movement patterns involved. This finding was held to indicate that mental imagery facilitates the symbolic coding of the 'ideational representation of the movements involved' (p. 113). For example, if you are a golfer, you could use imagery to practise putting in your mind. This might involve 'seeing' yourself in your mind's eye standing over a ball on the green and gently stroking it towards the hole while keeping your head steady.

By contrast with the neuromuscular account of MP, cognitive models attach little importance to what happens in the peripheral musculature of the performer. Instead, they focus on the possibility that mental rehearsal strengthens the brain's central representation or cognitive 'blueprint' of the skill or movement being visualised. In general, two types of evidence have been cited in support of cognitive theories of MP. To begin with, 'central' representation theories may explain why visualisation is especially suitable for mastering tasks (e.g., mirror drawing) which contain many 'cognitive' or 'symbolic' elements such as planning sequential movements (see the research findings on MP discussed previously). Interestingly, some anecdotal evidence complementing this finding comes from athletes who use mental imagery to anticipate what might happen in a forthcoming competitive situation. For example, as indicated at the beginning of this chapter, Mike Atherton, a former captain of the England cricket team, reported that he had used imagery so that nothing could come as a surprise to him in a test match. In addition, a cognitive explanation of MP is corroborated by research findings on bilateral transfer effects. So, Kohl and Roenker (1980) discovered that bilateral transfer of learning occurred even when the training task (involving the contralateral limb) was performed using mental imagery. In other words, when a task was physically performed with the left hand, people who had mentally practised it using their right hands performed as well as, or better than, people who had practised with their right hands. Despite such empirical support, however, cognitive theories of mental practice have at least three limitations.

To begin with, they cannot easily explain why MP sometimes enhances 'motor' or 'strength' tasks (Lebon, Collet and Guillot, 2010) which, by definition, contain few cognitive components. The second vexed issue for symbolic theories is that they find it difficult to explain how MP enhances the performance of experienced athletes who, presumably, already possess well-established blueprints or motor schemata for the movements involved. Finally, and perhaps most worryingly, most cognitive theories of MP are surprisingly vague about the theoretical mechanisms that are alleged to underlie imagery effects.

Bio-informational theory of mental practice

The bio-informational theory of imagery was developed by Lang (1979) in an attempt to understand people's emotional and psychophysiological reactions to feared objects. It was subsequently applied to research on MP in motor skills by Bakker, Boschker and Chung (1996).

Influenced by the imagery research of Pylyshyn (1973), Lang (1979) argued that mental images are not 'pictures in the head' but propositional representations – abstract, language-like cognitive codes that do not physically resemble the stimuli to which they refer. These representations are believed to contain three types of information about the imagined object or situation. First, 'stimulus' propositions are statements that describe the content of the material being imagined. For example, if one were to visualise a penalty kick in football, stimulus information might include the sight of the opposing goalkeeper, the sound of the crowd and the feel of the ball in one's hands as one places it on the penalty spot. Next, 'response' propositions are statements that describe how and what the person feels as she or he responds to the scenario imagined. For example, stepping up to take a penalty kick is likely to cause some degree of tension and physiological arousal in the player. Finally 'meaning' propositions refer to the perceived importance to the person of the skill being imagined. For example, if there were only a few seconds left in the match, and one's team is a goal down, then the hypothetical penalty kick is imbued with great significance. The information from these three types of propositions is believed to be organised in an associative network in the mind.

Within this network, the response propositions are of special interest to imagery researchers. This is because these propositions are believed to be coded as bodily responses, which are primed by 'efferent' outputs to the muscles of the body. In other words, the propositions regulating imagined responses reflect how a person would actually react in the real-life situation being imagined. Interestingly, Lang (1977, 1979) suggested that response propositions are modifiable. Therefore, based on this theory, it should be possible to influence athletes' mental practice by using imagery scripts that are heavily laden with response propositions. Although this suggestion attracted some initial support from researchers such as Bakker *et al.* (1996) and Hecker and Kaczor (1988), it has not been tested systematically in sport psychology in recent years. Clearly, additional research is required to validate Lang *et al.*'s (1980) theory that imagery scripts emphasising response propositions will elicit greater physiological activation than those mainly containing stimulus propositions.

In summary, according to bio-informational theory, imagery not only allows people to rehearse what they would do in certain hypothetical situations but also leads to measurable psychophysiological changes associated with the response and meaning propositions triggered by the situation being imagined. Based on this propositional model of imagery, several predictions from bio-informational theory can be specified. For example, imagery scripts that emphasise response propositions should elicit greater physiological activation than do those that are based only on stimulus propositions.

Although this theory has not been widely tested in sport and exercise psychology, it has interesting implications for at least three aspects of MP research. First, it encourages researchers to regard imagery as more than just a 'picture in the head'. To explain, Lang's (1977, 1979) theories postulate that for MP to be effective, both stimulus and response propositions must be activated by the imagery script used (Gould, Damarjian and Greenleaf, 2002a). Second, it postulates the importance of 'individualising' imagery scripts – or designing them to ensure that they take account of the personal meaning which people attribute to the skills or movements that they wish to rehearse (see also Holmes and Collins, 2002). Finally, bio-informational theory emphasises the need to consider emotional factors when designing imagery scripts – an issue which has been largely neglected by advocates of neuromuscular and cognitive theories of mental practice. Interestingly, there is now compelling evidence that visualising a stimulus has a similar effect on the body as actually seeing it. For example, recent neuroimaging research shows that fear-inducing imagery elicits increased activation in the brain's aversive system – which includes the amygdala and related paralimbic regions (Lang and Davis, 2006).

The PETTLEP approach to mental practice

The most recent theoretical approach to mental practice is the PETTLEP model (Holmes and Collins, 2001; 2002) – an acronym referring to physical, environmental, task, timing, learning, emotional and perspectival aspects of mental imagery. In this model, 'P' refers to the athlete's physical response to the sporting situation imagined, 'E' is the environment in which the imagery is performed, 'T' is the imagined task, 'T' refers to timing (i.e., the pace at which the imagery is performed), 'L' is a learning or memory component of imagery, 'E' refers to the emotions elicited by the imagery and 'P' designates the type of visual imagery perspective used by the practitioner (i.e., whether s/he imagines the movement from a 'first-person' perspective or from a 'third-person' perspective – see earlier in chapter). The PETTLEP model proposes that in order to produce optimal functional equivalence between imagery and motor production, and thereby to enhance subsequent sport performance, imagery interventions should replicate not only athletes' sporting situation but also the emotions that they experience when performing their skills. Although the predictions of the PETTLEP model have not been tested extensively, available empirical studies are generally supportive. For example, Smith *et al.* (2007) compared the use of PETTLEP imagery training with traditional mental practice techniques and also with physical practice in developing gymnastics jump skills. Results showed that the PETTLEP group improved its proficiency in these skills whereas the traditional imagery group did not.

Towards an integrated model of mental practice: Functional equivalence theory

Having considered the strengths and limitations of the neuromuscular, cognitive, bio-informational and PETTLEP theories of mental practice effects, what is the most plausible account at present? If we consider some recent neuropsychological research on mental imagery, an integrated model of mental practice can be developed. Briefly, two key propositions of this approach may be expressed as follows. First, neuroimaging studies suggest that imagery is 'functionally equivalent' to perception. To explain, mental imagery shares some neural pathways and mechanisms with like-modality perception and with the preparation and execution of motor movements. This postulated overlaps of neural representations between imagery, perception and motor execution is known as the 'functional equivalence' hypothesis (e.g., Jeannerod, 1994). Second, research indicates that mental practice is functionally equivalent to physical practice, in the sense that imagery is guided by the same kinds of central mental representations as are motor movements (Hall, 2001). Evidence to support this proposition comes from Decety and Ingvar (1990) who discovered that certain brain structures (e.g., the prefrontal areas, supplementary motor areas and cerebellum) show a pattern of neural activity during imagery that resembles the activity elicited by actual motor performance (see also Holmes and Collins, 2002). Taken together, these propositions suggest that MP is best understood, at present, as a centrally mediated cognitive activity that mimics perceptual, motor and certain emotional experiences in the brain. This view integrates the strengths of all four theories of mental practice – the neuromuscular account (because MP has neural substrates even though these are regulated centrally not peripherally), the cognitive model (because MP is believed to be mediated by a central mental representation) and the bio-informational and PETTLEP approaches (because MP elicits emotional reactions as well as cognitive and neural activity). Interestingly, Murphy, Nordin and Cumming (2008) proposed a 'neurocognitive model' of motor imagery which focuses mainly on the functions that imagery serves in regulating action (i.e., motor control) and emotional and motivational processes. It allocates a key role to working memory as the cognitive mechanism that mediates these imagery activities. Although this model integrates available evidence in an elegant manner, it requires validation by empirical research.

METHODS AND MEASURES

As outlined above, the effects of MP on skilled performance have attracted considerable research attention from psychologists. Systematic reviews of this large body of research literature (amounting to hundreds of studies) have been conducted by, in chronological order, Richardson (1967a, 1967b), Feltz and Landers (1983), Grouios (1992), Driskell, Copper and Moran (1994), Murphy and Martin (2002) and van Meer and Theunissen (2009).

In general, the experimental paradigm in MP research involves a comparison of the pre- and post-intervention performance of the following groups of participants: those who have been engaged only in physical practice of the skill in question (the 'physical practice' group, PP); those who have mentally practised it (the 'mental practice' group, MP); those who have alternated between physical and mental practice (PP/MP); and, finally, people who have been involved in a control condition. Historically, the target skills investigated in MP research have largely been relatively simple laboratory tasks (e.g., dart throwing or maze learning) rather than complex sports skills. After a pre-treatment, baseline test has been conducted on the specific skill involved, participants are randomly assigned to one of these conditions (PP, MP, PP/MP or control). Normally, the cognitive rehearsal in the MP treatment condition involves a scripted sequence of relaxing physically, closing one's eyes, and then trying to see and feel oneself repeatedly performing a target skill (e.g., a golf putt) successfully in one's imagination. After this MP intervention has been applied, the participants' performance on this skill is tested again. Then, if the performance of the MP group exceeds that of the control group, a 'positive' effect of mental practice is reported.

Based on this experimental paradigm, a number of general conclusions about mental practice have emerged (see also Kremer *et al.*, in press). First, relative to not practising at all, MP appears to improve skilled performance. Not surprisingly, however, it is less effective than physical practice. Thus a meta-analytic review by Driskell *et al.* (1994) showed that PP treatment conditions produced greater statistical 'effect sizes' than was evident in mental rehearsal conditions ('meta-analysis' is a quantitative statistical technique which combines the results of a large number of studies in order to determine the overall size of a statistical effect). Statistically, the relative effect sizes of physical practice and mental practice were estimated by these researchers as 0.382 and 0.261 (both Fisher's Z), respectively. These figures can be interpreted with reference to Cohen's (1992) suggestion that values of 0.20, 0.50 and 0.80 represent effect sizes that are small, medium and large, respectively. The second general finding from the research literature is that MP, when combined and alternated with physical practice, usually produces superior skill learning to that resulting from either mental or physical practice alone. Third, evidence suggests that mental practice improves the performance of 'cognitive' skills (i.e, those that involve sequential processing activities; e.g., mirror drawing tasks) more than it does for 'motor' skills (e.g., as balancing on a 'stabilometer'). Fourth, there seems to be an interaction between the level of expertise of the performer and the type of task that yields the best improvement from mental rehearsal (Driskell *et al.*, 1994). Specifically, expert athletes tend to benefit more from MP than novices, regardless of the type of skill being practised (i.e, cognitive or physical). Fifth, the positive effects of MP on task performance tend to decline sharply over time. Indeed, according to Driskell *et al.* (1994), the beneficial effects of visualisation are reduced to half their original value after approximately two weeks has elapsed. A practical implication of this finding is that in order to gain optimal benefits from mental practice, 'refresher' training should be implemented after this critical two-week period. Finally, there is evidence that imagery ability mediates the relationship between MP and motor skill performance. More precisely, athletes who display special skills in generating and controlling vivid images tend to benefit more from visualisation than counterparts who lack such abilities. In summary, there is now considerable evidence to support the efficacy of mental practice as a technique for improving the performance of a variety of sport skills. These skills include not only 'self-paced' actions (i.e, skills that are performed largely at one's own speed and with little or no interference from other people) such as golf putting or place kicking in rugby but also 'open' or 'reactive' skills (e.g., tactical movements in basketball; Guillot, Nadrowska and Collet, 2009).

Despite the preceding findings on the efficacy of MP, there is at least one vexed issue in this field. This issue may be called the 'validation problem' (Moran, 2012). Put simply, how do we know that athletes are actually using imagery when they tell us that they are doing so? In other words, how can we validate sport performers' subjective reports about their imagery experiences?

At the beginning of this chapter, we learned that Tiger Woods claimed to use mental imagery when playing golf. But how do we know that he is actually using imagery when he is engaged in MP? This is an important question because cognitive researchers (e.g., Nisbett and Wilson, 1977) and sport psychologists have warned us that people's retrospective reports on their own mental processes are open to a variety of memory biases and distortions (e.g., 'response sets' whereby people may wish to convey the impression that they have a 'good' or vivid imagination). Unfortunately, few MP researchers have addressed this issue. Nevertheless, two possible solutions to this imagery validation problem have been proposed. First, in an effort to tackle this problem, Moran and MacIntyre (1998) checked the veracity of canoe-slalomists' imagery reports by using a theoretical principle derived from chronometric research on mental imagery (e.g., Decety, Jeannerod and Prablanc, 1989). Using the *mental travel* chronometric paradigm (see review by Guillot and Collet, 2005), it is possible to investigate motor imagery objectively by comparing the duration required to execute real and imagined actions. The rationale underlying this approach is as follows. If, as the functional equivalence hypothesis postulates, imagined and executed actions rely on similar motor representations and activate certain common brain areas, then the *temporal organisation* of imagined and actual actions should also be similar. If that is so, then there should be a close correspondence between the time required to *mentally* perform a given action and that required for its *actual* execution. Put differently, the greater the congruence between the imagined time and the 'real' time required to complete a mental journey, the more likely it is that imagery is involved. By comparing the length of time it takes athletes to mentally perform a task with that required to physically do so, we can estimate the likelihood that mental imagery was involved. Using this logic, Collet *et al.* (2011) recently postulated a way of combining psychometric, psychophysiological and chronometric measures in order to measure motor imagery processes (see box below).

A second way of validating athletes' imagery reports is through functional equivalence theory (e.g., Jeannerod, 1994). Briefly, as explained earlier, mental imagery and perception are functionally equivalent, in the sense that they are mediated by similar neuropsychological pathways in the brain. As Kosslyn, Ganis and Thompson (2001) concluded, cognitive neuroscientists believe that 'most of the neural processes that underlie like-modality perception are also used in imagery; and imagery, in many ways, can stand in for (re-present, if you will) a perceptual stimulus or situation' (p. 641). If this theory is valid, then interference should occur when athletes are required to use perceptual and imagery processes concurrently in the same sensory modality. This 'interference' should manifest itself in errors and longer response times when athletes face this dual task situation.

Of course, the idea of using cognitive interference to validate imagery reports has certain obvious limitations. For example, apart from being modality-specific,

Motor imagery (MI) is a multidimensional construct that refers to the mental rehearsal of actions without engaging in the actual movements involved. More precisely, it is a dynamic mental state during which the representation of a given motor act or movement is rehearsed in working memory without any overt motor output (Collet *et al.*, 2011). Historically, attempts to measure motor imagery processes have involved standardised psychometric tests (e.g., the Vividness of Movement Imagery Questionnaire, VMIQ-R; Roberts *et al.*, 2008), qualitative procedures (Moran and MacIntyre, 1998), psychophysiological techniques (e.g., Guillot *et al.*, 2009) and chronometric tools (e.g., Guillot and Collet, 2005). Although these methods have provided some interesting insights into motor imagery, they have not yet been combined to yield an aggregate index of this construct. Recently, however, Collet *et al.* (2011) proposed a formula by which a novel 'motor imagery index' (MII) can be measured using a combination of six specific component scores. These scores include self-estimations of imagery quality, psychometric assessment of imagery vividness, three different psychophysiological indices (derived from electrodermal and cardiac recordings), and an estimation of the difference between actual and imagined duration of movement execution. According to Collet *et al.* (2011), the MII has at least at least three advantages for imagery researchers in sport psychology. First, it is relatively easy to calculate (see details in Collet *et al.*, 2011) because most of its components (specifically, the qualitative, psychometric and chronometric ones) do not require any specialist equipment. Second, the MII is a flexible metric because its weightings can be adjusted to take account of factors relating to specific features of the imagined movement as well as to individual characteristics of the participants involved. Finally, Collet *et al.* (2011) argued that due to its multicomponential origins, the MII provides a more valid measure of motor imagery than does the traditional use of just one index alone.

it is rather impractical, as it depends on finding a suitable pair of perceptual and imagery tasks for every MP study.

From the preceding findings, we can conclude that the imaginary rehearsal of motor movements and sport skills has a small but significant positive effect on their actual performance. But we must be careful not to extrapolate too much from this conclusion because MP effects are mediated by a host of intervening variables. These variables include the nature of the task or skill to be performed, the content of the imagery instructions provided, the duration of the imagery intervention employed, the extent of the performer's previous experience with the task, his or her imagery abilities, the level of expertise of the performer, the imagery outcome (i.e., success or failure) visualised and the type of imagery perspective adopted (i.e., internal or external). To illustrate one of these variables, consider the last mentioned factor – namely, the possibility that imagery *perspective* might affect skilled performance.

According to Mahoney and Avener (1977), the kinaesthetic feedback resulting from skilled performance increases when participants adopt an 'internal' (or 'first person') rather than an external (or 'third person') imagery perspective. To illustrate the difference between these rival perspectives, consider two different ways of visualising a golf putt. Here, external imagery would involve 'watching' oneself performing this skill from the perspective of an outside observer (e.g., as if one were looking at someone performing this skill on television). Conversely, an internal perspective would entail the simulation of what one would actually experience in all of one's senses if one were physically performing the same putt. For example, this might entail 'seeing' the ball in front of oneself and 'feeling' the muscular movements involved in the execution of the putting stroke. In short, an internal imagery perspective entails a simulation of the kinaesthetic sensations that would be experienced by the performer. Which of these imagery 'styles' or 'perspectives' is more effective for golf putting? Remember that Mahoney and Avener (1977) claimed that the internal imagery perspective should enhance the performance of 'postural' skills (e.g., gymnastics), which depend on kinaesthetic processes. However, White and Hardy (1995) discovered that external visual imagery was more effective than internal imagery in learning another type of postural process – a gymnastics routine. More recently, Hardy and Callow (1999) reported a series of experiments which showed that external visual imagery was superior to internal visual imagery in facilitating the acquisition and performance of a karate movement. Interestingly, Callow and Hardy (2004) found that kinaesthetic imagery may actually have a stronger relationship with an *external* imagery perspective than with an internal one.

In turning our attention to specific measures, we learnt earlier in this chapter that although mental images are ephemeral constructs, they differ from each other along two psychological dimensions, namely, vividness and controllability. These two dimensions of imagery form the basis of most psychological attempts to measure this construct. In general, two strategies have been pursued in order to assess these imagery dimensions. Whereas the subjective approach is based on the idea of asking people about the nature of their images, the objective approach requires people to complete visualisation tasks that have 'right' or 'wrong' answers (e.g., see Shepard and Metzler, 1971). The logic here is that the better people perform on these tasks, the more imagery skills they are assumed to possess.

The vividness of an image (which refers to its clarity or 'sharpness') can be assessed using self-report scales in which people are asked to comment on certain aspects of their mental representation. For example, close your eyes and form an image of your face. On a scale of 1 (meaning 'no image at all') to 5 (meaning 'as clear as in normal vision'), how vivid is your image of your face? Similarly, the vividness or clarity of an auditory image might be evaluated by asking people such questions as: 'If you close your eyes, how well can you hear the imaginary sound of an ambulance siren?' Unfortunately, subjective self-report scales of imagery have certain limitations (see Moran, 1993). For example, they are subject to contamination from response 'sets' such as 'social desirability'. Put simply, most people are eager to portray themselves as having a 'good' or vivid imagination regardless of their true skills in that area. For this reason, objective tests of imagery have been developed. Specifically, the controllability dimension of a visual mental image (which refers to the ease and accuracy with which it can be transformed symbolically) can be measured objectively by requesting people to complete tasks which are known to require visualisation abilities. For example, in the Group Mental Rotations Test (GMRT) (Vandenberg and Kuse, 1978), people have to make judgements about whether or not the spatial orientation of certain three-dimensional target figures matches (i.e., is congruent with) or does not match (i.e., is incompatible with) various alternative shapes. The higher people's score is on this test, the stronger are their image control skills. Interestingly, a recent study by MacIntyre, Moran and Jennings (2002) found that there was a significant correlation between the GMRT scores of elite canoe-slalom athletes and their World Cup race performance. For a more comprehensive account of the history of imagery measurement, see Richardson (1995) and Richardson (1999).

In general, two types of imagery instruments have been developed in sport psychology – tests of athletes' imagery abilities and tests of athletes' imagery use (Moran, 1993). Although space limitations preclude an exhaustive review of these types of measures, some general trends and issues in imagery measurement may be identified as follows.

First, among the most popular and psychometrically impressive tests of imagery skills in athletes are the Vividness of Movement Imagery Questionnaire (VMIQ) (Isaac, Marks and Russell, 1986) and the revised version of the Movement Imagery Questionnaire (MIQ-R) (Hall and Martin, 1997). The VMIQ is a 24-item measure of 'visual imagery of movement itself and imagery of kinaesthetic sensations' (Isaac, Marks and Russell, 1986, p. 24). Each of the items presents a different movement or action to be imagined (e.g., riding a bicycle). Respondents are required to rate these items in two ways – 'watching somebody else' and 'doing it yourself'. The ratings are given on a 5-point scale where 1 = 'perfectly clear and as vivid as normal vision' and 5 = 'no image at all'. Although not extensive, available evidence suggests that the VMIQ satisfies conventional standards of psychometric adequacy (Moran, 1993). Unfortunately, the VMIQ has several limitations. For example, it appears to confound two different imagery modalities – visual and kinaesthetic. Thus it requires respondents to imagine performing movements themselves but does not instruct them to use the kinaesthetic modality rather than the visual one. In addition, the VMIQ has not been subjected to confirmatory factor analysis – a technique commonly used to investigate the construct validity of a psychometric test. To overcome these and other problems with the VMIQ, Roberts *et al.* (2008) developed the Vividness of Movement Imagery Questionnaire – 2 (VMIQ-2). This test consists of 12 items and assesses the ability to form mental images of a variety of movements visually and kinaesthetically. The visual component is further sub-divided into 'external' and 'internal' visual imagery. Respondents are required to imaging each of the 12 movements and to rate the vividness of each item on a Likert-type scale from 1 ('perfectly clear and vivid') to 5 ('no image at all'). The VMIQ-2 displays impressive factorial validity and acceptable concurrent and discriminate validity. Next, the MIQ-R is especially interesting for sport researchers because it was designed to assess individual differences in kinaesthetic as well as visual imagery of movement. Briefly, this test contains 8 items that assess people's ease of imaging specific movements either visually or kinaesthetically. In order to complete an item, respondents must execute a movement and rate it on a scale ranging from 1 (meaning 'very hard to see/feel') to 7 (meaning 'very easy to see/feel'). Imagery scores are calculated as separate sums of the two subscales of visual and kinaesthetic imagery skills. Available evidence indicates that the MIQ-R displays adequate reliability and validity (Moran, 1993).

The Sport Imagery Questionnaire (SIQ) (Hall *et al.*, 1998) is also a popular and reliable tool for measuring imagery use in athletes. The SIQ is a 30-item self-report scale, which asks the respondent to rate (on a 7-point scale where 1 = 'rarely' and 7 = 'often') how often they use five specific categories of imagery. These categories include 'motivation general – mastery' (e.g., imagining appearing confident in front of others), 'motivation general – arousal' (e.g., imagining the stress and/or excitement associated with competition), 'motivation specific' (e.g., imagining winning a medal), 'cognitive general' (e.g., imagining various strategies for a competitive event) and 'cognitive specific' (e.g., mentally practising a skill). This test appears to have acceptable psychometric characteristics. For example, Beauchamp, Bray and Albinson (2002a) reported internal consistency values ranging from 0.72 (for a scale measuring motivational general–arousal) to 0.94 (for a scale assessing motivational general–mastery) for a modified version of the SIQ. Interestingly, a recent addition to measures in this field is a scale developed by Hausenblas *et al.* (1999) designed to measure exercise-related motivational and cognitive imagery. Preliminary psychometric analysis indicates that this test is a promising tool for the study of imagery processes in aerobics exercisers.

Unfortunately, despite considerable progress in imagery measurement in sport psychology, a number of conceptual and methodological issues remain in this field. For example, despite abundant evidence from neuroimaging research that imagery is a multidimensional construct, most imagery tests in sport and exercise psychology continue to rely on a single imagery scale score. Also, few imagery scales have an explicit or coherent theoretical rationale – despite the availability of many sophisticated models of imagery (e.g., see Murphy and Martin, 2002; Murphy, Nordin, S. Cumming, 2008). Finally, much of the psychometric evidence cited in support of imagery tests in sport psychology comes from the research teams that developed the tests.

PRACTICAL ISSUES AND INTERVENTIONS

Imagery interventions have attracted considerable research interest in sport psychology (see a comprehensive review by Cumming and Ramsey, 2009). Before we address this topic, however, a brief account of imagery use is necessary. As we discovered earlier in this chapter, people use mental imagery for a variety of purposes in everyday life. To illustrate, Kosslyn *et al.* (1990) asked a sample of university undergraduates to keep a diary or daily 'log' of their imagery experiences over the course of a week. Results revealed that imagery was used for such functions as problem solving (e.g., trying to work out mentally whether or not a new item of furniture would fit into a room), giving and receiving directions (e.g., using mental maps to navigate through an unfamiliar environment), recall (e.g., trying to remember where they had left a lost object), mental practice (e.g., rehearsing what to say in an important interview on the way to work) and motivation (e.g., using images of desirable scenes for mood enhancement purposes). This type of research raises a number of interesting questions. For example, how widespread is imagery use among athletes? Do elite-level athletes use it more frequently than their less proficient counterparts? For what specific purposes do athletes employ imagery?

Before we explore empirical data on these questions, let us consider briefly some anecdotal reports and textbook accounts of imagery use in sport. In this regard, many testimonials to the value of imagery have emerged from interviews with, and profiles on, athletes in different sports. For example, current and former world-class performers such as Jenson Button (motor racing), Michael Jordan (basketball), Tiger Woods and Jack Nicklaus (golf), John McEnroe and Andre Agassi (tennis) and Ronaldinho (football) all claim to have 'seen' and 'felt' themselves performing key actions successfully in their imagination before or during competition. As critical thinkers, however, we should be careful not to be too easily influenced by anecdotal testimonials. After all, no matter how colourful or evocative these examples are, they do not constitute empirical evidence. Psychologists are wary of attaching too much importance to people's accounts of their own mental processes, simply because such insights are often tainted by biases in memory and distortions in reporting. For example, athletes may recall more cases of positive experiences with imagery (i.e., occasions on which their visualisation coincided with enhanced performance) than negative experiences with it (where visualisation appeared to have no effect).

For what purposes do sport performers use mental imagery? According to Cumming and Ramsey (2009) and Murphy, Nordin and Cumming (2008), athletes' reasons for using imagery fall into two general categories – cognitive and motivational. Whereas *cognitive* reasons typically involve the use of imagery to enhance attention, skill-learning and skilled performance, motivational reasons include increasing self-efficacy and regulating emotions such as anxiety. So, a list of imagery uses in athletes includes such practices as:

- learning and practising sport skills (e.g., rehearsing a tennis serve mentally before going out to practise it on court)
- rehearsing and memorising strategy (e.g., vizualising a game plan before a match)
- attentional focusing/refocusing (e.g., focusing on the 'feel' of a gymnastics routine)
- arousal control (e.g., visualising oneself behaving calmly in an anticipated stressful situation)
- self-confidence (e.g., 'seeing' oneself as confident and successful)
- facilitating recovery from injury/managing pain (e.g., visualising healing processes)

In recent years, considerable research evidence has accumulated to support these uses of imagery among athletes. For example, there is evidence that imagery can be used for skill learning (Burhans, Richman and Bergey, 1988), strategic planning (MacIntyre and Moran, 1996), arousal control (Munroe *et al.*, 2000), developing confidence (Callow and Waters, 2005), improving concentration (Moran, 1996) and injury rehabilitation (Driediger, Hall and Callow, 2006). Typically, imagery use in athletes has been studied through descriptive and theory-driven studies (see Hall, 2001 and Martin, Moritz and Hall, 1999a for more detailed reviews of athletes' use of imagery). To explain the differences between these approaches, the descriptive strategy attempts to establish the incidence of imagery use in athletes, while the theoretical approach investigates specific categories of imagery functions in these performers.

In the descriptive approach, special survey instruments have been designed to assess imagery use in various athletic populations. This approach has led to some interesting findings. For example, successful athletes appear to use imagery more frequently than less successful athletes (Durand-Bush, Salmela and Green-Demers, 2001). Of course, this discovery is not really surprising in view of the fact that Murphy (1994) reported that 90 per cent of a sample of elite athletes at the US Olympic training centre claimed to use imagery regularly. Also, Ungerleider and Golding (1991) found that 85 per cent of over 600 prospective Olympic athletes employed imagery techniques while training for competition. Clearly, imagery is used extensively by expert athletes. By contrast, Cumming and Hall (2002b) found that recreational sport performers used imagery less than did more profi-cient counterparts (namely, provincial and international athletes) and also rated it as being less valuable than did the latter group. This trend was apparent even in the 'off season' (Cumming and Hall, 2002a). Moreover, as one might expect, visual and kinaesthetic imagery are more popular than other kinds of imagery in athletes (Hall, 2001). Although this descriptive research provides valuable base-line data on the extent of imagery use among different samples of athletes, it does not illuminate the precise functions for which visualisation is employed.

Therefore, another approach – theory-driven research – has emerged in the field of imagery studies in sport psychology since the late 1990s. For exam-ple, Hall et al. (1998) postulated a taxonomy of imagery use in athletes based on Paivio's (1985) theory that imagery affects both motivational and cognitive processes. As indicated earlier, the SIQ measures five different categories of such cognitive and motivational imagery use in athletes.

Although the SIQ is valuable in allowing researchers to explore the relation-ship between specific types of imagery use and subsequent athletic perform-ance, it has been criticised for the looseness of its categorical boundaries. To illustrate, Abma et al. (2002) pointed out that athletes who use cognitive-specific imagery regularly (e.g., in rehearsing a particular skill) may be classified as using motivation general-mastery if they believe that mental practice is the best way to boost their confidence.

Despite such criticisms, the theory-driven taxonomies developed by Hall et al. (1998) and Martin, Moritz and Hall (1999a) offer greater scope for research on imagery use by athletes than intuitive classifications promulgated in applied sport psychology. So what conclusions have emerged from research on imagery use in athletes? Based on reviews by Hall (2001) and Murphy, Nordin and Cumming (2008), research on this topic has led to the following general findings.

To begin with, there is evidence that athletes tend to use imagery more in pre-competitive than in practice situations – a fact which suggests that they tend to visualise more frequently for the purpose of mental preparation or performance enhancement in competition than for skill acquisition. A potential danger of engagement in pre-competitive imagery, however, is that it may hinder athletes' performance of 'open' or reactive skills (Murphy, Nordin and Cumming, 2008). Specifically, if an athlete is required to react quickly to an opponent's action (e.g., in returning a volley in a doubles match in tennis), then imagery may not be appropriate as it may be based on an incorrect anticipation of where the volley will be directed. Second, as indicated earlier, available evidence suggests that imagery is used by athletes for both motivational and cognitive purposes. Although the former category is rather 'fuzzy' and ill-defined, it includes appli-cations like 'seeing' oneself achieving specific goals and 'feeling' oneself being relaxed in competitive situations. For example, it is precisely this latter appli-cation that Richard Faulds pursued in creating an image prior to winning the

2000 Olympic gold medal for trapshooting: 'The image is the ice man. You walk like an ice man and think like an ice man' (Nichols, 2000, p. 7).

With regard to *cognitive* uses of imagery by athletes, two main applications have been discovered by researchers. On the one hand, as is evident from anecdotal and survey evidence, imagery is widely used as a tool for mental rehearsal (a cognitive-specific application). On the other hand, imagery is often used as a concentration technique (see also Chapter 5). To illustrate, consider how Ronaldinho, the Brazilian soccer star, used imagery as a focusing technique before matches: 'When I train, one of the things I concentrate on is creating a mental picture of how best to deliver the ball to a team-mates ... So what I do, always before a game ... is try and think up things, imagine plays, which no one else will have thought of' (cited in Cumming and Ramsey, 2009, p. 5). A third general research finding in this field concerns the *content* of athletes' imagery. In this regard, Hall (2001) claims that athletes tend to use positive imagery (e.g., 'seeing' themselves winning competitive events) and 'seldom imagine themselves losing' (p. 536). But is this really true? After all, everyday experience would suggest that many club-level golfers are plagued by 'negative' mental images such as hitting bunkers or playing the ball out of bounds. This observation raises an interesting question. Specifically, if athletes visualise the 'wrong' targets or experiences, is it possible that imagery could impair their sport performance? This possibility was considered by Greg Louganis (a former Olympic diving champion) who hit his head when diving in a qualifying round of the 1988 Games. Interestingly, he did not watch the replay of this incident afterwards because 'I didn't want that image in my head going into the competition' (Bartlett, 1994).

This issue of imagery content was examined by Murphy and Martin (2002), who have identified four situations in which a negative effect of imagery might occur:

1. Excessive anxiety: if athletes have a high degree of trait anxiety (see Chapter 6), the use of imagery before a competition may prove to be counter-productive as it may encourage rumination about what might go wrong.
2. Distractibility: athletes who are distractible may visualise the 'wrong' targets (see Chapter 5) before a competition and end up performing poorly as a consequence.
3. Lack of image control: athletes whose imagery control skills are deficient may become vulnerable to unwanted images.
4. Overconfidence: athletes who have a tendency to become overconfident before competition should avoid using imagery as it may exacerbate their problem.

Despite the possibility that imagery may have an adverse impact on athletes' psychological processes under certain circumstances, Hall (2001) suggested that, overall, athletes' imagery is usually accurate, vivid, positive in content and helpful to their athletic performance.

Practical guidelines on mental practice in sport are available in many text-books of applied sport psychology (e.g., see Kremer and Moran, 2008; Vealey and Greenleaf, 2010). Before concluding the chapter, we have provided details below on how to develop a mental practice programme for a practical athletic skill that you wish to improve. There are four key steps in the process of conducting mental practice. Before beginning, however, you must be clear about what specific sport skill or situation you wish to improve. Please take a moment to decide on what specific skill or situation you would like to practise in your mind. Ideally, it should be something that can be done alone and at an individual pace (e.g., a tennis serve, golf putt, penalty kick).

The four steps in visualisation are as follows. First, you must prepare properly by relaxing your mind and body. Second, you must create the mental image of the skill that you wish to practise. Third, you must experience a successful performance of that skill by 'replaying' it in your mind over and over again until it is automatic. Finally, you should programme it by combining it with a pre-performance routine (see also Chapter 5).

1. People visualise best when they are relaxed (e.g., daydreams are generated spontaneously by our minds when we feel relaxed). The easiest way to relax your body is to sit down in a quiet place and close your eyes. Slowly 'centre' your body by lowering your shoulders gently. Then gently 'flap out' the tension in your arms and legs. Take 5–10 deep breaths and make sure to push your stomach out slowly when you breathe in and pull in your stomach gently as you breathe out. You can train your body even better by saying the word 'RELAX' to yourself as you breathe slowly. Say 'RE' when you breathe in – and 'LAX' as you breathe out.

2. Now that you feel relaxed, you will find it easier to create the situation or skill that you wish to visualise. Focus on that skill or situation as well as possible. Close your eyes and imagine the venue where you will be performing this skill. Now try to see yourself doing this skill. Take two minutes to imagine this scene as vividly as possible – notice details of the sights, sounds and bodily sensations which you are experiencing.

3. See and feel yourself performing the skill slowly, smoothly and correctly. Notice how calm and confident you feel as you perform the movements in your mind. At first, it may help to slow down the movements – as though you're watching a slow-motion video of yourself playing the skill perfectly. As you get better at visualisation, however, you should form images in 'real time' (i.e., at the same speed as in real life). Watch yourself performing this skill over and over again for one to two minutes.

4. Combining visualisation with a 'pre-performance routine' can help to improve your concentration (see also Chapter 5). A 'pre-performance routine' is simply a series of actions which take you from thinking about a skill to actually doing it. It is like the steps of a stair, which take you from where

you are now to a quiet zone in your house where you will be free from all distractions. This quiet zone is your ideal performance state.

In conclusion, research evidence suggests that mental imagery (also known as 'visualisation'), or the ability to represent in the mind information that is not currently being perceived by the sense organs, is widely used by sport performers in an effort to enhance athletic performance. In this chapter, the role of imagery processes in sport was investigated. In the first part of the chapter, the nature of mental imagery and mental practice were examined and a brief summary was provided of the history of research on these constructs in sport psychology. In the second section, the strengths and weaknesses of various theoretical explanations of mental practice effects in sport were reviewed. The third section outlined the main methods and findings in the field of mental practice, while the final section reviewed and evaluated principal approaches to the measurement of mental imagery skills.

CASE STUDY

Hazel is a very talented 14-year-old tennis player who is about to take part in a series of trial matches for a place in the national junior elite tennis squad. With a month to go to the 'play-offs', however, she and her tennis coach, Angela, have approached you with the following problem. Briefly, Hazel seems to have lost confidence in her normal, aggressive 'serve–volley' style of play and competes increasingly from the baseline during rallies. As this 'baseline game' is not her natural style of play, Hazel has lost several matches recently. Angela suggests that Hazel's problems may be linked to a decline in the accuracy of her first service. Because of this inaccuracy, Hazel uses a soft second serve and stays at the back of the court as a result. Hazel agrees with her coach's diagnosis but says that she can't seem to clear negative thoughts from her mind as she steps up to serve in an important match. Although Angela has told Hazel repeatedly that 'it's all in her mind', the problem seems to be getting worse. At this stage, with time running out, Angela and Hazel are eager to hear what a sport psychologist can tell them about the cause and treatment of this problem.

1. With reference to the Theories and Models section in the chapter, how would you interpret what is happening in this case study?
2. With reference to Methods and Measures, what techniques would you employ to help to understand and quantify the issues?
3. With reference to Practical Issues and Interventions, how would you deal with this situation?

STUDY QUESTIONS

1. What is a 'mental image'? What were the main objections raised by J. B. Watson to this construct? Do you think that these objections have been answered satisfactorily by contemporary imagery researchers?
2. Outline and evaluate the neuromuscular, cognitive, bio-informational and PETTLEP theories of mental practice. Which of these theories is the most accurate, in your opinion? Where possible, support your answer with empirical research evidence.
3. Summarise three consistent findings from the research literature on mental practice. Do these findings have any practical implications for the learning and/or performance of sport skills?
4. In what ways do mental images differ from each other? What are the main difficulties encountered in measuring imagery in athletes? Do you think that the 'mental travel' paradigm could be combined successfully with psychometric methods of measuring imagery? If so, how?
5. There is general agreement among researchers that imagery is used by athletes for both cognitive and motivational purposes. By doing a literature search on 'uses of imagery', try to identify an evidence-based list of imagery uses by athletes within these cognitive and motivational categories. What uses of imagery fall outside these categories?

FURTHER READING

Cumming, J. and Ramsey, R. (2009). 'Imagery Interventions in Sport', in S. D. Mellalieu and S. Hanton (eds), *Advances in Applied Sport Psychology* (London: Routledge), 5–36.

Guillot, A. and Collet, C. (eds) (2010) *The Neurophysiological Foundations of Mental and Motor Imagery* (Oxford: Oxford University Press).

Moran, A. P. (2012) *Sport and Exercise Psychology: A Critical Introduction,* 2nd edn (London: Routledge).

Morris, T., Spittle, M. and Watt, A. P. (2005) *Imagery in Sport* (Champaign, Illinois: Human Kinetics).

Murphy, S., Nordin, S. and Cumming, J. (2008) 'Imagery in Sport, Exercise, and Dance', in T. S. Horn (ed.), *Advances in Sport Psychology*, 2nd edn (Champaign, Illinois: Human Kinetics), 297–324 and 463–7.

Weinberg, R. S. (2008). 'Does Imagery Work? Effects on Performance and Mental Skills?', *Journal of Imagery Research in Sport and Physical Activity*, 3, 1–21.

4 Motivation

INTRODUCTION, HISTORY AND DEVELOPMENT

From psychology's earliest days (James, 1890), the study of motivation has never been far from the core of psychological theory, research and application (Franken, 2007). Indeed, within the world of sport it can be argued that almost all applied sport psychology is concerned with motivation or the psychological processes that energise the individual and thereby influence behaviour. Equally the world of sport is littered with references to techniques for enhancing motivation and commitment, and including the sometimes-legendary stunts pulled by managers and coaches for motivating their charges. Some are praiseworthy for their invention if nothing else, whereas others should definitely carry a government health warning!

As other chapters in the book consider a range of practical interventions associated with motivation, the primary focus of this chapter will be on the more academic literature that considers how psychologists have helped to further our understanding of why we take up sport and exercise in the first place, what influences us to continue our involvement and what happens to make us discontinue or drop out. The chapter will consider not only theories and models of motivation that are well known within sport psychology but will also introduce readers to the separate literature dealing with motivation for physical exercise and activity in a more general sense. Make no mistake, the available literature in this field is vast and can be overwhelming to the uninitiated. Within the confines of a single chapter all we are able to do is offer a sketch or overview of main issues, and pointers as to where you can go to find more detailed information.

Understanding the factors that influence our engagement with sport and exercise has long preoccupied both sport and exercise psychology. To identify a definitive starting point for this work is not easy but certainly McClelland (1961) and Atkinson's (1964) research on achievement motivation has continued to make a significant impact on sport psychology from the late 1960s to the present day. In turn, the McClelland-Atkinson research was based on earlier drive theories of motivation and especially the work of Hull (1951) and Spence (1956). Today work on achievement motivation continues to resonate in contemporary perspectives and especially those concerned with intrinsic motivation.

The McClelland-Atkinson model (otherwise known as Need Achievement Theory) is based on earlier approach-avoidance models of motivation which predict that when faced with a challenge we are quite literally in two minds – do we fight or do we flight. According to the model our need to meet the challenge or achieve (nAch) will depend on the relative significance of two independent psychological constructs, our motive to achieve success (Ms) and our motive to avoid failure or fear of failure (Maf). Specifically our need to achieve (nAch) will depend on the size of the difference between the two motives (Ms – Maf) combined with our perception of the probability of success (Ps) and the incentive value of success (Is), that is, the value we place on rewards associated with success. 'Is' is thought to be inversely related to Ps and hence can be represented by the formula '1 – Ps = Is'. The final component is 'extrinsic rewards' which we believe we will receive if we are successful (Mext). Each ingredient is brought together in the following formula, where Ms and Maf are scored from 1 to 10 and the remaining factors from 0 to 1:

$$NAch = (Ms - Maf)(Ps \times Is) + Mext.$$

The predictive validity of the formula is hard to determine empirically but as an applied tool it remains of some predictive value. In general terms the model predicts that high achievers in sport, those who strive for success and have no fear of failure, will be drawn towards competition and difficult yet realisable challenges. By contrast, low achievers will avoid personal challenges, for example by only playing weaker opponents or by setting unattainable goals for an exercise regime that are not particularly threatening because failure is a high possibility.

Although considerable work has been conducted within the McClelland-Atkinson tradition, the empirical research within sport remains inconclusive (Roberts, 2001). Nevertheless, the model may still have practical utility in helping predict long-term patterns of motivation (Cox, 2002) or as a diagnostic aid for applied sport psychologists. More significantly the approach has helped to pave the way for later models of intrinsic motivation that consider the interaction between personal and situational variables in determining participation. Direct antecedents include the work of Spence and Helmreich (1983) who went on to describe achievement orientation multi-dimensionally, referencing three distinct responses or orientations to achievement situations – striving for excellence, emphasising hard work or desiring to outperform others. Diane Gill then took up this work within sport psychology (Gill, 1993), focusing on competitiveness as a sport-specific achievement construct that she measured in terms of three constructs (competitiveness, win orientation and goal orientation) using the Sport Orientation Questionnaire (SOQ; Gill, 1993), a scale that continues to generate interest and most especially with regard to competitiveness (Houston et al., 2002). At a more basic level, the focus of such endeavours on the importance of intrinsic motivators, and specifically achievement, is never far removed from the array of constructs and perspectives that characterise the contemporary literature. For example, recent work on both need satisfaction and autonomy-supportive environments continues to draw heavily on an array of constructs that would not have been unfamiliar to those working in the field many years ago (Gillet and Rosnet, 2008).

Across psychology in general the study of motivation advanced significantly with the development of social cognitive paradigms during the 1970s. Causal attribution theory, concerned with how we explain our social world, rose to prominence at this time and also made its mark within sport and exercise psychology, Weiner's (1979) attribution model took centre stage, the model providing a framework for understanding the explanations or causal attributions which people associate with success and failure in competitive sport. In sporting contexts the four main attribution elements have been labelled ability, effort, task and luck. In turn, these reflect on five primary constructs, whether factors are either internal or external, stable or unstable, intentional or unintentional, global or specific and controllable or uncontrollable (Hanrahan and Biddle, 2008).

Later writers also suggested that the feelings associated with external or internal attributions and the expectancy of future success or failure, will have a significant influence on achievement behaviours (Hanrahan and Gross, 2005). Mirroring work dealing with other life domains, research has shown that successful performance in sport is more likely to be attributed to stable, internal factors (such as ability) and most especially in sports involving interacting teams and where the attributions relate to team performance. However, there has not been the same support for the prediction that failure will tend to be attributed to external factors (task difficulty or luck). In general, research interest in attribution theory across psychology has waned, with criticisms that the theory lacks specificity in its predictions, hence being unable to explain individual differences in motivation. Instead commentators have called for more sophisticated models which can accommodate attribution processes alongside a wider range of psychological and contextual constructs and including those factors identified as significant motives for engagement in sport (Rees, Ingledew and Hardy, 2005).

Since the 1970s both sport and exercise psychologists have been interested in the wide range of motives associated with starting, participating and discontinuing programmes involving physical activity (Boiché and Sarrazin, 2008). In terms of participation in organised sport most of the literature has been gathered from young people (Sport England, 2005) whereas for participation in exercise programmes the tendency has been to consider adult populations (Weinberg *et al.*, 2000). Several reviews of the descriptive research in this area are available (see Biddle, Atkin and Pearson, 2007; Sallis, Prochaska and Taylor, 2000) and consistent patterns are identifiable. For example, the reasons that children typically offer for sport participation usually fall within one or more of five domains; competence; affiliation; fitness; fun and success. Motives connected with competence include skill acquisition, improvement and mastery and it is these inherent motives that have attracted the greatest attention. In contrast, until recently the motive of fun or hedonism has been largely ignored (McCarthy, Jones and Clark-Carter, 2008), yet it has been repeatedly shown that children very often first choose to participate for the sheer enjoyment and pleasure they associate with sport (Wankel, 1993).

As they grow older, the reasons that children cite for sport participation typically change, with an increasing concern with competition and fitness (Kremer, Trew and Ogle, 1997). Reasons for withdrawal from sport also begin to appear including a lack of progress or skill improvement; interest in/conflict with other activities; lack of fun; boredom; lack of playing time; excessive pressure from others; and increased time commitment (Foster *et al.*, 2007). Withdrawal from sport can be temporary or permanent and it can be either specific to a particular activity or total rejection of sport in all its forms. Estimates of attrition rates cite various percentages of youth sport withdrawal depending on the sports in question and the populations under scrutiny. However, an average rate of withdrawal of around one third is not uncommon across adolescent populations, with particular sports (e.g., swimming) revealing attrition rates that are far higher (Butcher, Lindner and Johns, 2002).

These descriptive studies are interesting insofar as they reveal social trends but they do not begin to answer theoretical questions about the process of motivation (Biddle and Nigg, 2000). In answer to the why questions such as, 'why do people take up a sport?'; 'why do some people drop out of sport?'; 'why do some and not others people decide upon a particular sport?' and 'why do some people persist at a sport despite setbacks?', we must turn to theories and models of motivation which move from description ('what, where, who and how') to deeper interpretation and inference ('why').

THEORIES AND MODELS

Self-determination theory

Most contemporary models of participation motivation owe a considerable debt to the pioneering work of Deci and Ryan (1985). In turn this work can be traced to both the McClelland-Atkinson tradition and the social cognitive movement of the early 1970s (Deci, 1971; 1975). Self-Determination Theory (SDT) considers how our innate need to show competence reflects in motivational types, including both the extrinsic and the intrinsic (Vallerand, Pelletier and Koestner, 2008). The term intrinsic motivation, so central to modern perspectives, was first coined by Deci in the early 1970s to describe psychological processes or drives where the individual feels competent and self-determining, and where continued participation is fuelled by intrinsic enjoyment of the activity itself (Deci, 1971). This stands in contrast with extrinsic motivation which is associated with a desire for external rewards, reinforcement or the drive to avoid punishment.

While SDT continues to enjoy prominence, it has become so large in scope that inevitably a number of 'sub-theories' have now developed to focus attention on particular issues. For example, Cognitive Evaluation Theory considers how contextual and environmental factors impact on intrinsic motivation via three processes – perceived locus of causality, perceived competence and finally, perception of events relevant to the initiation and regulation of behaviour (Deci, Koestner and Ryan, 1999).

SDT and related theories propose that we each have innate and spontaneous needs to display competence, autonomy/self-determination and relatedness within certain domains, and including the physical (Ryan and Deci, 2002; Vallerand, 2007). At any moment our motivation will be influenced by a hierarchy of social factors, including the *global* (i.e., the environment as a whole), *contextual* (i.e., usual response to a specific context, e.g., education, sport) and *situational* (i.e., specific activity at a given time), and the consequences can be affective, cognitive and/or behavioural.

According to the most recent version of SDT, motivation falls along a continuum of self-determination, with *amotivation* associated with the lowest level of self-determination, *intrinsic* motivation falling at the highest end of the continuum and *extrinsic* motivation located in the middle (Vallerand, 2007). Furthermore intrinsic motivation is then subdivided into three subtypes – motivation towards; (a) knowledge; (b) accomplishment; and (c) experiencing stimulation. Amotivation is regarded as the absence of motivation, purpose or expectation with regard to participation while extrinsic motivation is divided into four subcategories that vary in terms of the extent of self-determination. The lowest in relation to self-determination is known as *external_regulation*, where the aim is simply to achieve a reward or avoid punishment, followed by *introjected regulation* (participation out of pressure or coercion), *identified regulation* (participation from choice but not interest) and finally, *integrated regulation* (the values of the behaviour are integrated into personal values and belief systems).

Integrated regulation most closely resembles intrinsic motivation but is still regarded as qualitatively different as it involves achieving a goal that is socially valued but without necessarily embracing those social values within the self-concept (Vallerand, 2007). This it is not quite the equivalent of intrinsic motivation which is about engaging in an activity for its own inherent satisfaction rather than for any extrinsic reward or value.

Intrinsic motivation is the primary focus of SDT and the theory includes a number of propositions as to how different factors can have an influence on this. As already mentioned, the first suggests that intrinsic motivation is influenced by the person's degree of autonomy or self-determination. The person's perceived degree of control over any given behaviour will influence their future locus of causality or self-determination in similar situations, with an external perceived locus of causality reflecting low perceived control and hence likely to decrease intrinsic motivation in the future. In contrast, an internal locus of causality reflects a high degree of perceived control and is more likely to enhance longer term intrinsic motivation (Chatzisarantis *et al.*, 2003).

The hierarchical model suggests that self-determination influences motivation independently of other mediating variables such as competence and autonomy although the concepts of autonomy and self-determination do appear to be conceptually linked. Indeed, Markland (1999) suggests that viewing self-determination and competence as independent mediators of motivation contradicts Deci and Ryan's (1985) original assertions. Using regression analysis Markland found that self-determination and perceived competence accounted for 56 per cent of the variance in intrinsic motivation. Variations in perceived competence positively influenced intrinsic motivation only when self-determination was low. However, self-determination was also found to have a moderately strong independent relationship with intrinsic motivation.

Perceived competence and engagement with challenging activities also appear to mediate levels of intrinsic motivation. An activity can be considered as too easy, too difficult or challenging. Easy and difficult activities are thought to provide little information about a person's mastery or skill and so add little to their perception of competence. In contrast, a challenge that is both difficult and demanding but also attainable seems to strike the right balance (Hardy, Jones and Gould, 1996). It tests the person's ability on a task where they are unsure of the outcome and successful completion of the task enhances feeling of competence and mastery of the skill, thereby enhancing intrinsic motivation.

As the literature in this area continues to grow, so the relationship between extrinsic outcomes and intrinsic motivation appears increasingly complex. Deci (1975) originally proposed that the relationship was negative whereas later it was argued that outcomes can have both positive and negative relationships with motivation, dependent on the frequency of occurrence and the sex and age of participants. More recently, Deci and Ryan (2002) have revised their thinking and proposed that feedback and reinforcement outcomes interact with intrinsic motivation and this relationship is mediated by the functional significance or psychological meaning of each. The meaning of feedback and reinforcement can be perceived as either informational or controlling, with factors perceived as informational enhancing intrinsic motivation whereas controlling factors have little effect on motivation at all.

The issue of functional significance is also regulated by the individual's intrapsychic orientation (Vallerand, 2007). Echoing work on goal orientation theory (see below), an individual can be either ego involved or task involved in relation to their sport. Ego involved participants are motivated to perform in situations where there is the opportunity for self-reference, such as where the person is in competition with others. The processes of mastery and skill improvement tend to motivate those who are task orientated. It is thought that task-oriented people have a higher degree of self-determination and are more intrinsically motivated than ego oriented people.

RESEARCH BOX

For many readers, the list of theories and models that have been developed to understand why we take part in sport at times must seem very cold, dry and academic or in other words, passionless. This thought also occurred to one of the most pre-eminent researchers in this field, the Canadian psychologist Robert Vallerand. Professor Vallerand used the occasion of his Presidential Address to the Canadian Psychological Association in 2007 to outline his Dualistic Model of Passion (see text), a model that is now used extensively in a range of applied settings including sport. In one recent study, Lafrenière *et al.* (2011) used this model to look at how sport coaches' passion for coaching influenced the quality of the coach-athlete relationship, and what is more, how the type of passion experienced by the coach, either harmonious (positive) or obsessive (negative), impacted on the quality of this relationship. As many as 103 coaches and their athletes from a range of sports including soccer, gymnastics and volleyball were asked to complete questionnaires measuring the coaches' passion for coaching (both harmonious and obsessive), as well as their autonomy support and controlling behaviours. The athletes' perceived relationship quality and general happiness were also measured. The results obtained from these questionnaires were then analysed using structural equation modelling. The results clearly demonstrated that 'coaches' passion matters with respect to the quality of the coach-athlete relationship' (p. 150). More specifically, coaches with a healthy or harmonious passion for their sport often built high quality relationships that were characterised by autonomy-supportive behaviours which in turn were valued by athletes and increased their happiness. By contrast, those coaches who displayed obsessive passion towards their sport often engaged in overly controlling behaviour towards their athletes, although this did not necessarily reflect in poorer quality relationships between the athlete and the coach as perceived by the athlete. The implications of the study are significant. For a coach to be successful and to create a healthy coaching environment then passion does matter but it is the type of passion that is critical. To be effective, passion must be positive and harmonious and not driven to the point of obsession.

To many, SDT has now moved from an intuitively appealing approach to understanding human achievement motivation to a point where the levels of sophistication and complexity can easily become confusing. Perhaps as a reaction to this trend, most recently Robert Vallerand has shifted ground by arguing that while the three basic psychological needs of autonomy, competence and relatedness still underpin our motivation we should focus attention on the reasons why only certain activities seem to occupy our thoughts. Vallerand's Dualistic Model of Passion (Vallerand, 2008), maintains that these are best described as 'passionate activities' where passion is defined as a strong inclination toward a self-defining activity that one likes (or even loves), finds important, and in which one invests time and energy. Passionate activities are then characterised as either obsessive or harmonious. In line with SDT, obsessive passion results from a controlled internalisation of the activity into one's identity, where the values and regulations associated with the activity are not completely embraced. This type of passion can fuel an uncontrollable urge to participate whereas harmonious passion develops naturally from the true internalisation of the activity into the person's identity and occurs when the activity is accepted as important entirely in its own right. Not surprisingly, harmonious passion is associated with positive engagement in sport while obsessive passion is not.

Perceived Competence Theory

Harter's (1978) Perceived Competence Theory is based on the earlier theory of effectance as proposed by White (1959). White stated that a person is motivated to participate in activities associated with a variety of life domains (including sport) in order to demonstrate effectance (competence) and mastery over the situation. According to Harter, the motivational process is mediated by the influences of domain-specific perceptions of competence and control (Babkes and Weiss, 1999). Harter viewed perceived competence as a multidimensional construct with the individual striving for competence in each of the cognitive, social and physical domains.

Once the individual has engaged in a mastery attempt that person will receive feedback on competence from a variety of sources and including significant others (Amorose, 2007). This information will then influence the individual's perceptions of competence, control and affective reactions which, in turn, will influence the likelihood of the person repeating or avoiding the behaviour in order to demonstrate competence (Sundström, 2006). Success that is derived from either internal or external sources is accompanied by intrinsic pleasure, which raises perceived competence, which in turn increases achievement striving behaviour. Alternatively, failure may be accompanied by dissatisfaction and perceived incompetence that will result in fewer mastery attempts (Roberts, 1992). Thus, a person's motivation to demonstrate competence will not only mediate the start of a mastery attempt or participation but also the individual's continued engagement or withdrawal from that activity.

The theory suggests that those who have higher perceptions of competence should be more likely to be involved in sport. While this sounds sensible in theory, unfortunately research has shown that in practice this relationship is not always strong, even when employing modifications to Harter's original scale. As with SDT, perhaps this perspective is likewise not accommodating the diversity of reasons that participants cite for their sport involvement and including affiliation, fun and fitness. Put bluntly, are children involved in sport solely because they want to display competence or for a variety of reasons including wanting to spend time with friends? With this in mind, Klint and Weiss (1986) did find a relationship between perceptions of competence and domain-specific motives for participation. For example, those who entered sport for reasons of skill improvement or mastery had higher perceived physical competence whereas those who mentioned motives including group identity and affiliation had higher perceptions of social competence. Therefore, as any parent will testify, children are different and are motivated by different factors which in turn will reflect in different perceptions of competence. In a later study, Weiss, Amorose and Wilko (2009) found broad support for Harter's ideas, insofar as continued participation in an activity was not only influenced by the perceptions of ability in that activity but also by social acceptance among peers. The research also noted that supportive role models had an impact on perception of self worth and competency within different domains, and that feedback, whether positive or negative, was often regarded as valuable if it helped in the mastery of a new skill.

Harter's work emphasises that a person's motivational orientations are influenced by the outcome of mastery attempts and in turn these influence perceptions of competence. If a person chooses to focus on internal aspects of performance then they will evaluate performance with reference to internal criteria. In contrast, those who evaluate performance with reference to external social factors will have an extrinsic motivational orientation. Developmental and sex differences have been noted in individual perceptions of competence. For example, Van Wersch (1997) found that boys consistently rated themselves as being more physically competent than girls, a finding noted regardless of level of involvement or age.

Harter's theory implies that perceptions of competence can be influenced by social interactions with people such as coaches, teachers, parents or peers (Ullrich-French and Smith, 2006; Weiss, Amorose and Wilko, 2009). Feedback and positive reinforcement are two forms of information that can be given by parents or coaches to provide young people with information about their competence (Amorose, 2007). Allen and Howe (1998) stressed that females in particular rely heavily on evaluative feedback from significant others, be it in verbal or non-verbal form. However, this relationship is complex. The authors found that female athletes rated as high in ability by coaches and who received praise and information following success and less corrective information and encouragement following failure, then perceived themselves as highly competent. Those athletes who received more corrective information and encouragement following failure rated themselves as less competent. The researchers proposed that the athletes perceive corrective information as reflecting poorer ability and when given to one athlete and not another, indicates a perception of low ability. From an alternative viewpoint, it has been argued that those who take part in sport do so because they already perceive themselves as physically competent rather than their participation leading to higher perceived competence (Sundström, 2006). Parental influence may also play an important role in a child's response to sport participation. Babkes and Weiss (1999) found that the following parental characteristics (as seen by their children) were associated with children who had higher sport enjoyment, intrinsic motivation and perceived competence; positive belief in their child's ability, those who gave contingent reinforcement, and those who were seen as placing little pressure on their children. Peers may also provide a valuable source of information. For example, Horn and Amorose (1998) found that in pre and early adolescence, sport participants assess their own competence by cues gathered from peer interactions, while Smith *et al.* (2006) confirmed not only the significance of such peer relationships but also how the type of relationship had a profound effect on perceived competence.

Achievement Goal Theory

Achievement Goal Theory was original developed to explain educational achievement (Nicholls, 1984) and only later was it applied in the context of sport and exercise. The theory proposes that motivational affect, behaviour and cognition can each be understood in terms of particular achievement goals. The theory focuses on the beliefs or cognitions associated with achievement or success (Wang and Biddle, 2001) and proposes that an individual's goal orientations, characterised as either task (mastery) or ego (performance), will be shaped by the interplay between a range of dispositional and situational variables (Roberts, Treasure and Conroy, 2007). A task orientation, or involvement for the sake of mastery, refers to a self-referenced orientation where the person focuses on improvement and mastery of a skill. Typical behaviours associated with a task-orientation are persistence, optimal effort, choice of moderately challenging activities and the selection of competitive settings that will allow feedback on performance. Ego orientation or competitive involvement refers to a normative-referenced orientation, where the person is concerned with demonstrating ability in relation to others. Behaviours thought to be associated with this orientation include a perception of high ability and the selection of activities where the person feels that they will demonstrate superior ability in comparison to others. Where this cannot be achieved the person is thought to select goals that are either very difficult or which avoid failure, in both cases thereby protecting the ego.

Individual goal orientations have been examined in terms of a wide range of issues, including the perceived purpose of sport (Duda, 2005). Those adolescents with a high task orientation believe that sport will improve co-operation and mastery skills while those with a high ego orientation perceive the purpose of sport as being to improve social acceptance and competitiveness.

Duda (2005) further maintained that if an individual has a particular dispositional goal orientation then their attitude towards sport in general would reflect this perspective. Indeed it has been found that task-orientation is related to perceptions of exerted effort in competition while an ego-orientation is related to the demonstration of ability in competition (Boyd and Callaghan, 1994). Similarly Vlachopolos and Biddle (1997) found that participants with a high task-orientation viewed success as resulting from either personal effort, collaboration with team members or personally controllable attributions of past performance. In contrast, those with an ego-orientation saw success as dependent upon ability, deception and external factors. Duda (1996) also suggested that ego-oriented individuals more generally see the use of deception, aggression and unlawful methods as legitimate in sporting competition in order to gain the advantage over opponents. Not surprisingly the achievement orientation literature has tended to favour a task orientation as the more adaptive and desirable goal orientation but this may be a rather limited and perhaps over-simplistic view. For example, Hardy *et al.* (1996) point out that anecdotal evidence from elite athletes simply does not support the view that an ego orientation is maladaptive. Rather they suggest that many have a strong ego orientation, which is perhaps used to sustain long-term motivation. More recently, Hodge, Allen and Smellie (2008) found that a sample of over 300 elite athletes were characterised by a wide range of orientations, with no particular style dominating and at least five goal profiles being identifiable, and within which scores on task and ego orientation varied considerably.

Several studies have considered the relationship between participation motives and goal orientation. Those participants who are task-oriented tend to participate in sport for reasons of skill development, skill mastery, affiliation, and fitness while those with a strong ego-orientation tend to participate for recognition and social status (Duda, 2001). Such findings suggest that only those with an ego-oriented outlook will find competition meaningful, a view supported by Harwood, Hardy and Swain (2000). In contrast, other research has shown that participants with either a task or an ego orientation place a similar emphasis on competition; rather it is their subjective evaluation of the competitive context that is important not the context itself (Treasure *et al.*, 2001). White and Duda (1994) explained this difference as a 'function of an individual's goal orientation' (p. 16). Thus, the meaning of competition is different for each individual, reflecting his or her goal orientation.

Developmental differences in goal orientation have also been described. Originally, Nicholls (1978) proposed that children begin by being more task-oriented but as they approach adolescence so they tend to shift towards an ego-orientation. However, an ego-orientation has been noted in participants as young as 10 years (Boyd and Callaghan, 1994) and differences have also been observed between the sexes, with boys and men being viewed as more ego-oriented than girls or women (Roberts and Treasure, 1995). Also an ego-orientation varies across level of sport involvement whereas task-orientation is not a discriminatory variable across competitive level. In particular those competing at a high level of sport were found to have a high ego-orientation compared with high school or recreation sport participants (White and Duda, 1994).

Achievement Orientation Theory acknowledges the important influence of significant others on goal orientation, including peers, parents, teachers, coaches and instructors (Vazou, Ntoumanis and Duda, 2005; 2006). Researchers have consistently found that differences in the perceived motivational climate are associated with differences in motivational affect, cognition and behaviour (Ntoumanis and Biddle, 1999; White, 2007). Roberts, Treasure and Hall (1994) found that parents high in task-orientation tended to place importance on relationships with other team members whereas, parents high in ego-orientation tended to focus on normative standards and winning. Duda and Hall (2000) and White, Kavussanu and Guest (1998) found that those athletes with a high task- or ego-orientation tend to view their parents as having a similar goal orientation. However, both parents and their children proved inaccurate in predicting the actual goal orientation of the other (Duda and Hom, 1993). Thus it seems that it is not the actual goal orientation of the significant other that impacts upon the participant's goal orientation but rather how they interpret and perceive the actions of the other. White, Duda and Keller. (1998) found that athletes who perceived their parents as encouraging an ego-involving environment worried about their parent's reaction to mistakes made during learning. These children also tended to see their fathers as encouraging winning with minimal effort. This perceived view of parental attitude was not observed for athletes classified as high in task-orientation, these athletes saw their parents as encouraging learning and enjoyment (White et al., 1998). White (1998), who used Fox et al.'s (1994) four profiles to classify athletes, found further support for these findings. Those athletes with a dominant goal orientation had similar perceptions to those previously observed. With regard to athletes with high task and ego-orientation, White stated, 'The results indicated that when high task-orientation was coupled with high ego-orientation, perceptions of the motivational climate were less ego-involving' (p. 25).

The coach or teacher is another significant social influence upon sport participants. Yoo (2003) found that when athletes were assigned to tennis classes characterised by coaching styles and motivational climates that were either task or ego oriented, their subsequent performance changed. Those in the task condition improved their play and their anxiety levels dropped while performance dipped among those assigned to the ego condition, although anxiety levels remained unchanged.

Over recent years the theory has come under closer scrutiny and it is now argued that alongside the dichotomy between task and ego orientations there is a need to consider whether the person is driven by approach (challenge) or avoidance (fear) motives (Elliot and Conroy, 2005). In other words, performance goals that focus on challenge or striving to be competent differ from those that fear showing incompetence. The former is an approach goal and is likely to encourage persistence; the latter represents an avoidance goal, driven not by the desire to meet a challenge but to avoid failing, and hence is not likely to sustain motivation in the long term. In combination these then allow for four distinct achievement goals – mastery-approach (Map); Performance-approach (Pap); Performance-avoidance (PAv); and Mastery-avoidance (MAv). This new formulation has opened the way for interesting re-examinations of particular phenomena, for example perfectionism. In the past it was assumed that this trait was always maladaptive and was strongly associated with an ego orientation. Stoeber *et al.* (2008) discovered that when also taking into account approach – avoidance, that it was only a negative reaction to imperfection that was maladaptive and that striving for perfection was often a positive attribute.

Self-efficacy and social-cognitive theory

Self-efficacy refers to an individual's personal judgements of his or her capability or skill to perform (efficacy expectations) and judgements about the outcome of performance (outcome expectations) (Bezjak and Lee, 1990; Feltz, Short and Sullivan, 2008). It is the psychological construct that lies at the heart of both Self-Efficacy and Social-Cognitive Theories. Bandura's original work (Bandura, 1977a) suggested that four sources of information provide the individual with a sense of self-efficacy. These are *performance accomplishments* (past experience), *vicarious experience* (observation of others), *physiological states* (anxiety, stamina) and *verbal persuasion* (positive self-talk, instruction). Maddux (1995) later suggested that two additional sources of self-efficacy may exist, namely *emotional states* (mood) and *imaginal experiences* (mental imagery) (Maddux and Volkmann, 2010). Of these sources, performance accomplishments are regarded as the most influential source of efficacy information. These sources may also be used to enhance efficacy. If a participant has been successful in the past, they are more likely to feel efficacious in the future. In a further theoretical development, Bandura (1986) went on to say that Self-Efficacy Theory was too static and instead he argued there was a need to consider the ongoing and reciprocal interplay between the environment, our behaviour and our cognitions. This approach implies that psychological constructs, and including self-efficacy, will always be in a state of flux.

While this latter approach holds interesting possibilities for exploring which factors may determine the process of change, the majority of research continues to focus on the core construct of self-efficacy to the exclusion of all else (Feltz, Short and Sullivan, 2008). For example, self-efficacy has been shown to influence behaviours such as activity choice, level of effort, degree of persistence, and achievement (Propst and Koesler, 1998). Typically self-efficacy continues to be measured along three dimensions – _level_ (expected attainments), *strength* (certainty of expectations) and *generality* (number of domains). While the tendency may have been to regard self-efficacy as a psychological trait, it is now regarded as more context-specific than a trait. That is, a person who has high self-efficacy towards one activity may not have high efficacy for another although it may generalise across similar activities (Biddle and Nigg, 2000).

Self-efficacy has repeatedly been shown to be a strong predictor of physical activity (Bandura, 1997; Biddle and Nigg, 2000; McAuley, Pena and Jerome, 2001; Feltz, Short and Sullivan, 2008). For example evidence suggests that adults who are more physically efficacious are likely to attend exercise classes more regularly, expend greater effort, persist longer, have greater success and achieve better health related benefits from a return to exercise than adults with a low sense of physical efficacy (McAuley, Pena and Jerome, 2001). However, self-efficacy does not appear to be a strong predictor of continued adherence to exercise programs (Sallis *et al.*, 1986) though it is a significant predictor of long-term participation in exercise. Hence it appears that self-efficacy has a strong influence on the initiation or adoption of activity, is less important in the medium-term maintenance of activity but is significant in the long-term, continued involvement in activity. Finally, self-efficacy is also thought to mediate the influence of exercise upon affective responses such as anxiety and depression (McAuley and Courneya, 1992).

The power and applicability of self-efficacy in the prediction of participation in physical activity has been substantiated by its use by other theoretical approaches. In recent years, the construct self-efficacy has been incorporated into revisions of the Health Belief Model, Theory of Planned Behaviour and the Transtheoretical Model (see McAuley, Pena and Jerome, 2001 for a review).

Social Exchange theory and derivatives

The social psychological theory of Social Exchange, as originally proposed by Thibaut and Kelley (1959) to consider interpersonal relationships, has been incorporated into a number of sport-specific approaches over the years including Smith's (1986) Cognitive Affective Model, Gould's (1987) Motivational Model of Sport Withdrawal, Gould and Petlichkoff's (1988) Integrated Model of Sport Participation and Withdrawal, and Schmidt and Stein's (1991) Sport Commitment Model (see below for further detail). While research utilising social exchange principles within sport is not extensive, there is evidence to suggest that the underlying principles do have both practical and theoretical value in sport settings (Guillet *et al.*, 2002).

Three concepts outlined by Thibaut and Kelly (1959) have been emphasised in each of the sport-specific models mentioned above. These are *outcome, comparison levels* and *comparison levels_of alternatives*. The outcome of continued sport involvement involves the rewards and costs incurred by the participant. These can be either tangible (money or time) or psychological (competence or effort) (Schmidt and Stein, 1991). The individual is thought to weigh up the rewards against the cost of involvement. Each person has a comparison level that is made of expectations and perceptions of the activity. The comparison between cost and rewards against this level or threshold will determine a person's level of satisfaction with the sport i.e. above the threshold will result in satisfaction and below the threshold will result in dissatisfaction. However, the chosen activity is also compared to realistic alternative activities to determine continued involvement in an activity, which is the minimal outcome of an alternative needed in order to justify the cessation of the current activity (Hardy *et al.*, 1996).

Although the theory does appear to have intuitive appeal it has been criticised for its lack of sophistication and inability to explain certain aspects of sport withdrawal (Schmidt and Stein, 1991). Furthermore on the one hand it is argued that the capacity for engaging with an evaluation or cost-benefit analysis (Smith, 1986) may be beyond young children, while on the other hand such an evaluation may not reflect the full complexity of some individual's decisions to leave sport. Schmidt and Stein (1991) have argued that the theory cannot fully explain burnout from sport as it is unable to explain why athletes continue to persist with an activity to levels of chronic rather than acute stress, when clearly the costs outweigh the benefits. The theory is also unable to distinguish between those participants who dropout to those who burnout. The authors also maintain that social exchange theory may struggle to explain why someone would choose to continue in a sport when both under stress and faced with persistent dissatisfaction. To explain such behaviour they have proposed that commitment provides the key. That is, commitment is thought to mediate participation, explaining why people stay in sport in the absence of benefits and in the presence of increasing costs.

As with the other approaches outlined above it is unlikely that social exchange processes will provide a comprehensive explanation of participation motivation but it is yet another vital part of the jigsaw which when the pieces are all joined together, in combination aids our understanding.

Other perspectives

The majority of literature in sport psychology has focused on sport-specific theories such as those cited above. A further example is Vealey's (1986) Model of Sport Confidence, which was designed specifically to consider the role of self-confidence in determining the process of motivation in sporting contexts. The perspective argues that our self-confidence when faced with a particular competition or challenge (otherwise known as 'state sport confidence' – SC-state) reflects on both our underlying self-confidence or 'trait sport confidence' (SC-trait) and our 'competitive orientation'. Our performance then leads to 'subjective outcomes' (e.g., satisfaction, perceived success) which then influence our competitive orientation and trait self-confidence on future occasions. To support her approach, Vealey developed three separate measures of the three core constructs, known as the Trait Sport-Confidence Inventory, the State Sport-Confidence Inventory and the Competitive Orientation Inventory (Vealey, 1986), although primary research based on this model remains scarce.

Beyond sport psychology, those working in exercise psychology have been inclined to look elsewhere for their inspiration and including health and social psychology. In a review of theories of exercise behaviour, Biddle and Nigg (2000) suggested that theoretical explanations of motivation could be organised into four groupings, belief-attitude, control based, competence based and decision-making theories. Belief attitude theories include most notably the Health Belief Model (Becker *et al.*, 1977), the Theory of Reasoned Action (Ajzen and Fishbein, 1970; Fishbein and Ajzen, 1975) and the Theory of Planned Behaviour (Ajzen and Madden, 1986). Each has been applied to exercise settings, primarily to explain the uptake of and compliance with physical activity programmes among adult populations (Biddle and Mutrie, 2008).

The Health Belief Model proposes that beliefs about the health-enhancing value of exercise versus perceived costs of participation will determine actual participation (Graham, 2000), but driven by the core belief that we are motivated to be healthy. Research has also considered the influence of other mediating variables including social support (Kelly, Zyzanski and Alemagno, 1991) and self-efficacy (Rosenstock, Strecher and Becker, 1988). In terms of general understanding of participation motivation such health-oriented theories will always be limited in their predictive power as they tend to prioritise disease prevention above all other possible motives.

Within social psychology, the work of Ajzen and Fishbein has been very influential since the 1970s. The Theory of Reasoned Action and its successor, the Theory of Planned Behaviour, are both concerned with the relationship between our attitudes, social norms and subsequent behaviour. The Theory of Planned Behaviour introduced the additional variable of perceived behavioural control or the extent to which we believe that we can influence the behaviour in question (i.e., self-efficacy; McAuley, Pena and Jerome, 2001).

Both theories assume that our intention to behave reflects on both our personal beliefs (attitudes) about the behaviour, and what we believe significant others will think about our engagement in that behaviour (social norms). While the core of the perspective is well defined, over the years an increasing number of variables have come to be associated with each component, and therefore model testing has become increasingly sophisticated (Motl *et al.*, 2002). In general research suggests that behavioural intention is a good predictor of levels of physical activity (Godin, 1994; Hagger, Chatzisarantis and Biddle, 2002), but that the effect is mediated by a number of variables including gender, age and enjoyment (Motl *et al.*, 2002).

Control based theories include Locus of Control (Rotter, 1966) and Self-Determination Theory (Deci and Ryan, 1985), which are integrated into a number of other contemporary perspectives already outlined above.

The Transtheoretical Model of Behavioural Change or Stages of Change model (Prochaska and Di Clemente, 1983) is an example of a decision-making theory that incorporates cognitive and behavioural processes in a model of behavioural change. Primarily developed as a heuristic tool to help therapists deal with health-related problems, the process of change is described in terms of a series of stages which moves from pre-contemplation (no engagement) to contemplation ('thinking about doing it'), to preparation ('starting to try it'), action ('doing it') and finally maintenance behaviours ('regularly doing it'). While largely untested, the model has been applied to intervention programmes involving physical exercise and its simplicity has found to be attractive in applied settings (Cardinal, 1999).

METHODS AND MEASURES

Working within and sometimes without these theoretical paradigms, research has endeavoured to identify and quantify the psychological, social and structural factors that significantly influence initiating, continuing and discontinuing sport and exercise (see Boiché and Sarrazin, 2008; Cavill, Biddle, and Sallis, 2001). The key constructs that consistently have been shown to influence participation motivation in sport and exercise are described below, together with measures commonly associated with these constructs. Within this review the focus has been on specific psychological variables which have been associated with a number of theories, rather than constructs and measures associated exclusively with single theoretical perspectives, for example measures of motivation associated with Self-Determination Theory (see Li, 1999; Pelletier *et al.*, 1995; Vallerand and Fortier, 1998).

Psychological variables

Perceived competence. Research consistently indicates that intrinsic motives are predictive of adherence whereas extrinsic motives predict withdrawal (see Ryan *et al.*, 1997). More specifically, Harter (1978) has suggested that it is perceptions of competence that influence both initiation of participation and, more significantly, continuance (otherwise known as 'the success circle'). Despite these assertions, primary research in sport and exercise settings has not revealed a strong relationship (see Roberts, 2001) with research also highlighting the mediating influence of gender (Van Wersch, 1997) and context (Mullan, Albinson and Markland, 1997). More generally descriptive research shows that children and adults cite multiple reasons for participation, only one of which may be the demonstration of ability (Sallis, Prochaska and Taylor, 2000).

Feedback from a variety of sources during participation has been found to influence perceptions of competence and control as well as self-efficacy, affect and self-esteem (Feltz and Petlichkoff, 1983; Weiss and Frazer, 1995). In turn these will influence future participation i.e. the likelihood of repeating the activity to demonstrate competence or withdrawal to avoid failure. Therefore, motivation to demonstrate competence not only influences engagement in participation but also sustained involvement or withdrawal.

Perceived competence is commonly measured using Harter's own perceived competence scales or variations on those themes adapted to sport and exercise (Fox, 1998; Roberts, 1993). In her original work with children, the Self-Perception Profile for Children (Harter, 1985) measured the child's self perceptions in terms of five domains – athletic competence, physical appearance, scholastic competence, social acceptance, and behavioural conduct, together with global self-worth. Variations subsequently were developed to measure perceived self-competence among adolescents and adults, with the number of domains varying depending on age Harter, 1988; 1999; Messer and Harter, 1986; Neemann and Harter, 1986; Renick and Harter, 1988). For example, Marsh (1997) has developed a multidimensional measure of self-concept that includes four domains – academic, social, emotional and physical, along with global self-concept as the superordinate domain. Other writers have also employed hierarchical frameworks but have focused attention on only one domain, the physical. For example, the Physical Self-Perception Profile (Fox and Corbin, 1989) includes subscales measuring five dimensions of physical self-concept namely sports competence, physical condition, body attractiveness, physical strength and physical self-worth. The Physical Self-Description Questionnaire (PSDQ; Marsh, 1997) went further, including 11 subscales, namely strength, body fat, activity, endurance, sports competence, coordination, health, appearance, flexibility, global physical and global esteem. More recently, Milavić, Guć and Miletić (2010) have adapted Marsh's PSDQ and produced two scales measuring both General and Specific Perceived Self-Competence, although these scales require further validation at this time.

Despite the considerable literature now based in sport and exercise, albeit somewhat tenuously, on Harter's original propositions, a number of methodological concerns are still unresolved (Roberts, 2001). For example, children's capacity for accurate social comparison is questionable (Roberts, 1993). Mullan, Albinson and Markland (1997) further criticised the Athletic Competence Sub-scale for its orientation or bias towards competitive sport at the expense of other recreational or non-competitive activities that a child may be involved in. Mullan, Albinson and Markland (1997) later modified the scale to reflect physical activity in competitive sport, play activities and recreational games and found that children themselves tended to differentiate between these three types of physical activity. Boys were found to show higher perceived competence across all three categories while both boys and

girls rated competitive sport as the area where they had the least competence. Thus, sport participation as defined by Harter's (1985) scale may be an
inadequate reflection on actual types of participation.

Self-efficacy. This psychological construct makes an appearance in various theoretical perspectives including the theories or reasoned action and planned
behaviour (McAuley, Pena and Jerome, 2001), and the Transtheoretical Model
(Prochaska and Di Clemente, 1983). The latter proposes that self-efficacy is
one of a number of process variables that account for the movement of a
person from one stage of behavioural change to another.

Measurement of self-efficacy continues to present difficulties (Moritz *et al.*,
2000), not helped by the fact that Bandura's own position on the nature of
the construct changed over time. In his earlier theory, Self-Efficacy Theory
(Bandura, 1977), self-efficacy is determined by four sources of information -
performance accomplishment, vicarious experience, verbal persuasion and
emotional arousal. His later approach, Social-Cognitive Theory (Bandura,
1986), introduced a more dynamic element by suggesting that cognitions
(including self-efficacy), behaviour and the environment continue to interact in a reciprocal fashion over time. Hence self-efficacy is context-dependent
and in turn any measure must reflect that context. Bandura (1986) argues
that any measure must assess self-efficacy in terms of three dimensions –
level (expected level of attainment); *strength* (certainty that the level will be
attained); and *generality* (the fields across which the person feels capable).
This presents a real methodological challenge – to devise reliable and valid
techniques that are tailored towards particular activities and which reference all three dimensions (Moritz *et al.*, 2000).

Self-efficacy has been shown to be a significant predictor of exercise behaviour (McAuley, Pena and Jerome, 2001), with more recent research focusing
on how variables such as age, gender and socio-economic status mediate the
relationship between self-efficacy and participation (e.g., Allison, Dwyer and
Makin, 1999b). Self-efficacy is more specific than sport-confidence, as earlier proposed by Vealey (1986). Sport-confidence is a global measure of self-
confidence whereas self-efficacy deals with expectations of performance in
specific circumstances (Hardy *et al.*, 1996). Consistently research shows that
participation in physical activity, whether sport or exercise based, is positively correlated with self-efficacy (Roberts, 2001) while statistical modelling
suggests that self-efficacy is a significant predictor of exercise behaviour in
particular (McAuley, Pena and Jerome, 2001). With high expectations of a
successful outcome to participation and repeated success, a person will be
more likely to repeat and sustain involvement. Alternatively low self-efficacy
and unfavourable experiences are more likely to lead to withdrawal.

Schunk (1995) suggests that antecedent variables such as prior experience, social support and personality lead to variations in self-efficacy across
individuals and activities. During participation the person is influenced by

self-efficacy, personal goals, feedback and rewards which in turn influence subsequent self-efficacy and motivation toward sustained involvement. The influence of self-efficacy on exercise participation appears to be stronger in the early stages of exercise adoption (Poag and McAuley, 1992), while with repeated experience the activity inevitably becomes more routinised and the demands of participation less taxing, and hence the person relies less on self-efficacy and more on feedback.

In terms of specific demographic variables, men and those with higher socio-economic status are characterised by greater self-efficacy for physical activity compared with women or those with lower socio-economic status (Allison, Dwyer and Makin, 1999a; Gecas, 1989), although Biddle, Goudas and Page (1994) found that self-efficacy was a strong predictor of exercise participation for women but not for men, for whom attitude was the better predictor. Furthermore, self-efficacy has been found to increase until middle age where it peaks before decreasing after the age of 60 years (Gecas, 1989). Looking specifically at age related differences in childhood and adolescence, Chase (1998) suggests that different age groups rely on different sources of self-efficacy. For example, encouragement from significant others becomes an increasingly important source of self-efficacy information as we move to adolescence and specifically feedback from coaches and peers.

Goal-orientation. Over recent years a great deal of attention has been placed on one particular psychological construct, goal orientation (Wang and Biddle, 2007). Recent research continues to explore the relationship between goal orientation and participation through modelling the influence of goal orientations on intentions and perceived competence. With regard to the relationship between goal orientation and participation, research tends to focus on variables associated with participation rather than the process of participation in totality. Instead the implication is that goal orientation primarily discriminates between reasons for participation. A notable exception to this trend is the work of Papaioannou and Theodorakis (1996) on determinants of intention to participate in physical activity. Using structural equation modelling techniques, they found that ego orientation was not related to intention to participate and that task orientation positively influenced intention only indirectly through interest in the activity and attitudes towards involvement. Furthermore the influence of perceived competence on participation was thought to occur independently of goal orientation. The authors suggest that perceived competence influences intention to participate through behavioural control as well as those paths through which task orientation is thought to exert its influence. However, in a further study employing SEM techniques Wang and Biddle (2000) found that goal orientations influenced intention to participate through perceived competence. The inference to be drawn from such research is that task orientation has some predictive power in terms of participation although its influence may be mediated by other psychological constructs, while ego orientation has less predictive power (Whitehead, 1995).

Goal orientation has also been used to explain differences in activities, meaning attached to activity, attitudes towards activity, beliefs about success, and the motivational climate of the activity (Duda, 2005). Constructs such as perceived competence, enjoyment, competitiveness, intrinsic motivation, self-efficacy and self-esteem have also been associated with differences in goal orientation (Duda and Hall, 2000) along with factors including the level of involvement, age and gender of the participant. Those involved in competitive sport outside school have been found to have a higher ego orientation than those involved at school or recreational level. In contrast, task orientation has not been found to discriminate between participants according to level of involvement (White and Duda, 1994). Developmental changes in goal orientation have also been noted; children are thought to be more task-oriented but as they move into adolescence so ego orientation is thought to increase (Nicholls, 1978). Finally, with regard to gender, boys and men are thought to be more ego-oriented than girls and women (Roberts and Treasure, 1995; White and Duda, 1994).

Goal-orientations have been typically measured using either the Perception of Sport Questionnaire (POSQ; Roberts, Treasure and Balague, 1998) or the Task and Ego Orientation Sports Questionnaire (TEOSQ; Duda, 1989; Duda and Whitehead, 1998), the latter measuring both sport-specific and domain-general goal orientation. While the original theory implies the existence of an orthogonal relationship between the two orientations (Duda, 1989) unfortunately much of the literature chooses to classify participants according to a dominant goal-orientation (Hardy et al., 1996; Harwood, Hardy and Swain, 2000; Harwood, 2002). In the words of Hardy et al. (1996), 'Such comparisons are not really logical, since they confound two independent variables and amount to a comparison of apples and oranges' (p. 77).

Relying on the orthogonal relationship, Fox et al. (1994) characterised schoolchildren according to four distinct goal profiles. The first two groups include those who have similar scores for task- and ego-orientation, whether low or high on both. The second two groups include individuals who have a dominant goal profile; thus the person could be highly task-orientated with a low ego-orientation or vice versa.

A number of attempts have been made to test the validity of goal profiles using cluster analysis (Hodge and Petlichkoff, 2000; Wang and Biddle, 2001). When the two goal orientations are correlated, researchers have found a weak correlation, suggesting support for orthogonality rather than bi-polarity (Chi and Duda, 1995: Roberts, Treasure and Kavussanu, 1996). Another issue to consider is that there is a qualitative difference between dispositional (i.e., a tendency towards) goal orientations and situational (i.e., perceptions in a specific context) goal orientations (Harwood, 2002). Like other areas of research dealing with individual differences clarity as to whether states or traits are being measured should be paramount (Harwood, Hardy and Swain, 2000; Treasure *et al.*, 2001).

Goal profiles were traditionally calculated by the use of mean or median splits in the data (Meece and Holt, 1993). However, this is a rather crude measure especially in the case of those participants whose scores fall close to the measure of central tendency (Hodge and Petlichkoff, 2000). By using the more sophisticated technique of cluster analysis the authors found no evidence of a bifurcation of profiles by each orientation. By contrast they found that goal profiles of; low ego/moderate task (rather than low/low); high ego/moderate task (rather than high/high); low ego/high task and high ego/low task provided a better explanation of variations in goal orientation. Clearly there remain significant issues to be resolved in terms of operationalising these psychological constructs.

Competitive orientation. A related literature considers goal orientation within the context of our orientation towards competition itself, as a sport-specific achievement construct. Derived from a number of theoretical traditions associated with achievement orientation, Diane Gill and colleagues developed the Sport Orientation Questionnaire (Gill and Deeter, 1988). The 25-item questionnaire measures three orientations, Competitiveness (enjoyment of competition and the desire to strive for success through competition), Win orientation (interpersonal comparison and 'winning'), and Goal orientation (personal performance standards). Perhaps not surprisingly, research reveals that athletes tend to outscore non-athletes on all three subscales but the Competitiveness subscale is the most powerful discriminator (Gill, 1993).

Affect/mood state. On the one hand the sport and exercise literature suggests a positive relationship between participation and affect in terms of contentment, satisfaction and enjoyment. On the other hand increased negative affect (depression, anxiety, tension) is associated with withdrawal from activity. However, as yet the causal nature of this relationship is unclear with studies exploring the mediating role played by factors such as self-efficacy (Rudolph and Butki, 1998), intrinsic motivation (Frederick, Morrison and Manning, 1996), and significant others (Carron, Hausenblas and Mack, 1996).

This work may have been fettered previously by reliance on inappropriate measures of affect but more recent studies employed measures such as Watson, Clark and Tellegen's (1988) Positive Affect Negative Affect Schedule (PANAS) (e.g., Crocker, 1997) are providing more revealing results. Any analysis of the relationship between affective states and participation must accommodate both positive (contentment, satisfaction, enjoyment) and negative (depression, anxiety, tension) affect as independent constructs. According to Lawton (1994) frequency of engagement in leisure activity is associated with positive affect whereas negative affect is not associated with participation but may be linked to withdrawal from activity (Frederick, Morrison and Manning, 1996).

Rudolph and Butki (1998) suggest that affect and self-efficacy are significantly related as a function of exercise participation. McAuley (1991) found that participants who reported increased self-efficacy also reported increased positive affect and decreased negative affect after participation. Subsequent path analysis indicated that it was self-efficacy that had a direct effect on exercise related positive affect (b=0.21, p>0.05). The authors found that participation in exercise led to increased positive well-being and decreased psychological distress even after ten minutes of exercise. In turn the relationship between positive affect and intrinsic motivation has also been considered. Frederick, Morrison and Manning (1996) found that intrinsic motivation was a significant predictor of positive affect, which in turn influenced adherence to activity, perceived competence and satisfaction.

Carron, Hausenblas and Mack (1996), in a meta-analysis of the effect that social influence has on participation, found that support from significant others had a strong relationship with affective response. They suggested that support from significant others leads to a perception that participation is a favourable activity. This then sustains a self-fulfilling prophecy and consequently positive affect including enjoyment and satisfaction. In support of these findings, Smith (1999), using structural equation modelling techniques, found that among adolescents, friendship had a direct influence on affect. Affect in turn was found to have a direct effect on motivation and participation. Affect was also influenced indirectly by peer acceptance and physical maturity, through self-worth. Among the elderly, friendship was also found to enhance positive affect (Lawton, 1983).

Enjoyment. A construct related to positive mood or affect, enjoyment, continues to be seen as significant in determining adherence to exercise (McCarthy, Jones and Clark-Carter, 2008). Despite its importance in the motivation literature the concept of enjoyment remains poorly defined and is often misinterpreted. One definition of sport enjoyment is that provided by Scanlan and colleagues (Scanlan and Lewthwaite, 1986; Scanlan and Simons, 1992; Scanlan, Stein and Ravizza, 1989). To them, enjoyment is viewed as a positive affective response to physical activity. Unfortunately this view fails to recognise enjoyment as a motivator that initiates participation as well as sustaining involvement. Boyd and Yin (1996) describe enjoyment as a process that influences commitment, which in turn influences participation, Other literature tends to cite enjoyment as a specific measure of the more global term of positive affect. Another view is that held by Csikszentmihalyi (1990) who defined enjoyment in terms of flow. On the basis of this definition, enjoyment is seen as a process of which one product may be positive affect. Thus, previous research addressing the influence of enjoyment on participation has been bedevilled by a range of definitional issues that may have hindered progress (Kimiecik and Harris, 1996).

Among adults, Ashford, Biddle and Goudas (1993) found that the best predictors of enjoyment were sports mastery, performance, sports importance and socio-psychological well-being. Boyd and Yin (1996) suggested that significant sources of sport enjoyment in physical activity of adolescents include greater task-orientation, greater perceived competence and increased number of years involved in the activity. Learned helplessness was negatively related to enjoyment, indicating that a lack of persistence and avoidance of challenging behaviours can be associated with lower levels of enjoyment. Similar sources of enjoyment in youth athletes were found by Scanlan *et al.* (1993a) including effort, mastery, satisfaction with performance, peer and coach support. As can be seen from all these studies, enjoyment tends to be associated with intrinsic rather than extrinsic factors (McCarthy, Jones and Clark-Carter, 2008).

It is apparent that the variable of enjoyment is important in understanding participation. Thinking about participation temporally, enjoyment may provide important information on affect, behaviour and cognition connected with initiation, sustained involvement or withdrawal from physical activity. However, there is a clear need for further research examining this concept, its definition and its measurement.

Contextual variables

Significant others. Undoubtedly significant others play a key role in determining participation and continuance throughout our lives, although who is significant at each stage of our life varies considerably (Sport England, 2005). Among adults, it is work colleagues, health professionals, family and friends who have the strongest influence on exercise adherence (Carron, Hausenblas and Mack, 1996) whereas peer influence is particularly important in adolescence (Horn and Amorose, 1998) and during early to middle childhood parents seem to influence participation and adherence to physical activity programmes.

The preponderance of research in this area has focused on the social influences that determine participation among young people. As one example, Smith, Smoll and Smith (1989) referred to the 'athletic triangle', namely that of the athlete, coach and parent, but it is peer influence that has been found to be of particular importance during early adolescence (Sallis, Prochaska, and Taylor, 2000). Peer comparison and evaluation are seen as particularly important cues or sources of competence feedback at this age (Horn and Amorose, 1998). Duncan (1993) suggested that peers will influence the child's enjoyment, companionship and recognition and these in turn will influence perceptions of competence and affective responses to participation. Using structural equation modelling, Smith (1999) found that peer friendship (companionship and support) does not directly influence either motivation or physical activity but does have an indirect influence through mood state or affect. Peer acceptance (status and value) again was found to influence motivation and participation independently first through self-worth and then through affect. Although Smith tested his model independently for sex differences, identical paths were found for both boys and girls with only a small variation in the strength of the pathways.

Alongside peers, coaches and parents are responsible for creating a motivational climate connected with physical activity among young people (Amorose and Horn, 2000). Work in this domain tends to be couched in terms of Achievement Orientation Theory, suggesting that coaches and parents emphasise either a mastery/task orientation or a competitive/ego orientation. Consistently researchers have found a significant correlation between differences in motivational climate and motivational affect, behaviour and cognition (Ntoumanis and Biddle, 1999). Thus if a child perceives parents or coaches as showing preference for certain objectives associated with physical activity, this perception of motivational climate will subsequently influence enjoyment, satisfaction and beliefs about involvement (Seifriz, Duda and Chi, 1992).

The role of the coach or teacher is hugely influential to a young person's participation and motivation. They provide not only the necessary tuition for skill acquisition but also cues regarding ability, progress and acceptance through offering encouragement, feedback, reinforcement, and hence generating a particular motivational climate. However, the influence of the coach is tempered by how the participant perceives these cues and then acts upon them. For example, Allen and Howe (1998) suggest that children in a team situation perceive those who receive praise as competent and those who receive corrective feedback as having less ability. A coach's influence will also vary by such variables as age, gender, physical maturity and sporting experience (Allen and Howe, 1998; Brustad, 1996; Martin *et al.*, 1999).

In terms of children's participation, parents or guardians play their most significant role in the early to middle childhood years (Jambor, 1999). Parental characteristics (as perceived by the child) associated with greater enjoyment, intrinsic motivation and perceived competence include contingent reinforcement, little pressure and a positive view of the child's ability (Babkes and Weiss, 1999). This is supported by the work of Kendall and Danish (1994) who suggested that rather than providing a physical role model for their children, parents offer a key source of support and encouragement through their attitudes, opinions and behaviour.

As an aside, Weiss and Hayashi (1995) highlight the reciprocal nature of social influence on the activities of those involved. For example, if a child is involved in a sport then family life is adjusted to accommodate practice and competitions. Parents and other siblings may choose to support from the sidelines or become actively involved in that sport or adopt a more active lifestyle. 'Parents, especially, reported attitudinal and behavioural changes as a consequence of their son's or daughter's intensive sport involvement, supporting the existence of reverse socialisation effects through sports participation' (Weiss and Hayashi, 1995, p. 46).

Turning finally to adults, more limited research demonstrates that it is family members and important others (including work colleagues, health professionals and friends) who seem to have the greatest influence on adults' participation in sport and exercise. Carron *et al.* (1996) found that important others and a task-cohesive group provided the strongest source of influence on patterns of exercise adherence, whereas the influence of family support is stronger for affective responses to involvement and compliance with exercise programmes, such as those associated with health rehabilitation.

Health and fitness. A number of studies consistently point to the significance of health related motives for participation (e.g., Buonamano, Cei and Mussino, 1995), and most especially as we grow older. For example, Weiss and Chaumeton (1992) suggest that 'fun' is the most important motive for children and older adults, whereas health and fitness occupies pole position for young and middle-aged adults. The alternative foci of sport-related and exercise-related theories of motivation are more easily understood in the light of this finding.

Activity choice. Given the extensive array of activities that involve physical activity, it would seem sensible to consider how participation motivation may relate to activity choices, for example in terms of either team or individual sports. There is an extensive literature that describes demographic patterns of leisure activity among young people although such work tends not to consider these social trends in relation to underlying theories. This work does reveal however that certain types of activity are more attractive than others. For example, when asked to state a preference, boys will tend to choose team sports while girls will select individual, non-competitive activities (Kremer, Trew and Ogle, 1997). Furthermore, among adolescents over recent years there has been a shift away from organised activities and towards less structured pastimes (De Knop *et al.*, 1999).

Focusing on choice of team or individual sports, it is interesting that work on goal orientation has revealed that task orientation is positively associated with the belief that co-operation and collaboration will lead to team success and that a task-oriented motivational climate is associated with greater team and task cohesion (Duda, 2001). Hence it could be inferred that those with a task orientation may be drawn to team sports in the first place, and in turn make better team players than those with an ego orientation. Furthermore, work on self-efficacy suggests that collective efficacy may be more significant to a team's success than each player's self-efficacy beliefs (Beauchamp, 2007), and hence the type of sport may mediate the significance of self-efficacy in determining motivational strength.

Once involved with a sport, team dynamics may then come to play a significant role in personal motivation. For example, team cohesion has been found to influence rates of dropout (Carron, 1982) and to determine levels of absenteeism for practices (Carron *et al.*, 2002). With regard to intention to participate, Spink (1995) questioned athletes about their intention to return for the next season and found that high perceptions of social cohesion were associated with the intention to return.

Structural barriers. There is a real danger that a review of participation motivation will focus undue attention on the psychological factors and in the process unwittingly ignore practical issues that may have a more profound influence on motivation (Pratt, Macera and Blanton, 1999; Davison and Lawson, 2006). For example, Sleap and Wormald (2001) found that young adolescent women were aware of the potential benefits of exercise but it was barriers, whether genuine or perceived, which prevented regular participation. Likewise Coakley and White (1992) found that adolescents and young adults who did not engage in physical activity gave reasons that included both personal constraints (low perceived competence, boredom and perceived negative evaluation by peers) and external constraints (money, lack of choice, support from significant others, opposite sexed friends and past experience). Indeed this classification of barriers as either personal or external has been supported in the literature (Allison, Dwyer and Makin, 1999b; Gould, 1987; Sleap and Wormald, 2001). Among adolescents lack of time and conflict with other activities are cited as the most important reasons for poor adherence to physical activity programmes (Butcher, Lindner and Johns, 2002), whereas Gebhardt, Van Der Doef and Maes (1999) list four primary reasons for non-participation – chores, entertaining/socialising with friends, watching TV and 'being cosy at home'. With age, perceived risk of injury becomes increasingly important (Biddle and Nigg, 2000) while gender differences constantly appear. Overall Allison, Dwyer and Makin (1999b) found that female adolescents reported more barriers to participation in physical activity than males, with embarrassment regarding body shape and evaluation of appearance by peers (and especially boys) of particular concern. Adolescent females interviewed by James (2000) described the lengths they went to in order to avoid others seeing their bodies in swimming pools, and such practical issues should never be ignored when considering motives for engaging in sport and exercise. While traditional gender stereotypes may be increasingly challenged there is still evidence to suggest that subtle stereotypical gender roles may still operate to discourage girls from entering the world of sport. In the words of Culp (1998), 'it is unacceptable for girls to get dirty ... males are considered tougher or more competitive' (p. 366).

PRACTICAL ISSUES AND INTERVENTIONS

As should be readily apparent there is no shortage of primary research in this area. However, examples of this research being translated into practical interventions are not commonplace. The reasons why this should the case are not immediately apparent. Perhaps the levels of sophistication and theoretical abstraction are now so great that practical remedies are increasingly difficult to devise? Perhaps the lack of consensus discourages action, or perhaps all forms of intervention are implicitly underpinned by the principles associated with this literature? Whichever argument has greater veracity it does seem imbalanced that so much energy continues to be devoted to primary research while so little is applied to positive action measures in the real world.

In terms of encouraging young people to take up sport, the majority of reported intervention programmes do not have a strong theoretical underpinning (Leslie, Sparling and Owen, 2001; Stone *et al.*, 1998). While the absence of theory-driven interventions is generally true there are exceptions to the rule. As already mentioned, the Transtheoretical Model of Behaviour has been employed to provide a framework for deciding which strategy may be most effective for encouraging participation and continuance at different stages (Cardinal, 1997). Harwood and Biddle (2002) describe an intervention programme based on Achievement Goal Theory, which follows Ames (1992) TARGET strategy, developed for use in classrooms as a technique for creating a mastery motivational climate.

A further example is work on goal-setting which has enjoyed considerable prominence within applied sport psychology over several decades and yet which in many respects stands apart from the other perspectives described in the chapter to this point. This is one occasion where it could be argued that action has been allowed to take precedence over research for too long, and particularly sport-specific research.

Goal setting

Famously, Burton (1992) once described goal setting as the Jekyll and Hyde of sport psychology, perhaps not without some justification (Burton, Naylor and Holliday, 2001; Weinberg and Weigand, 1993). The use of goal setting as a performance enhancement technique in sport is derived from Edwin Locke's Goal Setting Theory (Locke, 1968). According to Locke and Latham (1994), goals affect performance by way of four mechanisms. First, goal setting focuses attention, second it mobilises effort in proportion to the demands of the task, third goals enhance persistence, and finally goals have an indirect effect in that they encourage the individual to develop strategies for achieving their goals. Furthermore, Locke and his co-workers claim that a number of features or principles relate to these performance effects. The four principles which should characterise effective goal setting are Difficulty, Specificity, Acceptance and Feedback. Although developed primarily with business and industry in mind, goal setting procedures have been embraced enthusiastically by sport psychologists (Hall and Kerr, 2001) as an integral part of psychological skills training programmes. For example, there are very few sport psychologists who would not be familiar with SCAMP or SMART, the two acronyms commonly used to remind athletes of goal setting principles (SCAMP – Goals should be Specific; Challenging and Controllable; Attainable; Measurable and Multiple; and Personal. SMART – Goals should be Specific; Measurable; Action-oriented; Realistic; and Timely).

Advocates of goal setting would argue that when used appropriately it is able to nurture precisely the kind of motivation that many contemporary theories of motivation regard as vital, driven by personal achievement and intrinsic reward, with a primary but not exclusive focus on process and performance (which may be controllable) rather than outcome or result (which may be determined by external forces beyond our control) (Locke and Latham, 1994). Unfortunately, the reality of intervention has not always met expectations, and several reasons for this shortfall have been advanced. Some would argue that interventions have ignored fundamental differences between the worlds of work and sport (Hall and Kerr, 2001; Kremer and Scully, 1994) and indeed examples where sport and work differ are not hard to find. First, in the world of work intra-organisational competition may be confined to particular functions and indeed may be positively discouraged among co-workers. In sport, and particularly individual sports, competition is considered to be an essential component, whether during training or competition. Second, the extrinsic rewards which accrue from work stand in contrast to the intrinsic motivators which have been identified as being so crucial to maintaining an interest in sport. Third, performance enhancement in business is normally directly related to an end product, increased productivity, while in sport it is argued that goal setting should focus on the process and not the outcome (Bull, 1991). Finally, goals in business and industry tend to be imposed on the individual by external forces whereas sport psychologists advocate that the individual should take control and have ownership of their goals.

Despite these reservations, the limited research that is available suggests that while the positive effects may not be as great as in the world of work goal setting techniques can enhance sporting performance (Burton, and Weiss, 2008; Kyllo and Landers, 1995) and what is more many athletes perceive that they derive benefit from adopting goal setting procedures (Weinberg, Burke and Jackson, 1997). Evaluating the effect of goal setting in sport is not easy because the positive effects do appear to be highly sensitive to individual and contextual variables and effective implementation does require a degree of procedural rigour which is not always matched by the real-world practice of intervention (Weinberg, 1996) For example, those athletes who are not achievement oriented to begin with may find that goals which are either too distant or too challenging may actually de-motivate and hence inhibit rather than enhance performance (Hall and Kerr, 2001). Furthermore, while some athletes may have the single-mindedness to adhere to a well-defined goal setting programme, through hell or high water, others may struggle with the perceived structure and potential constraints that they associate with this level of prescription. Others who may already be sufficiently achievement oriented may not derive benefit from additional attention of this type, while others may feel that the focus on process or personal performance may detract from competition itself which they both enjoy and find motivating. Hence while the general principles are sensible and may have general applicability it would appear that the theory has some way to go before a precise set of guidelines can be drawn up which will accommodate significant individual, social and structural differences.

Integrative models

It could be argued that until a consensus becomes more apparent within the literature, then the translation of theory to practice will continue to be a fraught process. With this in mind, the following quote from Roberts' (1992) seminal text *Motivation in Sport and Exercise* is very revealing:

> We must consider the multivariate complexity of information processing, bi-directional causality, cognitions, and feedback, because such concern is more likely to capture the individual and social reality of individuals in sport and exercise. In the real world, effects are the result of multiple causes in complex interactions. Thus, we must spend more time creating appropriate hypotheses that emanate from an understanding of both the cognitive complexity of the individual and the situational constraints of the contexts. We need to describe, document and conceptually represent the cognitive functioning of exercise and sport participants. Only then can we begin to consider which intervention strategies may be appropriate for particular cognitive deficits underpinning deviant, inappropriate or ineffectual behaviour.
>
> (p. 29)

While this was written nearly 30 years ago, the sentiment still rings true to this day. Until a stronger theoretical consensus emerges across the literature and this consensus is captured by genuinely integrative models of participation motivation then it may be premature to devote too much attention to developing programmes of intervention. Existing theories may help inform elements of intervention programmes, but what of the bigger picture?

Looking at history of work on this task, within exercise psychology Sonstroem's (1988) Psychological Model for Physical Activity Participation was an early but still significant attempt to consider why we engage in any form of physical activity. He suggests that our involvement increases ability which in turn raises self-esteem and which then creates a cycle of activity. Within sport psychology, one of the earliest models to address sport motivation in a holistic fashion was the Model of Youth Sport Withdrawal (Gould, 1987). Intrapersonal, motivational and situational influences associated specifically with competitive sport were initially considered, and it was found that factors affecting withdrawal included conflicts of interest, lack of playing time, lack of success, lack of skill improvement, stress, lack of fun, dislike of coach, boredom and injury. Both of these approaches are reflected in more recent models, the most significant of which are outlined below.

The integrated model of youth sport participation and withdrawal

Building on Dan Gould's earlier work, Gould and Petlichkoff (1988) developed their model to account for behaviour associated with initiation, continued participation and attrition from sport by young athletes in particular, and incorporated elements of competence motivation, achievement orientation and cognitive-stress research, as outlined earlier.

The model contains three components; motivation for participation and withdrawal; cost-benefit analysis and implications of involvement and withdrawal. The first component can be sub-divided in two. Gould and Petlichkoff cited various 'surface-level motives' (p. 172), which are described by children as their motives for participation and withdrawal. These take the form of individual, psychological and physical motives as well as situational motives. Underlying these surface-level motives are the theoretical constructs gathered from three different theories. Included are achievement orientations, competence motivation and cognitive-affective stress (Smith, 1986). These theoretical constructs are said to provide the psychological explanation of motivation.

The second component is concerned with a 'decision making process' (p. 175), which occurs when the young person weighs up the pros and cons of participation against the viable alternative activities based on principles of social exchange. Gould and Petlichkoff (1988) stressed the fact that the cost-benefit analysis is based on the participant's perceptions of their situation at that moment in time.

The third and final component suggests that sport involvement can be of varying intensities and can be sport specific or domain general. This reflects the individual differences that exist in youth sport participation. With regard to withdrawal, Gould and Petlichkoff (1988) recommend that observers view this process as a continuum from sport specific to domain general i.e. withdrawal from a specific level of a sport to withdrawal from all sporting activities.

Gould and Petlichkoff (1988) contend that 'young athletes motive for participation and withdrawal can be explained by the same processes and are influenced by a common set of factors' (p. 171). This view of the relationship between motivation to participate and withdraw from sport provides the justification for the model and seems appealing in its simplicity, although Weiss and Petlichkoff (1989) argue that this is an assumption, which still has very little empirical support.

Sport Commitment Model

Schmidt and Stein (1991) Sport Commitment Model was an attempt to elaborate upon social exchange principles in order to explain participation motivation in sport. Citing Kelley (1983) and Rusbult's Investment Model (Rusbult, 1983) they suggest that commitment is a construct that may help explain why an individual will continue to engage with an activity beyond the time that a pure social exchange analysis would suggest is reasonable. Their concept of commitment is not synonymous with dependence but is stable and is associated with positive states including love, enjoyment and satisfaction (Schmidt and Stein, 1991). Rusbult proposed that commitment could be predicted by variables such as satisfaction, alternatives and investments (intrinsic or extrinsic). Schmidt and Stein adapted Rusbult's three categories of people in relationships to three types of athlete involved in sport, namely stayers, leavers (dropouts) and entrapped (burnouts). Dropout can be distinguished from burnout with reference to investments and alternatives. The individual who drops out may have made fewer investments to the chosen activity and perceives alternatives as much more enticing. However, the burnout prone individual perceives their investments as considerable and hence they will tend to persevere with an activity in the hope good times are just around the corner. In support of these proposals, Raedeke (1997) found that athletes who felt entrapped by or obligated to their sport had higher burnout scores than those athletes who felt attracted or indifferent to the sport.

The model as originally outlined by Schmidt and Stein was later revised, and the Sport Commitment Model then became the subject of extensive research during the 1990s (Carpenter, Scanlan, Simons and Lobel, 1993; Carpenter, 1995; Scanlan et al., 1993a; Scanlan et al., 1993b; Scanlan et al., 1993c; Scanlan, and Simons, 1992). Scanlan et al. (1993b) defined sport commitment as, 'a psychological construct representing the desire and resolve to continue sport participation. It represents athletes' psychological states of attachment to their participation' (p. 6). This definition of commitment regards the concept as a general psychological state or motivational force and thus should not be confused with either a specific intention or behaviour. Scanlan and colleagues were also quick to point out that sport commitment should never be confused with either its antecedents or behavioural consequences and that sport commitment can be sport specific or domain general.

The updated model attempted to explain the relationship between various constructs, which determine commitment and general motivational force. Antecedent constructs include sport enjoyment, involvement alternatives, personal investments, social constraints, and involvement opportunities and these can influence commitment in two ways. The person will either 'want to' or feel they 'have to' continue involvement.

The model has been tested on various populations and it has been found that while each of the antecedents has been shown to predict sport commitment

(Carpenter *et al.*, 1993), it is 'sport enjoyment' and 'personal investments' that are the strongest predictors of commitment (e.g., Carpenter and Scanlan, 1998), while 'personal investments' and 'involvement alternatives' have proved more difficult to quantify.

Scanlan and colleagues classify enjoyment as a positive affective response reflecting generalised feelings of pleasure, liking and fun. However, Kimiecik and Harris (1996) argue that this interpretation may be flawed. They define enjoyment in terms of *flow* or the feelings experienced during an enjoyable activity. This perspective considers enjoyment as a process rather than the outcome of the process, and it would seem there is a degree of ambiguity over terminology that needs to be resolved. Further, the large bulk of research focuses exclusively on young people, and the limited research that is available with adult populations would suggest that the model may need further revision to accommodate important age differences (Casper, Gray and Babkes Stellino, 2007).

The integrated model of sport participation

Weiss and Chaumeton (1992) proposed their integrated model of sport participation in an attempt to bring some coherence to previous research findings. The model suggests that motivation is a process that encapsulates both individual differences and outcomes.

In common with previous cognitive theories, it is suggested that the individual has an orientation that is primarily either intrinsic/mastery (process) or extrinsic/outcome (product). Performance will lead to many outcomes and, according to the participant's personal motivational orientation, each individual will focus upon particular outcomes. A mastery-oriented participant will attune to skill improvement and comparison to past performance whereas an outcome-oriented participant will focus on the social or competitive outcome of the performance. Feedback and reinforcement will also play a role at this point in the model, be it given by the coach, parent or peers. With this information the participant begins to develop his/her own internal or external reward system and sets goals accordingly. Perceived competence and control are also included in the model, along with positive and negative affect. As suggested by Scanlan and Simons (1992) sport enjoyment is part of positive affect and is a 'response to the sporting experience that reflects generalised feelings such as pleasure, liking and fun' (p. 203).

Weiss and Chaumeton (1992) have proposed that individual differences and contextual factors exert influence over the paths taken through their model of motivation. Individual differences include gender, cognitive and physical maturity, while contextual factors include coaching style, sport type and reward structure.

The model certainly appears to provide a useful framework for considering the range of variable that may impact on the process of motivation although it does not appear to have generated much research interest since its introduction in the early 1990s.

The youth physical activity promotion model

Welk's model aims to provide an explanation of youth participation in physical activity and accommodates the influence of personal, social and environmental factors (Welk, 1999). He argues for a distinctive model of motivation for children, in recognition of developmental, psychological and behavioural differences between children and adults. Welk suggests that personal variables such as age, gender, culture and socio-economic status (SES) have a primary influence over all other constructs within the model.

First the model suggests that enabling factors such as access to equipment and facilities, level of fitness and skill determine if a person can become involved in sport. Second reinforcing factors such as the influence of parents, peers, coaches and teachers will come to play an important role in enabling participation. These factors are directly affected by the demographic variables mentioned earlier. Thus if a child is from a low SES background and has inactive parents they are less likely to participate in a sport that requires a considerable time and financial commitment from themselves and their parents.

These enabling, reinforcing and demographic factors consequently influence the child's cognitions about participation. Welk (1999) frames these cognitions in terms of two basic questions, 'Is it worth it?' and 'Am I able?'. 'Is it worth it?' refers to cognitions about the costs and benefits of participation and to affective responses such as enjoyment and interest. 'Am I able?' deals with perceptions of competence, locus of control, self-efficacy and self-worth. These factors are thought to predispose children towards physical activity.

The model has integrated concepts from several approaches previously cited in this chapter and appears useful in clarifying the links between several factors involved in the process of motivation. However, the model remains untested and furthermore, it restricts itself to a consideration of the initiation of physical activity. Initiation is only the first stage of the process of participation and it would be hoped that a comprehensive, integrative model would aspire to account for not only initiation but also continued participation, as well as withdrawal of drop out.

The integrated theory of intrinsic and extrinsic motivation in sport

Yet another attempt to integrate this disparate literature was made by Vallerand and Losier (1999). Their theory takes as its core Self-Determination Theory, as described previously. Social factors (i.e., success/failure, competition/co-operation, coaches' behaviour), mediated by psychological factors (i.e., perceptions of competence, autonomy and relatedness) then determine motivation. Motivation is conceptualised, in line with the work of Deci, as falling along a continuum of self-determination ranging from amotivation through extrinsic motivation to intrinsic motivation. Although there is limited research specifically designed to test the model, there are signs that particular components stand scrutiny and including the relationship between social factors, psychological mediators and subsequent intrinsic and extrinsic motivation (Kowal and Fortier, 2000). However, while other research has provided general support for the model, the self-determination construct has been found to be less robust (Ferrer-Caja and Weiss, 2000).

The cognitive behavioural process model of participation motivation

Kremer, Busby and Lowry began the process of attempting to synthesise existing research into a single, integrated model of participation (Kremer and Busby, 1998; Lowry, 2002). The core of the emerging model is based on well established principles derived from the process models of work motivation primarily associated with Porter and Lawler (1968) and Vroom (1964), otherwise known as VIE Theory (Valence, Instrumentality, Expectancy; Pinder, 1991; Van Eerde and Thierry, 1996) and also incorporating principles derived from Adams' Equity Theory (Adams, 1965). Motivation is defined as a process which links effort to performance to reward and finally to satisfaction, with the strength of motivation determined by the product of valence (the value we place on anticipated rewards), expectancy (our belief that our effort will reflect in changed performance) and instrumentality (our belief that our performance will be rewarded). Using this relationship to form the spine of the model, the authors then endeavoured to introduce the numerous components that previous research has associated with participation motivation at appropriate stages from the predisposition to participate to decision-making, to participation, rewards and evaluation of rewards. Furthermore the model endeavours to introduce a temporal dimension by indicating how this motivational process may determine the individual's willingness to continue to engage in the physical activity, or choose an alternative activity, or drop out entirely.

An initial qualitative study (Busby, 1997, 1999; Busby and Kremer, 1999) confirmed the core features of the model when describing patterns of physical activity over time among a group of life sentence prisoners. Further components of the model were then tested using structural equation modelling. Analysis of two large data sets, based on 2000 young people, generally confirmed the structure of the model, although a number of amendments were also made (Lowry, 2002). The most recent version of the model is shown in Figure 4.1.

In conclusion, our understanding of participation motivation has progressed slowly, from early endeavours to identify individual factors responsible for motivation; to an examination of the influence of attributions on subsequent sports involvement; to piecemeal observations of factors affecting participation; and finally, towards the development of integrative cognitive-behavioural process models. As yet these integrative models still remain in their infancy but they do represent an attempt to bring the sport and exercise psychology literature yet closer to the heart of mainstream psychology and this is trend is surely to be encouraged.

Figure 4.1 *Revised cognitive-behavioural process model of participation motivation*

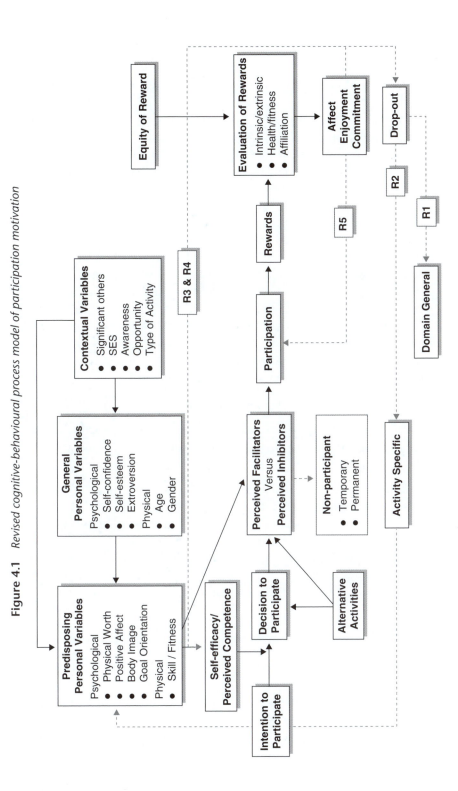

CASE STUDY

From an early age it was obvious that Paul was likely to excel in sport. At primary school he was an automatic choice on every team, he played soccer for a local youth side, and ran in the county cross country championships, which he won easily. His sport came easily to him and he enjoyed trying out new activities and meeting friends. Both his parents were very supportive. His mother had been a county hockey player and his father had played rugby and was president of the local rugby club. At his secondary school Paul was encouraged to play soccer, and scouts from several professional clubs came to watch him play. One offered him the opportunity of an apprenticeship but his parents were keen for him to continue his education and go on to university if possible. The school principal was an ardent soccer fan and coached the First XI himself. His father was involved with mini rugby at his club and Paul would play rugby in the morning before playing soccer in the afternoon. On occasions where there was a school soccer game then he had to miss mini-rugby which his father accepted but he never went to watch him play football. His PE teacher was a keen athletics coach and Paul would still compete although he did not have time for specific training. His natural talent and fitness ensured that he continued to show great promise. At the age of 15 Paul began to find that his enthusiasm for his sport was waning and he found it increasingly difficult to find time for all his sports. He began to miss matches because of injury and on one occasion was late for the bus and was left behind. His father could not persuade him to go to rugby and he showed his obvious displeasure. Paul began to spend more time playing on his compute or hanging around with his friends.

1. With reference to the Theories and Models section in the chapter, how would you interpret what is happening in this case study?
2. With reference to Methods and Measures, what techniques would you employ to help understand and quantify the issues?
3. With reference to Practical Issues and Interventions, how would you deal with this situation?

STUDY QUESTIONS

1. Compare and contrast the key constructs of self-determination theory, perceived competence theory and achievement goal theory.
2. Review the evidence suggesting that self-efficacy can predict participation in physical activity.

3. Consider the contextual variables that have been shown to influence the initiation, continuation and discontinuation of sport and exercise, with particular reference to the measures commonly associated with these variables.
4. What are some of the limitations of goal setting as a psychological intervention?
5. Outline and evaluate the integrative models that have been developed in relation to participation in sport and exercise, looking for commonalities and differences.

FURTHER READING

Duda, J. L. (2005) 'Motivation in Sport: The Relevance of Competence and Achievement Goals', in A. J. Elliot and C. S. Dweck (eds), *Handbook of Competence and Motivation* (New York: Guildford Publications), 318–35.

Elliot, A. J. and Conroy, D. E. (2005) 'Beyond the Dichotomous Model of Achievement Goals in Sport and Exercise Psychology', *Sport and Exercise Psychology Review*, 1, 17–25.

Feltz, D. L., Short, S. E. and Sullivan, P. J. (2008) *Self-Efficacy in Sport: Research and Strategies for Working with Athletes, Teams and Coaches* (Champaign, IL: Human Kinetics).

Hagger, M. S. and Chatzisarantis, N. L. D. (2007) (eds) *Intrinsic Motivation and Self-Determination in Exercise and Sport* (Champaign, IL: Human Kinetics).

Roberts, G. C. (2001) (ed.) *Advances in Motivation in Sport and Exercise* (Champaign, IL: Human Kinetics).

Vallerand, R. J. (2008) 'On the Psychology of Passion: In Search of What Makes People's Lives Most Worth Living', *Canadian Psychology*, 49, 1–13.

5 Concentration

INTRODUCTION, HISTORY AND DEVELOPMENT

Many athletes have discovered from personal experience that attentional processes such as the ability to concentrate effectively are essential for optimal performance in sport. For example, Petr Cech, the Chelsea goalkeeper who set a record by keeping 24 'clean sheets' in the UK Premiership in 2005, claimed that 'everything is about concentration' (cited in Szczepanik, 2005, p. 100). Perhaps not surprisingly, lapses in concentration can mean the difference between success and failure in competitive sport. To illustrate, at the 2004 Olympic Games in Athens, Matthew Emmons, the American rifle-shooter, missed an opportunity to win a gold medal in the 50m three-position target event when he suddenly lost his focus and shot at the wrong target – thereby squandering a three-point lead and almost certain victory in the event. In the light of such incidents, it is not surprising that athletes, coaches and psychologist agree that paying attention to the task at hand is vital for success in sport. But from a psychological perspective, what does 'paying attention' actually mean? What principles govern effective concentration in athletes and why do people seem to 'lose it' so easily in competitive situations? More importantly, what practical techniques can performers use to achieve an optimal focus in sport?

In cognitive sport psychology, 'concentration', or the ability to focus mental effort on the task at hand while ignoring distractions (Moran, 1996), is regarded as one component of the tri-dimensional construct of 'attention'. For cognitive psychologists, this latter term denotes the process of exerting mental effort 'on specific features of the environment, or on certain thoughts or activities' (Goldstein, 2008, p. 100). The three dimensions of attention may be explained as follows.

The first dimension of 'attention' denotes a perceptual skill, which enables a sports performer to 'zoom in' selectively on task-relevant stimulus information while ignoring distractions. To illustrate, a goalkeeper who is preparing to defend a corner kick must be able to visually 'track' the flight of the ball while simultaneously ignoring the jostling and sudden movements of players who are crowded in the penalty area. The second dimension of attention refers to a type of mental 'time sharing' ability in which an athlete has learned, through extensive practice, to perform two or more concurrent skills equally well. In other words, she or he has learned to divide his or her attention effectively. For example, a proficient basketball player can dribble with the ball while simultaneously looking around for an opportunity to pass the ball to a better-placed team mate. Interestingly, people seem to be capable of doing two or more things at the same time provided that at least one of them is highly practised and the tasks operate in different sensory modalities. If neither task has been practised sufficiently or if the concurrent activities are in the same sensory system, then errors will probably occur. The third dimension of attention is 'concentration' or the ability to exert deliberate mental effort when focusing on what is most important in any given situation. For example, a hockey player tries to 'concentrate' when paying attention to coaching instructions delivered before an important match. In this case, concentration can be described as the conscious experience of investing mental effort in a task. To summarise, the construct of 'attention' refers to three different cognitive processes – selectivity of perception (i.e., selective attention), the ability to coordinate two or more actions at the same time (divided attention) and concentration or 'effortful' awareness.

Having explained the constructs of 'attention' and 'concentration', let us now consider the importance of focusing on the task at hand in sport (see Figure 5.1). At least three sources of evidence may be cited in support of the claim that concentration is vital for success in sport. This evidence comes from interviews with athletes (anecdotal evidence), studies of 'peak performance' experiences (descriptive evidence) and research on the efficacy of concentration strategies on athletic performance (experimental evidence). Let us now consider each of these types of evidence in turn.

To begin with, many world-class athletes ascribe their success to the focusing skills that they have learned through competitive experience. For example, Trevor Immelman (South Africa) attributed his victory in the 2008 US Open golf championship to the fact that, mentally, he had been 'totally in the present' in his final round in this event (McRae, 2008, p. 6). Secondly, studies of 'peak performance' experiences or 'flow states' in athletes highlight the importance of absorption in or concentration on the task at hand (see Jackson, 1996; Jackson and Kimiecik, 2008; Kimiecik and Jackson, 2002). To explain, in these coveted but elusive states of mind, there appears to be no difference between what athletes are thinking about and what they are doing. This fusion of thought and action lies at the heart of the 'flow' experience. Thus Jackson *et al.* (2001) defined 'flow' as a 'state of concentration so focused that it amounts to absolute absorption in an activity' (p. 130). Similarly, Kimiecik and Jackson (2002) concluded that a 'complete focus on the task at hand stands out as the clearest indication of flow' (p. 506). A good example of this phenomenon occurred in the case of Roger Bannister who ran the first sub-4 minute mile in Oxford in 1954: 'There was no pain, only a great unity of movement and aim. The world seemed to stand still ...' (Bannister, 2004, p. 13).

Figure 5.1 *Concentration is vital for success in sport*

Source: Photograph courtesy of Department of Sport, University College, Dublin and Sportsfile.

Paradoxically, athletes often report feeling that their minds were 'empty' during peak performances. In this regard, when Pete Sampras won the 1999 Wimbledon Championship, he told reporters afterwards that 'there was absolutely nothing going on in my mind at that time' (cited in Barnes, 1999, p. 14).

The final source of evidence on the importance of concentration in sport comes from experimental research. For example, Wulf (2007) reviewed a number of laboratory experiments indicating that an external focus of attention (where athletes direct their attention at the effects that their movements have on the environment) is usually more effective than an internal one (where athletes focus on their own bodily movements) in the learning and perform-ance of motor skills. The preceding lines of evidence, therefore, converge on the conclusion that concentration is vital for success in sport.

THEORIES AND MODELS

The construct of attention has attracted research interest from psychologists since the dawn of experimental psychology. Thus Abernethy, Summers and Ford (1998) claimed that 'understanding attention ... has been one of, if not the, cen-tral research issue' (p. 175) within cognitive psychology. Not surprisingly, research on attention has become central to cognitive neuroscience because it addresses such fundamental questions as how 'voluntary control and subjective experi-ence arise from and regulate our behaviour' (Posner and Rothbart, 2007, p. 1). Since the cognitive revolution of the 1950s, the mind has been regarded as a lim-ited capacity, information processing system (e.g., see Broadbent, 1958). Within this cognitive research tradition, three key metaphors of attention emerged. The first of these was the idea that attention resembled a physical device (or 'filter'), which 'screened' information as it flowed into the mind. The next metaphor postulated that attention was a 'spotlight' or 'zoom lens' which could illuminate or enlarge what we focused on in the world. Finally, the energy or 'resource' metaphor arose from research on 'divided' attention or our capacity to perform two or more concurrent tasks equally well.

Attention as a 'filter'

The first cognitive metaphor of attention evolved from the research on how people can manage to follow just one conversation at a party when several peo-ple are talking around them at the same time. This question became known as the 'cocktail party' problem. In a clever laboratory analogue of this real-life situation, Cherry (1953) asked people to listen to different messages played on headphones to their two ears. Their task was to pay attention to and repeat aloud (or 'shadow') the message to a designated ear while ignoring the mes-sage presented to the other ear. Results showed that although listeners could recall accurately the content of the shadowed message, they extracted very little information from the unattended ear. For example, they rarely noticed what words were used in the unshadowed message or even when this message suddenly changed from English to a foreign language. However, they almost always detected 'physical' variations in the unattended information such as the pitch of the speaker's voice. This finding led Cherry to conclude that unattended auditory information receives very little processing.

In an effort to explain Cherry's (1953) findings, Broadbent (1958) coined the metaphor of attention as a 'filter' or 'bottleneck'. Briefly, he proposed that when people pay auditory attention, they block out all stimuli except those on which they are focusing. In other words, attention resembles a filter because only one channel of information is allowed to pass through on its way to the brain. However, certain physical aspects of the unattended information (e.g., its loudness and/or the pitch of the speaker's voice) are also allowed through the filter. This 'bottleneck' theory of attention is an 'early selection' approach because it assumes that only a minimal amount of information processing is conducted on the stimulus input prior to attentional selection. Subsequently, however, Broadbent's (1958) theory was challenged by Gray and Wedderburn (1960) who found that some of the unattended information had been processed semantically. For example, salient information in unshadowed messages (such as the sound of the listener's own name) 'grabbed' people's attention in a way that Broadbent could not explain. This finding led rival researchers (e.g., Deutsch and Deutsch, 1963) to conclude that the 'bottleneck' in the processing system probably occurs later than had been envisaged originally. Although there was some disagreement between proponents of 'early selection' theory and their 'late selection' rivals, this debate faded away because an important methodological change occurred in attentional research. Specifically, from the early 1970s, most investigators in this field switched from using auditory to *visual* stimuli. This happened not only because people tend to rely more on vision than on hearing in daily life but also because experimenters could measure more precisely the presentation times and sequences of visual stimuli than their auditory equivalents. As a consequence of this upsurge of interest in visual processing of information, a new and more dynamic metaphor emerged – that of attention as a 'spotlight' and/or 'zoom lens'.

Attention as a 'spotlight' or 'zoom lens'

For over three decades, the study of visual attention has been dominated by the 'spotlight' metaphor (e.g., Posner, 1980) – the idea that our minds pick up information by directing a beam of light at target stimuli around us. A related metaphor is the 'zoom lens' model (Eriksen and St James, 1986), which suggests that the attentional beam can be broadened or narrowed in the same way that one can adjust the focus of a camera. According to this latter metaphor, broadening the beam weakens the resolution of the attentional lens but narrowing the beam has the converse effect. In other words, the resolution of the lens (processing efficiency) decreases as the size of the area inspected increases (see Cave and Bichot, 1999 for a review of this metaphor). One implication of this metaphor is that attention was no longer regarded as an inflexible screening device (i.e., a filter) but as a flexible lens which can intensify perceptual analysis of stimuli. Interestingly, there is some evidence that expert athletes (e.g., boxers) can switch attention (disengage their attentional spotlight) from one location to another more quickly than novices (e.g., see Nougier, Stein and Bonnel, 1991). Subsequently, as a result of the increasing influence of neuroscience on cognitive psychology, researchers began to explore the possibility that the attentional spotlight is directed not at the visual field around us but at the brain areas that specialise in visual perception. Therefore, as Fernandez-Duque and Johnson (1999) pointed out, there has been a shift from 'an attention-spotlight shining on objects in a visual or auditory field to an *inner neural spotlight* shining on brain areas' (p. 99, emphasis added). In other words, the spotlight metaphor of attention has become the 'spotlight in the *brain*' metaphor.

What are the strengths and weaknesses of the spotlight metaphor of attention? On the positive side, it suggests that sports performers cannot ever 'lose' their concentration because their mental spotlight has to be directed somewhere – either at the external world or internally at the private world of their own thoughts and feelings. We shall return to this important idea later in the chapter. Another benefit of the spotlight metaphor is its implication that in order to focus properly, we need to shine our mental beam at a specific target. However, it is only recently that sport psychologists have begun to explore the question of what exact target athletes should focus on when they are exhorted to 'concentrate' by their coaches. For example, Castaneda and Gray (2007), addressed this question by requiring highly skilled and less skilled baseball players to participate in four conditions in a baseball simulator – two that directed attention to skill execution (i.e., 'skill-internal' or movement of the hands; and 'skill-external' or movement of the bat) and two that directed attention to the environment (i.e., 'environment-irrelevant or auditory tones and 'environmental/external' or the ball leaving the bat). Results showed that batting performance for the highly skilled players was significantly better in the two skill conditions than in either of the two environmental conditions. On the negative side, however, the 'spotlight' metaphor of attention is plagued by two main problems. First, it has not adequately explained the mechanisms by which executive control of one's attentional focus is achieved (Fernandez-Duque and Johnson, 1999). Put simply, who or what is directing the spotlight? Second, this metaphor places too much emphasis on what is illuminated by the spotlight and neglects the issue of what lies 'outside' the beam of our concentration. In other words, it ignores the possibility that unconscious factors can affect attentional processes. We shall return to this issue when we consider how unconscious sources of distraction can affect athletes.

Attention as a 'resource'

Whereas filter theories were concerned mainly with identifying how and where selective perception occurred in the information processing system, capacity or resource theories of attention (e.g., Kahneman, 1973) were developed to explain how people can manage to perform two or more simultaneous actions success-fully. Research on this type of mental 'time sharing' ability is relevant to sport psychology because it illuminates various constraints on dual-task perform-ance. For example, research suggests that people can perform two simultaneous tasks successfully only if these tasks rely on different sensory modalities (e.g., vision and hearing) and/or if at least one of the tasks is so highly practised that it is 'automatic' (i.e., does not need to be monitored consciously). Conversely, two tasks will probably interfere with each other if they share the same sensory modality (e.g., whistling and listening require audition) or if either of them has not been practised extensively (Eysenck and Keane, 2010).

Originally, resource theorists (e.g., Kahneman, 1973) postulated that atten-tion resembled a limited 'pool' of undifferentiated mental energy, which could be allocated flexibly to task demands according to certain psychological princi-ples (e.g., motivation, arousal and practice were alleged to increase spare atten-tional capacity whereas factors like task difficulty were assumed to reduce it). Subsequently, Navon and Gopher (1979) argued that people may have *multi-ple* attentional resources rather than a single resource. Each of these 'multiple pools' may have its own capacity and specialised functions. For example, the attentional resources required for selecting a finger to make a movement may be separate from those required to facilitate jaw movements in saying a word (Schmidt and Lee, 2011). Therefore, these two operations should be able to run concurrently without any interference between them. How have resource theo-ries helped us to understand attentional processes? Perhaps the greatest con-tribution here is in the general idea that task performance is constrained by available mental resources – especially those regulating working memory (our mental system for storing and manipulating currently relevant information for a brief period of time). To explain, in most sport situations, athletes face the challenge of selecting task-relevant information from a surfeit of stimulation while simultaneously ignoring distractions. A possible weakness of resource models of attention, however, stems from the danger of circularity in key terminology. Specifically, as Eysenck and Keane (2010) pointed out, resource theorists can always 'explain' dual-task interference effects by assuming that the resources of some central attentional capacity have been exceeded by the demands of the concurrent tasks. But this is just a re-description of the find-ings – not really an explanation – because there is no independent measure of attentional resources.

In general, cognitive models of attention (whether based on spotlight or resource metaphors) have two major limitations. First, they have been preoccupied mainly with external (or environmental) determinants of attention and have largely overlooked 'internal' factors (e.g., thoughts and feelings) which can distract athletes. For example, consider what happened to Sonia O'Sullivan, the 2000 Olympic silver medallist in the 5000m event in Sydney, who allowed her concentration to slip in the 10,000m race at the same Games. According to her, the thought of the medal she had won prevented her from focusing properly in the next race:

> If I hadn't already got a medal, I might have fought a bit harder. But when you have a medal already, maybe you think about that medal for a moment. It probably was only for a lap … but that is all it takes for a race to get away from you.
>
> (Cited in Curtis, 2000, p. 29).

The second weakness of cognitive models of attention is that they largely ignore the influence of emotional states. This neglect is lamentable because it is widely known in sport psychology that anxiety impairs attentional processes. For example, the phenomenon of 'choking under pressure' (whereby an athlete's normally expert level of performance deteriorates suddenly and significantly under conditions of perceived pressure; Kremer *et al.*, in press; see also Chapter 6), illustrates how the 'beam' of one's attentional spotlight can be directed inwards when it should be focused only on the task at hand.

METHODS AND MEASURES

Three main approaches may be identified in the attempt to measure attentional processes in athletes. These approaches are the psychometric (or 'individual differences'), experimental and neuroscientific paradigms. What follows is a summary of these approaches. Readers may also wish to consult other reviews of these paradigms in Summers and Moran (in press).

Psychometric approach

The psychometric approach to the measurement of attention is based on the assumption that people can provide valuable self-report evidence on their own focusing habits, skills, preferences and problems, Based on this assumption, sport psychologists have attempted to measure individual differences in attentional processes in athletes using specially designed 'paper-and-pencil' tests.

For example, the Test of Attentional and Interpersonal Style (TAIS) (Nideffer, 1976) was a popular inventory in this field in the 1980s and 1990s and was used as a screening device in applied settings, such as the Australian Institute for Sport (Bond and Sargent, 1995; Nideffer *et al.*, 2001). It contains 144 items, organised into 17 subscales, which purport to measure people's attentional processes in everyday situations. Although the original version of this test was not intended for use with athletic populations, several sport-specific versions of the TAIS have emerged in recent years. The TAIS is based on Nideffer's model of attention, which can be outlined briefly as follows. According to Nideffer, people's attentional focus varies simultaneously along two independent dimensions, 'width' and 'direction'. With regard to 'width', attention is believed to range along a continuum from a 'broad' focus (where one is aware of many stimulus features at the same time) to a 'narrow' one (where irrelevant information is excluded effectively). Attentional 'direction' refers to the target of one's focus (i.e., either external or internal). These dimensions of 'width' and 'direction' may be combined factorially to yield four hypothetical attentional 'styles'. To illustrate, a 'narrow external' attentional focus in sport is implicated when a golfer looks at the hole before putting. By contrast, a 'narrow internal' focus is required when a gymnast mentally rehearses a skill (such as a back flip) while waiting to compete. Despite its plausibility and popularity, however, this test has several flaws which we shall describe shortly.

The TAIS (Nideffer, 1976) has 17 subscales, of which nine assess the manner in which a person is likely to behave in a variety of interpersonal situations (e.g., item 60, 'People fool me because I don't bother to analyse the things that they say; I take them at face value'). Another six subscales are held to assess attentional processes (specifically, various combinations of attentional 'width' and 'direction') and the remaining two scales are alleged to measure behavioural and cognitive control. The constructs alleged to be measured by the six attentional subscales are:

1. 'broad external focus', (BET), or the capacity 'to effectively integrate many external stimuli at one time' (Nideffer, 1976, p. 397); or 'good environmental awareness and assessment skills' (Nideffer, 1987, p. 19) – measured by such items as 'I am good at rapidly scanning crowds and picking out a particular person or face' (Van Schoyck and Grasha, 1981, p. 152)

2. 'external overload', (OET), external distractibility, or the performer's propensity to make 'performance errors due to attending to irrelevant external distractions' (Nideffer, 1987, p. 19), as measured by items like 'At stores, I am faced with so many choices I can't make up my mind' (Van Schoyck and Grasha, 1981, p. 152)

3. 'broad internal focus', (BIT), or the ability to think of several things at once when it is appropriate to do so, as measured by such items as 'I theorise and philosophise' (Van Schoyck and Grasha, 1981, p. 152)

4. 'internal overload', (OIT), internal distractibility, or a susceptibility to 'thinking about too many things at once' (Nideffer, 1976, p. 397), as assessed by items like 'When people talk to me I find myself distracted by my own thoughts and ideas' (Van Schoyck and Grasha, 1981, p. 152)

5. 'narrow attentional focus', (NAR), or the ability to narrow attention effectively when required, as assessed by statements like 'When I read it is easy to block out everything but the book' (Van Schoyck and Grasha, 1981, p. 152)

6. 'reduced attentional focus', (RED), or a propensity to make errors by narrowing attentional processes excessively as assessed by 'I make mistakes because my thoughts get stuck on one idea or feeling' (Van Schoyck and Grasha, 1981, p. 152).

Among its advantages are the fact that it seems to make 'intuitive sense to coaches and athletes' (Bond and Sargent, 1995, p. 394) and that volleyball players who had been rated by their coaches as 'good concentrators' in competition scored significantly lower on the BET ('broad external' focus) and BIT ('broad internal' focus) subscales than did 'poor concentrators' (Wilson, Ainsworth and Bird, 1985). Unfortunately, these advantages must be weighed against the following weaknesses. First, it is questionable whether athletes are capable of evaluating their own attentional processes using self-report instruments (Boutcher, 2008). Second, the TAIS assesses perceived, rather than actual, attentional skills. Therefore, we cannot be sure that athletes who complete it are distinguishing accurately between what they actually do and what they would like us to believe that they do in everyday situations requiring attentional processes. Third, the TAIS fails to differentiate between athletes of different skill levels in sports in which selective attention is known to be important (Summers and Ford, 1990). Fourth, Nideffer's theory is conceptually flawed because it does not distinguish between task-relevant and task-irrelevant information in sport situations. In view of these difficulties, the construct validity of the TAIS appears to be questionable. In summary, the TAIS has "limited validity and predictive properties for sport performance' (Boutcher, 2008, p. 330). Nevertheless, the psychometric approach has yielded several other instruments that purport to measure concentration processes in sport. For example, Hatzigeorgiadis and Biddle (2000) developed a 17-item test called the Thought Occurrence Questionnaire for Sport (TOQS) which attempts to assess the degree to which athletes experience cognitive interference from distracting thoughts (e.g., about previous mistakes that they have made) during competition. This test contains three subscales which use a standard stem item ('During the competition, I had thoughts ...') that purport to measure 'task-related worries' (e.g., '... that other competitors are better than me'), 'task-irrelevant thoughts' (e.g., '... about what I'm going to do when I'll go home') and 'thoughts of escape' ('... that I cannot stand it any more'). The reliability of each of these subscales appears to be impressive but the construct validity of the TOQS requires additional empirical scrutiny. Another psychometric test that assesses cognitive interference is the Sport Anxiety Scale-2 (SAS-2; Smith *et al.*, 2006) which contains a 'concentration disruption' sub-scale that appears to be quite reliable.

Neuroscientific approach

The second general measurement paradigm in this field involves the search for reliable psychophysiological and neural substrates of attentional processes in athletes. Among the earliest indices of attention that have been studied in this regard are heart rate (HR), electroencephalographic (EEG) measures and event-related potentials (ERPs or 'cortical evoked potentials') (see Hatfield and Kerick, 2007; Janelle and Hatfield, 2008). More recently, sophisticated neuroscientific techniques such as transcranial magnetic stimulation (TMS; a method in which a magnetic coil is placed over the scalp either to inhibit or to stimulate selectively certain parts of the cortical surface) have been used to identify the neural mechanisms underlying attentional processes such as action anticipation in professional basketball players (Aglioti, Cesari, Romani and Urgesi, 2008).

In an early study in this field, Lacey (1967) proposed the 'intake-rejection' hypothesis to account for a pattern of psychophysiological activity that appears to be correlated with attentional focus. Specifically, he postulated that when a task is performed that requires an 'external' attentional focus, a slowing down or 'deceleration' of heart rate occurs immediately before skill execution. Conversely, this hypothesis predicts that when people focus on internal stimuli, their heart rate will increase. This hypothesis has received some empirical support. Thus there is some evidence of cardiac deceleration among elite rifle shooters just before they pull the trigger. This finding is interesting because it suggests that expert target shooters may be able to 'switch on' their attention at will. Another neuroscientific technique that has been used to study attentional processes in athletes is electroencephalography – a method that provides researchers with a continuous record of the spontaneous electrical potentials that are generated by nerve cells in the brain. A typical finding on EEG data concerns cerebral asymmetry effects in target sports. To explain, research suggests that in the milliseconds before expert marksmen (e.g., pistol shooters) prepare to shoot, their EEG records tend to display a distinctive shift from left hemisphere to right hemisphere activation. This shift may indicate that elite marksmen 'are less and less reliant on verbal-analytical processes associated with the left temporal region as they successfully approached the trigger pull' (Hatfield and Kerick, 2007, p. 91). Clearly, such EEG alpha band synchrony (or 'idling'; ibid.) in the left temporal region is a distinctive feature of the preparation of elite marksmen in various sports (e.g., pistol-shooting, archery).

Unfortunately, despite yielding such findings, the EEG is regarded as a relatively blunt instrument because it is typically measured independently of external stimulus events. Arising from this latter limitation, the method of measuring ERPs was developed in order to assess electrical activity in the brain which is 'time locked' to designated eliciting stimuli. Therefore, unlike the EEG, ERPs reflect transient changes in the brain's electrical activity that are 'evoked' by certain information processing events. Typically, ERPs display characteristic peaks of electrical activity beginning a few milliseconds after the onset of a stimulus and continuing for almost a second afterwards. These electrical peaks and troughs are labelled either 'positive' (P) or 'negative' (N) and are designated by their latency in milliseconds from stimulus onset. Using this method, the 'P300' has become an ERP index of attention (Polich, 2007; see also Zani and

Rossi, 1991). More recently, neuroscientific imaging techniques such as functional magnetic resonance imaging (fMRI) and 'positron emission tomography' (PET) have been developed to enable researchers to identify which areas of the brain 'light up' when cognitive activity (such as attention) takes place there (Ward, 2010). Unfortunately, considerable caution is required in the interpretation of data yielded by neuroscientific techniques in psychology. Specifically, we should be wary of the speculative and atheoretical use of such techniques. As Cacioppo, Berntson and Nusbaum (2008) warned, 'neuroimaging is an important new tool in the toolbox of psychological science, but one that is most productive scientifically when its use is guided by psychological theories and converging methodologies' (p. 67). In the absence of critical thinking about the validity of neuroimaging techniques, there is always the danger that they may promote a form of 'neurological reductionism' (Herlihy and Gandy, 2002), in which neural correlates of a cognitive process are mistakenly confused as 'explanations' for that activity.

Experimental approach

The third approach to the measurement of attentional processes in athletes is the 'dual-task' paradigm, which comes from experimental psychology (Eysenck and Keane, 2010). The theoretical rationale for this approach is derived from 'capacity theory' (Kahneman, 1973), which we mentioned in our earlier discussion of resource theory. Briefly, capacity theory proposed that attention may be defined operationally in terms of the interference between two tasks (a 'primary' task and a 'secondary' task) that are performed simultaneously. If these two tasks can be performed as well simultaneously as individually, then it suggests that at least one of them was automatic (i.e., demanding minimal attentional resources). However, if the primary task is performed less well when it is combined with the secondary task, then both tasks are believed to require some attentional resources. In the dual-task paradigm, two tasks are typically performed over three conditions. In condition one, the person has to perform the primary task on its own. In condition two, she or he must perform the secondary task on its own. In condition three, the tasks are performed concurrently.

When this method is applied to sport psychology, the 'primary task' usually consists of a self-paced or 'closed' skill (i.e., one that can be performed without interference from others, e.g., target shooting in archery), whereas the 'secondary task' typically requires the subject to respond to a pre-determined 'probe' signal (e.g., an auditory tone). Following comparison of performance between these three conditions, conclusions may be drawn about the attentional demands of the primary and secondary tasks. Using this method, sport psychologists are usually interested in people's performance in condition three – the concurrent task situation. In this condition, participants are required to perform a primary task that is interrupted periodically by the presentation of a 'probe' stimulus (e.g., an auditory tone). When this probe signal occurs, the person has to respond to it as rapidly as possible. It is assumed that the speed of responding to the probe is related inversely to the momentary attention devoted to the primary task. Therefore, if a primary task is cognitively demanding, then a decrement should be evident in secondary task performance. But if the performance of the secondary task in the dual-task condition does not differ significantly from that evident in the relevant control condition, then it may be assumed that the primary task is relatively effortless (or automatic).

In summary, the dual-task paradigm is an attempt to measure the spare mental capacity of a person while she or he is engaged in performing some task or mental activity. To illustrate this approach, consider a study by Wilson *et al.* (2007) that was designed to explore the effects of anxiety on skilled performance. More precisely, these authors used a dual-task research design to investigate the effects of manipulating people's focus of attention (i.e., either explicitly on their own driving or on a distracting secondary task) on performance on a driving simulator under either low- or high-anxiety provoking conditions. In this experiment, participants were required to perform a primary task (i.e., simulated rally driving) as fast as possible while responding as accurately as possible to one of two theoretically-derived secondary tasks. The skill-focused secondary task required participants to respond to an auditory tone by indicating at that moment whether their left hand on the steering wheel was higher, lower or at the same height as their right hand. The distraction secondary task required people to try to remember the pitch of an auditory tone presented while they were driving. Each condition was completed under evaluative and non-evaluative instructional sets that were designed to manipulate the level of anxiety experienced by the drivers. Results showed that racing performance effectiveness (as measured by lap times) was maintained under anxiety-provoking conditions – although this occurred at the expense of reduced processing efficiency (see 'processing efficiency theory', Chapter 6). More recently, Gabbett, Wake and Abernethy (2011) used the dual-task paradigm to investigate sport skill assessment and enhancement (see box below).

Unfortunately, despite its elegance and ingenuity, the dual-task paradigm from experimental psychology has several weaknesses when applied to athletic performance situations (although it may offer researchers a way of validating athletes' reports of their imagery experiences – see Chapter 3). For example, as Wilson *et al.* (2007) acknowledged, the dual tasks used by researchers in this field are 'somewhat contrived and arbitrary' (p. 454). Also, few criteria are available to guide researchers on the selection of appropriate secondary tasks

To summarise this section of the chapter, three approaches to the measurement of attentional processes in athletes have been reviewed. Unfortunately, no consensus has emerged about the best combination of these methods to use when assessing athletes' attentional processes in applied settings. Nevertheless, the self-report paradigm is perhaps the most popular of the three on account of its brevity, convenience and simplicity. Of course, a major problem with

---

RESEARCH BOX

Dual-task methodology, which requires participants to perform two concurrent activities, is typically used to investigate the attentional demands of a given skill. Recently, however, Gabbett, Wake and Abernethy (2011) reported a study that investigated the degree to which dual-task training methods could improve the performance of 'draw' and 'pass' skills in rugby players – activities that require the ball-carrier to draw opposing defenders in a certain direction in order to expose gaps which can be exploited for attacking purposes. In this study, 21 elite young rugby league players were randomly allocated to either a single-task (*n*=10) or dual-task (*n*=11) training group. Each group performed one training session per week for 8 weeks between the pre- and post-test sessions. The training activities included 6–7 minute sessions of draw and pass drills. The single-task training group performed these activities in isolation whereas the dual-task training group performed them concurrently with an arithmetical secondary task that required counting backwards in 3's from a designated number. In order to assess the learning and transfer of these skills to field settings, a simulated game was developed in which players were required to execute the skills of drawing and passing. Draw and pass skills were assessed by video and coded by independent judges. Results revealed that although statistically non-significant, there was a greater mean score improvement for draw and pass skill proficiency in the dual-task training group than in the single-task training group. Gabbett, Wake and Abernethy (2011) recommended that further research is required to establish the degree to which dual-task training methods may serve to improve sport skills in team games.

---

this approach is that few self-report measures of attention deal explicitly with concentration skills.

Effective concentration

At least five theoretical principles of effective concentration in sport may be identified from reviews of the research literature on the relationship between attention and athletic performance (Kremer and Moran, 2008; Moran, 2012). These principles are summarised in Figure 5.2.

The first principle of effective concentration is that athletes must prepare to achieve a focused state of mind. In other words, it requires deliberate mental

Figure 5.2   *Concentration principles*

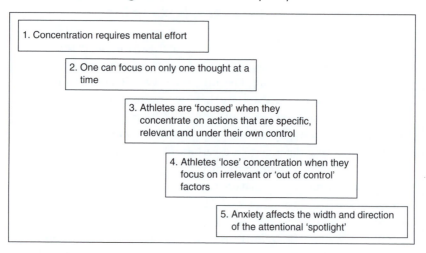

1. Concentration requires mental effort

2. One can focus on only one thought at a time

3. Athletes are 'focused' when they concentrate on actions that are specific, relevant and under their own control

4. Athletes 'lose' concentration when they focus on irrelevant or 'out of control' factors

5. Anxiety affects the width and direction of the attentional 'spotlight'

Source: Based on Moran, 1996

effort and intentionality on the part of the performer. This principle is understood intuitively by many leading athletes. For example, Ronan O'Gara, the Irish and Lions' rugby out-half, revealed that 'I have to be focused. I have to do my mental preparation. I have to feel that I'm ready' (cited in English, 2006, p. 70). Second, although skilled athletes have developed the ability to divide their attention successfully between two or more concurrent actions (see earlier account of 'dimensions of attention'), they focus optimally when they have only *one thought* at a time. This 'one thought' principle has some neurological plausibility because research shows that the working memory system (which regulates conscious awareness) is limited in capacity and duration. For example, according to Garavan (1998), the focus of attention in working memory is limited to a *single item* at a time. Third, as we explained in our discussion of peak performance experiences (e.g., Jackson, 1995, 1996), athletes' minds are focused optimally when there is no difference between what they are thinking about and what they are doing. In other words, sport performers tend to concentrate most effectively when they direct their mental spotlight at actions that are specific, relevant and under their own control. Fourth, research shows that athletes tend to 'lose' their concentration when they pay attention to events and experiences that are in the future, out of their control or otherwise irrelevant to the task at hand (Moran, 1996; 2012). The final principle of effective concentration acknowledges the potentially disruptive influence of emotions such as anxiety. In particular, anxiety impairs athletes' concentration in several distinctive ways. For example, it overloads their working memory with worries (or cognitive anxiety), narrows the beam of their mental spotlight and redirects it inwards onto self-referential stimuli. Interestingly, self-focus models of choking under pressure (e.g., Masters,

1992; Masters and Maxwell, 2008; see also Chapter 6) postulate that anxiety causes people to focus their attention inwards and attempt to consciously control skills that are usually executed automatically – thereby precipitating a form of skill failure known as paralysis by analysis (see also Chapter 6). Anxiety also influences people to focus on task-irrelevant information. So, Janelle, Singer and Williams (1999) discovered that anxious drivers who participated in a motor racing simulation were especially likely to attend to irrelevant cues. Anxiety also influences the direction of athletes' attentional focus by encouraging them to dwell on real or imagined personal weaknesses (self-focused attention) and on potential threats in the environment. In short, anxiety affects the content, direction and 'width' of the spotlight of athletes' concentration (see also Moran, Byrne and McGlade, 2002). But why do sport performers 'lose' their concentration in the first place?

Why do athletes 'lose' their concentration?

Despite the importance of attentional lapses in sport, little research has been conducted on the reasons why highly skilled and motivated athletes 'lose' their concentration in sport (Moran, 1996). From Figure 5.2 above, however, we propose that this latter problem occurs whenever sport performers focus on factors that are either irrelevant to the job at hand or beyond their control. But is concentration ever really 'lost'? As we explained earlier when discussing the 'spotlight' metaphor of attention, concentration cannot really be lost – only misplaced. This experience is very common in everyday life. For example, have you ever had the experience of finding yourself reading the same sentence in a textbook over and over again because your mind was 'miles away'? If so, then you have distracted yourself by allowing a daydream or other distraction to become the target of your attention. Incidentally, this problem can be overcome by writing down two or three specific study questions before you approach a textbook or notes (see advice in Moran, 2010).

In general, psychologists distinguish between external and internal sources of distraction (Moran, 2012). Whereas the former category involves objective stimuli which divert our attentional spotlight away from its intended target, internal distractions include a vast array of thoughts, feelings and/or bodily sensations (e.g., pain, fatigue) which impede our efforts to concentrate on the job at hand. Using this distinction, what types of distraction have affected athletes' concentration and performance in sport?

Typical external distractions include sudden changes in ambient noise levels (e.g., the click of a camera), gamesmanship ploys by opponents (e.g., at corner kicks in football, opposing forwards often stand in front of goalkeepers in order to distract them), unpredictable playing surfaces or weather conditions (e.g., a golfer may become distracted by windy conditions) and audience behaviour. Invariably, these distractions lead to impaired athletic performance. For example, consider what happened to Vanderlei De Lima, the Brazilian marathon runner, while competing in the Olympic Games in Athens in 2004. Leading the race comfortably, he was completely taken aback when a spectator jumped out from the crowd and wrestled him to the ground. Not surprisingly, De Lima's concentration was disrupted and he eventually finished third in the event (Goodbody and Nichols, 2004). By contrast with such external threats to attentional processes, internal distractions are self-generated cognitive concerns that arise from athletes' own thoughts and feelings. Typical examples in this category include wondering what might happen in the future, regretting what has happened in the past, worrying about what other people might say or do and/or feeling tired, bored or otherwise emotionally upset. A good example of a potentially costly self-generated distraction occurred in the case of the New Zealand golfer Michael Campbell at the 2002 European Open Championship at the 'K Club' in Kildare, Ireland. To explain, he was leading the field by five strokes with four holes to play when he made the cardinal error of thinking too far ahead: 'I was in cruise mode but I got too far ahead of myself. I started thinking of my speech, the sort of thing you're not supposed to do, and I suffered the consequences' (cited in Reid, 2002, p. 1). Fortunately for Campbell, he managed to overcome this distraction and won the tournament by one stroke.

Surprisingly few studies have been conducted by psychologists on the phenomenology of distraction in athletes. This neglect of distractibility is a consequence of two main factors – one theoretical and the other methodological. First, for many years (e.g., dating back to the 'multi-store' model of memory; see Eysenck and Keane, 2010, for details) cognitive researchers assumed falsely that information flows into the mind in only one direction, from the outside world inwards. In so doing, they ignored the possibility that distracting information could travel in the opposite direction, namely from long-term memory into the working memory system or current awareness. A second reason for the neglect of internal distractions in psychology stems from a methodological bias. To explain, researchers focused on external distractions simply because they were easier to measure than self-generated distractions. As a result of this bias, the theoretical mechanisms by which internal distractions disrupt concentration remained largely unknown until recently. Fortunately, Wegner (1994) developed a model that rectifies this oversight by purporting to explain why people tend to lose their concentration 'ironically', or at precisely the most inopportune moment. So, why do people's minds wander at the wrong time?

According to Wegner (1994), the mind wanders *because* we try to control it. Put simply, trying *not* to think about something may paradoxically increase the prominence of this thought in our consciousness. This idea accords readily with certain everyday experiences. For example, if you try hard to fall asleep, you will inevitably end up staying wide awake! Similarly, if you attempt to suppress a certain thought in your mind, it will probably become even more prominent in your consciousness. Interestingly, there are many situations in sport in which such ironic failures of self-regulation occur. For example, issuing a negative command to a golfer who faces a short putt ('whatever you do, don't miss it!') may make him or her miss it. So why does this happen?

The 'ironic processes model' of mental control (Wegner, 1994) suggests that when people try to suppress a thought, they engage in a controlled (conscious) search for thoughts that are different from the unwanted thought. At the same time, however, an automatic (unconscious) search takes place for any signs of the unwanted thought. Therefore, the intention to suppress a thought activates an automatic search for that very thought in an effort to monitor whether or not the suppression has been successful. Normally, the conscious intentional system dominates the unconscious monitoring system. But under certain circumstances (e.g., when our working memories are overloaded or our attentional resources are depleted by fatigue or stress), the ironic system prevails and an 'ironic intrusion' of the unwanted thought occurs. Wegner (1994) attributes this 'rebound' effect to the impact of cognitive load. Specifically, whereas this load is believed to disrupt the conscious mechanism of thought control, it does not interfere with the automatic (and ironic) monitoring system. Thus Wegner (1994) proposed that 'the intention to concentrate creates conditions under which mental load enhances monitoring of irrelevancies' (p. 7). To summarise, Wegner's (1994) research helps us to understand why athletes may find it difficult to suppress unwanted or irrelevant thoughts when they are tired or anxious.

Interestingly, the ironic character of mental lapses in sport has been known for many years. For example, Herrigel (1953) observed that 'as though sprung from nowhere, moods, feelings, desires, worries and even thoughts incontinently rise up, in a meaningless jumble, and the more far-fetched and preposterous they are, the more tenaciously they hang on' (p. 53). In recent years, Wegner's model has attracted increasing attention from sport psychology researchers – especially with regard to ironies of *action* rather than those of thought. For example, Woodman and Davis (2008) explored the effects of ironic processes on golf putting performance. They discovered that when players were under pressure (e.g., by competing for a prize), they committed ironic errors when putting (e.g. in over-shooting the hole when instructed *not* to do so). Clearly, this finding raises doubts about the validity of asking anxious athletes not to worry about an important forthcoming athletic event or outcome. This finding also underlines the danger of providing negative instructions (e.g., 'don't get caught offside') to athletes before they take part in competitions. Such instructions may encourage indecision or tentative play among the athletes concerned.

Practical issues and interventions

Over the past decade, a variety of strategies that purport to improve concentration skills in athletes have been advocated by sport psychology researchers (e.g., see Kremer and Moran, 2008). In general, the objective of these concentration strategies is to help athletes to focus only on 'what is important at that moment for executing the skill to perfection' (Orlick, 1990, p. 18). But what exactly do these strategies consist of and how effective are they in enhancing concentration and athletic performance?

In general, focusing skills interventions may be divided into two broad categories: concentration training exercises and concentration techniques (Moran, 1996, 2003, 2012). The difference between these activities is that whereas the former are intended for use mainly in athletes' training sessions, the latter are designed primarily for competitive situations.

Among the toolbox of concentration exercises recommended by some sport psychologists over the past two decades are such activities as the 'concentration grid' (a visual search task endorsed by Weinberg and Gould, 2007, in which the participant is required to scan as many digits as possible within a given time limit), watching the oscillation of a pendulum (which is alleged to show how 'mental concentration influences your muscle reactions'; Weinberg, 1988, p. 87) and looking at a clock 'and saying 'Now' to yourself every alternate 5 and 10 seconds' (Hardy and Fazey, 1990, p. 9). Unfortunately, few of these activities are supported either by a plausible theoretical rationale or by adequate evidence of empirical validity. For example, take the case of the ubiquitous concentration grid – which is also endorsed by Williams *et al.* (2010). Surprisingly, no references were cited by Weinberg and Gould (2007) to support their claim that this grid was used 'extensively in Eastern Europe as a precompetition screening device' (p. 391) or that 'this exercise helps you learn to focus your attention and scan the environment for relevant cues' (p. 392). Similarly, there does not appear to be any empirical evidence to justify the claim that watching a pendulum will enhance one's concentration. Interestingly, this pendulum exercise has a long and controversial history. According to Spitz (1997), it was a precursor of the Ouija board and has been used in the past for water divining, diagnosing physical illness and even for alleged 'communication' with the dead. To summarise, there appears to be little empirical justification for the use of generic visual search and/or vigilance tasks in an effort to improve athletes' concentration skills.

In contrast to the previous concentration exercises, 'simulation training' (Orlick, 1990) may have a satisfactory theoretical rationale. This exercise, which is also known as 'simulated practice' (Hodge and McKenzie, 1999) and 'distraction training' (Maynard, 1998), proposes that athletes can learn to concentrate more effectively in real-life pressure situations by simulating them in practice conditions.

Anecdotal testimonials to the value of simulation training have emerged in recent years in sports such as soccer and cricket. For example, Javier Aguirre, the coach of the Mexican national soccer team, instructed his players to practise penalty taking after every friendly match in the year leading up to the 2002 World Cup in an effort to prepare his players for the possibility of penalty shoot-outs in that tournament. He justified this decision by explaining that 'there will always be noise and that is the best way to practise' (cited in Smith, 2002,

p. S3). Simulation training has also been used in cricket. For example, consider the mental preparation techniques employed by the batsman Mike Atherton, a former captain of the England team, in preparation for test matches:

> For me it begins with practice over those two days. It is a conscious thing, a full dress rehearsal. I treat nets absolutely as a match situation. So, as you walk into the net you give yourself the same thought processes as you might in a match, you take guard and do all your trigger movements the same and you are very, very hard on yourself. This is not just an occasion to go in and hit the ball.
>
> (cited in Selvey, 1998, p. 2)

Unfortunately, despite its intuitive appeal, simulation training has received little or no empirical research evaluation as a concentration strategy (but see Moran, 2009c, for a list of possible simulation techniques used in soccer coaching). However, some support for its theoretical rationale may be adduced from certain findings in cognitive psychology research. For example, research on the 'encoding specificity' principle of learning shows that people's recall of information is facilitated by conditions which resemble those in which the original encoding occurred (Eysenck and Keane, 2010). Based on this principle, the simulation of competitive situations in practice should lead to positive transfer effects to the competition itself. In addition, adversity training may counteract the tendency for novel or unexpected stimuli to distract athletes in competition. Therefore, the simulation of these factors in training should reduce their attention-capturing qualities subsequently. To summarise, it seems plausible that simulation training could enhance athletes' concentration skills. However, this conclusion remains tentative for one important reason. It is doubtful if simulations can ever replicate the arousal experienced by athletes in 'real match' competitive situations. For example, Ronan O'Gara, the Ireland and Lions rugby

Figure 5.3 *Concentration techniques*

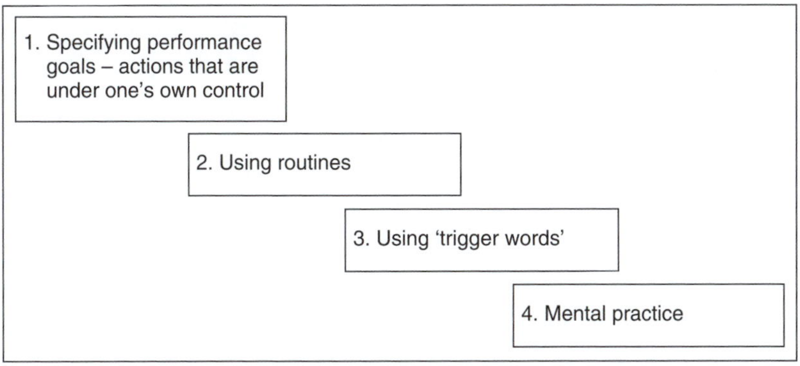

Source: Based on Moran, 1996, 2003, 2012

out-half, admitted that although one can practise taking penalty kicks in training, 'it's completely different in a match where my heartbeat is probably 115 beats a minute whereas in training it's about 90–100' (cited in Fanning, 2002, p. 6). Clearly, it is difficult to simulate emotional aspects of competitive action.

Having reviewed some popular concentration exercises, let us now turn to the second type of attentional skills intervention used in sport psychology, namely the concentration techniques listed in Figure 5.3.

Specifying performance goals

'Goals' are targets or objectives which people strive to attain. Although research suggests that setting goals can significantly improve athletic performamce (Kingston and Wilson, 2009), not all goals are equally effective in this regard. To explain, Weinberg (2009) distinguished between 'outcome' or 'result goals' (or those that refer to the outcome of a sport contest – namely, winning or losing), 'performance goals' (or specific actions lying within the athlete's control such as preparing a stroke early in a rally in tennis) and 'process' goals (or the actions that facilitate a given performance goal – such as swinging from low to high when playing a backhand stroke in tennis). Using this distinction, many coaches and psychologists encourage athletes to set performance goals for themselves in an effort to improve their concentration. For example, penalty takers in soccer are often advised to focus only on their proposed target and not to worry about whether or not the goalkeeper will save their shot. This advice seems plausible theoretically because performance goals encourage athletes to focus on task-relevant information and controllable actions. Interestingly, some empirical support for this idea stems from research on the correlates of 'best' and 'worst' athletic performances. Accordingly, Jackson and Roberts (1992) found that collegiate athletes performed *worst* when they were preoccupied by *result* goals. Conversely, optimal displays tended to coincide with a deliberate focus on performance goals. Similarly, Kingston and Hardy (1997) discovered that golfers who focused on specific action goals improved both their performance and concentration. In summary, there is both conceptual and empirical support for the validity of specifying performance goals rather than result goals as a technique for improving concentration skills in athletes.

Using pre-performance routines

Most top-class athletes display characteristic sequences of preparatory actions before they perform key skills. For example, basketball 'free throwers' and tennis players tend to bounce the ball a set number of times before playing their shots. These preferred action sequences are called 'pre-performance routines' (PPRs; see Cotterill, 2010; Kremer *et al.*, in press) and are typically performed prior to the execution of 'self-paced' skills (i.e., actions that are carried out largely at one's own speed and without interference from other people) (see Figure 5.4).

Figure 5.4 *Pre-performance routines help athletes to concentrate effectively when performing self-paced skills*

Source: Photograph courtesy of Department of Sport, University College, Dublin and Sportsfile

Three types of routines are used by athletes. First, 'pre-event' routines are preferred sequences of actions in the 'run up' to competitive events. Included here are stable preferences for what to do on the night before, and the morning of, the competition itself. Second, 'pre-performance' routines are preferred sequences of task-relevant thoughts and actions which athletes engage in prior to their performance of specific sport skills – as in the case of tennis players bouncing the ball before serving. Finally, 'post-mistake' routines are action sequences which may help performers to 'let go' of errors so that they can refocus on the task at hand. For example, a golfer may 'shadow' the correct swing of a shot that had led to an error.

Support for the value of PPRs as concentration techniques comes from both theoretical and empirical sources. Theoretically, pre-performance routines may improve concentration for several reasons. First, they are intended to encourage athletes to develop an appropriate mental 'set' for skill execution by helping them to focus on task-relevant information. For example, rugby place kickers tend to walk back from the ball a consistent number of paces before steadying themselves to concentrate on the kick being undertaken. Second, routines remind athletes to concentrate on the 'here and now' rather than on past events or possible future outcomes. This 'present mindedness' is vital in sport. Indeed, Paul Azinger, the American golfer and former US Ryder Cup captain, proclaimed that 'staying in the present is the key to any golfer's game: once you start thinking about a shot you just messed up ... you're lost' (cited in MacRury, 1997, p. 116). Finally, pre-performance routines may prevent athletes from devoting too much attention to the mechanics of their well-learned actions – a habit that can unravel even the most automatic of skills (Beilock, 2010; see also Chapter 6). In other words, routines may help to suppress the type of inappropriate conscious control that often occurs in pressure situations.

Complementing this theoretical rationale, empirical evidence from case studies suggests that routines can improve athletes' concentration skills and performance. For example, Cotterill, Sanders and Collins (2010) interviewed a sample of amateur international golfers to elicit their views on the efficacy of PPRs. Results revealed that these golfers used routines extensively for attentional purposes such as attempting to 'switch on and off' (p. 55) and for 'staying in the present and not dwelling on the past or engaging in fortune telling' (p. 55). However, research suggests that the routines of expert athletes may actually be far more *variable* than had been believed. For example, Jackson and Baker (2001) analysed the pre-strike routine of the prolific former Welsh international rugby kicker, Neil Jenkins. As expected, he reported using a variety of concentration techniques (such as thought-stopping and mental imagery) as part of his pre-kick routine. But surprisingly, these researchers discovered that Jenkins varied the timing of his pre-kick behaviour as a function of the difficulty of the kick he faced. This finding shows that routines are not as rigid or stereotyped as was originally believed.

Apart from their apparently inherent variability, pre-performance routines have two other limitations. First, they may lead to superstitious rituals on the part of the performer. For example, before he plays a competitive match, the tennis champion Rafael Nadal, insists on having two perfectly aligned water bottles beside the court - with their labels facing the baseline (Hyde, 2009). Similarly, Tiger Woods feels compelled to wear a red shirt when competing on the final day of tournaments (Preston, 2000). Interestingly, some athletes seem to be unable to differentiate between superstitious rituals and PPRs. For example, consider how Serena Williams explained her defeat at the Fench Open tennis championship in 2007: 'I didn't tie my laces right and I didn't bounce the ball five times and I didn't bring my shower sandals to the court with me … I just knew fate, it wasn't going to happen' (cited in Hyde, 2009, p. 3).

But how can we distinguish between such superstitious behaviour and a rational pre-performance routine? One way of differentiating between routines and superstitions is to examine the issue of *control*. To explain, superstitious behaviour rests on the belief that one's fate is governed by factors that lie outside one's control. But the virtue of a routine is that it enables athletes to exert complete control over their preparation. Therefore, whereas players may shorten their pre-performance routines in adverse circumstance (e.g., bad weather conditions), superstitions tend to grow longer over time as performers 'chain together' more and more illogical links between behaviour and outcome. A second problem with routines is that they need to be revised regularly or else they may become mindless rituals for sports performers. To explain, if athletes maintain the same pre-performance routines indefinitely, they may become so accustomed to them that their minds may begin to wander or 'tune out'. Clearly, an important challenge for applied sport psychologists is how to help athletes to attain an appropriate level of conscious control over their actions before skill execution.

Before concluding this section of the chapter, it may be helpful to provide an example of a pre-performance routine in action. In this case, the routine (adapted from Moran, 2000) is designed to help individuals 'focus' before serving in tennis. The purpose of any pre-shot routine is to take you smoothly and at your own pace from thinking to acting – or from conscious control to automatic pilot. Based on what top tennis players do, the following is a pre-serve routine that can be used to improve serving skills. There are four steps involved in this process:

1. Pick your target (e.g., your opponent's forehand or backhand side) and decide on the type of serve that is required. Would you like to swing the ball out wide or would you prefer to aim down the middle? Are you going to go for placement, power or spin?
2. Pause, get into the ready position, glance at your target, exhale gently and bounce the ball three times for rhythm.
3. Try to 'see' and 'feel' the type of serve that you want to play. Once you have pictured this serve mentally, glance at your target once again.

4. Clear your mind, toss the ball up high and let your body and racket arm do the rest.

'Trigger words' as cues to concentrate

It has long been known that athletes talk to themselves either silently or out loud when they train or compete. This 'self-talk' is usually intended to improve athletes' concentration by instructing or exhorting themselves to engage in specific task-relevant actions. For example, gymnasts may say 'forward' as a reminder to push their bodies upwards while practising a floor routine. Similarly, basketball players may say 'rhythm' when dribbling with the ball and tennis players may say 'low to high' when preparing for a backhand topspin shot. Athletes' self-talk can be either overt (words spoken out loud) or covert ('spoken' inside one's head) and its content may involve praise (e.g., 'Yes! That's good'), criticism ('You fool – what a stupid mistake!') and/or instruction (e.g., the use of a trigger word such as 'turn'). In an effort to measure the content of athletes' self-talk, Zourbanos *et al.* (2009) developed a test called the Automatic Self-Talk Questionnaire for Sports (ASTQ). Preliminary psychometric analysis indicates that this test has acceptable reliability and factorial validity.

A good example of trigger words in action occurred during the 2002 Wimbledon ladies' singles tennis final between Serena Williams and her sister Venus (who she defeated 7–6, 6–3). During the changeover time between games in this match, Serena read notes that she had written to herself as instructional cues to remind her to 'hit in front of you' or to 'stay low' (Williams, 2002, p. 6). Interestingly, there is evidence that instructional self-talk is superior to motivational self-talk in enhancing the performance of tasks that require precision and fine motor coordination (Theodorakis *et al.*, 2000) and in improving athletes' skills in basketball (Perkos, Theodorakis, Y. and Chroni, 2002) and ice hockey (Rogerson and Hrycaiko, 2002).

As a cognitive self-regulatory strategy, self-talk has been recommended as a technique for focusing attention (Weinberg, 1988; Zinsser, Bunker and Williams, 2010). In support of this strategy, Landin and Herbert (1999) discovered a link between training in trigger words in tennis (such as 'split, turn') and self-reported improvements in concentration on court. Although there is considerable evidence that self-talk can improve athletic performance (e.g., see review by Hardy, Oliver and Tod, 2009), there is a dearth of published studies on the question of whether or not it actually improve athletes' concentration skills. However, on a theoretical basis, it is possible that positive and/or instructional self-statements could enhance attentional skills by reminding athletes about what to focus on in a given situation. To conclude, it seems intuitively plausible that to be effective, trigger words must not only be short and vivid but must also emphasise positive targets (what to aim for) rather than negative ones (what to avoid) – recall the implications of Wegner's (1994) ironic processes model discussed earlier.

Mental practice

The term 'mental practice' (MP) or 'visualisation' refers to the systematic use of mental imagery in order to rehearse physical actions (see Chapter 3 for a review of the role of mental imagery in sport). In short, it involves 'seeing' and 'feeling' a skill in one's imagination before actually executing it (Kremer *et al.*, in press; Moran, 2012). Although there is considerable empirical evidence that MP facilitates skill learning and performance, its status as a concentration technique remains uncertain. Judging from anecdotal evidence, however, imagery is used widely by athletes for focusing purposes. For example, consider golfer Darren Clarke's use of imagery to block out distracting thoughts: 'Visualizing things is massively important. If you don't visualize, then you allow other negative thoughts to enter your head. Not visualizing is almost like having a satellite navigation system in your car but not entering your destination into it. The machinery can only work if you put everything in there' (Clarke, 2005, p. 3). In addition to its use as a tool to block out distracting thoughts, mental imagery can also help athletes to prepare for various hypothetical scenarios in impending competitive encounters. For example, the rugby star Jonny Wilkinson, a World Cup winner with England in 2003, uses imagery extensively: "This visualization technique is a sort of clarified daydream with snippets of the atmosphere from past matches to enhance the sense of reality. It lasts about twenty minutes and by the end of it I feel I know what is coming. The game will throw up many scenarios but I am as prepared in my own head as I can be" (Wilkinson, 2006, p. 58).

If this quote is representative of other athletes' experiences with imagery, it suggests that visualisation helps sports performers to prepare for various imaginary scenarios that ensure that they will not be distracted by unexpected events. Unfortunately, this hypothesis has not been tested empirically as yet. Therefore, despite the fact that mental imagery is known to improve athletic performance (Moran, 2012), its status as a concentration technique is uncertain.

In conclusion, attentional processes such as concentration, or the ability to focus mental effort on what is most important in any situation while ignoring distractions, are a crucial prerequisite of successful performance in sport. Unfortunately, despite a century of empirical research on attentional processes, there is still a great deal of confusion about what concentration is and how it can be measured and improved in athletes. We began this chapter by explaining the nature and importance of 'attention' and 'concentration' in sport psychology. Then, we traced the evolution of various metaphors and theories of attention within cognitive psychology. The third part of the chapter explored three main paradigms used by psychologists to measure attentional processes – the psychometric, neuroscientific and experimental approaches. Next, some principles of effective concentration were presented along with a brief analysis of why athletes 'lose' their focus so easily. In the final section, we reviewed the nature and efficacy of various practical exercises and techniques that are alleged to improve concentration skills in athletes.

CASE STUDY

Paul is a 20-year-old professional soccer goalkeeper attached to a Premiership football club but who has recently been sent 'on loan' to a lower division team. Although he played international football at under-18 level, he has been disappointed with his performances over the past two seasons and feels that he needs to play well in his new club or else his contract with his Premiership team may not be renewed. During a discussion, he reveals that some of his difficulties stem from a tendency to 'lose my focus' during matches – especially when the ball is in the opposing team's half of the pitch. His goalkeeping coach has criticised him repeatedly for taking up 'bad positions' in the penalty area at set pieces (e.g., corner kicks) and also for kicking the ball aimlessly up-field rather than directing it to a teammate. He says that he has never considered any form of mental preparation for matches because 'you either have it or you don't' but he is willing to try anything that will help him to play better.

1. With reference to the Theories and Models section in the chapter, how would you interpret what is happening in this case study?
2. With reference to Methods and Measures, what techniques would you employ to help to understand and quantify the issues?
3. With reference to Practical Issues and Interventions, how would you deal with this situation?

STUDY QUESTIONS

1. What do the terms 'concentration' and 'attention' mean in sport psychology? How do we know that concentration is essential for athletic success?
2. Compare and contrast the filter, spotlight and resource models of attention. What are the main limitations of these cognitive approaches to attention?
3. What are the three main paradigms or approaches used by sport psychologists to measure attentional processes in sport? Give an example of a measurement technique arising from each of these paradigms.
4. Why do athletes 'lose' their concentration? Give examples of external and internal distractions in sport. How can these distractions be overcome?
5. What practical techniques are recommended by sport psychologists for improving athletes' concentration skills? Which of these techniques is most useful for an athlete performing an individual sport (e.g., golf)? Which of

them is most useful for team sport performers (e.g., football players)? Does the nature of a sport affect the type of concentration technique that is most suitable for it?

FURTHER READING

Abernethy, B., Maxwell, J. P., Masters, R. S. W., Van der Kamp, J. and Jackson, R. C. (2007) 'Attentional Processes in Skill Learning and Expert Performance', in G. Tenenbaum and R. C. Eklund (eds), *Handbook of Sport Psychology,* 3rd edn (New York: John Wiley), 245–63.

Boutcher, S. D. (2008) 'Attentional Processes and Sport Performance', in T. S. Horn (ed.), *Advances in Sport Psychology*, 3rd edn (Champaign, Illinois: Human Kinetics), 325–38 and 467–70.

Moran, A. P. (2012) *Sport and Exercise Psychology: A Critical Introduction*, 2nd edn (London: Routledge).

Moran, A. P. (2009a). 'Attention in Sport', in S. D. Mellalieu and S. D. Hanton (eds), *Advances in Applied Sport Psychology* (London: Routledge), 195–220.

Moran, A. P. (2009c). 'Attention, Concentration and Thought Management', in B. W. Brewer (ed.), *Sport Psychology* (Handbook of Sports Medicine and Science) Oxford: Wiley-Blackwell, 18–29.

6 Anxiety

INTRODUCTION, HISTORY AND DEVELOPMENT

The ability to cope with pressure situations on the 'big day' of competitive action is widely regarded as a key determinant of success in sport. Evidence to support this claim comes from at least two sources. At an anecdotal level, many top athletes experience anxiety before they compete in major athletic tournaments. For example, Rebecca Adlington, the first British woman to win two Olympic gold medals for swimming, admitted that she had to lie down on the floor before her races in the 2008 Games in Beijing in order to avoid 'standing up and being sick, because I was more nervous than I'd even been in my life' (cited in Moss, Cochrane and Burnton, 2008) Augmenting this anecdotal evidence are psychological profiles of elite athletes (e.g., Dugdale, Eklund and Gordon, 2002; Gould, Dieffenbach and Moffett, 2002; Krane and Williams, 2010) that indicate that the ability to regulate arousal levels is associated with optimal performance in sport. Taken together, anecdotal and descriptive evidence highlight the need for anxiety control skills among elite sport performers. But what exactly is 'anxiety' and how does it affect athletic performance? Where does it come from and how can it be measured? Why do some athletes 'choke' under pressure? Lastly, what practical strategies can help athletes to cope with anxiety in sport situations? The purpose of this chapter is to provide answers to these questions by exploring what is known about the nature, correlates and control of anxiety in sport.

The chapter is organised as follows. To start with, we examine the nature, characteristics and types of anxiety. In this section, we also distinguish anxiety from the related construct of 'arousal'. The next part of the chapter reviews the main theories and models of the anxiety–performance relationship in sport. Then, we explore the principal methods used to measure anxiety processes in athletes. After that, we investigate the various coping techniques used by athletes to reduce competitive anxiety. Finally, as a case study of anxiety in action, we investigate the phenomenon of 'choking' under pressure. Some of these issues have been addressed by Fletcher, Hanton and Mellalieu (2006), Kremer *et al.* (in press) and Moran (2012).

According to Cashmore (2008), the term 'anxiety' refers to an unpleasant emotion, which is characterised by vague but persistent feelings of apprehension and dread. In a similar vein, Buckworth and Dishman (2002) defined this emotion as a state of 'worry, apprehension, or tension that often occurs in the absence of real or obvious danger' (p. 116). Typically, the tension felt by anxious people is accompanied by a heightened state of physiological arousal that is mediated by the autonomic nervous system. This system regulates the body's 'internal' biological environment, which includes the heart, lungs, digestive system and glands.

Psychologists view 'anxiety' as a multidimensional construct with three key elements: cognitive; somatic (from the Greek word soma meaning 'body'); and behavioural (Gould, Greenleaf and Krane, 2002). These dimensions can be described briefly as follows. 'Cognitive' anxiety involves negative appraisal of situational factors as well as of the self (Smith, Smoll and Wiechman, 1998). It is also characterised by intense worries about the future situation and/or one's athletic performance. In particular, cognitive anxiety denotes 'negative expectations and cognitive concerns about oneself, the situation at hand and potential consequences' (Morris, Davis and Hutchings, 1981, p. 541). Although few studies have been conducted on the worries of competitive athletes, Dunn (1999) identified four principal themes in his analysis of cognitive anxiety in ice hockey players. These themes were a fear of performance failure, apprehension about negative evaluation by others, concerns about physical injury or danger, and an unspecified 'fear of the unknown'. Similar concerns were reported by Martinent and Ferrand (2007) who discovered that competitive athletes worried about poor performances – especially the possibility of making mistakes. In general, cognitive anxiety has a debilitating effect on athletic performance (Cashmore, 2008). We return to this issue in the third section of the chapter when we explore why some athletes 'choke' under pressure.

The second component of the construct of anxiety involves 'somatic' or bodily processes. 'Somatic' anxiety refers to the physical manifestation of anxiety and may be defined as 'one's perception of the physiological-affective elements of the anxiety experience, that is, indications of autonomic arousal and unpleasant feeling states such as nervousness and tension' (Morris, Davis and Hutchings, 1981, p. 541). In sport, this component of anxiety is evident in such symptoms of autonomic arousal as neuroendocrine secretions (e.g., of cortisol, a hormone released when people are under stress), rapid heart beat, increased perspiration, shortness of breath, clammy hands and a feeling of 'butterflies' in the stomach. Interestingly, Strahler *et al.* (2010) used the 'cortisol awakening response' (CAR) to investigate athletes' anxiety levels before an important competition. Surprisingly, their results showed that although these athletes reported experiencing a significant increase in somatic anxiety as day of the competition approached, no significant increase in CAR activity was evident. This result suggests that neuroendocrine indices of somatic anxiety may not correspond with subjective experience of stress in athletes. The third component of anxiety is behavioural. Here, indices of anxiety include tense facial expressions, agitation and restlessness (Gould, Greenleaf and Krane, 2002). Interestingly, in spite of being overtly perceptible, the behavioural dimension of anxiety has received relatively little research attention in sport. However, Pijpers *et al.* (2003) studied the behavioural correlates of anxiety in people scaling an indoor climbing wall. They found that, using kinematic measures, the bodily movements of anxious climbers were jerkier and displaced more from their centre of gravity than were those of less anxious counterparts.

In general, two types of anxiety have been identified by researchers (Spielberger, 1966). On the one hand, 'state' anxiety (or 'A-state') is a transient, situation-specific form of apprehension. On the other hand, 'trait' anxiety (also known as 'A-trait') refers to a general, enduring and relatively stable personality characteristic of 'anxiety-proneness' in people. It is a pre-disposition to perceive certain situations as threatening or anxiety-provoking. Technically, state anxiety is 'subjective, consciously perceived feelings of tension and apprehension' (Spielberger, 1966, p. 17) whereas trait anxiety describes a general disposition among people to feel anxious in certain environmental situations (e.g., when playing an important match).

Let us now consider how anxiety may be distinguished from 'arousal'. This distinction is important because research on anxiety processes in sport has been hampered by semantic confusion (Fletcher, Hanton and Mellalieu, 2006; Gould, Greenleaf and Krane, 2002; Thomas, Melleliau and Hanton, 2009). In sport psychology, the term 'arousal' has been used interchangeably with bodily alertness, 'drive' and activation to refer broadly to the intensity of behaviour (Smith, Smoll and Wiechman, 1998). Therefore, arousal is probably understood best as a type of undifferentiated energy, which 'primes' or prepares the body for emergency action such as the 'fight or flight' response. More precisely, it denotes a 'general physiological and psychological activation of the organism which varies on a continuum from deep sleep to intense excitement' (Gould, Greenleaf and Krane, 2002, p. 227). Physiologically, feelings of arousal are mediated by the sympathetic nervous system (which is that part of the autonomic nervous system that prepares the body to 'fight or flight' in the face of perceived danger). Therefore, when we become aroused, our brain's reticular activating system triggers the release of biochemical substances like adrenaline and noradrenaline into the bloodstream so that our body is 'energised' appropriately for action.

Anxiety can be distinguished from arousal in at least one important way. Specifically, whereas 'arousal' involves *undifferentiated* bodily energy, 'anxiety' is an emotional label for a *negatively* interpreted arousal experience (Hardy, Jones and Gould, 1996). In short, anxiety is a negatively charged emotional state. This idea that anxiety has an 'interpretative' component is central to some recent theoretical models of the construct. For example, Gould, Greenleaf and Krane (2002) postulated that cognitive anxiety emerges from the interpretation or 'appraisal' of arousal. Therefore, 'anxiety' can be regarded as negatively interpreted arousal. But this view of anxiety raises an interesting conceptual issue. Specifically, if arousal is amenable to interpretation, then how can we be sure that different athletes will interpret a given state of arousal in the same way? This question raises the issue of whether top athletes view anxiety as a friend or as a foe.

In this regard, some sports performers view anxiety as something that is essential for optimal performance. For example, Christine Ohuruogu, the 400 m sprinter who won a golf medal for Britian in the 2008 Olympic Games, claimed that 'you need some level of pre-race nerves to get the adrenaline gling but it is crucial to keep it under control' (cited in *Guardian*, 2009, p. 35). Interestingly, Mahoney and Avener (1977) found that successful gymnasts (i.e., those who qualified for the 1976 US Olympic squad) tended to perceive pre-competitive anxiety as a form of anticipatory excitement – a view that facilitated their subsequent performance. Conversely, less successful counterparts (i.e., athletes who failed to qualify for the US team) tended to treat their arousal levels negatively, interpreting them as unwelcome signs of impending disaster. Subsequently, a series of studies by Jones and Swain (1992, 1995) and Hanton and Jones (1999) showed that anxiety can either have a facilitative or debilitative effect on sport performance, depending on athletes' perception of their arousal symptoms (see review by Hanton, Neil and Mellalieu, 2008). To explain, if athletes perceive their anxiety to be positive, then it will probably facilitate their performance. The converse prediction also applies. Interestingly, Jones and Swain (1995) supported this 'directional interpretation hypothesis' (Jones and Swain, 1992) when they discovered that elite cricketers interpreted their anxiety symptoms as being more facilitative of competitive performance than did less successful counterparts, despite similar anxiety intensity. To summarise, the way in which athletes label their arousal may determine whether they feel challenged or overwhelmed by a pressure situation. Methodologically, this finding suggests that self-report measures of anxiety should include a scale to assess the 'direction' as well as the intensity of the symptoms experienced.

A key idea from the preceding studies is that similar arousal experiences can be labelled differently. In other words, 'pleasant excitement' for one athlete may appear to be 'unwanted stress' for another performer. To illustrate a positive interpretation of a state of arousal, consider what Sam Torrance, captain of the victorious European team that won the 2002 Ryder Cup, advised his players before the match: 'If you're not nervous, then there is something wrong with you. Nerves create adrenaline and I told them to use that, use it in your own advantageous way, to make you feel better, get pumped up' (cited in O'Sullivan, 2002, p. 19). By contrast, a low level of arousal may be experienced either as a relaxed state or as a 'flat' or 'sluggish' feeling. Thus as Lazarus (2000) pointed out, 'too little anxiety can ... be counterproductive. To turn in a top performance requires the mobilization of sustained effort rather than relaxation' (p. 245).

THEORIES AND MODELS

The relationship between anxiety and athletic performance has attracted a great deal of attention from researchers over the past century (see reviews by Gould, Greenleaf and Krane, 2002; Landers and Arent, 2010). What theories and models have guided this research and what findings have emerged? In general, the most influential theories of the anxiety–performance relationship in sport have been (in chronological order): the 'inverted-U hypothesis' (based on Yerkes and Dodson, 1908); 'catastrophe theory' (e.g., L. Hardy, 1990; Hardy and Parfitt, 1991); the 'conscious processing hypothesis' (Masters, 1992; Masters and Maxwell, 2008) and 'attentional control theory' (Eysenck et al., 2007). As we shall see, earlier unidimensional models of anxiety (e.g., the inverted-U approach and drive theory) have been superseded by later multidimensional approaches such as attentional control theory.

The inverted-U hypothesis

According to the 'inverted-U hypothesis' (e.g., see Oxendine, 1984), the relationship between arousal and performance is *curvilinear* rather than linear. As Landers and Arent (2010) explained, this hypothesis postulates that 'as arousal increases from drowsiness to alertness, there is a progressive increase in performance efficiency. However, once arousal continues to increase beyond alertness to a state of high excitement, there is a progressive decrease in task performance' (p. 229). Put simply, the inverted-U hypothesis claims that increased arousal improve performance up to a certain point, beyond which further increases in arousal may impair it. This theory that arousal has diminishing returns on performance is derived from the Yerkes–Dodson law (Yerkes and Dodson, 1908). Briefly, this latter principle proposed that there is an optimal level of arousal for performance on any task. Specifically, performance tends to be poor at low or high levels of arousal but is best at intermediate levels of arousal.

If the Yerkes–Dodson theory is correct, then athletic performance which occurs under conditions of either high or low arousal should be inferior to that displayed at intermediate levels. Some evidence exists to support this hypothesis. For example, Klavora (1978) found that within a sample of high school basketball players, the highest levels of performance were displayed by people who reported moderate levels of somatic anxiety. However, the question how much arousal is optimal for athletic performance is a complex one that is influenced by several intervening variables. For example, as Landers and Arent (2010) pointed out, the nature of the task and its cognitive demands appear to play key roles in mediating the relationship between arousal and performance. For example, in the case of precision tasks (such as golf-putting) that require fine-motor skills and a steady hand, a small amount of arousal can sometimes impair performance. By contrast, tasks (such as weightlifting) that require gross motor skills, are rarely impaired by low levels of arousal. Similarly, motor tasks that are cognitively demanding (e.g., in requiring many decisions) seem to be more affected by arousal than are tasks that are less demanding in this way. Because there are multiple mediators of the relationship between arousal and athletic performance, it has proved difficult for researchers to test the predictions of the 'inverted-U' hypothesis. This problem is exacerbated by several other methodological issues in this field. For example, it is not easy to devise independent measures of the construct of 'arousal'. As a result, researchers find it difficult to decide whether a given arousal level is 'too low' or 'too high' for a performer. Furthermore, as researchers cannot predict in advance the point of 'diminishing returns' for the effects of arousal on skilled performance, the inverted-U hypothesis is 'immune to falsification' (Neiss, 1988, p. 353). Finally, how can researchers induce different levels of arousal in participants? Clearly, unlike Yerkes and Dodson (1908), they cannot use electric shocks or other forms of aversive stimuli for this purpose. In summary, the inverted-U theory has several flaws as a possible explanation of the link between arousal and performance. Perhaps most significantly, it does not elucidate putative theoretical mechanisms that might account for the link between arousal and performance. Thus the inverted-U is 'a general prediction, or a theory that explains how, why, or precisely when arousal affects performance' (Gould, Greenleaf and Krane, 2002, p. 214).

Catastrophe theory

The 'catastrophe theory' of anxiety (e.g., L. Hardy, 1990; Hardy and Parfitt, 1991; Hardy, Beattie and Woodman, 2007) postulates that physiological arousal interacts with anxiety (in this case, cognitive state anxiety) to influence athletic performance. Its central tenet is that physiological arousal is associated with athletic performance in a manner described by the inverted-U curve, but only when athletes have low cognitive state anxiety (i.e., when they are not worried). When cognitive anxiety (worry) is high, however, increases in arousal tend to improve performance up to a certain point, beyond which further increases may produce a swift, dramatic and discontinuous (hence 'catastrophic') decline in performance rather than a slow or gradual deterioration. Furthermore, catastrophe theory claims that once athletes have capitulated to the effects of anxiety, they cannot simply go back to where they were previously. Instead, they must go back to a lower level of anxiety and start again. In summary, Hardy and his colleagues postulated that arousal may have different effects on athletic performance, depending on prevailing levels of cognitive anxiety in the performer.

Based on this theory, at least two predictions are possible (Gould, Greenleaf and Krane, 2002). First, the interaction of physiological arousal and cognitive state anxiety will determine athletic performance more than the absolute value of either variable alone. So, high cognitive anxiety should enhance performance at low levels of physiological arousal but should hinder performance at relatively higher levels of arousal. This prediction is interesting because it suggests that contrary to popular opinion, cognitive anxiety does not always hamper performance (Hardy, 1997). In addition, when an athlete experiences high cognitive anxiety, then the arousal–performance curve should follow a different path under conditions of increasing versus decreasing physiological arousal (a phenomenon known as 'hysteresis'). Although catastrophe theory has received some empirical support (see Edwards *et al.*, 2002; Vickers and Williams, 2007), its complexity (in particular, its three-dimensional nature) makes it difficult to test empirically. Another limitation of the catastrophe model is that it is primarily descriptive rather than explanatory. In other words, it does not specify adequately the mechanisms by which anxiety is believed to impair performance.

Conscious processing or 'reinvestment' hypothesis

The 'conscious processing' or 'reinvestment hypothesis' (Masters, 1992; Masters and Maxwell, 2008; Masters, Polmanand and Hammond, 1993) suggests that sudden deteriorations of skilled performance under anxiety-provoking conditions are caused by a 'reinvestment of controlled processing' or a 'tendency to introduce conscious control of a movement by isolating and focusing on specific components of it' (Masters, Polmanand and Hammond, 1993, p. 664). In other words, this theory proposes that anxiety encourages athletes to attempt to control their movements using explicit rules rather than automatic, implicit habits. For example, an anxious tennis player who is serving at match point may become so preoccupied with technical coaching instructions (e.g., 'throw the ball up high and slowly let your serving arm drop behind your shoulder') that he or she freezes – a phenomenon known colloquially as 'paralysed by analysis'. This skill failure happens, according to Masters and his colleagues, because the 'reinvestment' of conscious processes in automatic skills is time-consuming and ineffective. In short, Masters, Polmanand and Hammond (1993) proposed that skilled performance tends to deteriorate whenever people try to exert conscious control over movements that had been previously under automatic control.

Although the phenomenon of 'paralysis by analysis' has been known for a long time, Masters (1992) added a subtle 'twist' to it. Briefly, skill failure under pressure appears to occur largely because performers regress to earlier, verbal models of control of actions. But what if it were possible to learn a new skill without acquiring explicit verbal knowledge about it? If this happened, there would be nothing for performers to regress back to in pressure situations. Therefore, such a skill should not fail under pressure. In an effort to test this hypothesis for the skill of golf putting, Masters (1992) devised an intriguing experimental paradigm. Briefly, participants were required to perform putting skills in a training and a testing phase. Two conditions were crucial to the experiment. In the 'explicit' condition, participants were instructed to read coaching manuals on golf putting. Conversely, in the 'implicit' condition, participants were given no instructions but had to putt golf balls while performing a secondary task (which had been designed to prevent them from introspecting on the 'rules' of the skill). There were four training sessions in which participants had to try to 'hole' 100 golf balls. The number of putts holed was measured in each case. After the fourth training session, a source of stress was introduced. This stress was induced by a combination of evaluation apprehension (e.g., requesting an alleged golfing expert to judge their putting performance) and financial inducement. Results suggested that, as predicted by the 'reinvestment hypothesis', the implicit learning group showed no deterioration in performance under

---

RESEARCH BOX

The term 'choking under pressure' refers to a phenomenon in which an athlete's normally expert level of performance deteriorates suddenly and significantly under conditions of perceived pressure spite of high levels of motivation and incentives for success (see more detailed discussion later in the chapter). Although evidence is accumulating to suggest that skill failure under pressure in motor tasks is associated with a mental process known as 'reinvestment' (i.e., the propensity to engage in conscious control activities when under pressure), relatively little is known about the relationship between reinvestment and performance deterioration in cognitive task (e.g., those that require working memory). In an effort to address this unresolved issue, Kinrade, Jackson and Ashford (2010) investigated the role of reinvestment in choking under pressure on motor and cognitive tasks. Participants completed the Reinvestment Scale as well as variety of low-and high-complexity tasks eliciting motor (e.g., peg-board) and cognitive (e.g., modular arithmetic problems tapping working memory) processes in low- and high-pressure conditions. Results revealed that pressure had a detrimental effect on performance in the peg-board motor task, Damarjianled to faster but more error-prone performance in the card-sorting task and led to increased errors in the high-complexity cognitive (modular arithmetic) tasks. Furthermore, high reinvestment scores were significantly associated with performance decrements in both the peg-board and modular arithmetic tasks. These findings led Kinrade, Jackson and Ashford (2010) to conclude that reinvestment is associated with choking under pressure in cognitive as well as in motor tasks. More generally, this study supports the theory (e.g., see Masters and Maxwell, 2008) that high reinvesters are more susceptible to the detrimental effects of pressure than are low reinvesters.

stress in contrast to the golfers in the explicit learning condition. Masters (1992) interpreted this to mean that the skills of athletes with a small pool of explicit knowledge are less likely to fail than those of performers with relatively larger amounts of explicit knowledge. In other words, anxiety appears to have different effects on performance, depending on how the skill was acquired in the first place (i.e., through explicit or implicit learning). In an effort to measure individual differences in dispositional reinvestment (or people's tendency to attempt to gain conscious control over an automatic skill in pressure situations), Masters, Polmanand and Hammond, (1993) developed a 20-item Reinvestment Scale. Put simply, this scale purports to measure the extent of people's self-consciousness in everyday situations. Sample items include 'I'm aware of the way my mind works when I work through a problem' and 'I'm concerned about my style of doing things'. Interestingly, Jackson, Ashford and Norsworthy (2006) reported evidence that supports the predictive validity of this scale when they found that high 'reinvesters' displayed greater susceptibility to skill failure under pressure than did low 'reinvester' counterparts. More recently, Kinrade, Jackson and Ashford (2010) investigated the relationship between reinvestment and choking under pressure (see above).

To summarise, the conscious processing hypothesis predicts that athletes whose cognitive anxiety increases will tend to revert to conscious control of normally automatic skills. Although this theory has received impressive empirical support to date (see review by Masters and Maxwell, 2008), additional validation evidence is required.

Attentional control theory

Attentional control theory (ACT; Eysenck *et al.*, 2007; Derakshan and Eysenck, 2009), which is a successor to 'processing efficiency theory' (PET; Eysenck and Calvo, 1992), was postulated to investigate theoretical relationships between anxiety, working memory (our mental system for storing and manipulating currently relevant information for a brief period of time) and skilled performance. Both ACT and PET assume that we can distinguish between performance effectiveness (i.e., the quality of task performance) and performance efficiency (i.e., the relationship between performance effectiveness and use of processing resources) and that anxiety impairs processing efficiency more than performance effectiveness. Both theories also assume that cognitive anxiety (or worrying) impairs the efficiency of the central executive component of the working memory system. ACT, however, goes beyond PET in addressing the theoretical mechanisms by which anxiety impairs cognitive performance.

A central prediction of ACT is that anxiety hampers performance via 'attentional control' – which is a key function of the central executive. According to Corbetta and Shulman (2002), there are two attentional systems – one influenced by a person's current goals and expectations (a top-down goal-driven system) and the other, a bottom-up, stimulus driven system which is triggered by salient environmental events. According to ACT, anxiety affects attentional control. Specifically, it 'disrupts the balance between these two systems by enhancing the influence of the stimulus driven, bottom-up processes over the efficient top-down goal-driven processes' (Derakshan and Eysenck, 2009, p. 170). Furthermore, ACT predicts that anxiety 'increases attention to task irrelevant stimuli (especially threat-related)' (p. 170) and 'reduces attentional focus on concurrent task demands' (p. 170). More precisely, ACT predicts that anxiety disrupts performance not only by impairing *attentional inhibition* (the process by which, under normal circumstances, people can restrain themselves from directing their attention at task-irrelevant factors) but also by impairing attentional shifting (the process by which people can normally switch their attention in response to changing task requirements).

Recent research provides some empirical support for the predictions of ACT. For example, Wilson, Wood and Vine (2009) used eye-tracking technology to analyse the visual search strategies of expert soccer players as they prepared to take penalties in five-a-side matches (where there is smaller distance between the goal-posts than in normal eleven-a-side matches) under various conditions of anxiety. Their results corroborated a key prediction of ACT in showing that anxious penalty-takers displayed an attentional bias towards salient and threat-related stimuli (in this case, kicking towards the goalkeeper) rather than towards the ideal target for their kicks (i.e., a point just inside either goal-post, beyond the goalkeeper's reach). Clearly, further research is required in sport psychology to test the predictions of this emerging theory of the relationship between anxiety and performance.

Early research in sport psychology was guided by the assumption that the relationship between anxiety and performance was linear and inverse. In short, the more anxious athletes are, the worse they perform. But with the advent of more sophisticated theoretical models in the 1990s (see e.g., catastrophe theory, the conscious processing hypothesis), a different picture of the anxiety–performance relationship has emerged. This shift in understanding is evident in four main ways. First, a crucial factor that mediates the relationship between anxiety and performance is the way in which athletes *interpret* the anxiety that they experience. In general, if it is perceived as 'energising' performance, then it will probably help the athlete to do well. But if it is seen as a threat to performance, then the athlete will probably do badly. Second, as anxiety is a multidimensional construct (with cognitive, somatic and behavioural components), it is not surprising that different types of anxiety may have different effects on skilled performance. For example, catastrophe theory suggests that a high degree of cognitive anxiety (or 'worry') is not always detrimental to performance. This view is shared by the processing efficiency model, which argues that worry can sometimes motivate anxious performers to invest

more effort in the tasks that they are performing. But this increased investment of effort may come at a price, namely a concomitant decline in processing efficiency. Third, in order to explore adequately the effects of anxiety on
performance, researchers will have to use indices of processing efficiency (e.g.,
as is evident from certain aspects of visual search behaviour; see Williams
et al., 2002a) as much as measures of overall task performance. Finally, most
models of anxiety in sport agree that skilled performance tends to 'unravel'
when athletes think too much about themselves (self-consciousness) or about
the mechanics of the tasks that they are trying to perform ('paralysis by analysis'). The issue of how to maintain an optimal attentional focus in sport performance is considered in Chapter 5.

METHODS AND MEASURES

Before reviewing current measures of anxiety in sport psychology, two general
points should be noted. First, despite the three-dimensional nature of anxiety,
sport psychology researchers have tended to ignore the behavioural component of this construct in their measurement strategies (but see Pijpers *et al.*,
2003, for an exception to this trend). Second, as a consequence of their convenience, brevity and ease of scoring, the most popular anxiety measures in sport
psychology are 'self-report' scales.

Physiological measures

As anxiety is a type of fear reaction, it has a strong physiological basis. Thus
Spielberger (1966) proposed that anxiety states are 'accompanied by or associated with activation of the autonomic nervous system' (p. 17). As we have seen,
this activation results in such typical symptoms of anxiety as elevated heart
rate, increased blood pressure, fast and shallow breathing, sweaty palms and
tense musculature. If such indices could be measured conveniently, they would
facilitate research on anxiety, as they are relatively unaffected by response 'sets'
such as people's tendency to present themselves in a favourable light when
answering questionnaire items (a tendency called 'social desirability').

Unfortunately, physiological measures of anxiety such as heart rate, blood
pressure or the 'galvanic skin response' (GSR, an electrical measure of the amount
of sweat on the skin indicative of relatively high arousal) are not widely used
in sport psychology for at least three reasons. First, there is no single, universally agreed physiological index of anxiety. Second, as athletes differ in the way
in which they interpret autonomic arousal (e.g., as being either facilitative or
debilitative of their performance), physiological measures of anxiety are of limited value. Finally, physiological assessment of athletes is usually complex and
time-consuming. Nevertheless, as mentioned earlier in this chapter, researchers
such as Strahler *et al.* (2010) have pioneered the use of neuroendocrine indices

such as 'cortisol awakening response' (CAR) to investigate anticipatory anxiety in athletes. In summary, for a variety of reasons, physiological instruments have not been popular among sport psychologists who wish to measure anxiety processes in athletes.

Self-report instruments

Given their simplicity and convenience, paper-and-pencil tests of anxiety have proliferated in sport psychology research in recent years. Among the most popular self-report instruments in this field are the Sport Competition Anxiety Test (SCAT) (Martens, 1977), the Sport Anxiety Scale (SAS) (Smith, Smoll and Schutz, 1990) and its successor, the Sport Anxiety Scale-2 (SAS-2) (Smith *et al.*, 2006), and the Competitive State Anxiety Inventory-2 (CSAI-2) (Martens *et al.*, 1990) and its successor, the Revised Competitive State Anxiety Inventory (CSAI-2R) (Cox, Martens and Russell, 2003). These tests can be described briefly as follows.

The SCAT (Martens, 1977) is a 10-item inventory that purports to measure trait anxiety in sport performers. Parallel versions of this test are available for children (aged 10–14 years) and adults (15 years and above). Typical items include 'When I compete I worry about making mistakes' and 'Before I compete I get a queasy feeling in my stomach'. Respondents are required to indicate their agreement with each item by selecting their preferred answer from three categories: 'hardly ever', 'sometimes' and 'often'. Reverse scoring is used on certain items (e.g., 'Before I compete I feel calm'). Scores on this test range from 10 to 30. Internal consistency coefficients range from 0.8 to 0.9 and test-retest reliability values cluster around 0.77 (Smith, Smoll and Wiechman, 1998). Validation studies suggest that the SCAT is mainly a measure of somatic anxiety (ibid.). Evidence of the test's convergent validity comes from studies which show that it is correlated moderately with various general anxiety inventories. Overall, Smith, Smoll and Wiechman (1998) concluded that although the SCAT 'has been a very important research tool within sport psychology' (p. 117), it needs to be revised as a multidimensional test, reflecting the accepted distinction between somatic and cognitive anxiety.

The SAS (Smith, Smoll and Schutz, 1990) is a sport-relevant multidimensional test of cognitive and somatic trait anxiety. It contains 21 items, which are divided into three subscales: Somatic anxiety (9 items such as 'I feel nervous'), worry (7 items such as 'I have self-doubts') and a 'concentration disruption' (5 items such as 'My mind wanders during sport competition') subscale. Reliability data for this scale are encouraging, with internal consistency estimated at between 0.88 (somatic anxiety), 0.87 (worry) and 0.69 (concentration disruption) (Dunn *et al.*, 2000) and test-retest figures at 0.77 for an inter-test interval of 18 days (Smith, Smoll and Schutz, 1990.). Evidence of convergent validity for this scale was reported by Smith, Smoll and Schutz (1990) who calculated significant correlations (ranging between 0.47 and 0.81) between its subscales and SCAT

(Martens, 1977). Discriminant validity for the SAS is supported by evidence of low correlations between it and general mental health measures (see Smith, Smoll and Wiechman, 1998). Factor analyses have also confirmed that the SAS assesses three separate dimensions: somatic anxiety, cognitive anxiety/worry, and concentration disruption (Dunn *et al.*, 2000). More recently, Smith *et al.* (2006) developed the Sport Anxiety Scale-2 (SAS-2). This test is a multidimensional 15-item instrument that, like its predecessor, purports to measure individual differences in somatic anxiety, worry and concentration disruption – but this time for children as well as for adults. According to the authors, the SAS-2 shows evidence of convergent validity due to its high correlation with the SAS. These researchers also report that the reliability of the SAS-2 is impressive with internal consistencies estimated at 0.84 (for the somatic anxiety sub-scale), 0.89 (for the worry sub-scale) and 0.84 (for the concentration disruption sub-scale).

The CSAI-2 (Martens *et al.*, 1990) is a multidimensional test of state anxiety. It has 27 items divided into 3 subscales (each containing 9 items): cognitive anxiety; somatic anxiety; and self-confidence. A sample item in the cognitive anxiety subscale is 'I am concerned about losing'. Typical items in the somatic anxiety subscale are 'I feel nervous' and 'My body feels tense'. The 'self-confidence' subscale is included in the test because a lack of confidence is believed to be a sign of cognitive anxiety (ibid.). On a 4-point scale (with 1 = 'not at all' and 4 = 'very much so'), respondents are required to rate the intensity of their anxiety experiences prior to competition. Following a review of 49 studies using the CSAI-2, Burton (1998) reported that internal consistency estimates for these three subscales ranged from 0.76 to 0.91. However, doubts about the factorial composition of this test were expressed by Lane *et al.* (1999), who reported that researchers in this field 'cannot have faith in data obtained using the CSAI-2 until further validation studies have been completed' (p. 511). In response to some of these issues, the Revised Competitive State Anxiety Inventory (CSAI-2R) was developed by Cox, Martens and Russell (2003). This 17-item scale purports to measure the intensity components of cognitive anxiety, somatic anxiety and self-confidence. Unfortunately, according to Uphill (2008), the construct validity of this test remains equivocal.

A key limitation of the CSAI-2 stems from its neglect of the fact that anxiety can be interpreted differently by different athletes – the 'direction' of anxiety issue (see Jones, 1995). A possible solution to this problem is to add a directional measure to the CSAI's traditional 'intensity' approach of anxiety. Adopting this strategy, Jones and Swain (1992) asked respondents firstly to complete the CSAI-2 in order to elicit the intensity with which they experienced the 27 symptoms listed in this test. Then they asked these participants to rate the degree to which the experienced intensity of each symptom is facilitative or debilitative of subsequent athletic performance. A 7-item Likert response scale was used, with values ranging from –3 (indicating 'very negative') to +3 (indicating 'very positive'). To illustrate, an athlete might respond with a maximum '4' to the statement 'I am concerned about losing' but might then rate this concern with a +3 on the interpretation scale. By doing this, the performer is indicating that he or she feels that this concern about losing is likely to have a facilitative effect on his or her forthcoming performance. In the CSAI-2, 'direction of anxiety' scores can vary between –27 and +27. Internal consistency reliability estimates for this facilitative/debilitative measure range from 0.72 (for the somatic anxiety subscale) to 0.83 (for the cognitive anxiety subscale) (Swain and Jones, 1996). When this 'directional modification' scale has been used in conjunction with the CSAI-2, the resulting instrument is called the 'DM-CSAI-2' (Burton, 1998). But how valid is this procedure? Several studies have supported the validity of the DM-CSAI-2. E.g., Jones *et al.* (1994), following a comparison of elite and non-elite swimmers, discovered that the elite athletes had reported interpreting cognitive and somatic anxiety as being more facilitative of their performance than their less successful counterparts. As one might expect, however, a significant proportion of the non-elite swimmers reported anxiety as being debilitative to their performance.

Practical issues and interventions

In this section of the chapter, we explore various practical coping techniques used by athletes (but see Thatcher, Lavallee and Jones, in press, for a more comprehensive account of research in this field). Before we tackle this issue, however, we need to learn more about the main causes of anxiety in sport performers. According to Uphill (2008) and Moran (2012), the following factors may precipitate anxiety in athletes:

■ Predispositions, trait anxiety: many sport psychologists (e.g., Anshel, 1995) believe that athletes' levels of trait anxiety are important determinants of the amount of state anxiety which they are likely to experience in a given situation. But is it valid to use a personality trait as an 'explanation' for a mental state? After all, one cannot explain aggressive behaviour by saying that a person has 'aggressive' traits. Clearly, we must be careful to avoid circular reasoning when seeking to explain why athletes become anxious in certain situations. Nevertheless, research suggests some reasons why athletes differ in their level of pre-competitive trait anxiety.

■ Perceived importance of the result/competition: in general, the more importance attached to a forthcoming competition by an athlete, the more anxiety he or she is likely to experience in it.

■ Negative attributions: an 'attribution' is a perceived cause or explanation of something that happens in one's life. It seems likely that if athletes attribute unsuccessful outcomes (e.g., defeats, poor performances) to internal and stable factors (e.g., a lack of technical proficiency), they may learn to associate anxiety with competition.

■ Perfectionism: athletes who set excessively high standards for their performances may feel anxious when things do not go smoothly for them. Thus Flett and Hewitt (2005) suggested that perfectionism is mainly a negative factor that 'contributed to maladaptive outcomes among athletes and exercisers' (p. 14).

■ Fear of failure: athletes who endorse a 'win at all costs' mentality may become vulnerable to performance anxiety. For performers whose self-esteem is defined solely by what they achieve, defeat is a catastrophe as it indicates personal failure. Interestingly, a fear of failure emerged as a powerful source of anxiety in the figure skaters studied by Gould, Finch and Jackson (1993).

■ Time to competition: Research suggests that different types of anxiety display different temporal patterns of emergence before a given competition. For example, whereas cognitive anxiety tends to remain high and stable in the days preceding a competition, somatic anxiety remains relatively low until one or two days before the evemt – after which point is may increase until the competition begins (Uphill, 2008).

Having identified some common determinants of anxiety in sport, let us now explore research findings on the practical strategies used by athletes to cope with such sport-related pressure situations (see also reviews by Nicholls and Polman, 2007; Thomas, Mellalieu and Hanton, 2009). According to Lazarus and Folkman (1984), we can distinguish between two types of coping responses used by people to counteract stressful situations – 'problem-focused' and 'emotion-focused' strategies. Whereas problem-focused coping strategies seek to reduce the stress experienced by tackling the stressful situation directly (e.g., by obtaining more information about it), emotion-focused strategies attempt to help the person to reduce the emotional distress caused by the stressful situation (e.g., by practising relaxation techniques when the stress is experienced).

Early research revealed that athletes tend to use a wide variety of strategies to cope with competitive stress. For example, Gould, Finch and Jackson (1993) interviewed 17 current or former US national champion figure skaters about the way in which they coped with competitive stress. Coping techniques reported by at least 40% of these athletes included rational thinking and self-talk, 'positive focus', social support (i.e., seeking advice from coaches, friends or family members), time management strategies, pre-competitive mental preparation, anxiety management (e.g., relaxation, visualisation; see also Chapter 3 on imagery), training hard, and attempting to avoid the source of stress. Clearly, this study suggests that athletes tend to use multiple strategies to counteract the unwanted effects of anxiety in sport. More recently, researchers have attempted to explore theoretical links between specific stressful events and resultant coping strategies in various sports. For example, Weston et al. (2009) investigated the stressors faced, and coping strategies used, by a sample of single-handed, round-the-world sailors. In response to various stressors identified (e.g., isolation, sleep deprivation, yacht-related problems), these sailors reported using a combination of problem-focused (e.g., making detailed plans for 'what-if' scenarios) and emotion-focused (e.g., seeking support from others where possible) coping strategies. With regard to the *efficacy* of coping strategies, research evidence is available to support the proposition (Folkman, 1991) that whereas problem-focused coping techniques are usually preferable for stressful situations that are *controllable*, emotion-focused techniques are usually more appropriate for *uncontrollable* stressors. Further information on the nature and efficacy of coping strategies in sport may be found in Thatcher, Lavallee and Jones (in press).

Understanding that 'pressure' is a perception not a fact: Restructuring the situation

People experience 'pressure' or anxiety symptoms whenever they believe that they will not be able to cope with the demands of a current or impending situation. For example, a footballer may dread playing in an important match for fear of making a mistake. But athletes need to be taught that 'pressure' is a perception or interpretation of a situation – not a fact. Therefore, by restructuring the situation differently in our minds (see practical strategies offered by Hanton, Thomas and Mellalieu, 2009), we can learn to interpret it as a challenge to our abilities rather than a threat to our well-being. For example, the anxious footballer could look at the anxiety-provoking situation differently by saying to himself or herself: 'I'm looking forward to this match because it gives me a chance to show how well I can play'. An example of restructuring in action comes from Ian Thorp, the former Australian swimmer and five-time Olympic gold medallist, who revealed how he had coped with the pressure imposed by people's expectations of him when he competed in Sydney at the 2000 Games: 'For me, Sydney was a dream ... I guess there was always a lot of attention on me, a lot of expectation on me to perform well and if you turn those into a positive thing it becomes support, whereas if you turn it into a negative thing it becomes pressure' (cited in Hanton, Thomas and Mellalieu, 2009, p. 31).

To experience restructuring for yourself, try the exercise below to learn more about how to turn a source of pressure into a challenge. The purpose of this exercise is to show you how to use a technique called 'cognitive restructuring' to turn a feared pressure situation into a manageable challenge. To begin, think of a situation in your sport or daily life that usually makes you feel anxious. Now, describe this situation by finishing the following sentences:

- 'I hate the pressure of ...'
- Fill in the missing words with reference to the pressure situation you have experienced. For example, you might write down 'I hate the pressure of serving for the match when playing tennis'. Alternatively, it could be 'I hate the pressure of facing exams when I have not studied for them'. Now, I would like you to think of this pressure situation again. But this time, you have to restructure it in your head so that you think about it differently.
- 'I love the challenge of ...'

■ Please note that you are not allowed to simply repeat what you wrote before. For example, you cannot say 'I love the challenge of serving for the match when playing tennis'. Instead, you have to pick something else to focus on in that pressure situation besides the fear of making mistakes. As we shall see in Chapter 5, the secret of holding your focus under pressure is to concentrate on something that is specific, relevant and under your own control. Usually, that means concentrating on some aspect of one's preparation for the feared situation. For example, you could write 'I love the challenge of preparing in the same way for every serve – no matter what the score is in the match'. Notice how restructuring a situation can make you feel differently about it. You no longer see it as something to fear, but as something that challenges your skills.

Interpreting arousal signals constructively

Despite their talent and experience, many athletes have a poor understanding of what their body is telling them when they are anxious. In particular, they need to be educated to realise that anxiety is not necessarily a bad thing, but merely a sign that one cares about what one is doing. Without such education, athletes tend to make the mistake of misinterpreting physical signs of readiness (e.g., a rapid heart beat, a surge of adrenaline) as unwelcome harbingers of impending disaster. Therefore, sport performers must learn to perceive somatic arousal as an essential prerequisite of a good performance. Some players realise this intuitively when they concede that they cannot play well unless they feel appropriately 'juiced' or 'pumped up' for a contest. For example, Martin Corry, the former England and Lions rugby player, spoke of the importance of arousal enhancement as part of his pre-match preparation: 'Back in the dressing-room, we'll put on our proper kit and the noise levels will rise significantly. Everyone's pumped up, the captain will give us the big 'come-on' and we're out the tunnel' (cited in Corry, 2007, p. 3). In summary, the first step in helping athletes to cope with anxiety is to educate them as to what it means and how to detect it. The principle here is that awareness precedes control of psychological states.

Physical relaxation techniques

In the heat of competition, athletes tend to speed up their behaviour. The obvious solution to this problem is to train them to slow down and relax whenever tension strikes. Of course, this advice must be tailored to the demands of the sport in question. Thus the feasibility of using physical relaxation techniques (e.g., progressive muscular relaxation; see practical tips offered by Williams, 2010) depends heavily on the amount of 'break time' in the sport in question. For example, in 'stop-start', untimed sports like golf or tennis, it may be possible to lower one's shoulders, flap out the tension from one's arms and engage in deep-breathing exercises. By contrast, in sports where play is fast and continuous (e.g., hockey), such relaxation techniques may not be possible. The importance of relaxation for peak performance has been recognised intuitively by top-class coaches and managers. For example, the late Brian Clough (who led Nottingham Forest to two consecutive European Cup triumphs) proclaimed that 'when footballers go out on the field they have to be relaxed not frightened' (cited in Walker, 2008, p. 7).

Giving oneself specific instructions

Anxiety is unhelpful because it makes people focus on what might go wrong (i.e., possible negative consequences) rather than on what exactly they have to do (the immediate challenge of the situation). Therefore, a useful way to counteract pressure in a competition is to ask oneself: 'What exactly can I do right now?' By focusing on what they have to do, athletes can learn to avoid the trap of confusing the facts of the situation ('we're 1–0 down') with an anxious interpretation of those facts ('it's no use, we're going to lose'). Therefore, when athletes experience pressure, they should focus outwards and give themselves specific commands which help them to concentrate on actions that can be performed right now (Kremer and Moran, 2008).

Adhering to pre-performance routines

Most athletes use 'pre-performance routines' (PPRs), or systematic sequences of preparatory thoughts and actions, to concentrate effectively before they execute important skills (e.g., golf putts, penalty kicks in football and rugby; see also Chapter 5). Apart from their value as concentration techniques, these routines serve as a cocoon against the adverse effects of anxiety. Specifically, by concentrating on each step of the routine, athletes learn to focus only on what they can control – a vital principle of anxiety management in anxiety-provoking situations.

Simulation training

An interesting approach to helping athletes to prepare for competitive stress is to simulate aspects of the anxiety-provoking situations in practice. For example, Gould (2009) proposed that simulation training or 'having athletes and teams practise in environments that are as similar to the competitive environment as possible' (p. 58) can reduce uncertainty – a key contributor to anxiety in athletes. Simulation training has been practised informally by coaches for many years. For example, Bob Bowman, the renowned swimming coach who guided Michael Phelps to become the most successful Olympic athlete of all time, deliberately broke Phelps' goggles during practice races so that he could learn to swim without them if they were damaged during a competitive event. Remarkably, this latter situation transpired in the 2008 Games in Beijing when

Phelps won the 200m butterfly race even though his goggles has been broken for the last 100m of this event (Whitworth, 2008).

In conclusion, this section of the chapter suggests that athletes can learn to cope with pressure situations by using at least four psychological strategies. First, they must be trained to believe that 'pressure' lies in the eye of the beholder. Therefore, they must be taught to cognitively restructure competitive events as opportunities to display their talents (the 'challenge' response) rather than as potential sources of failure (the 'fear' response). Second, athletes must learn for themselves that systematic preparation tends to reduce pressure. Third, athletes who experience anxiety can learn to talk themselves constructively through the feared situation. Finally, when anxiety strikes, athletes must be prepared to deepen their routines and use physical relaxation procedures in accordance with the temporal demands of their sport.

'Choking' under pressure

The term 'choking under pressure' refers to a phenomenon in which an athlete's normally expert level of performance deteriorates suddenly and significantly under conditions of perceived pressure (Kremer *et al.*, in press). Two aspects of choking are especially important. First, as Hill *et al.* (2010) pointed out, the athlete who is alleged to have 'choked' must be shown to have been capable of, and motivated to achieve, a significantly higher level of performance than that which was evident. In addition, as the term 'anxiety' is derived from the Latin *angere*, which means 'to choke' (Onions, 1996), it is clear that the concepts of choking and anxiety are inextricably linked. Although choking is pervasive in sport, it is especially prevalent among performers of self-paced skills in precision activities such as golf or tennis (Beilock, 2010). For example, consider the case of the French golfer Jean van de Velde who squandered a 3-shot lead on the final hole of the 1999 Open Championship in Carnoustie due to a series of poor decisions that bore all the hallmarks of excessive anxiety. But choking is also evident in team sports. For example, some of the world's best soccer players have missed penalties in 'shootouts' in major championships (Jordet, 2009). Given the dramatic nature of choking in sport, what do we know about the nature and causes of this problem?

In sport psychology, 'choking under pressure' can be a very debilitating and persistent problem for athletes – especially those who compete in precision sports like golf, snooker and darts. Many athletes have experienced bouts of 'choking under pressure' in their careers. Some notable examples from golf, darts and tennis include the following:

At least three types of symptom characterise the experience of 'choking'. First, the afflicted athlete tends to believe that the harder she or he tries, the worse the problem becomes. This experience is curious because increased 'drive' often leads to enhanced performance. Second, just like any other anxiety disorder, choking produces such symptoms as tense muscles, shaky limbs, rapid heart and pulse rates, shortness of breath, butterflies in the stomach, 'racing' thoughts and feelings of panic. Finally, athletes who 'choke' often find it difficult to perform skills that used to be automatic for them. Therefore, golfers who suffer from the 'yips' may find it impossible to complete a putting stroke. Likewise, bowlers in cricket who suffer from the 'iron elbow' may suddenly feel as if they cannot release the ball. Choking reactions may also be characterised by a tiny muscular spasm which also occurs just as the stroke is about to be executed. For example, Eric Bristow, a world champion in darts for three consecutive years, revealed that 'I had it so bad I was even getting it when I was practising ... It took me six or seven years to sort it out' (cited in Dobson, 1998, p. 16).

Most sport psychologists regard 'choking' as an anxiety-based *attentional* difficulty rather than as a mental weakness. Given this view, it is probably inaccurate and unfair to describe someone as a 'choker' because *any* athlete's performance can be impaired if she or he concentrates on the 'wrong' target (i.e., himself or herself or the mechanics of the skill that she or he is trying to perform).

In contemporary sport psychology, two main approaches to understanding choking behaviour have come to the fore – distraction theories (e.g., processing efficiency theory, PET; Eysenck and Calvo, 1992; mentioned briefly earlier in chapter) and self-focus theories (e.g., Beilock and Carr, 2001; Masters, 1992). In general, distraction theories suggest that anxiety situations create a distracting environment which causes athletes to shift their attention away from *task-relevant* information and towards *task-irrelevant* issues (e.g., worries about the consequences of performing poorly in the situation). By contrast, self-focus theories of choking postulate that anxiety increases athletes' level of self-consciousness to the point where they consciously attend to, or think too much about, skills that are normally performed automatically – thereby precipitating skill failure. Although it is difficult to arbitrate empirically between these two rival theories of choking, Gucciardi and Dimmock (2008) suggested a possible resolution as follows. Specifically, empirical support for distraction theories seems to be strongest in the case of cognitive tasks (e.g., mathematical reasoning) that depend heavily on working memory resources for execution. By contrast, self-focus theories of choking appear to be supported best for motor performance in which few demands are made on working memory (e.g., in the case of executing a golf-putt). In summary, although no consensus has been reached as yet about the theoretical mechanisms that underlie choking under pressure, most theories of this phenomenon agree that anxiety impairs performance by inducing the athlete to regress to an earlier stage of skill acquisition.

In conclusion, it is widely agreed that athletic success depends significantly on the ability to regulate one's arousal levels effectively. Put simply, sport performers need to know how and when to either 'psych themselves up' or 'calm themselves down' in competitive situations. In the first section of the chapter, we examined the nature, characteristics and types of anxiety, and also distinguished between anxiety and 'arousal'. The next part of the chapter was devoted to reviewing the principal theories and models of the anxiety–performance relationship in sport. After that, we critically evaluated the main methods used to measure anxiety processes in athletes. Then, we investigated the various coping techniques used by athletes to reduce competitive anxiety. Finally, in order to examine anxiety in action, we investigated the phenomenon of 'choking' under pressure.

CASE STUDY

David is a 23-year-old amateur international golfer with a plus-two handicap who is considering a professional career in this sport. Despite the fact he has been a member of the men's senior elite golf squad for the past three years, he has yet to win a major amateur tournament. Nevertheless, he has been a runner up in such events on four occasions. At first, this lack of a tournament victory did not bother him and he was able to console himself with the thought that success would come in time. Unfortunately, over the past six months he is beginning to wonder why he seems fated to be always 'second best'. As a result of this worry, he has become quite nervous about 'closing out' games against opponents in match play situations and/or about playing the last few holes of stroke play events. Sometimes, David becomes so anxious that he can almost feel the club shaking in his hands as he chips onto the green or prepares to line up a putt. Although he tells himself that there is nothing to worry about, he wonders if he is really mentally tough enough to cope with the pressure of playing golf professionally. He has read a lot about golf psychology and wonders if he has the 'yips'. He has come to you for advice about this problem.

1. With reference to the Theories and Models section in the chapter, how would you interpret what is happening in this case study?
2. With reference to Methods and Measures, what techniques would you employ to help to understand and quantify the issues?
3. With reference to Practical Issues and Interventions, how would you deal with this situation?

STUDY QUESTIONS

1. What does the term 'anxiety' mean in sport psychology? How does it differ from 'arousal'? What are the main components of the construct of anxiety?

2. Is anxiety always associated with poor performance in sport? Answer this question with reference to the predictions of three of the following theories: the inverted-U hypothesis, drive theory, catastrophe theory, processing efficiency theory and the conscious processing hypothesis.
3. What are the advantages and disadvantages of using self-report scales and physiological measures when attempting to assess anxiety in athletes? What can you conclude from the relatively low correlations typically obtained between these two types of measures of this construct?
4. What practical advice would you give to a top-class athlete who suffers from 'performance anxiety'?
5. What psychological theories have been proposed to explain why some athletes 'choke' under pressure? Which of these theories do you believe is most accurate? Give reasons for your answer.

FURTHER READING

Beilock, S. (2010) *Choke* (New York: Free Press).

Landers, D. M. and Arent, S. M. (2010) 'Arousal-Performance Relationships', in J. M. Williams (ed.), *Applied Sport Psychology*, 6th edn (New York: McGraw-Hill), 221–46.

Masters, R. S. W. and Maxwell, J. P. (2008) 'The Theory of Reinvestment', *International Review of Sport and Exercise Psychology*, 2, 160–83.

Nicholls, A. R. and Polman, R. C. (2007) 'Coping in Sport: A Systematic Review', *Journal of Sports Sciences*, 25, 11–31.

Thomas, O., Mellalieu, S. D. and Hanton, S. (2009) 'Stress Management in Applied Spprt Psychology', in S. D. Mellaliru and S. D. Hanton (eds), *Advances in Applied Sport Psychology: A Review* (London: Routledge), 124–61.

7 Sport Expertise

INTRODUCTION, HISTORY AND DEVELOPMENT

The study of expertise in sport has great intuitive appeal for spectators and scientists alike. We marvel at the performances of sporting legends, looking on in awe at the gracefulness and athleticism of their performances, and perhaps occasionally with envy as to the superior gifts or abilities that they are perceived to possess over and beyond mere mortals. Regardless of its intuitive appeal, the study of expertise in sport provides a window for understanding the acquisition of skill across domains (see Williams *et al.*, 2011). The identification of essential attributes that distinguish individuals who are skilled from those less skilled highlights those factors that potentially limit high-level performance and provides a principled basis for determining which types of practice are most likely to be beneficial for performance enhancement. Such knowledge is relevant when designing appropriate training interventions as well as for those involved in the process of talent identification and selection (Williams, 2000; Williams and Reilly, 2000). Moreover, the study of expertise in sport can be helpful in evaluating the explanatory power of theories and models of expertise developed in other domains.

The impetus for studying the psychology of expert performance in sport came from the classic work of de Groot (1965) with Chess Grandmasters. When chess Grandmasters were shown game configurations for intervals of 5–10 seconds, they were able to recall the position of chess pieces almost perfectly from memory. The level of performance declined very rapidly below the Grandmaster level, from a recall accuracy of 93 per cent to a value of 51 per cent for club level players. Chase and Simon (1973a, 1973b) reported similar conclusions, but included a control condition where pieces were arranged randomly on the board rather than in a structured fashion. In this condition, there were no differences between Grandmaster and club level players. The authors concluded that the superior recall of experts on structured chess stimuli could not be attributed to differences in visual short-term memory capacity, rather the advantage was due to their advanced task-specific knowledge bases and the more rapid and efficient retrieval of this information from memory. The expert players were able to chunk together individual chess pieces into larger and more meaningful playing patterns, circumventing the limited capacity of short-term memory and facilitating the recall process.

The systematic study of expertise in sport became prominent in the early 1980s and perhaps owes as much to developments in the related field of skill acquisition as to corresponding developments in cognitive psychology. Fran Allard and colleagues (e.g., Allard, Graham and Paarsalu, 1980; Allard and Starkes, 1980) at the University of Waterloo in Canada carried out the seminal work on perceptual-cognitive expertise in sport. They replicated the work of Chase and Simon (1973a, 1973b) using groups of basketball players and non-players and discovered that experts in sport possess the same cognitive advantage over novices as those in other domains. At around the same time, others, such as Jones and Miles (1978) at the University of Wales, Bangor became interested in anticipation skill in fast ball sports. They showed that experts were quicker and more accurate than novices at anticipating the direction of serve in tennis using realistic, film-based simulations of the return of serve scenario. Similarly, Bard and colleagues at Laval University in Canada became the first to systematically investigate skill-based differences in visual search behaviours in sport (e.g., Bard and Fleury, 1976; 1981).

Since these early days, several prominent scientists such as Bruce Abernethy, while based both at the University of Queensland, and the University of Hong Kong, and Janet Starkes at McMaster University were instrumental in the development of what is now a vibrant and accepted area of academic study in its own right. This observation is confirmed by the number of new scientists entering the field (e.g., see Farrow, Baker MacMahon, 2008), the recent publication of meta-analytic reviews (Mann *et al.*, 2007; Voss *et al.*, 2010) and the publication of several journal special issues on this theme in sport and mainstream psychology journals (e.g., see Williams and Ericsson, 2007; 2008; Ericsson and Williams, 2007).

THEORIES AND MODELS

An abundance of theories and models have been proposed to account for the specific mechanisms underpinning superior performance in sport. However, a difficulty is that these are not theories and models relating to the development of expertise more broadly per se, but rather they are typically causal accounts that predict how some of the specific skills underpinning expertise are acquired. Thus far, there are no unifying frameworks that would integrate distinct theories and models that consider the perceptual, cognitive and motor processes governing expertise and its acquisition in sport (Williams and Ward, 2007). Moreover, the existing conceptual frameworks are fairly diverse, often embracing different epistemological and methodological approaches to the study of expertise.

The most popular theories and models employed by researchers in this field have embraced the metaphors of cognitive psychology with a focus on mapping and predicting the expert performer's more refined and organised memory and/or task-specific knowledge structures (e.g., Anderson, 1992; Ericsson and Kintsch, 1995, 2000; Gobet, 1998; Gobet and Simon, 1996; Tienson, 1990). These approaches have typically employed a reductionist approach, where laboratory-based tasks are often employed to identify fundamental mechanisms. One of the most popular frameworks has been long-term working memory theory proposed by Ericsson and co-workers (e.g., Ericsson and Delaney, 1999; Ericsson and Kintsch, 1995). In this theory, it is argued that experts bypass the limitations of short-term working memory by acquiring skills that promote rapid encoding of information in long-term memory and allow selective access to this information when required. After extended practice with the domain of expertise, performers index information in such a way that they can successfully anticipate future retrieval demands.

A central proposal of the long-term working memory theory proposed by Ericsson and colleagues is that retrieval cues kept in short-term working memory facilitate access to information stored in long-term memory. Skilled performers develop more flexible and detailed representations than less skilled athletes allowing them to adapt rapidly to changes in situational demands. A particularly relevant aspect of the theory is the notion that experts construct a retrieval structure 'on-the-fly', enabling them to adapt rapidly to the changing nature of the situation. The construction-integration (CI) model provides a detailed explanation and computational mechanism for building a situation model and arriving at an appropriate response, albeit in text comprehension (see Kintsch, 1988). The model is supported by empirical evidence that has since been extended to explain dynamic and 'real-world' tasks such as computer programming and piloting an airplane (e.g., Doane and Sohn, 2000).

Alternative theoretical accounts of expertise have been proposed from the perspectives of ecological psychology and dynamical systems theory. These frameworks are characterised by a marked reluctance to resort to cognitive structures to explain human behaviour, focusing instead on the need to identify mutual synergies between performer and environment without the need to resort to internal representations to guide perception and action. At least at a philosophical level, the focus methodologically is on maintaining the close functional links between perception and action by gathering data in situ and manipulating various constraints on performance (see Phillips *et al.*, 2010).

A number of reviews and books had been written to illustrate the potential value of these two theoretical frameworks for the study of expertise in sport (e.g., Beek, *et al.*, 2003; Davids, Button and Bennett, 2008; Williams, Davids and Williams, 1999). The notion, grounded in ecological psychology, of educating attention (i.e., the process of picking up specifying, higher-order invariants at the expense of non-specifying information) and freezing and exploiting perceptual degrees of freedom (see Savelsbergh *et al.*, 2004) may provide useful perspectives on the process of perceptual expertise and learning. Similarly, the dynamical notion of reducing dimensionality (i.e., the process of harnessing control over essential, and relinquishing nonessential, degrees of freedom for effective performance) attempts to provide an explanation of how skilled performers develop more effective coordination dynamics when compared with less skilled performers (Huys, Daffertshofer and Beek, 2004).

METHODS AND MEASURES

Ericsson and Smith (1991) proposed a three-step approach for studying expertise across domains, termed the *expert performance approach*. The first step in this approach is to identify a representative task(s) from the domain of expertise that is replicable under standardised conditions either in the laboratory or the field. The design of a representative task should not only differentiate skilled from less skilled individuals, but also capture the essence of specific facets of expertise under investigation. Initially, sports psychologists tended to rely on paradigms developed to study expertise in mainstream psychology, without modifying the task to elicit truly representative performance (see Abernethy, Thomas and Thomas, 1993). The propensity was to employ static slide presentations of sport stimuli and pen-and-paper response measures. Although such paradigms were successful in highlighting differences between participants who were relatively disparate in ability, they tended to lack sensitivity when attempting to differentiate those closer together in age and/or skill level (Ward and Williams, 2003). The suggestion is that the more realistic the experimental protocol the greater the expert advantage over the novice (Abernethy, Thomas and Thomas, 1993; Williams, Davids and Williams, 1999). As the field has developed over recent years, researchers have made use of advancements in technology by employing life-size, video-projected images, and requiring participants to move in response to dynamic, action sequences (for detailed reviews of these developments, see Hodges, Huys and Starkes, 2007; Williams and Abernethy, in press; Williams and Ericsson, 2005; Williams *et al.*, 2011). For example, recent advances in technology have enabled data to be gathered in situ in the actual performance environment (e.g., see Causer *et al.*, 2010; Panchuck and Vickers, 2008).

The second step in the expert performance approach is to analyse the stable characteristics of expertise through the use of process tracing measures such as verbal reports, the recording of visual gaze characteristics and/or representative task manipulations. For example, using verbal protocol analysis, Ericsson and colleagues (Ericsson and Charness, 1994; Ericsson and Delaney, 1999; Ericsson and Kintsch, 1995) demonstrated that experts acquire mental representations and memory skills that mediate performance, facilitate cognitive adaptability, aid in monitoring and controlling their performance, promote planning and reasoning about future events, and permit future retrieval demands to be anticipated. This step in the expert performance approach allows key mediating mechanisms to be examined via analysis of the processes that lead to superior performance.

In the sports domain, several authors have attempted to determine the processes and mechanisms underpinning expert performance using eye movement recording, verbal reports, film-based occlusion techniques, point-light displays and most recently, neuroimaging techniques such as fMRI (for recent reviews, see Williams and Ericsson, 2005; Williams *et al.*, 2011; Williams and Abernethy, in press). However, sports psychologists have been criticised for bypassing this step within the expertise approach, undertaking work that is essentially descriptive, merely outlining expert–novice differences rather than trying to identify underlying processes and provide theoretical explanation (Williams and Ward, 2007).

The final phase in the expert performance approach involves efforts to detail the adaptive learning and explicit acquisition processes relevant to the development of expertise. Ericsson, Krampe and Tesch-Römer (1993) attempted to outline the type of activities and acquisition processes that result in concomitant increases in performance in the deliberate practice framework. In the sports domain, several researchers have extended the work of Ericsson and colleagues (e.g., Ford, Ward and Williams, 2009; Helsen, Starkes and Hodges, 1998; Hodges and Starkes, 1996; Starkes *et al.*, 1996; Ward *et al.*, 2007). The typical approach has been to document the practice histories of athletes and, on the basis of these data, try and infer those activities likely to promote expert performance. Other researchers have attempted to develop specific training interventions to facilitate the acquisition of expertise. For example, Williams and colleagues (see Smeeton *et al.*, 2005; Williams *et al.*, 2002a; Williams, Ward and Chapman, 2003) have shown that perceptual and cognitive skills can be improved using training interventions based on video simulation, instruction and feedback.

Perceptual and cognitive expertise in sport

In sports psychology, the majority of those interested in expertise have focused on identifying the perceptual and cognitive skills underpinning anticipation and decision making. Several researchers have attempted to develop representative tasks to recreate the sporting environment under controlled conditions in order to identify some of the important processes that differentiate skilled from lesser skilled performers. In this section, a brief review of some of the main findings that have emerged from this body of work is presented.

Identifying patterns of play: the recall and recognition of game structure

Following on from the classic work of Chase and Simon (1973a, 1973b), Allard, Graham and Paarsalu (1980) showed that expert basketball players were able to recall patterns of play from within their domain of expertise better than novice players. Players were presented with brief four-second slide presentations of basketball configurations, following which they were asked to indicate where players were positioned on a schematic representation of the court. Both structured (sequences taken directly from match play) and unstructured (e.g., teams warming up prior to a match) slides were presented. The experts were more accurate in recalling player positions than novices on the structured configurations only. The expert basketball players were able to cluster or group individual elements (i.e., player positions) into larger and more meaningful units (i.e., game configurations). This process, referred to as 'perceptual chunking', can be integrated with high-level cognitive processes such as schematic knowledge and planning through complex data structures referred to as 'templates' (Gobet and Simon, 1996). No differences were observed across groups on the unstructured trials. These findings have subsequently been extended to a variety of other sports such as field hockey, rugby, soccer and volleyball (for a review, see Williams et al., 2011).

An alternative methodological approach is to present performers with slide or film presentations of structured and unstructured situations, some of which have been previously viewed whilst others have not. The task for the participants is to indicate quickly and accurately those clips they have and have not seen before. Typically, expert sports performers are better than novices at recognising structured configurations only. Experts are thought to encode structured, sport-specific information to a deeper and more meaningful level, thus facilitating the recognition of particular patterns of play. Allard and colleagues (1980) carried out the seminal work using this paradigm in basketball; subsequently, similar findings have been reported in American football (Garland and Barry, 1991), field hockey (Starkes, 1987; Smeeton, Ward and Williams, 2004) and soccer (Williams et al., 1993, 2006). The ability to recognise structured patterns of play is thought to be an important component of anticipation skill, particularly in team games such as soccer (North et al., 2009; Williams and Davids, 1995). If players are able to recognise a particular pattern of play early in its evolution, they can anticipate their opponents' intentions and plan ahead as to the most appropriate course of action.

A more recent development has been a focus on identifying the specific information that players use to make these recognition-based judgements. For example, verbal reports, eye movement data, and manipulations to stimuli using spatial occlusion and point-light display techniques have been used to identify the essential information upon which such judgements are made (see North et al., 2009, 2011; Williams et al., 2006). Also, the extent to which performance on anticipation and recognition tasks is correlated has been examined as well as the underlying processes employed when the making each type of judgement (see Canal-Bruland and Williams, 2010; North et al., 2009, 2011).

RESEARCH BOX

North *et al.* (2011) examined the mechanisms underlying skilled antici-pation and recognition in soccer. Skilled and less-skilled players viewed 5-sec film clips involving offensive sequences of play taken directly from soccer matches. In one condition, participants were required to antici-pate the end action in the sequence (e.g., pass destination), whereas in another condition they were asked to make a familiarity-based decision as to whether or not they had seen the sequence in an earlier viewing phase. In the recognition phase, sequences were presented as regular film clips and as point light displays (PLD). In the PLDs, players were represented as points of light against a black background. Players from one team were represented as red points of light, while those on the opposing team were represented as green points of light, and the ball as a white point of light. Verbal reports on the thought processes employed when performing each task were gathered from players immediately after certain trials using methods adapted from the Ericsson and Simon (1993).

A significant difference in anticipation accuracy was reported between skilled and less-skilled players. The skilled participants were more accurate (M *% accuracy* = 65.3 vs. 46.8) when making anticipa-tion judgements when compared with less-skilled players. A significant difference between skill groups was also observed on the recognition test with the skilled players being more sensitive (M *d'* = 0.80 vs. 0.36) in distinguishing previously seen from novel stimuli than less-skilled participants. No significant effects were observed for display type (PLD vs. Film) and there were no interactions between skill group and dis-play. The skilled players showed superior performance when recognis-ing sequences presented in film and PLD format.

The superior anticipation and recognition performance reported by the skilled participants may be due to their more extensive task-specific retrieval structures in memory when compared to less-skilled players (see Williams *et al.*, 2011). Skilled players are predicted to index and store the encoded information into complex representations so as to allow efficient retrieval at a later time (i.e., during recognition). The interactive encoding model presented by Dittrich (1999) suggests that skilled players perceive, encode and store these types of displays based on the relational information that exists between features (e.g., relative motions between players), thereby explaining why the skilled group maintained its advantage over less skilled players in recognition performance across film and PLD conditions. In contrast, less-skilled players are thought to perceive and encode these sequences in memory using more superficial, surface-level display features.

The verbal reports of the thought processes employed during anticipation and recognition supported the use of more refined and enriched memory structures by the skilled compared to less skilled players when engaging in both types of judgments. When compared to their less skilled counterparts, the skilled participants made significantly more high-level evaluation (M = 10.9 vs. 6.4) and prediction (M = 3.2 vs. 1.5) statements on the anticipation task, whereas there were no differences across groups in the number of low-level monitoring statements that were verbalised. Also, the skilled players made more high-level rather than low-level statements when engaging in the recognition task when compared with their less-skilled counterparts, but the representations activated during recognition were less complex than those employed when making anticipation judgements in both groups, implying that performance on these two tasks is guided by slightly different underlying processes. As predicted by Long Term Working Memory theory (Ericsson and Kintsch, 1995), superior performance on tasks requiring anticipation and recognition is supported by engagement in forward planning rather than thinking only about immediately available surface information and commenting on on-going events.

Reading an opponent's intentions: using advanced visual cues.

The ability to anticipate future events based upon visual information or cues from an opponent's postural orientation is essential in sport, particularly in ball games where the speed of play dictates that decisions must often be made in advance of the action. A variety of techniques have been used to examine whether experts are able to pick up postural cues better than novices. The most frequently used approach has been the film-based, 'temporal occlusion paradigm', originally employed by Jones and Miles (1978) in tennis. In this approach, the action under investigation (e.g., return of serve in tennis or penalty kick in soccer) is filmed from the performer's customary perspective. The film is then selectively edited to present a varying extent of advance and ball flight information. A repeated measures design is employed whereby the same sequence of action is presented under different temporal occlusion conditions. For example, the action may be occluded prior to, at, or after ball contact with a racket as in the tennis serve scenario or a limb as would be the case in the soccer penalty kick. Participants are required to indicate either using a pen-and-paper response

154

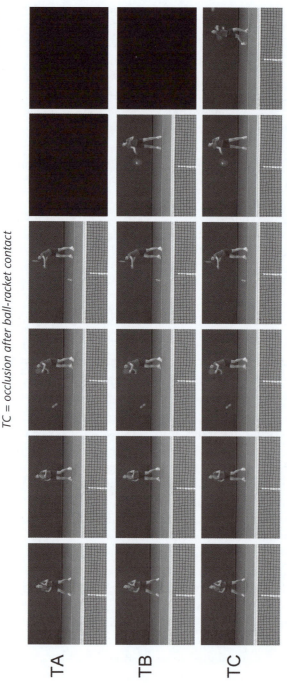

Figure 7.1 *An example of the typical stimuli employed in a temporal occlusion study involving the tennis forehand drive shot. Three temporal occlusion periods are illustrated. TA = occlusion before ball-racket contact; TB = occlusion at the moment of ball-racket contact; TC = occlusion after ball-racket contact*

or by moving as if to respond to the action where the opponent intends to place the ball. An illustration of the temporal occlusion paradigm is presented in Figure 7.1.

Typically, experts are more accurate than novices in anticipating an opponent's intentions at the earliest (i.e., pre-event) occlusion conditions, with this superiority decreasing as the length of the viewing period increases. The expert's ability to make more effective use of advance visual cues to anticipate future events is one of the most robust findings in the expertise literature, having been confirmed in a variety of sports and using a range of laboratory- and field-based techniques (for a detailed review, see Williams and Ericsson, 2005; Williams, Davids and Williams, 1999).

In a closely related area of study, researchers have attempted to determine what is the specific source(s) of information guiding skilful action? This question is typically addressed using spatial/event occlusion procedures. In the spatial/event occlusion approach, participants are presented with film sequences where a specific information source (e.g., racket, arm, head) has been occluded. If there is a decrement in performance on the trial when a particular cue is occluded, compared with a full vision control condition, then the importance of the occluded source of information is highlighted. The time of occlusion of each cue can also be manipulated to provide a clearer indication of what sources of information are important at each stage in the action. Abernethy and colleagues (Abernethy, 1988, 1990; Abernethy and Russell, 1987; Müller, Abernethy and Farrow, 2006) have undertaken the majority of work using this approach.

A more recent argument is that performers are likely to extract global, motion-related information from an opponent's postural orientation rather than a specific information cue. The suggestion is that skilled performers use the relative motion between joints and/or limbs to guide skilful action rather than a specific information cue(s). The performer's ability to perceive biological or relative motion is normally examined by presenting information in the form of a point-light display. A retro-reflective marker or small light source is positioned at each of the major joint centres of the body and the action is then filmed under darkened viewing conditions, thereby providing a series of lights against a black background. Alternatively, data may be captured used an optoelectronic motion analysis system. Ward, Williams and Bennett (2002) used this type of approach to show that expert tennis players were better than novices at anticipating the direction of forehand and backhand shots presented as point-light displays (cf. Abernethy *et al.*, 2001). Some recent adaptations to this approach have involved removing (Abernethy, Zawi and Jackson, 2008) or distorting (Huys *et al.*, 2008, 2009; Williams *et al.*, 2009) access to the information presented in point-light displays. An example of the point-light presentations employed by Ward *et al.* (2002) is presented in Figure 7.2.

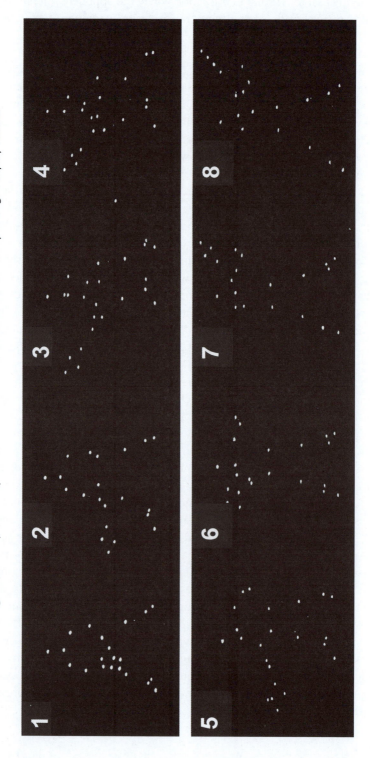

Figure 7.2 *A pictorial representation of the tennis forehand drive shot in point-light display format*

Looking the right way: visual search behaviour

Another approach that has been employed to determine the information used to guide action in sport has involved the measurement of visual search behaviours using eye movement registration systems. These systems record participants' eye movements and interspersed visual fixations as they perform on the task. The duration of each fixation is presumed to represent the degree of cognitive processing, whereas the point-of-gaze is assumed to indicate areas of interest. An example of the typical system used to record visual point-of-gaze in a sport setting is provided in Figure 7.3.

The majority of researchers have examined the visual search behaviours employed by experts and novices using film simulations of sport situations, although new technology has enabled researchers to collect data in the field setting in sports like basketball (Vickers, 1996), shooting (Causer *et al.*, 2010), table tennis (Rodrigues, Vickers and Williams, 2002), tennis (Singer *et al.*, 1998), and ice hockey (Panchuck and Vickers, 2006). The consensus is that experts' focus their gaze on more informative areas of the display compared to novices, enabling them to more effectively anticipate action requirements (for a detailed review, see Vickers, 2007; Williams, Davids and Williams, 1999; Williams *et al.*, 2004).

Although experts are more selective in the manner in which they gaze upon selected areas of the display, the search strategy employed is at least partly determined by the nature of the task and the performer's physical and emotional reaction to competition. In team sports such as soccer different search strategies

Figure 7.3   *An example of data being gathered using a head-mounted, corneal reflection system. a) The image from an external camera focusing on the shooter; b) an image of the eye picked up by the head-mounted camera; c) an image of the scene with the visual point-of-gaze highlighted*

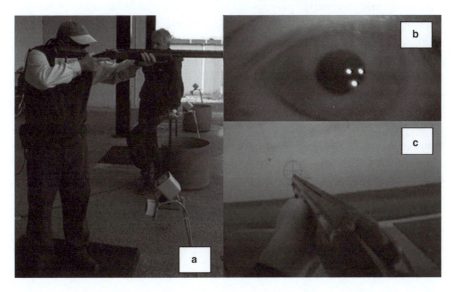

are employed when viewing the whole field (i.e., 11 vs. 11 simulations) compared to micro-situations within the game (i.e., 3 vs. 3 or 1 vs. 1 situations), and when participants are presented with offensive compared with defensive simulations (e.g., see Helsen and Pauwels, 1993; Vaeyens *et al.*, 2007; Williams *et al.*, 1994; Williams and Davids, 1998). Similarly, changes in search behaviour are commonly observed when performers are placed under conditions involving emotional or physiological stress (e.g., see Causer *et al.*, in press; Janelle, Singer and Williams, 1999; Vickers and Williams, 2007; Williams and Elliott, 1999).

The visual search strategy employed may be reflective of the relative involvement of central (the fovea) and peripheral vision during task performance. The technology employed only provides a measure of the orientation of the fovea towards selected areas of the display (i.e., visual point-of-gaze). However, there is evidence to suggest that sports performers often use peripheral and central vision in an integrated manner to extract relevant information from the display. Several researchers have noted that experts are more inclined to fixate gaze centrally in an attempt to pick up an opponent's relative motion profile using peripheral vision (e.g., Ripoll, 1991; Williams and Davids, 1998).

What happens next? Knowledge of situational probabilities

In addition to their ability to extract meaningful contextual information from the display, there is evidence to suggest that, when compared to novices, experts have more accurate expectations of the events most likely to occur in any given scenario. Alain and colleagues (e.g., Alain and Proteau, 1980; Alain and Sarrazin, 1990; Alain, Sarrazin and Lacombe, 1986) carried out the seminal work in this area. Alain and Proteau (1980) examined the extent to which players in various racket sports made use of situational probabilities to anticipate the shots available to their adversaries. The decision-making behaviour of squash, tennis, badminton and racquetball players was studied in the game situation by filming some of the rallies, allowing participants to view the film, and then asking them specific questions regarding shot selection during the rally. Players were asked to comment on the subjective probabilities they had assigned to their opponents' shots. Players evaluated the probability of each possible event that could occur and then used this information to maximise the efficiency of subsequent behaviour. It appears that players' initial anticipatory movements were guided by their expectations, with subsequent corrective or confirmatory movements being made on the basis of current information.

A similar approach was employed by Ward and Williams (2003) who asked elite and sub-elite soccer players to assign probability values to the 'best passing options' available to a player in possession of the ball. Film sequences were paused immediately prior to the ball being passed and participants were required to highlight likely passing options. The elite players were better than the sub-elite group at identifying those who were in the best position to receive the ball and were more accurate in assigning an appropriate probability to players in threatening and non-threatening positions, as determined by a panel of expert coaches. It appears that experts 'hedge their bets' more than novices, judiciously putting both their expectations and the more effective processing of contextual information to effective use. The sub-elite players, in contrast, were less efficient in their selection of critical and non-critical players and were not as adept at assigning a hierarchy of probabilities to likely events.

McRobert and colleagues (2010) employed a novel approach to examine the role of expectations or contextual information in cricket. Skilled and less skilled batters played simulated strokes in response to life-size filmed representations of bowlers. In one condition, the batsmen viewed a total of 36 random deliveries from ten different bowlers, whereas in a second condition batters were presented with an entire over each (i.e., six consecutive deliveries) from six bowlers who had delivered only one ball each in the first condition. The performance of the batsmen on the final delivery from each six-ball over in the second condition was compared with that on the same delivery when presented as an independent trial in the first condition. The batsmen improved their accuracy in making anticipation judgments and modified their visual search behaviours and thought processes (as elicited by verbal report protocols) in the condition which contained additional contextual information when compared to the random viewing condition. The batsmen spent more time fixating on central (i.e., head-shoulder region) rather than peripheral (i.e., ball-hand) areas and articulated deeper thought processes involving prediction and planning rather than monitoring and evaluation statements when additional contextual information was presented. The importance of contextual, game-related information in making anticipation judgments has also been reported in baseball (McPherson and MacMahon, 2008) and tennis (Crognier and Fery, 2005).

The different perceptual-cognitive skills outlined in this section are thought to interact in a dynamic manner during performance, with the relative importance of each one likely differing as a function of the various constraints impacting on performance at any point in time (Williams, 2009). Unfortunately, there have been no systematic attempts to examine empirically how these different skills interact in order to influence anticipation and decision-making in sport.

Practical issues and interventions

An important task for those interested in expertise in sport is to determine how skill is acquired and whether its rate of acquisition can be facilitated through practice and instruction. Bloom (1985) carried out the pioneering research in this area. He identified three important phases in the development of expertise: initiation; development; and perfection. During the initiation phase, the child is exposed to the domain under playful conditions. If some degree of success is achieved, interest in the task increases, regular practice habits are established and more formal instruction provided. After an extended period of practice, normally in the early or mid-teens, the child is encouraged to make a major commitment toward reaching the elite level.

Ericsson and colleagues (e.g., Ericsson, 1996; Ericsson, Krampe and Tesch-Römer, 1993) extended the work of Bloom by trying to identify those training activities that are most closely related to the development of expertise. Ericsson, Krampe and Tesch-Römer (1993) asked musicians of varying levels of expertise to indicate the amount of hours they had spent practising different types of music-related activities and to rate each activity in terms of its relevance to performance, inherent enjoyment and the amount of effort required. The expert musicians practised alone for more than 25 hours per week, more than three times the number of practice hours reported by less accomplished musicians. The quantity and quality of practice was closely related to the level of attained performance. In attaining excellence, the musicians had engaged in over 10,000 hours of effortful, deliberate practice with the specific intention of improving performance. According to this theory, practice should be not overly enjoyable, challenging in relation to its level of difficulty, informative due to the availability of feedback, and repetitive with an opportunity to detect and correct errors (for a review, see Ericsson, Nandagopal and Roring, 2009).

The role of deliberate practice in developing expertise in sport

The theory of deliberate practice introduced by Ericsson, Krampe and Tesch-Römer (1993) has subsequently attracted interest from sport psychologists. Several researchers have provided support for the proposal that there is a very strong relationship between the amount of practice that performers have accumulated during their careers and the eventual level of success achieved within the sport. The relationship between practice and level of attainment has been demonstrated using retrospective recall of practice history profiles in individual sports such as wrestling (Hodges and Starkes, 1996), figure skating (Starkes *et al.*, 1996) and karate (Hodge and Deakin, 1998). Those practice activities most related to actual performance (such as sparring in wrestling or skating practise in figure skating) were judged the most effortful or demanding of concentration. However, in contrast to expert musicians, the elite athletes reported that the most relevant practice activities were also the most enjoyable. The average amount of practice per week in each of these sports is consistently high (26.2 hours/week in karate, 28 hours/week in figure skating, 24.9 hours/week in wrestling), and comparable with those reported by Ericsson and colleagues for expert musicians.

Also, there have been attempts to examine the applicability of deliberate practice theory in team sports such as soccer and field hockey (Ford, Ward and Williams, 2009; Helsen *et al.*, 2000; Ward *et al.*, 2007). Helsen *et al.* (2000) examined the practice history profiles of international, national and provincial soccer players in Belgium. The amount of time spent in team practice was the strongest discriminator across groups. However, the international players spent more time in individual practice than the national and provincial players at 6 years into their careers

(11 years of age). The international and national players reached their peak in regard to the number of hours per week spent in practice (individual plus team practice) at 15 years into their career (around 20 years of age). At 18 years into their careers, the international, national and provincial players had accumulated a total of 9332, 7449 and 5079 practice hours, respectively. As reported for individual sports, those activities considered most relevant for improving performance were also the most enjoyable. The most enjoyable aspects of practice for the soccer players were mainly team-related and included work on technical skills, games and tactics. The activities rated least enjoyable were running, game analysis and cycling. In contrast to musicians, expert soccer players find the competitive and physical nature of the sport, as well as the social activity surrounding participation, enjoyable.

A novel, quasi-longitudinal design was used by Ward *et al.* (2007) to assess practice history profiles in elite and sub-elite soccer players in the United Kingdom between 9 and 18 years of age. The intention was to examine the relative contribution of sport-specific and non-sport-specific activities to the development of elite performance. The mean number of hours per week that the elite and sub-elite players spent in soccer-specific team and individual practice, playful soccer activity and match play is highlighted in Figure 7.4. The amount of time spent in soccer-specific team practice was the strongest predictor of skill. The elite players spent twice the amount of hours per week in team practice compared to the sub-elite players in each age category. However, Ford and colleagues (2009) have recently highlighted the importance of sport-specific play, or non-coach led activity in discriminating between elite players who progress to professional status at the age of 16 years compared to those players who had progressed through the same development process but were not offered a scholarship contract at the same age.

Ward and colleagues (2007) also examined the participation history of the players in activities other than soccer to determine whether skill groups could be differentiated on activities such as practice, play and match play in other sports and games. The intention was to examine differences in sporting diversity and its influence upon skilled behaviour within the specialist domain. There were no differences between the elite and sub-elite players in the number of hours accumulated in other sports, the number of sports played or the age at which players stopped participating in other sports. These findings contradict those reported by Côté and colleagues (2001) who proposed that expert participants demonstrate greater diversity in the nature of their involvement in other sports than less expert performers.

Although the deliberate practice theory proposed by Ericsson and colleagues has been criticised (e.g., see Abernethy, Farrow and Berry, 2003), it has nonetheless focused attention on the nature of the practice activities underlying the acquisition of expert performance. The issue of whether endless hours of deliberate practice is sufficient in itself to attain expertise is perhaps less important than the realisation that a long-term, focused commitment to practice is necessary to achieve excellence in any domain.

Figure 7.4 *Hours per week spent in team practice, individual practice, match play and playful activities in soccer for elite (a) and sub-elite (b) soccer players*

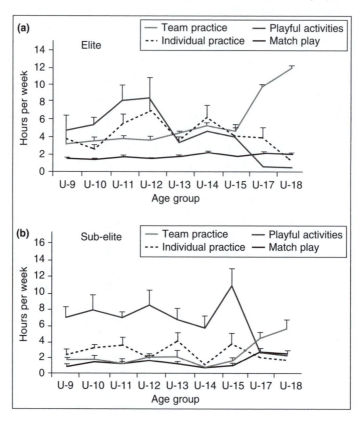

Source: Adapted from Ward et al. (2007)

Can we develop perceptual and cognitive expertise through appropriate training interventions?

There now exists an extensive knowledge base on expertise in sport and, as highlighted in this chapter, many of the characteristics that differentiate experts from novices have been identified. In contrast, attempts to facilitate the acquisition of perceptual and cognitive expertise in sport through the implementation of suitable training interventions are rather scarce in the literature. Although there are a few published papers on this topic, unfortunately much of the research is plagued by methodological shortcomings. For example, researchers have typically neglected to employ suitable control and placebo groups to ensure that improvements in performance represent a meaningful training effect rather than the result of increased test familiarity. Similarly, there have few attempts to determine whether any improvements observed in the laboratory actually transfer to the performance setting or are retained over prolonged periods of time (for detailed reviews, see Ward, Williams and Hancock, 2006; Williams, Janelle and Davids, 2004).

Williams and colleagues (e.g., Smeeton *et al.*, 2005; Williams *et al.*, 2002a; Williams, Ward and Chapman, 2003) have attempted to rectify these perceived shortcomings in the literature. In one study, Williams, Ward and Chapman (2003) showed that the ability of novice field hockey goalkeepers to make anticipation judgments at the penalty-flick was improved as a result of 60 minutes of video simulation training where the important information cues underlying performance were highlighted. The improvements in performance were observed on a film-based laboratory test and on a field-based test of anticipation skill that involved frame-by-frame video analysis of the goalkeepers' actual response to each penalty. In contrast, no significant pre- to post-test differences were observed in participants assigned to a control (completed pre- and post-tests only) or placebo (received technical instruction on hockey goalkeeping) group.

In another study, Williams *et al.* (2002a) employed a similar design to train anticipation skill in tennis. However, an interesting addition to this study was the comparison between participants that received explicit instruction as to the important cues underlying anticipation of tennis forehand and backhand shots and those who were encouraged to identify these cues for themselves through guided discovery learning. In the latter condition, participants were directed to focus on general areas of the display and discover through trial and error learning the various relationships between their opponent's postural orientation and eventual shot placement. The two groups of participants that underwent 90 minutes of training significantly improved their performance when compared to control and placebo groups on a film-based test of anticipation and an on-court test that required them to move in response to actual tennis shots performed by an opponent. No significant differences were apparent across the two training groups. Longer training periods and a delayed retention test that involves an anxiety-provoking manipulation were notable omissions from this study (see Smeeton *et al.*, 2005). Participants undertaking instruction through guided discovery are likely to take longer to learn than those exposed to explicit instruction. However, skills learnt through guided discovery may be more resilient to forgetting and the potentially negative effects of emotional stress than those acquired through more explicit instruction strategies (Masters, 1992; Hardy, Mullen and Jones, 1996b).

Another avenue of investigation undertaken by Williams and colleagues (2004) focused on the relative effectiveness of a training intervention that requires participants to verbally indicate the direction of an opponent's serve in tennis (perception only) compared with another condition whereby learners attempted to execute the service return shot (perception–action coupling). Participants who received technical instruction as to how to play forehand and backhand return shots were included as controls. Anticipatory performance was assessed pre- and post-test using on-court measures involving frame-by-frame video analysis. The findings are presented in Table 7.1. The perception–action and perception only training groups significantly reduced their response times from pre- to post-test compared with the control group. No significant differences were observed between the perception–action and perception only training groups. It appears that anticipation skill can be improved through appropriate instruction, regardless of whether the learner has to physically respond to the action or merely make a perceptual judgement as to the likely destination of an opponent's serve. A possible implication is that video simulation training with a verbal or pen-and-paper response may be at least as effective as on-court instruction, allowing coaches to make alternative use of on-court practice time.

Although significant progress has been made in determining the type of training interventions most likely to facilitate the acquisition of perceptual and cognitive expertise, there remain a number of unanswered questions. These include: How should information be conveyed to the learner (e.g., explicitly, implicitly or via guided discovery)? What is the optimum frequency, duration and scheduling for this type of intervention? Can other perceptual and cognitive skills such as pattern recognition or knowledge of situational probabilities in sport be improved? Should these skills be trained in an integrated manner or can training in isolation result in performance benefits? At what age and skill level should this type of instruction be introduced?

In conclusion, a brief overview of the research work on expertise in sport was presented in this chapter. It appears that skilled sport performers have much in common with experts in other domains. In particular, expert sport performers possess an elaborate sport-specific cognitive knowledge base that enables them to interpret events similar to those previously experienced. When compared to their novice counterparts, experts are faster and more accurate in recognising and recalling patterns of play from within their domain of expertise, are better at anticipating their opponents' actions based on advance visual cues, employ more effective and appropriate visual search behaviours, and are more accurate in their

Table 7.1 *Mean performance scores and standard deviations on the pre- and post-tests for the three groups of participants*

		Pre-test		Post-test	
Group		DT (ms)	RA (%)	DT (ms)	RA (%)
Perception–action	M	1437.8	89.4	998.6	84.3
training	SD	72.1	4.2	192.5	9.79
Perception only	M	1492.5	90.0	1163.9	87.5
training	SD	72.6	11.0	179.6	5.9
Technical	M	1402.7	90.0	1360.7	91.3
training	SD	67.6	13.4	84.6	13.5

Source: Adapted from Williams *et al.* (2004)

expectation of what is likely to happen given a particular set of circumstances. The experts' superior knowledge and skills are developed through sport-specific practice, rather than as a result of maturation. There is evidence to suggest that the development of perceptual and cognitive expertise can be facilitated through appropriate interventions using various forms of instruction and feedback.

An important factor to emerge from the study of expertise is an increased understanding of what it takes to attain excellence in any domain. Expert sports performers invest an incredible amount of practice time in order to achieve prominence within their chosen sport. These performers are dedicated to achieving excellence and develop a 'rage to master' from an early age (Winner, 1996). Those with such precocity for learning classically possess high levels of intrinsic motivation and an intense and often obsessive interest with their domain of expertise. The commitment and motivation to spend many hours in deliberate practice activities with the specific intention to improve performance may well prove to be the most important attribute to possess on the road to excellence in sport.

CASE STUDY

Stephanie is an elite tennis player who is having difficulty moving up the LTA rankings. Her coach feels that she is having problems in anticipating the shots played by her opponents and this is proving particularly difficult when attempting to return serve. Stephanie has worked hard to improve her fitness as well as the effectiveness of her forehand and backhand return shots, but her success rate at returning serve is below those players above her on the LTA rankings.

1. How could you assess Stephanie's skill in anticipating an opponent's actions in the service return scenario? What type of tests and measures would you employ to identify areas for improvement?
2. Provide some examples of how you could go about developing a training programme to improve her ability to read an opponent's serve?
3. How could you monitor the effectiveness of this training programme?

STUDY QUESTIONS

1. With reference to a sport of your choice, consider how you would design representative tasks to assess perceptual and cognitive expertise.
2. Consider the relative importance of pattern recognition skill and advance cue usage in the following sports: soccer, volleyball, field hockey, tennis and cricket.

3. Discuss how situational probabilities may be important to anticipation in your sport. Provide some specific examples of situational probabilities and how they may impact on performance.
4. Discuss the relative importance of practice/experience and innate abilities in the acquisition of expertise.
5. With reference to the sport or activity that you consider yourself to be most accomplished in performing, outline the age at which you began participating, the typical number of hours per week that you spent in practice activities and the nature of these practice activities. Compare your findings with those from another sport or activity where you would consider yourself to be a less accomplished performer.
6. Outline how you would develop a training programme to improve anticipation in a sport of your choice.
7. In implementing a training programme to improve anticipation, consider the relative merits of explicit instruction and guided discovery techniques. Would you recommend one approach over the other? Provide some illustrations to highlight the differences between each mode of instruction.

FURTHER READING

Ericsson, K. A. Charness, N., Feltovich, P. J. and Hoffman, R. R. (2006) (eds) *The Cambridge Handbook of Expertise and Expert Performance* (New York: Cambridge University Press).

Farrow, D., Baker, J. and MacMahon, C. (2008) (eds) *Developing Sport Expertise: Researchers and Coaches Put Theory into Practice* (London: Routledge).

Starkes, J. L. and Ericsson, K. A. (2003) (eds) *Expert Performance in Sports: Advances in Research on Sport Expertise* (Champaign, IL: Human Kinetics).

Vickers, J. N. (2007) *Perception, Cognition, and Decision Training: The Quiet Eye in Action* (Champaign, Il: Human Kinetics).

Williams, A. M., Davids, K. and Williams, J. G. (1999) *Visual Perception and Action in Sport* (London: Routledge).

Williams, A. M. and Hodges, N. J. (2004) (eds) *Skill Acquisition in Sport: Research, Theory and Practice* (London: Routledge).

8 Acquiring Sport Skills

INTRODUCTION, HISTORY AND DEVELOPMENT

The ability to execute movement skills effectively is fundamental to any level of performance in sport. In fact, performance in predictable, closed sports such as gymnastics and dance is based almost solely on the ability to reproduce movement in a consistent and efficient manner. In more unpredictable, open sports such as soccer and tennis technical skill is also paramount to successful performance, albeit in combination with other skills such as anticipation and decision making. Given the importance of movement skills in sport, and in everyday life, it is not surprising that sport psychologists have devoted much research to providing coaches and practitioners with guidance as to how best to facilitate the acquisition of such skills (e.g., see Williams and Hodges, 2004, 2005).

The study of motor skill learning has a rather long history, with its foundations stemming from experimental psychology. Some of the earliest published papers on motor skill acquisition were the classic works of Bryan and Harter (1897, 1899) on the sending and receiving of Morse code messages. In this task, skill is related to the speed with which operators can translate between English and Morse code and execute the required key taps. Bryan and Harter compared expert and novice telegraphers and, in a later study, examined the acquisition of skill in several operators over a 40-week practice period. They concluded that learning proceeds through distinct phases, including periods of no improvement (learning plateaus), and that the rate and manner of learning may be somewhat unique from one individual to another. At a similar time, Thorndike (1927) published other classical work on the role of reward and error information (knowledge of results) in strengthening behaviour (law of effect) and on the transfer of training (for a detailed historical review, see Adams, 1987; Summers, 2004).

During the period 1940–70, labelled by Adams (1987) as the 'middle period', more systematic programmes of work emerged. This renewed interest in motor skills research was brought about by the advent of the Second World War and the need to address task-centred questions based on the selection and training of military personnel. Several researchers focused on the importance of individual differences and abilities in selection (e.g., Fleishman, 1956), whereas others worked on learning-related issues such as the importance of knowledge of results (feedback) and massed versus distributed practice (e.g., Ammons, 1950; Bilodeau and Bilodeau, 1958). Fitts and Posner's (1967) attempts to characterise the different stages of skill learning (cognitive, associative, autonomous) is also worthy of note. The research on motor learning was strongly influenced by the principles of conditioning advocated by Hull (1943) in his 'general learning theory'. The theory attempted to explain how fatigue and recovery processes affected the acquisition of motor skills over long practice periods. Another important development at this time was the application of 'cognitive information-processing models' to performance and learning, based on the brain–computer analogy first coined by Craik (1948). The information-processing models that emerged at this time went on to dominate the psychological and skill acquisition literature in the late 1970s and 80s (e.g., see Neisser, 1976), and still have a significant influence today.

Towards the end of this period, the work of Franklin Henry is seen as being instrumental in the development of the field, ably supported by A. W. Hubbard and A. T. Slatter-Hammel. While based at the University of California at Berkley, Henry was the first to apply principles of psychology within the context of physical education and sport. Several of his doctoral students went on to take up prominent positions in physical education departments in the United States, leading to a significant growth of interest in issues related to motor learning during the 1970s. Similarly, at the University of Illinois, Jack Adams provided the first major theory of motor learning (Adams, 1971), while several of his doctoral students including Richard Schmidt and Karl Newell became leading figures in the field. In Europe, John Whiting and his group at the University of Leeds led the way in the late 1960s and early 1970s with their systematic programme of research on acquiring ball skills. The work emanating from these groups paved the way for the expansion and renewed interest in skill acquisition at the end of the last millennium.

Although cognitive psychology has provided the conceptual backdrop for the majority of post-war skill acquisition research (e.g., Schmidt's (1975) Schema Theory being one of, if not the, most cited theoretical papers), towards the latter decades of the last millennium alternative theoretical frameworks emerged from the fields of ecological psychology and dynamical systems theory. The original work of American psychologist James Gibson (1979) on direct perception and Russian physiologist Nikolai Bernstein (1967) on the control and coordination of movement has influenced the writings of several prominent scientists such as Scott Kelso, Peter Kugler and Michael Turvey at the Haskins Laboratories, University of Connecticut (e.g., Kelso, 1995; Kugler, Kelso and Turvey, 1982; Kugler and Turvey, 1987). This perspective used physical biology as its basis and suggests that coordinated movement emerges as a function of the constraints placed on individuals during performance and learning. This alternative perspective provided a timely challenge to those undertaking work from the traditional cognitive perspective and further stimulated interest in the field of skill acquisition.

THEORIES AND MODELS

Those typically undertaking research work in the area of motor behaviour have embraced either the cognitive or ecological/dynamical perspective on skill acquisition, although there have been several attempts at integrated modelling (e.g., see Davids *et al.*, 2001). Cognitive theories of motor control and learning are heavily dependent on prescription (i.e., symbolic knowledge structures or schema stored in memory) to mediate the translation of information from (sensory) input to (motor) output. It is presumed that these knowledge structures contain the relevant commands needed for movement to be controlled through hierarchical (top-down) processes.

Perhaps the most prominent theoretical framework for motor learning research within the cognitive domain has been 'schema theory' developed by Richard Schmidt in the mid-1970s. According to Schmidt (1975), the learner develops through practice an expansive, generative 'rule' or generalised motor programme to cope with a variety of similar but different instances (see Magill, 2007; Schmidt and Lee, 2011; Schmidt and Wrisberg, 2009). Each class of actions or skill is thought to have its own generalised motor programme. This generalised motor programme is presumed to have invariant (i.e., consistent) characteristics such as relative timing and force and changeable parameters such as overall force and time. A learner, for example, may develop a generalised motor programme for kicking a soccer ball. Aspects of the movement would be fixed from one attempt to another, such as the timing of joint flexion and extension or the relative amount of force produced by each muscle, whereas other components such as the overall force produced or timing of the movement could be modified in order to be able to pass the ball accurately over varying distances. From this perspective, learning is based on principles of regression, such that variability of practice within a particular class of actions is essential in developing flexible and adaptable schemata (Shapiro and Schmidt, 1982).

In contrast, ecological/dynamical systems theories suggest that perception and action are grounded in physical terms and natural law rather than symbolic structures and computation. These models invest control in hetrearchical (bottom-up) control processes, and assume that movement is self-organised as a result of the constraints acting on the performer at any given moment. Constraints, which may be internal (e.g., morphology of the body) or external (e.g., strategy and tactics) to the learner, are important influences, guiding and shaping functional coordination states (Newell, 1985). As learning progresses, performers become more refined at mapping/coupling perceptual information onto the dynamics of the system in a way that is consistent with these constraints (for a detailed review, see Davids et al., 2008; Williams et al., 1999). The emphasis on a constraints-led approach has led researchers to try and identify the key constraints under which skilled behaviour emerges in sport (see Phillips et al., 2010). It has also been argued that an important role for the coach is to understand the nature of the constraints acting on each athlete so that these can be manipulated effectively during practice (Davids et al., 2008; Williams and Hodges, 2005).

The majority of the research work on skill acquisition presented in this chapter is from the perspective of cognitive psychology. However, the intention is not to suggest that this approach offers several advantages over and above other theoretical viewpoints. The content of the chapter merely reflects the fact that the vast majority of current research work has been undertaken from this perspective. Thus far, there remains far less work on skill acquisition from the ecological/dynamical systems camp, although later in this chapter the issue of how best to manipulate constraints to facilitate effective learning is discussed in greater detail.

METHODS AND MEASURES

Motor learning is defined as 'a set of processes associated with practice or experience that leads to relatively permanent changes in the capability for movement' (Schmidt and Lee, 2011). Although changes in central nervous system function occur as a result of learning, the process itself is difficult to quantify since it can only be inferred from changes in performance (i.e., observed behaviour). This difficulty is compounded by the fact that performance is relatively transient or temporary in nature, with significant variations in behaviour possible due to factors other than learning such as, for example, changes in motivation, anxiety or fitness levels. Learning can therefore only be inferred by observing changes in performance over an extended period of time.

This distinction between learning and performance is crucial for scientists and practitioners since many of the typical interventions employed by coaches have varying effects on these two processes. As highlighted throughout this chapter, a number of instructional procedures have a detrimental effect on performance while, at the same time, being beneficial to skill learning and vice versa. What you see is not always what you get as far as the process of skill acquisition is concerned.

Typically, learning is assessed by plotting performance across time (i.e., performance curves). An agreed measure of performance is required in order to determine whether improvements are observed. The learner normally undertakes a pre-test to determine initial performance levels before participating in some form of structured intervention. A post-test is then administered to determine the change in performance. Occasionally, more than one form of intervention may be compared (e.g., various levels of feedback precision), and a control group is employed to ensure that any pre- to post-test improvement is a meaningful training effect rather than a by-product of increased test familiarity or habituation. In order to measure learning accurately, retention or transfer tests must be used in association with performance curves. A retention test necessitates that the player is retested after a period of time when the transient effects of performance have subsided. In contrast, a transfer test requires the learner either to perform the skill that has been practised in a new situation or to perform a variation of the practised skill.

The majority of researchers working in the area of motor learning have relied on outcome measures of performance that specify whether the desired task (e.g., hitting the target) has been achieved. These have included error scores, response time and accuracy, and movement time (for a review, see Magill, 2007; Schmidt and Lee, 2011; Schmidt and Wrisberg, 2009). The disadvantage of relying purely on outcome measures is that the learner may record accurate outcome scores at the expense of developing a more appropriate movement form that may facilitate better performance in the long term. Alternatively, no change in outcome scores may be apparent following a particular intervention, implying that no learning has taken place, whereas the learner may demonstrate a significant improvement in movement form. Consequently, researchers have attempted to record process measures of learning that describe the movement itself in conjunction with outcome scores (e.g., see Horn, Williams, and Scott, 2002). For example, changes in movement kinematics such as limb position, velocity and acceleration have been examined using high-speed video or optoelectronic systems. Other measures of learning have included electromyography to assess muscle activity, eye movement recording and various measures of brain activity such as electroencephalography, event-related potentials and functional magnetic resonance imaging (see Janelle, Duley and Coombes, 2004). These developments, which have partly been driven by advancements in measurement technology, have provided the researcher with more sensitive measurement tools to address theoretical and practical issues.

PRACTICAL ISSUES AND INTERVENTIONS

The main aim of the instructional process is to provide an environment whereby skills can be learnt in a safe and efficient manner. An important role for sport psychologists with an interest in the skill acquisition process is to provide practitioners and coaches with guidance as to how best to teach movement skills to beginners, and those more advanced in skill and experience. Some of the important procedures within the instruction process are highlighted in Figure 8.1, and a review of current knowledge within each of these areas follows.

Figure 8.1   *Some of the important factors underlying effective instruction*

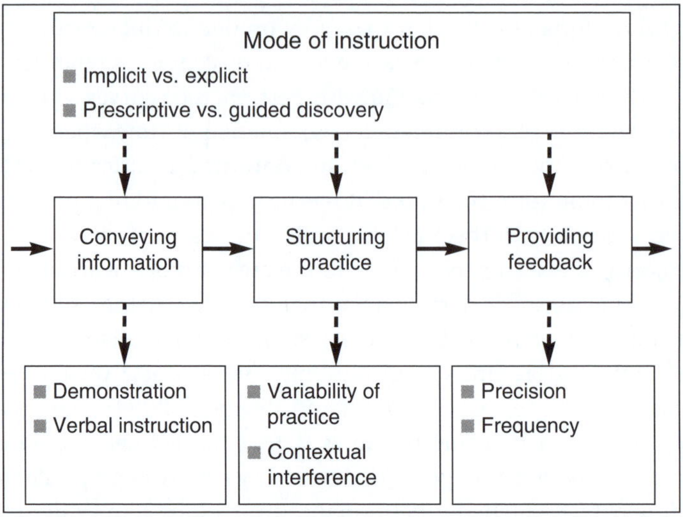

```
┌─────────────────────────────────────────────────────────────────┐
│         ┌─────────────────────────────────────────────┐          │
│         │            Mode of instruction              │          │
│         │  ▨ Implicit vs. explicit                    │          │
│         │  ▨ Prescriptive vs. guided discovery        │          │
│         └─────────────────────────────────────────────┘          │
│              ┆               ┆               ┆                    │
│      ┌──────────────┐ ┌──────────────┐ ┌──────────────┐          │
│  →   │  Conveying   │→│  Structuring │→│  Providing   │  →       │
│      │ information  │ │   practice   │ │   feedback   │          │
│      └──────────────┘ └──────────────┘ └──────────────┘          │
│              ┆               ┆               ┆                    │
│  ┌──────────────────┐┌──────────────────┐┌──────────────────┐   │
│  │ ▨ Demonstration  ││ ▨ Variability of ││ ▨ Precision      │   │
│  │                  ││   practice       ││                  │   │
│  │ ▨ Verbal         ││ ▨ Contextual     ││ ▨ Frequency      │   │
│  │   instruction    ││   interference   ││                  │   │
│  └──────────────────┘└──────────────────┘└──────────────────┘   │
└─────────────────────────────────────────────────────────────────┘
```

Conveying information: verbal instructions and demonstrations

Coaches need to decide how best to convey information to the learner about the skill to be performed. The majority of coaches rely heavily on demonstrations to inform the learner as to the desired movement form and outcome; the assumption being that information is presented most effectively in visual rather than verbal form, as highlighted by the old adage 'a picture paints a thousand words'. However, are demonstrations always the most effective manner to convey information? Are there situations where verbal instructions may be better than demonstration, or when learners should be left to their own devices to solve the movement problem?

Demonstrating the skill

The process of learning from a demonstration is referred to as 'observational learning'. The presumption is that demonstrations provide a model or visual template of the action that learners can copy and attempt to imitate. The learner formulates a 'symbolic' representation or 'cognitive blueprint' in memory that serves to aid subsequent recall and reproduction of the skill. In Bandura's (1977b, 1986) 'cognitive mediation theory', four interrelated processes in the acquisition of movement skill are highlighted. These processes are: attention; retention; motor production; and motivation. Initially, the learner must focus attention on, and extract from the model, the relevant sources of information needed to guide subsequent reproduction of the skill. The learner must then retain this information by constructing a symbolic or cognitive representation of the skill in memory. Cognitive activities such as rehearsal, labelling and organisation are involved in the retention process. This representation or schema is then used to guide subsequent attempts at reproduction, supported by feedback and instruction. The learner's motivation to reproduce the observed action is paramount to refinement and further development of the skill.

The majority of research on observational learning has tested Bandura's (1977a) prediction that observers pay closer attention to models possessing symbols that reflect status, such as age and skill level. The general consensus from this body of work is that learners pay more attention to a model that is highly respected by the group, whereas the accuracy of the demonstration is seen to be important since observational learning is based on direct imitation of the visually presented skill (McCullagh and Weiss, 2001). However, several authors have voiced the opinion that observing a learning model is at least as beneficial as viewing a skilled model since the former actively engages the learner in a problem-solving process (e.g., see Domingue and Maraj, 1998; McCullagh and Meyer, 1997). The benefits of using a learning model may be heightened if the observer is also able to hear the prescriptive feedback provided to the model by the coach. For example, McCullagh and Caird (1990) reported that participants who observed a learning model perform a timing task and listened to the feedback provided by the instructor showed better performance compared with those who viewed a skilled model only.

Another issue that has received considerable interest, particularly with regard to the process of motor reproduction, is whether the effectiveness of demonstrations varies depending on the skill to be learnt. One suggestion is that demonstrations are only effective when they convey a clear movement strategy that is reproducible by the learner. It may be that demonstrations are no more effective than verbal instruction or practice alone when the information conveyed is low and/or when the task requires that the learner develop a feel for the movement (Horn and Williams, 2004; Williams *et al.*, 1999). The likelihood is that a demonstration would be most effective when it clearly highlights the strategy required for successful performance and the learner has the necessary movement skill and motivation to apply the strategy conveyed in an effective manner.

More recently, researchers have attempted to determine the nature of the information picked up by the learner when observing a model (for recent reviews, see Hodges *et al.*, 2007; Maslovat *et al.*, 2010). Scully and Newell (1985) argued that learners pick up the relative motions between the key body parts (i.e., the movement's topological characteristics) rather than specific information cues about the movement. According to this perspective, demonstrations should be most effective early in learning, referred to by Newell (1985) as the coordination stage, when the player is trying to acquire a new movement pattern (Magill and Schoenfelder-Zohdi, 1996). In this situation, the movement of various body parts in relation to each other defines the action pattern required for successful performance. Later in learning when the performer is trying to parameterise or 'scale' an existing movement pattern, demonstrations are presumed to be no more effective than verbal instructions or continued practice on the task (Scully, 1988).

The learner's ability to pick up relative motion information has been nicely demonstrated in a series of studies by Horn and colleagues (e.g., Horn, Williams and Scott, 2002; Horn and Williams, 2004) using point-light displays, whereby only the major joint centres of the body were visible as white dots against a black background. Participants who viewed either a video or point-light demonstration of a soccer chip pass towards a target did not differ in their effectiveness in at imitating the model's action both with and without the presence of intrinsic feedback

Figure 8.2   *Mean absolute (AE) and variable error (VE) scores for the three groups of participants during acquisition and retention*

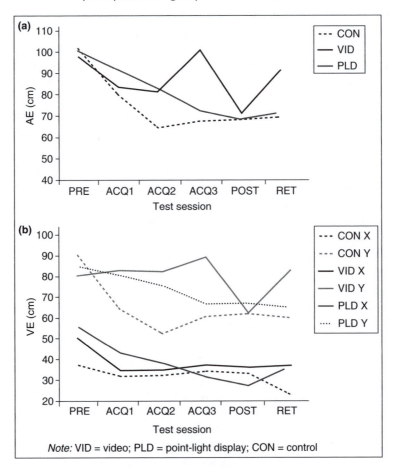

Source: Adapted from Horn, Williams and Scott, 2002

regarding the ball's landing position. No differences were observed between groups in performance outcome or in coordination, while both treatment groups outperformed a no-model control group. The vertical (Y) and horizontal (X) radial and variable error scores are presented in Figure 8.2. Similarly, Scully and Carnegie (1998) reported that participants who viewed a point-light representation of a ballet sequence approximated the model's landing position, angular displacement and relative timing more successfully than those who observed a video presentation of the action. The removal of structural information via the presentation of a model in point-light form rather than using video may make it easier for the learner to pick up crucial relative motion information. The advent of computerised motion analysis systems has simplified markedly the process of creating point-lights and, consequently, such images are easily created for skill instruction purposes.

Providing verbal instructions about the skill

Another method that coaches could employ to convey information to the learner is verbal instruction. Verbal instructions may be provided prior to, or after, attempting to perform the skill or as verbal guidance during the demonstration. Several factors need to be taken into account when providing verbal instruction. In particular, instructions should be kept brief and simple because players have a limited capacity to absorb information, particularly when performing a new skill. The language employed should be non-technical and appropriate to the age of the players. Verbal instruction should complement the demonstration by giving the players a general idea of how to perform the skill; it should give them the 'big picture' in as few words as possible. Verbal instruction and subsequent feedback should also be compatible (Hodges and Franks, 2001). If instruction is focused on a particular aspect of behaviour (e.g., keeping the head steady when putting in golf), then attention should be directed towards this aspect of performance using verbal prompts and subsequent feedback (Magill, 2007).

Masters and colleagues (e.g., Liao and Masters, 2001; Masters, 2000; Masters and Maxwell, 2004) have argued that verbal instructions may be particularly effective when used to provide the learner with heuristic instruction. This technique, referred to as 'analogy learning', reduces the amount of information that the learner has to process by grouping task-relevant rules or instructions into a single, all-encompassing metaphor or heuristic. When attempting to teach the tennis serve, for instance, the coach could tell the learner that the service action is similar to an overarm throwing action. Liao and Masters (2001) used this type of approach to teach a group of novices the topspin table tennis forehand shot. The learners were instructed to draw a right-angle triangle with the bat (hypotenuse uppermost) and to strike the ball as the bat travelled up the hypotenuse of the triangle. The analogy group outperformed a group that were provided with a set of explicit instructions regarding the drive shot that were adapted from a table tennis coaching manual.

An alternative perspective is that verbal instructions can sometimes have detrimental effects on learning (see Hodges and Lee, 1999; Wulf and Weigelt, 1997). Wulf and Weigelt (1997) found that 'expert strategy' instruction given to beginners when learning to move on a ski-simulator was actually detrimental to acquisition, as compared to a group who did not receive any technique instruction. The authors suggested that instructions and movement demonstrations direct attention inappropriately to the body, at the expense of a goal-related focus on the effects of the action (which might be encouraged by withholding instruction and promoting more discovery learning conditions). The suggestion that an external rather than internal focus of attention may be more beneficial to skill acquisition has subsequently been supported in a number of studies (for a detailed review, see Wulf, 2007). Further research is necessary to determine the specific role of verbal cues and narration during the instruction process.

Practice scheduling

An important issue for coaches is how best to structure practice sessions for effective learning. Skills may be practised in many ways, for varying periods of time, under a range of conditions and according to different schedules. A key task for the coach is to manipulate these practice variables to meet the learner's needs. The most important questions relate to the extent to which practice conditions need to be highly variable and, if practising more than one skill per session, should practice be structured in a blocked or random manner? These issues are referred to as 'variability of practice' and 'contextual interference effects' respectively, and both areas of study have attracted significant research interest.

Variability of practice

According to Schmidt's (1975) schema theory, when practising skills, variability in movement and context characteristics is essential in order to develop a more expansive, generative rule or generalised motor programme to cope with a variety of similar yet different situations. When variability is introduced into the practice environment, the learner has to parameterise the motor programme differently from one trial to the next, resulting in a more flexible and adaptable movement representation.

Although there is some contradictory evidence, the proposition that variable practice results in greater accuracy and consistency than specific repetition of the same skill has received considerable support (for a review, see Lee, Magill and Weeks, 1985; Van Rossum, 1990). McCracken and Stelmach (1977) carried out one of the earliest studies using a task that required learners to move their right arm to knock over a barrier with a constant 200 ms movement time. The distances to the barrier could be changed during practice to create four different conditions (15, 35, 60, and 65 cm). A constant practice group, made up of four subgroups, performed 300 practice trials at each of the barrier distances. The variable practice group performed 75 trials at each of the four conditions, with these trials being presented in a random order. In the transfer phase, a novel (50 cm) distance was employed immediately and two days after acquisition. As expected, the four constant practice groups had smaller absolute error scores during acquisition compared with the variable practice group. However, the variable practice group showed much better performance on the immediate and delayed transfer tests. It appeared that variability of practice allowed participants to learn the task more effectively, permitting them to perform much better than the constant practice group on a novel variation of the same task. Variable practice increases the applicability of the skill, enabling novel variations of the task to be performed effectively and accurately.

The benefits of variable practice appear to be particularly pronounced with children (e.g., see Wulf, 1991; Yan, Thomas and Thomas, 1998). When teaching children the soccer instep pass, for instance, coaches should ensure that they vary practice conditions by manipulating factors such as distance, speed, height or direction of the pass and that the practice session mimics the range of variations experienced during a match. However, coaches should not make the variation in practice so great that the task becomes a different skill to that originally practised. For example, with regard to the example of instep passing, coaches should ensure that however they vary conditions, the same generalised motor programme is employed by the learner to perform the skill. The suggestion is that variable practice is most effective when coupled with a random rather than blocked practice schedule, as discussed in the next section (Lee, Magill and Weeks, 1985).

A recent issue that has attracted interest is the phenomenon of 'especial skills'. The proposal is that especial skills develop through the accumulation of significant amounts of specific practice at a task. Keetch and colleagues (2005, 2008) showed that skilled basketball players develop exceptional levels of performance at the free throw shot distance (i.e., 15ft from the basket), with accuracy scores significantly higher than would be predicted based on the regression model predicted by a generalised motor program view of performance. There has been some debate as to the factors responsible for this enhanced performance as well as the extent to which the notion of an 'especial skill' is generalisable to other tasks and sports (see Breslin *et al.*, 2010).

Contextual interference effects: blocked versus random practice

Contextual interference occurs when several skills are learnt within the same practice session (Battig, 1979). A low contextual interference practice schedule may involve practising one skill per session, or perhaps two separate skills

RESEARCH BOX

Ford, Yates, and Williams (2010) examined the practice activities and instructional behaviours employed by 25 youth soccer coaches during 70 different training sessions. A video-based, time-use analysis was undertaken to identify the specific activities that the coaches had players practice during each session, whereas a lapel microphone was used to record their verbal comments. A modified version of The Arizona State University Observation Instrument (Lacy and Darst, 1985) was employed to code coach behaviours. Altogether, 9 of the coaches worked with an under-9 years age group, 8 with an under-13 years age group, and 8 with the under-16 years age group. Moreover, 9 coaches were recorded working with elite, 8 with sub-elite and 8 with non-elite players.

The activities employed were coded into two categories termed as Training Form (i.e., work on fitness, technique and skills practices) and Playing Form (i.e., small-sided games, conditioned games and phase of play activities) respectively. The Playing Form activity was judged to be more game-like and specific to the demands of competition than Training Form activity. Coach behaviours were coded into four categories, namely, Instruction, Support and Encouragement, Management and Prolonged Silence.

Overall, the proportions of time spent in Training Form and Playing Form activity was 65% and 35% respectively. Only minor variations in these proportions were noted across the different age and skill groups. It appears that the majority of training time is spent in activities that may be deemed less specific to the demands of competition and match play. Although it is possible that Training Form activities may be modified to better reflect the demands of match-play, the amount of time spent in more realistic Playing Form activities was very low.

The analysis of coach behaviours during training revealed that coaches provided high levels of instruction (circa 30% of coach behaviours) and management (circa 24% of coach behaviours), irrespective of the practice activity in which players engaged. A lack of differences in the nature of the instructional behaviours employed across practice activities and skill and age groups was notable, implying the absence of any age- or skill-related progressions in practice activities or instructional behaviours.

The authors highlight the growing body of empirical evidence supporting use of more realistic practice activities that mimic the specific perceptual, cognitive and motor demands of match-play. A concern is raised that Coaches may be creating a learning environment that is overly prescriptive with too much time spent in structured practice activities that do not recreate effectively the demands of competition. The need to use empirical processes to evaluate effective practice activities and coach behaviours is highlighted, as well as the need to ensure that contemporary literature from the learning sciences and areas associated with instructional systems design are more strongly embedded in coach education programmes.

(e.g., shooting and passing in basketball) in blocks of 20 to 30 minutes each (i.e., blocked practice). In contrast, much higher levels of contextual interference would arise if a variety of skills (e.g., shooting, passing, dribbling) were practised in a somewhat random manner throughout the session (i.e., random practice). In the most random practice schedule, a player never practises the same skill on consecutive trials. The degree of contextual interference can be considered as a continuum, with a totally random order of skill practices at one end (high contextual interference) and blocks of practice on one skill at the other (low contextual interference; see Magill, 2007).

Shea and Morgan (1979) were the first to identify the contextual interference phenomenon within the context of motor learning. They compared two groups of individuals who practised three versions of a laboratory task for a total of 54 trials (18 trials per version). The task required participants to knock over three (of six) small wooden barriers as quickly as possible using a tennis ball. The three tasks differed in terms of the specific barriers that had to be struck during the movement, with each version of the task being instigated by a different colour stimulus light. The blocked practice group completed all 18 trials on the first task, before switching to the second and finally the third task. The random practice group completed all 54 trials in a randomised manner, with no more than two trials in succession being performed on any one task and no more than three trials on any task within each set of nine trials.

The blocked practice group recorded faster response times than the random practice group during acquisition, particularly during the first block of nine trials. In contrast, the pattern was reversed in the random and blocked retention tests completed 10 minutes and 10 days following the practice period, with the random practice group outperforming the blocked practice group. It appears that while blocked practice facilitated a more rapid performance improvement, random practice was better for learning as determined by immediate and delayed retention tests.

Several researchers have subsequently confirmed that a random or high contextual interference practice schedule, while detrimental to short-term performance, is better for long-term retention and learning than blocked conditions (for a more detailed review, see Magill, 2007; Schmidt and Lee, 2011; Schmidt and Wrisberg, 2009). These findings have been demonstrated using sport-related skills such as badminton (Goode and Magill, 1986), baseball (Hall, Domingues and Cavazos, 1994), volleyball (Bortoli *et al.*, 1992), and kayaking (Smith and Davies, 1995). The clear message is that coaches should try and avoid repetitious, blocked practice by presenting a variety of skills within the same session. The benefits of random practice also appear to be enhanced when skills differ more markedly (e.g., dribbling and the chest pass may be more distinct than the chest pass and the overhead pass in basketball) (for an interesting discussion, see Brady, 1998). An exception to this rule may potentially arise very early in learning where there is some evidence to suggest that blocked practice may be better (Shea, Kohl and Indermill, 1990). Since performance during acquisition is likely to be poorer under random compared with blocked practice conditions, learners may feel that they are making relatively little progress and be discouraged from continuing with practice (see Simon and Bjork, 2001). A key role for the coach therefore is to achieve a balance between performance and learning, ensuring effective skill development on the one hand while continuing to engage the individual in practice on the other.

A variety of theoretical accounts have been proposed to account for the positive effects of contextual interference on skill learning. The majority of these suggest that random practice schedules facilitate learning either by encouraging the performer to undertake more elaborate and distinctive processing from one trial to the next (Shea and Morgan, 1979) or through the forgetting and subsequent reconstruction of an action plan each time a skill is performed (Lee and Magill, 1985). Regardless of the ongoing controversy about the mechanisms underpinning the contextual interference phenomenon, the benefit of random over blocked practice is one of the most established findings in the motor learning literature.

A key issue is that the demands of practice must match the demands of competition, particularly in dynamic fast ball sports and team games where variability and randomness are an integral part of the performance environment. Coaches should consistently reflect on whether or not their practice sessions match the competition environment. The possibility of a theory-practice divide exists, with recent published reports suggesting that coaches may be devoting too much time to technical training rather than having athletes practice skills under realistic match conditions (e.g., see Ford, Yates and Williams, 2010).

Providing feedback

During practice, feedback is provided to the learner about the correctness of the movement performed and whether the outcome has been achieved. This feedback, which is available intrinsically (i.e., via the performer's own sensory mechanisms) and/or extrinsically (i.e., from an external source such as a coach), is regarded as one of the most important factors underpinning skill learning. The coach typically provides information after the skill has been performed, referred to as terminal or post-event augmented feedback. Although learning can occur in the absence of augmented feedback, the provision of such information results in more efficient learning, ensures correct development of the motor skill and better eventual performance. Information relating to the nature of the movement itself is termed 'knowledge of performance', whereas that referring to the outcome of the task, relative to some external goal, is termed 'knowledge of results'. This distinction is not always apparent, especially when the goal of the action is a particular movement pattern or technique.

The majority of researchers have manipulated the provision of knowledge of results in order to determine its effects on skill learning, mainly because of the difficulties in providing knowledge of performance within a controlled experimental setting and trying to measure changes in movement form and topology. However, in most instructional settings where learners are able to see whether they have been successful in achieving the intended goal, coaches are far more likely to provide knowledge of performance (Magill, 2007). The learner is presumed to process these two sources of feedback in a similar manner (Wulf and Shea, 2004), although this has yet to be verified empirically. Several factors relating to the provision of feedback have been examined in the literature, such as its role and importance at each stage of learning as well as the optimal levels of precision and frequency for effective skill learning (for detailed reviews, see Magill, 2001, 2007; Schmidt and Lee, 2011; Schmidt and Wrisberg, 2009).

Feedback and stage of skill learning

Is feedback important at every stage within the learning process? Newell (1974) reported one of the earliest studies to address this particular question. The task required participants to learn to make a rapid ballistic movement by sliding a handle/rod down a track a distance of 24 cm in 150 ms. Participants knew the distance to move, but not the correct speed of movement. Feedback was provided as absolute error in milliseconds. Six groups of participants had feedback withdrawn after 2, 7, 17, 32, 52 trials or not withdrawn at all (75 trials). The groups that had feedback withdrawn after 52 and 75 trials were able to perform the lever movement task very accurately on later trials with no feedback, whereas those that had feedback withdrawn early during acquisition were far less accurate on the no-feedback trials. It appears that feedback is essential early in learning to help to establish a reference of correctness for the movement, whereas after a certain amount of practice learners are able to detect and correct their own errors and are less dependent on prescriptive feedback (see also Schmidt and White, 1972).

Skilled players often have a good indication of where they are going wrong and how they can attempt to rectify the problem on future attempts. It is important for the coach to develop intrinsic error detection and correction mechanisms in their athletes. Too much feedback can prevent learners from evaluating their own performance and cause them to become dependent on augmented feedback from the coach. A solution may be to provide more descriptive rather than prescriptive feedback as skill develops. Prescriptive information may be provided early in learning to correct the errors made during performance, whereas as learning progresses feedback can be more descriptive in order to encourage players to acquire the ability to detect their own errors (Magill, 2007). The provision of descriptive feedback may be coupled with a question and answer approach. Questions such as 'What could you have done better on that attempt?' encourage learners to think about their own performance and develop greater sensitivity for the movement (see Liu and Wrisberg, 1997).

Precision of feedback

The precision of feedback relates to how detailed or specific augmented feedback should be in reference to the learner's performance on the skill. This information can be very specific or general in nature. The traditional view is that more precise information is better for skill learning than less precise information (Reeve and Magill, 1981; Smoll, 1972). However, this statement needs to be tempered somewhat since the optimal level is dependent on a range of factors including the difficulty of the task and the age and skill level of the learner (for a detailed review, see Magill, 2001, 2007).

Another suggestion is that more detailed feedback may benefit learners only after they have had sufficient practice on the task. Magill and Wood (1986) required participants to learn a complex arm movement task in which they had to move their arm through a series of small wooden barriers to produce a six-segment pattern within a specified movement time. Participants either received qualitative feedback (i.e., too fast or too slow) or quantitative feedback (i.e., number of ms too fast or too slow) at the end of each trial. Although no differences were evident between the two groups during the first 60 trials of acquisition, the quantitative feedback group showed better performance on the final 60 trials of acquisition, and better learning as judged by performance on 20 no-feedback retention trials. The implication is that early in practice qualitative feedback is sufficient for the learner, whereas more detailed and specific information is required after extended practice on the task.

Frequency of feedback

According to the guidance hypothesis proposed by Salmoni, Schmidt and Walter (1984), providing feedback on every trial has a beneficial effect on performance but a detrimental effect on skill learning. Providing feedback on every practice attempt can lead to an 'overload' of information, result in overreliance on augmented feedback and prevent the learner from participating in trial and error problem solving. The optimal frequency of feedback appears to be dependent on the player's stage of learning as well as the complexity or difficulty of the task. In the initial stages of learning or when the task to be learnt is fairly difficult, players may require prescriptive feedback more frequently to improve performance (Wulf, Shea and Matschiner, 1998). As skill develops, the frequency of feedback provision may be reduced or 'faded out' to encourage learners to detect and correct their own errors. This latter observation appears somewhat contradictory to the earlier statements made in relation to feedback precision. However, the key difference is that as learning progresses, the frequency of feedback should be decreased while, as discussed earlier, the level of precision may need to be increased.

The frequency of feedback provision can be reduced using 'summary' or 'bandwidth techniques' (see Magill, 2007; Schmidt and Lee, 2011; Schmidt and Wrisberg, 2009, Wulf and Shea, 2004). The former technique involves giving the learner a summary of performance after a certain number of practice trials, whereas the latter refers to the provision of feedback only when errors are outside a predetermined range of correctness. The suggestion is that summary feedback should be given less frequently and/or the bandwidth for feedback provision should be increased as learning progresses (Guadignoli, Dornier and Tandy, 1996). These approaches have the desired effect of reducing the number of trials following which feedback is provided, encouraging learners to seek their own solutions to the problem at hand. The difficulty for the coach is deciding when and how to use these techniques effectively.

Mode of instruction

Closely related to the issue of how best to provide feedback to the learner is the mode of instruction that should be employed by the coach. Coaches are likely to have their own preferred mode of instruction, with this varying in the extent to which they consider their role to be fairly prescriptive and 'hands-on' or less prescriptive and more 'hands-off'. In the latter approach the learner is guided rather than cajoled through the skill acquisition process. Historically, coaches have adopted a fairly prescriptive approach to the learning process through liberal use of verbal instruction, demonstration and feedback to coerce the learner to adopt the desired movement behaviour (e.g., see Ford, Yates and William, 2010). Is this prescriptive approach the most appropriate for effective motor skill instruction? This issue has attracted considerable interest in the skill learning literature, highlighted by the current debate regarding the relative benefits of explicit versus implicit instruction and prescriptive coaching versus guided discovery learning (see Williams and Hodges, 2005).

Explicit versus implicit learning

Explicit processes are conscious, verbally based and open to introspection, whereas implicit processes are generally unavailable for conscious introspection, independent of working memory and difficult to verbalise (Gentile, 1998). Implicit processes are thought to be more resistant to the effects of psychological stress, more durable and less prone to forgetting over time than explicit processes (Abrams and Reber, 1988; Allen and Reber, 1980). The assumption, in traditional theories of learning (e.g., Anderson, 1983; Fitts and Posner, 1967), is that skills are initially learnt using conscious, verbal rules and that these are forgotten and task-relevant processing becomes sub-conscious as skill develops. However, a recent suggestion is that movement skills may be learnt effectively in an implicit manner, without reference to conscious, control processes.

Masters (1992) carried out one of the earliest studies to examine the relative effectiveness of implicit and explicit learning strategies in the acquisition of sports skills. Participants learned a golf putting skill either with or without the performance of a secondary task that involved random letter generation. The secondary task was expected to overload working memory capacity, thereby making it harder for learners to accumulate explicit knowledge by preventing the rehearsal and storage of task-relevant information. As predicted, those who performed the secondary task during acquisition failed to develop as many explicit rules as those who performed the putting task only. However, the performance of the implicit group improved during acquisition and retention and did not differ from that of the explicit group, demonstrating that learning can occur in the absence of explicit rule formation.

Perhaps the most interesting finding reported by Masters (1992) was that the performance of those who learnt the putting skill implicitly was more robust to disruption from evaluation-induced anxiety. He claimed that those who had learnt the skill explicitly reinvested effort in the processing of explicit, verbal knowledge related to the mechanics of the putting action; commonly referred to as 'paralysis by analysis'. In contrast, participants in the implicit group did not have access to explicit knowledge or rules and were therefore more immune to the effects of anxiety. The reinvestment hypothesis proposed by Masters, Polman and Hammond. (1993) has subsequently received support from several authors (e.g., Hardy, Mullen and Jones, 1996b; Mullen and Hardy, 2000; Smeeton et al., 2005).

In a series of follow-up studies, Masters and colleagues (e.g., Maxwell, Masters and Eves, 1999; Maxwell et al., 2001) have explored a variety of different methods to encourage implicit learning processes. These techniques have included guided discovery, analogue learning, errorless learning and the withholding of outcome feedback (for a review, see Masters, 2008; Masters, Law and Maxwell, 2002; Masters and Maxwell, 2004). Although there have been criticisms of the approach adopted by Masters (e.g., see Beek, 2000), this body of work has highlighted several potential advantages with implicit learning strategies over and beyond traditional explicit learning approaches.

Prescriptive coaching versus guided discovery

Although the guided discovery approach to instruction has been proposed as an effective method to reduce reliance on explicit learning processes, its appropriateness as an instructional strategy has also been strongly endorsed by those embracing the ecological/dynamical approach to skill acquisition (e.g., see Davids, Button and Bennett, 2008). Coaching strategies that are overly prescriptive are likely to impose artificial constraints on learning, producing temporary and inefficient movement solutions. In contrast, guided discovery techniques are proposed to guide learners to search, discover and exploit their own, perhaps unique, solutions to the movement problem, through a less prescriptive, more hands-off approach to instruction. Coaches are encouraged to facilitate exploratory behaviour by manipulating the constraints of the learning environment (see Williams and Hodges, 2005). In this constraints-led approach to instruction, coaching is about creating the optimal environment for changes in movement form to emerge through self-exploration or discovery learning. Some of the constraints that may be manipulated for the purposes of encouraging effective learning include the nature of the equipment used during practice, the structure and organisation of activities that coaches use to simulate performance demands, such as small-sided or conditioned games, and the availability of environmental information.

The size and mass of a piece of equipment such as a ball or a racket relative to relevant limb segments such as the hand or arm has a direct effect on the behaviour employed by the learner. When catching a ball, for instance, if the ball is too large to catch using one hand, then it is likely that the learner would revert to two-handed catching. Similarly, if a tennis racket is too heavy for a child to perform an overhead smash, then he or she may wait for the ball to bounce before undertaking a forehand or backhand drive shot. It is therefore important that the dimensions of sports equipment and playing areas are appropriately scaled to the body dimensions of the learner, particularly where young children are concerned (Haywood and Getchell, 2001).

Weigelt, Williams and Wingrove (2001) provided an example of how equipment constraints can be manipulated to encourage effective learning using the Futebol de Salão ball to develop ball control and juggling skills in intermediate soccer players. The Futebol de Salão ball is smaller, heavier and has different bounce characteristics than a regulation soccer ball. In this study, participants underwent a three-week training period in which feet-only juggling was practised for 15 minutes, four times per week either using the Futebol de Salão or a regulation soccer ball. Participants were tested on their juggling and ball control performance using a standard ball. In the juggling task, participants attempted to keep a ball in the air using their feet only for as many 'touches' as possible. The control task required participants to stop an approaching ball with one touch only inside a marked target area. Participants who practised with the

Futebol de Salão ball significantly improved their ball juggling skills from pre- to post-test compared to those who practised with the regulation soccer ball, and a control group that participated in regular training only. It appears that the characteristics of the Futebol de Salão created a unique learning environment that encouraged the development and transfer of juggling and, to a lesser extent, ball control skill. The relative improvement in performance from pre- to post-test on the juggling and ball control tasks is presented in Figure 8.3.

Coaches are also encouraged to structure and organise practice sessions in order to elicit certain types of behaviours from the learner. For example, in soccer, conditioned games involving one- and two-touch practices constrain the learner to search for suitable passing opportunities prior to receiving the ball, while games which allow goals to be scored solely from crosses encourage teams to employ width in offensive play as well as developing the skills of heading

Figure 8.3   *The mean relative improvement in performance from pre- to post-test for participants on the juggling and ball control skill tests*

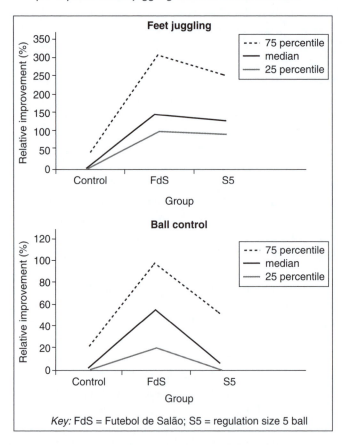

Source: Adapted from Weigelt, Williams and Wingrove, 2001

and volleying. Other constraints that may be employed to promote discovery learning include the implementation of tight time constraints, the restriction of space through use of playing areas or zones, and the selective use of opponents to manipulate 'pressure'. Coaches need to be thoughtful and creative in designing conditioned games and practices that enable relevant skills to emerge in learners (e.g., see Charlesworth, 1994; Thorpe, 1996).

Another suggestion is that coaches can manipulate access to various sources of environmental information, particularly vision, in order to facilitate skill acquisition. Williams *et al.* (2002b) used this type of approach to develop ball control skill in novice, 12-year-old soccer players. The children were tested on their ability to control an approaching soccer ball within a designated target area. Varying amounts of practice were provided either under full vision or in a condition where sight of the foot was occluded throughout each trial, before being transferred to the alternative viewing condition. Participants who practiced under occluded viewing conditions showed greater relative` improvement in performance over practice and transfer sessions compared with a full vision control group (see also Bennett, Davids and Woodcock, 1999; Bennett *et al.*, 1999). Children unable to see the foot during practice were constrained to try and pick up information relating to foot orientation and positioning from alternative sources, presumably facilitating the shift from visually driven to proprioceptive control processes that is often characteristic of expert performance (Fleishman and Rich, 1963).

In conclusion, the aim in this chapter was to provide a brief summary of major findings that have emerged from the skill acquisition literature since development of the area some 100 years or so ago. The intention was not to provide an exhaustive review, but rather to highlight those findings with particular relevance to coaches and potentially others involved in the instruction process such as physical and speech therapists. A model was presented to highlight some of the important processes involved in skill instruction. This was accompanied by a review of the relevant literature in each area and an attempt to provide guidance as to how best to convey information, structure practice sessions and provide feedback so as to optimise practice time. Finally, the relative merits of more or less prescriptive approaches to instruction were considered, with particular reference to the potential benefits provided by strategies that promote implicit learning and guided discovery over and above more traditional instructional approaches.

It was proposed that demonstrations provide an effective method of conveying information, particularly when they present a clear movement strategy that is reproducible by the learner. Verbal instructions are likely to be as effective as demonstrations when the information conveyed is fairly simple or when the task necessitates that the learner develops a feel for the movement. Verbal cues or prompts may be employed at the same time as a demonstration, and appear to be most effective when they focus the learner on the outcome of the movement rather than the movement itself. When structuring practice sessions, coaches should ensure that the learner experiences a variety of practice opportunities and is encouraged to improve a range of skills. While feedback regarding task performance is essential for skill learning, learners should try and develop their own error detection and correction capabilities rather than relying too heavily on augmented, extrinsic information provided by the coach. A variety of techniques are available to the coach when encouraging the learner to become less dependent on augmented information such as fading, bandwidth and summary feedback and adopting a question and answer approach to instruction. Implicit learning and guided discovery techniques may be used to further encourage learners to find their own unique, adaptable and effective solutions to movement problems. In particular, exciting opportunities exist for innovative coaches to determine how best to manipulate the constraints of the learning environment to facilitate skill acquisition. Although significant progress has been made in highlighting the important factors underlying skill acquisition, considerable scope still exists for sport psychologists to make a meaningful contribution to performance enhancement in sport.

CASE STUDY

The coach at a local soccer club has been working with the under-12 team for a number of years. The players under his guidance have always worked hard during practice and have had reasonable success in match play. However, the players' performance during competitive games has not always matched that observed in training and practice matches. Also, the teams under his guidance have generally underperformed in important cup matches. The coach has relied on relatively traditional instructional techniques, making frequent use of demonstration and verbal instruction, drill-based practice sessions and providing regular feedback to players regarding their performance. The coach is anxious about the upcoming season and is considering how best to alter practice in order to avoid similar problems to those encountered previously.

1. Outline some possible reasons for the difficulties encountered.
2. How might the coach alter his or her practice session or instructional strategy to overcome some of these potential problems? What might the coach consider doing differently this season compared to previous campaigns?
3. How could the coach assess whether the changes that have been made to the practice and instruction process are likely to be successful, particularly when it comes to an important cup match?

STUDY QUESTIONS

1. With reference to a sports skill of your choice, outline how you would measure motor learning over protracted periods of practice. What factors may affect performance on this task from one practice session to the next?
2. What would be the advantages involved in recording process measures of performance in addition to outcome scores?
3. With reference to a variety of different sports skills, consider when and in what context would a demonstration likely be most effective in conveying information to learners.
4. Consider how you could create variable practice conditions when teaching a sport skill of your choice.
5. Provide some examples of high and low contextual interference practice sessions in a sport setting.
6. When teaching motor skills to a group of young children, consider how best to employ blocked and random practice conditions.
7. What procedures can reduce the dependency-producing effects of providing feedback on each learning trial? Provide some examples of how these techniques could be used in a sport of your choice.
8. Provide examples of how coaches could manipulate constraints to facilitate skill acquisition in sport.

FURTHER READING

Davids, K., Button, C. and Bennett, S. J. (2008) *Dynamics of Skill Acquisition* (Champaign, IL: Human Kinetics).

Magill, R.A. (2007) *Motor Learning: Concepts and Applications*, 8th edn (New York: McGraw-Hill).

Schmidt, R. A. and Lee, T. A. (2010) *Motor Control and Learning: A Behavioral Emphasis*, 5th edn (Champaign, IL: Human Kinetics).

Schmidt, R. A. and Wrisberg, C. A. (2009) *Motor Learning and Performance: From Principles to Practice*, 4th edn (Champaign, IL: Human Kinetics).

Williams, A. M. and Hodges, N. J. (2004) (eds) *Skill Acquisition in Sport: Research, Theory and Practice* (London: Routledge).

9 Teams

INTRODUCTION, HISTORY AND DEVELOPMENT

The world of sport presents a great opportunity to consider social processes and most especially in the context of teams. This may either be how individuals respond in team settings or a reflection on team dynamics and team performance. Work in this field has progressed from a relatively narrow research base to a position where the understanding of team processes is now good, and fully integrated with wider developments across social psychology in particular (Forsyth, 2009). For example, Kremer (2007) argued that the position had changed significantly from the early 1990s. At that time, work on the social psychology of sport had been characterised by an over-reliance on outmoded theories whereas by 2007 the scene had changed dramatically with many innovatory approaches to group dynamics being pioneered within sport and exercise psychology itself, as reflected in a growing number of textbooks dedicated specifically to the social psychology of sport (e.g., Beauchamp and Eys, 2007; Carron, Hausenblas and Eys, 2005; Hagger and Chatzisarantis, 2005; Jowett and Lavallee, 2007). Across social psychology as a whole, the heyday for group dynamics research was not in the immediate past but tended to coincide with the experimental, reductionist tradition that characterised social psychological research leading up to the 1980s (Jackson, 1988). At this time writers such as Bales (role differentiation), Steiner (taxonomy of group types), Zimbardo (social norms), Asch (conformity), Milgram (social influence), Leavitt and Shaw (communication networks) and Stoner and Janis (group decision-making) laid the empirical base for understanding group dynamics, and the models and theories associated with these writers have remained influential to the present day (see Forsyth, 2009). More recently, within social psychology as a whole these fields have tended to be ignored as attention has focused on social cognition and intergroup relations, a trend that can be confirmed by a scan of topics included in any contemporary social psychology textbook.

At the same time, the breadth of topics which are still potentially germane to team dynamics is considerable. In order to consider all relevant material in this chapter the literature on team dynamics has been subdivided into five areas in subsequent sections:

1. Defining teams
2. Individual performance in teams
3. Team dynamics
4. Teams in context
5. Team roles

Defining teams

Before embarking on a consideration of team dynamics and performance it may be useful to define the subject matter – that is, what is a group and, in turn, what is a team? Definitions of groups abound in the literature, each focusing on particular elements such as communication, influence, interaction, inter-dependence, interrelations, psychological significance, identity and structure. Of all these the overarching construct appears to be interdependence (Lewin, 1947) and, by inference, interaction and influence. Hence a group can be defined as, 'Two or more interdependent individuals who influence one another through social interaction' (Forsyth, 2009, p. 5). In turn, each group can then be characterised by its profile in relation to five qualities: interaction; structure; cohesiveness; social identity; and goals.

A team may not be qualitatively different from a group but instead it may be best thought of as having surpassed a threshold which defines 'teamness' on all five of the grounds noted above. For example, a group of friends who regularly jog together may already qualify on three of the five criteria (interaction, struc-ture, cohesiveness) but would only be regarded as a team when they decide on a common goal (e.g., running a marathon relay) and share a common identity (e.g., a name or kit).

Within sport psychology research, in reality the issue of definition is often academic as the team is already self-defined prior to investigation, for example, by club allegiance. However it is not unusual to discover that even within one 'team' there may be several 'teams' and especially whenever a common goal is not shared. For example, the bench and court teams in a basketball team may operate to different agenda and respond emotionally in different ways to success and failure. Following the work of Henri Tajfel and social identity theory (Tajfel, 1982) such issues raise interesting possibilities for exploring intergroup relations *within* sport teams rather than *between* teams, but to date such opportunities have rarely been taken.

Within social psychology, traditionally groups are classified according to task demands associated with the group (Steiner, 1972). According to Steiner's Social Combination Theory, tasks can be categorised first as either *unitary* (where the task cannot be broken down and where group members typically work together on the single task, e.g., a rowing eight) or *divisible* (where the task can be bro-ken down to smaller units and where group members can be assigned to par-ticular tasks, for example, a medley relay team in swimming). Second, some tasks require quantity of contribution (known as *'maximisation'*, e.g., tug-of-war) whereas others require quality of contribution (*'optimisation'*, e.g., golf).

Furthermore, tasks require contributions to be brought together in different ways. *Additive tasks* sum individual contributions, hence they are often divis-ible and maximising (e.g., a rugby scrum). *Disjunctive tasks* are those where the task involves only one group solution, which may be reached by one or more members (e.g. a mountaineering expedition). *Conjunctive tasks* are only finished when every group member arrives or completes the task (e.g., a relay race, a team equestrian event). Compensatory tasks are uncommon in sport but not in sport adjudication (e.g., diving, ice skating judges), and are those where the solution is an average of each member's contribution, while Discretionary tasks are rare and are those where groups members can operate discretion as to how inputs are combined when reaching a solution (e.g., a treasure hunt).

Across social psychology this taxonomy has been employed to provide a yard-stick against which to compare actual and potential performance on particular tasks and thereby determine the extent of losses attributable to group processes. In summary, this work demonstrates that groups rarely perform at a level above that which would be predicted on the basis of individual members' potential contributions (Forsyth, 2009; Laughlin, 1996). The reasons for the gap between actual and potential team performance will be explored later in this chapter but with few early exceptions (Gill, 1979; Jones, 1974; Landers, 1974; Melnick and Chemers, 1974), the gap itself has not been a topic for specific investigation in sport psychology. One reason may be that real-life groups, including sport teams, are notoriously difficult to categorise using this taxonomy, rarely falling conveniently under any single heading and thereby rendering comparisons tricky.

Within sport psychology a more common taxonomy used for classifying team sports is based on the extent of interaction between those in the team (Landers and Lueschen, 1974). At one extreme, *interactive sports* involve ongo-ing coordination of actions between team members (e.g., soccer, rugby, netball, basketball, hockey). Alternatively, *coactive sports* involve team members per-forming individually but in a team context (e.g., golf, bowls, archery, skiing, shooting, darts, snooker). Once more, sports in the real world generally defy simple categorisation and most team sports cannot be easily labelled as exclu-sively interactive or coactive sports. Take either baseball or cricket as examples. Each contain individual (e.g., batting and pitching/bowling) and collective (e.g., fielding) activities, and players move between these different roles during the course of any game. Broadening the example, almost any team event will include elements that represent an amalgam of both coactive and interactive activities and yet despite this problem with categorisation, the gross distinction between predominantly interactive and coactive team sports may still be of some value in helping understand collective phenomena including the effects of team cohesion on performance, and should be borne in mind when reading the following sections.

Individual performance in teams

Research dealing with social influences in teams has a very long if narrow history (Aiello and Douthill, 2001) with the majority of work focusing around two topics, *social facilitation* and *social loafing* (Carron and Brawley, 2008; Jones, Bray and Lavallee, 2007). Norman Triplett's work on 'dynamogism' among cyclists (see Chapter 1; Triplett, 1898) was the precursor for a rich tradition of research dealing with social facilitation effects that has continued to the modern day (Strauss, 2002). This research generally confirms that the presence of others does have an influence on individual performance but the effect depends crucially on the task demands. Dominant, well-learned responses tend to be facilitated while non-dominant while novel responses are inhibited by the presence of others, and these effects are often attenuated when these others (either co-actors or spectators) are known to be evaluating performance.

While most research is based on laboratory tasks, a small number of field experiments suggest that the effect is ecologically robust. For example, a rarely cited pioneering study by Meumann (1904) found that when the experimenter returned unannounced to a weights room one evening, where a number of participants had been asked to routinely 'pump iron', performance which had been constant over several days suddenly improved considerably. Much more recently, Michaels *et al.* (1982) found that the performance of above average and below average pool players either improved or deteriorated respectively when a group of people came to stand and watch them play in a local pool hall.

According to Diane Gill (2000, p. 275), social facilitation research has waned over recent years because of difficulties in demonstrating consistent effects in the real world of sport, although equally it could be argued that the difficulties may stem from methodological issues rather the social phenomenon itself. Certainly a classic meta-analysis, based on 241 studies and involving a total of 24,000 participants, did confirm the effect and most especially social inhibition on complex tasks (Bond and Titus, 1983), and there is no *prima facie* reason to suggest why sport teams should be immune from the effects of social facilitation in comparison with all other small groups.

Social loafing is a term with a history nearly as long as social facilitation. In 1913, a French agricultural engineer called Max Ringelmann (Ringelmann, 1913) discovered that, on average, one man pulling on a rope was likely to pull twice as hard (an average of 63 kgs) as when his efforts were combined as part of a team of eight (an average of 31 kgs). Later studies involving a range of coactive tasks (e.g., hand clapping) have confirmed that the gap between actual group performance and individual potential productivity (Steiner, 1972) cannot be explained by co-ordination losses alone (Ingham *et al.*, 1974), with a substantial residual effect reflecting a personal, motivational deficit. This deficit, the Ringelmann effect or social loafing, is defined as the reduction of individual effort when working as part of a group or team (Latané, Williams and Harkins, 1979), and has been the subject of close attention by both social and sport psychologists (Hanrahan and Gallois, 1993; Hardy, 1990; Heuze and Brunel, 2003; Karau and Williams, 1997; 2001).

A substantial literature demonstrates that many factors impact on the extent of social loafing (Heuze and Brunel, 2003) including group size, the identifiability of individual effort, the strength of group identity, the nature and attractiveness of the task, the degree of trust between group members, the interdependence of group members, the extent of involvement with the group, group cohesiveness, intergroup comparisons and personal responsibility (Karau and Williams, 1993; 1997).

While historically the two phenomena have been looked at in isolation over recent years there has been a tendency to describe team influences simultaneously (Aiello and Douthill, 2001), most significantly in the work of Karau, Williams and colleagues (see Karau and Williams, 2001), and this work will be considered under *Theories and Models* below.

Team dynamics

Within social psychology small group dynamics have been a focus for research for a considerable time, with most attention falling on topics including group decision making, communication networks, social influence, group structures, conflict, cooperation and competition, group development and role differentiation (Forsyth, 2009). Sport psychologists, not surprisingly, have tended to concentrate their energies on a subset of those topics that are especially salient to sport (see Carron, Hausenblas and Eys, 2005) and one topic in particular, team cohesion (Carron, Eys and Burke, 2007). This work continues to be groundbreaking within psychology as a whole, offering genuine and unique insight into the intricacies of group cohesion in general. The research reveals that cohesion itself is multifaceted and includes at least two primary dimensions, task and social cohesion, with other secondary dimensions contingent on the type of group (Cota *et al.*, 1995). Second, research shows that a number of factors interact to determine levels of group cohesion, and that cohesion is not a particularly reliable predictor of group performance or success (Carron, Bray and Eys, 2002; Hardy, Eys and Carron, 2005; Hemmings, 2001).

In terms of the determination of group or team cohesion, numerous factors have been identified as influential (Bray and Whaley, 2001; Carron, 1988; Kozub and Button, 2000; Mudrack, 1989), including group size, propinquity (i.e., physical proximity between members), the costs incurred in joining the group, leadership styles, competition, success and similarity. The final factor, similarity or homogeneity, has been the focus of considerable interest, with some authors arguing that similarity encourages cohesiveness (Eitzen, 1975) while others maintain that it may inhibit healthy group development (Janis, 1982). In an unpublished meta-analysis incorporating over 200 studies, Anthony and Mullen (1993) found that there was a tendency for groups that were made up of similar members to be more cohesive although this was more evident in laboratory than real groups and the effect was dependent on group size. Overall the strength of the relationship was described as significant but 'weak', indicating that the issue has yet to be satisfactorily resolved.

In recent years a complementary literature has developed around the constructs of role efficacy in teams and collective efficacy (Beauchamp, 2007; Chow and Feltz, 2007). This work is derived from Bandura's construct of self-efficacy and considers not only team members' belief in the ability of the team but also the team's collective beliefs. Role efficacy is defined as a person's confidence in his/her capabilities to take on interdependent role responsibilities within the team, for example, in relation to his/her position, and has often been considered alongside role ambiguity (Beauchamp et al., 2005). Typically, it has been found that the two are orthogonally related, that is, higher role ambiguity corresponds with lower role efficacy. Collective efficacy is the team's confidence in their collective capabilities to perform collective tasks (Beauchamp, 2007, p. 183) and comprises two elements, collective resources and coordinative capabilities, The former refers to belief in the extent of the team's abilities to produce certain outcomes while the latter considers the level of cooperation that exists in order to harness these abilities for the common good. Research shows that teams with higher collective efficacy are characterised by more positive cognitions, including commitment, affective responses (e.g., satisfaction) and behaviours (e.g., performance and effort) (Bray, 2004; Chow and Feltz, 2007).

Looking beyond cohesion and collective-efficacy, the maturity of teams has long been a topic of interest. Despite the significance of group development in general for understanding performance in sports that involve a high degree of interdependence, and the prominence attached to stage models of team development in the literature (e.g., Tuckman, 1965; Tuckman and Jensen, 1977), there is little contemporary sport related research dealing with group development and performance. During the 1970s a number of significant archival studies had set the scene by identifying the relationship between team maturity and success. Research using data derived from sports such as soccer, baseball, basketball and gymnastics demonstrated that turnover rates of players and performance were negatively related, and also revealed large differences between sports in terms of the time taken for a team to reach maturity and then to maintain excellence. For example, Loy, McPherson and Kenyon (1978) cite a breakdown of results of American Football teams in the National Football League between 1955 and 1959 by length of member tenure within the team. Mature teams (i.e., with 2.25 years or more average playing experience together per player) had a winning record which was 17 per cent higher than those with immature teams (less than 2.25 years). The 'shelf-life' of a successful team is likely to depend on many factors including the age of players, the type of sport and various facets of group dynamics including cohesiveness and role differentiation. However, these issues remain largely unexplored in contemporary research.

The concept of team identity itself has rarely attracted much attention in the sport psychology literature although fans' identification with teams is better researched (Jacobson, 2003; Wann *et al.*, 2001). By contrast, within social psychology work on social identity in small groups has been prominent from the 1970s onwards (see Ellemers, Spears and Doosje, 1999). According to the dominant European perspective, social identity theory (Stets and Burke, 2000), the more closely an individual identifies with a group, and hence defines him or herself in terms of group membership, then the more that person will be inclined to maximise differences between the ingroup and the outgroup. This is also likely to reflect in competitiveness and an increase in effort expended in striving for common goals. Hence the extent to which players identify with the club or the team is likely to have a considerable bearing on performance but as yet has not been investigated widely within sport psychology.

Teams in context

In contrast the contextual variables that can influence team performance have been subject to close scrutiny and in particular the effects of home advantage on team performance (Carron, Loughhead and Bray, 2005; Nevill and Holder, 1999). Intuitively we would guess that playing at home, for whatever reason, brings an advantage but what does the archival research suggest is the case? In an early review, Schwartz and Brasky (1977) collated and catalogued the results of several thousand professional games played in the United States. The authors did indeed find evidence of home advantage in the four high profile sports of baseball (53% home wins), ice hockey (64%), American football (60%) and basketball (64%). Likewise Edwards (1979) found that in a variety of sports, including both college (59% home wins) and professional American football (54% home wins), and professional baseball (56% home wins) that home advantage held, and the effect was most noticeable for those teams, which were already on a tide of success. Nevill and Holder (1999) also revealed home advantage in their overview of home win percentages (or hwp) across five US sports, baseball (54.3% hwp), American football (57.3% hwp), ice hockey (61.2% hwp), basketball (64.4% hwp) and soccer (68.3% hwp). Furthermore, Thomas, Reeves and Bell (2008) found that all teams in rugby's Six Nations scored more points at home compared to when they played away while teams that played the second leg of soccer's Champions League ties at home were found to be more likely to progress to the next round as a consequence (Page and Page, 2007). In a similar vein, Bray (1999) and Madrigal and James (1999) both confirmed home advantage for ice hockey and basketball, with the quality of the team also playing a mediating role. Specifically, high quality teams appear to be given an added lift by home support whereas poorer teams may actually play better away from home.

In an analysis that considered games at various stages of tournaments, Baumeister and Steinhilber (1984) found that home advantage actually disappeared in the latter stages of major baseball and basketball competitions. In an extension of this work, Benjafield, Liddell and Benjafield (1989) considered all World Series (baseball) games between 1924 and 1982, NBA (basketball) play-offs between 1967 and 1982, and NHL (ice hockey) Stanley Cup games between 1968 and 1988. Overall they found home advantage did appear to be evident in deciding games but not when the team was defending a title. What may be equally significant is the expectation of players that there is a home advantage (Bray and Widmeyer, 2000), although what is meant by 'home' may be worthy of a closer look. Studying a US college basketball team that had to play at five different home venues while its stadium was being rebuilt, Moore and Brylinsky (1995) found that home advantage was still evident despite the lack of familiarity with the 'home' venues. Maybe a case of home is where the fans are?

Increasingly research indicates that the home advantage effect is dependent on a number of factors (Courneya and Carron, 1991; 1992; Nevill and Holder, 1999) including the types of behaviour associated with a particular sport. For example, Glamser (1990) found professional English soccer players from a particular club were more likely to be either booked or sent off the further away from home they played. Similarly, Varca (1980) found that American professional basketball players displayed 'functionally aggressive behaviour' at home, whereas away players were more likely to exhibit 'dysfunctionally aggressive behaviour', in other words they accumulated more recorded fouls.

In addition, the nature and density of the crowd, as well as the design of the venue itself, may be significant in eliciting certain effects (Nevill, Balmer and Williams, 2002). For example, Paulus, Judd and Bernstein (1976) did not find that crowd size *per se* influenced batting performance in major league baseball, instead it is crowd density rather than size that is more significant factor in baseball along with other sports (Agnew and Carron, 1994; Carron, Loughhead and Bray, 2005). In terms of the nature of the crowd itself, research shows that verbally aggressive crowds have been shown to have a powerful inhibitory effect on away teams (Greer, 1983), once more suggesting that it is the nature of the crowd, whether large or small, that is of key significance.

Team roles

For those well versed in leadership research outside sport psychology, the literature within sport psychology will appear familiar. The history of leadership research in general is fascinating (Bass, 1990; Bass and Riggio, 2006), moving from simple and sovereign explanations to an acknowledgement that the construct 'leadership' subsumes a number of functions associated with social influence that facilitate progress towards individual and group goals. Modern approaches acknowledge that no single theory can adequately explain the entire gamut of leadership behaviour but instead look to how a variety of perspectives are able to complement each other in furthering understanding. Within sport psychology some of these perspectives have been brought to bear on a number of discrete issues, including the relationship between centrality of playing position, captaincy and future management roles (e.g., Norris and Jones, 1998), techniques for measuring coaching behaviours and the relative effectiveness of different coaching styles (e.g., Smith and Smoll, 2007), decision-making and styles of coaches (e.g., Chelladurai and Doherty, 1998) and the expectations and experiences of coaches by athletes, and vice versa (e.g., Chelladurai, 1993; Olympiou, Jowett and Duda, 2008).

More recently an interesting and related literature has started to develop around role conflict and role ambiguity in sports teams (Beauchamp *et al.*, 2002). This literature suggests that while role conflict (where the player is dealing with incongruent expectations about their role in the team) is generally dysfunctional (Carron and Hausenblas, 1998), the relationship between role ambiguity (where there is uncertainty about role expectations associated with task performance) and performance may be more complex. For example, with a defensive role an absence of ambiguity may be important whereas for an attacking role a degree of ambiguity may be positively associated with creativity and flair (Beauchamp, 2002). Related constructs include role efficacy, role conflict and role overload, with distinctions between each not always immediately obvious (Eys, Beauchamp and Bray, 2006).

THEORIES AND MODELS

Individual performance in teams

In attempting to understand the effects of others on performance, traditionally, it has been Zajonc's drive theory of social facilitation (Zajonc, 1965) that has been to the fore, arguing that the mere presence of others increase levels of arousal or drive which thereby facilitates the production of dominant responses and inhibits the execution of novel skills or responses. Over the last thirty years support for this theory has diminished with evidence that it is not merely presence but also concern with evaluation or conflict between evaluation and presence that may be important (Strauss, 2002). While both evaluation apprehension and 'mere presence' may be significant, all-embracing answers to the 'why' questions still remain elusive, with a number of different explanations still in competition. To some authors, social facilitation relates to physiological drive and our ability to evaluate others, to others it relates to attentional overload, to others attentional shift, and to others attentional conflict (Aiello and Douthill, 2001; Harkins and Szymanski, 1987).

As regards social loafing, likewise a number of competing theoretical explanations are also available (Karau and Williams, 1993). Several of these perspectives concentrate on the psychological consequences of placing people in situations where they know their efforts are not easy to identify and where they are not being personally evaluated. Drawing loosely on Social Impact Theory (Latané, 1997), coupled with the notion of diffusion of responsibility, it is argued that in a group we feel able to share responsibility with other group members and this may well lead to a diminution of effort. Other commentators, more influenced by Social Exchange Theory (Homans, 1961), emphasise the strategies that people will use to 'get by' in groups. It is assumed that we are motivated to exert the minimum effort for the maximum reward, otherwise referred to as free riding or, more politely, the allocation strategy (Widmeyer, Brawley and Carron, 1992). A further approach emphasises group identity and cohesiveness, arguing that the more closely we identify with the group then the less likely we are to loaf (Hogg, 1992).

In early attempts to integrate existing research, Harkins and Szymanski (1987) and Mullen and Baumeister (1987) both considered social loafing and social facilitation as related social phenomena. Harkins and Szymanski emphasised the effects of evaluation by either self or others while Mullen and Baumeister utilised related constructs from Self-Attention Theory to consider our self-awareness in a variety of social contexts, arguing that in some circumstances self-awareness may increase effort while in others it may not.

Following from this work, Brehm and Kassin (1996) and Sanna (1992) formulated a set of four principles, which capture succinctly the combined effects of social facilitation and social loafing:

- When the presence of others increases evaluation of an individual's work then performance on an easy or 'dominant' task will be enhanced because we are more motivated.
- At the same time, performance on more difficult (non-dominant) tasks may become worse because of an increase in arousal/stress.
- When the presence of others decreases evaluation of an individual's work, performance on easy tasks will be impaired because we do not care (social loafing).
- However, performance on difficult tasks will be enhanced because we are less anxious in a group setting ('social security')

These principles go some way towards integrating facets of social influence in groups although Karau and Williams' (2001) Collective Effort Model goes yet further by incorporating ideas from a number of perspectives including social impact theory, drive theory, evaluation apprehension and diffusion of responsibility (or 'dispensability of effort'). Their model is based on a VIE (valence, instrumentality, expectancy) model of motivation (see Chapter 4), arguing that individual performance will only be enhanced in a team setting if the team member anticipates that the increase in effort will be matched by an increase in personal, valued rewards. The authors go on to suggest that individual effort can be maximised when personal involvement in the task is highlighted, when individual and collective performance is known to be evaluated, when the individual believes that their personal contribution is valued and is indispensable, when there are clearly defined goals which are challenging but attainable, when the team is unified in purpose, and when collective efficacy (the belief that the team is capable of achieving its targets) is high. In an alternative formulation, Aiello and Douthill (2001) outlined an integrative unifying theory, principally to consider social facilitation effects but incorporating social loafing at the same time. The model considers how situational factors (e.g., sensory cues, proximity of others, feedback and climate), presence of others (e.g. type of presence, roles of others, salience of presence, relationships and length of presence) and task characteristics (e.g., difficulty, cognitive/motor characteristics and time) combine to influence the individual's perceptions, cognitions, reactions and finally, performance. Although not well researched to date, both models provide useful frameworks for understanding the totality of forces that may influence individual performance in a team setting, and move us beyond the confines of a perspective that sees social facilitation and loafing as separate and distinct social phenomena.

Team dynamics

While traditionally work addressing team dynamics in sport psychology has tended to be dominated by the theme of team cohesion, more recently the research base has widened to encompass related constructs including collective efficacy and roles in the context of team dynamics(e.g., role ambiguity, role conflict, role efficacy and role overload). Over the last 30 years one author, the Canadian sport psychologist Bert Carron, along with his many associates, has dominated this field. Carron (1982) has been influential in modelling what cohesion is (defining cohesion), how it develops (the antecedents of cohesion), and how it subsequently influences group and individual performance (the consequences of cohesion). To date, while not all parts of Carron's model of team cohesion have been tested empirically, by far the greatest attention has been devoted to the relationship between cohesion and performance (Carron and Brawley, 2000; Carron, Eys and Burke, 2007).

Carron's work hinges on a significant distinction between two types of group cohesion, task and social. Task cohesion refers to how well the group or team operates as a working unit while social cohesion refers to how well members like each other and the extent of team identity. In later work, Carron and his co-workers then went on to make more subtle distinctions between these terms, and specifically how cohesion is perceived by team members. Four categories of perceptions were then described, based on the two major categories of cohesion (Group Integration; Individual Attractions to the Group) being further subdivided into the task and social domains. 'Group Integration' (task or social) is defined as members' perceptions of the group as a totality, while 'Individual Attractions to the Group' (task or social), as the name suggests, represents each members' personal attractions to the group.

In a further elaboration of this basic model, Cota *et al.* (1995) drew a distinction between primary and secondary dimensions of cohesion. Primary dimensions or components include the task/social and individual/group considerations as proposed by Carron, Widmeyer and Brawley (1985), along with normative views among group members (Yukelson, Weinberg and Jackson, 1984) and the group's resistance to disruption. Secondary dimensions may include particular features of a group that predispose it towards certain states. For example, Cota *et al.* (1995) suggest that the dimension identified as 'valued roles' by Yukelson, Weinberg and Jackson (1984) may be relevant, particularly where roles are strongly defined and not easily interchangeable, including positions on a team in certain sports.

According to Carron (1982) there are four primary factors that will influence the development of a highly cohesive team. These are situational factors (e.g., size, organisational orientation, geographical variables, contractual responsibilities, normative pressures, intergroup conflict), personal factors (e.g., gender, maturity, personal attributes, shared perceptions, individual satisfaction, similarity), leadership factors (e.g., coach and captaincy behaviour and styles, communication, coach-athlete relationship, decision-making style) and team factors (e.g., relationships, task characteristics, ability, achievement orientation, homogeneity, intragroup cooperation, experience, norms, stability and team maturity). To date there has been support for the role which many of the elements associated with each of these set of factors may play in determining team cohesion (Carron, Eys and Burke, 2007; Carron, Hausenblau and Eys, 2005) although given the wide range of factors under consideration it would be difficult to analyse interactions between all variables simultaneously.

When considering the outcome of team cohesion, there has been a tendency to focus attention primarily on team performance and success (Carron, Bray and Eys, 2002). Unfortunately, this focus may detract from a more fine-grained analysis of how cohesion may impact on each team member and the group's dynamic, in the short and longer term. To achieve this degree of sophistication it is necessary to disaggregate outcomes into either team or individual. Team outcomes can include performance, success rate, team stability, interactions and communication, synergy and collective efficacy. Individual outcomes can include personal satisfaction along with improved personal states (e.g., self-esteem, self-efficacy, trust, reduced anxiety, increased role clarity, role acceptance and role performance) (Terry, 2000). At the very least it would seem appropriate to consider not only performance but also satisfaction when evaluating the effects of team cohesion but to date research has tended to place greater emphasis on the former and it is towards this relationship in particular which we now turn.

It would be fair to say that despite the high level of interest in measurement and in theoretical debate, primary sport-related research is thin on the ground. In terms of the relationship between sporting success and cohesiveness the conclusions that have been reached from this research have been equivocal (e.g., Grieve, Whelan and Meyers, 2000). For example, Hardy, Eys and Carron (2005) found that over 50 per cent of athletes that they interviewed were able to identify possible disadvantages attaching to high levels of social cohesion within a team, with 31 per cent reporting disadvantages associated with high task cohesion. On the one hand, studies of team sports, including basketball, American football, soccer, volleyball and baseball, at various times have shown that the success of teams can depend more on cohesion than skill level of individual members (Carron, Eys and Burke, 2007). However, equally research has shown that conflict and rivalry within a team can be a spur to success, or can drive individual team members to great things. One example of this was the German rowing eight in the 1960s, who were on the point of breaking up because of internal disputes and yet went on to win Olympic gold in 1968 (Lenk, 1969).

In an earlier review, Widmeyer, Carron and Brawley (1993) argued that of the studies that had directly examined the relationship between performance and cohesion, at least four out of five (83%) had found a positive correlation between team success and cohesion, while only a small number of studies reported a negative relationship. Furthermore, only one study had found no relationship. It is revealing that only certain types of sport appear to characterise studies where a relationship has been demonstrated. In particular, those that had revealed a positive relationship include basketball, hockey, volleyball, American football, ice hockey and golf (i.e. predominantly interactive sports), while those showing a negative relationship included shooting, rowing and bowling (co-acting sports).

While these studies consider relationships between success and cohesion rarely do they consider the thorny issue of causality and specifically, does cohesion engender success or does success engender cohesion? A significant meta-analysis by Mullen and Copper (1994) went some way towards answering this question. Their analysis concluded that a cohesion-effectiveness relationship does exist in small groups and that it is often most apparent in sport teams. Indeed the difference between sports teams and other non-sport real-life groups was so noticeable that the authors actually caution generalising from one set of studies to the other. They also confirmed that the effect derives most significantly from task commitment or cohesion and not from social or interpersonal cohesion. A vital conclusion derived from a select sample of longitudinal studies was that the stronger direction of effect seemed to be from performance to cohesiveness, and not vice versa. This is not to argue that cohesion cannot influence performance but that the performance to cohesion link is the more definite, a conclusion endorsed by other researchers. Reflecting this conclusion, Slater and Sewell (1994) suggest a circular or reciprocal relationship between team cohesion and performance, although noting that the strongest influence is in the direction of performance to cohesion.

Looking to the future, it has been argued that more sport-based research is needed and that this research must be rooted in theory, it must adopt a longitudinal perspective, use multivariate analyses and look at a wider range of groups in different competitive and recreational sports.

An associated facet of group dynamics concerns team development and maturity. Within social psychology, Tuckman (Tuckman, 1965; Tuckman and Jensen, 1977) described group development in terms of four basic stages. First, the group comes together and works through an orientation or initial 'getting to know you' stage (*forming*), normally characterised by an air of formality. Next, there may well be heightened tension associated with role differentiation and competition for status and influence (*storming*), before norms, rules and standards of behaviour begin to stabilise (*norming*). Finally, the group will have matured to a stage where it is able to work together as a unit (*performing*), before moving to closure if the team disbands (*adjourning*).

While this stage model provides a broad framework for understanding how a team may come together in its early stages of existence, it does not offer great insight into the personal, social and contextual variables which may influence development, nor cycles of change over longer periods of time, nor the levels of tension or conflict which are appropriate at each stage. More recently, building on the earlier Equilibrium Model of Group Change (Bales, 1965), Punctuated Equilibrium Models suggest that groups go repeatedly through cycles of change as they continue to work together over time (Arrow, 1997; Arrow and McGrath, 1995). These stages involve constant oscillations between activities associated with both task and social cohesion, along with rapid adjustments in response to changes in personnel or task demands. This work strongly suggests that Tuckman may have downplayed the ongoing significance of conflict and its management in effective team functioning, where ongoing tensions may actually encourage individual expression (Keashly, 1997) and help avoid unhealthy atmospheres associated with 'tight' groups, such as manifest in the phenomenon of groupthink (Janis, 1982; Mullen *et al.*, 1994).

Teams in context

Many of the studies dealing with contextual determinants traditionally did not operate from any obvious theoretical perspective but it is interesting to note how these are slowly emerging in the latest research. For example, an increasingly sophisticated literature describes the phenomenon of home bias in terms of factors including support, familiarity, characteristics of the crowd (including size, intimacy, hostility, noise and density), characteristics of the venue (e.g., indoor -v- outdoor), characteristics of the team (e.g., quality), perceptions of the team and type of sport (interactive -v- co-active, contact -v- non-contact, team -v- individual) (Baumeister, 1995; Carron, Loughhead and Bray, 2005).

In the meanwhile, theoretical perspectives are now being employed to explain certain aspects of team performance. For example, Baumeister and Steinhilber (1984) suggest that the reduction of home advantage in the later rounds of tournaments can be explained with reference to heightened self-attention when performing in front of an evaluative home crowd. Likewise the influence of crowd density as opposed to crowd size (Agnew and Carron, 1994) may reflect on processes associated with social facilitation and hence Karau and William's (2001) Collective Effort Model may be invoked.

Team roles

Traditionally the greatest volume of research on team roles focused on leadership in teams, whether coaches or captains, with the former in particular generating a very extensive literature (e.g. Cassidy, Jones and Potrac, 2004; Jones, 2006) When discussing leadership roles, a wide range of contingency models are routinely referenced across sport psychology, each focusing on a particular function, including situational control, motivation, decision-making and followers' maturity. While each model has a different focus and uses different terminology, common themes are identifiable. For example, each contingency approach acknowledges that there is no magic formula for predicting who will be a successful leader. In addition, no single leadership, captaincy, management or coaching style will ever be successful across a range of situations. Instead, the only general advice which can be offered is that to be as effective as possible then sports' coaches, managers or captains must develop the ability to assess changing situations and employ a leadership style which is in keeping with circumstance, satisfying the needs of their followers and the demands of the situation (Riemer, 2007). A brief overview of the major contingency models that have influenced contemporary thought is offered below.

Fiedler's Contingency Model of Situational Control – Fiedler's model still enjoys considerable popularity, despite the accumulated criticisms which it has attracted from within occupational psychology (e.g., Stewart and Latham, 1986). In common with other contingency approaches, Fiedler (1967) argued that different individuals will be more or less effective as leaders in different situations. Individuals are categorised by their score on the Least Preferred Co-worker scale (or LPC), a scale which measures what the individual thinks of the person s/he least liked working with. Team or group situations are categorised in relation to three factors (task structure, leader-member relations and position power of the leader), factors which are thought to influence the degree of control that the leader is likely to exert in a given situation. Of all the criticisms levelled against Fiedler's work perhaps the most fundamental is that which attacks his contention that our LPC score is stable over time. According to Fiedler, we are low, moderate or high LPC people. Hence when operating as leaders, we are best advised to manipulate situations to suit our trait or predisposition rather than adapt our preferred leadership style to the circumstance. This sentiment is enshrined in his Leader-Match programme for managers (Fiedler and Chemers, 1984). Fiedler himself did work with certain sports, including basketball, in the development of his original theory (Fiedler, 1967), although subsequent research in the sport domain has been both very limited and equivocal in terms of offering support for the model.

Vroom and Yetton's Normative Theory – Vroom and Yetton (1973) argue that one of the primary leadership functions is decision-making. When making decisions, the theory postulates that a leader or manager must weigh up two considerations. These are the quality of the decision and the acceptance of the decision by those who must implement it. On some occasions it is vital that the decision itself is of high quality irrespective of its acceptance by the group, on other occasions acceptance is of paramount concern while on other occasions both may be equally important. Depending on circumstance then one or more leadership styles are likely to be most effective. The way in which these ideas are traditionally presented is in the form of a decision tree, where questions are asked sequentially from left to right until a terminal mode is reached that determines which leadership style to adopt in those particular circumstances.

Chelladurai and Haggerty (1978) adapted this model for use with sports' coaches in their *Normative Model of Decision Styles in Coaching* (Chelladurai and Doherty, 1998). As with the original model, decisions lead sequentially on to further questions before reaching a terminal node signifying a leadership style. The seven key questions or dimensions are: time pressure (quick decision?), decision quality requirement (quality required?), the source and quality of information (good information?), the complexity of the problem (complex problem?), the need for the group or team to be behind the decision (acceptance critical?), the manager/coach's power base (strong power base?) and the extent of group integration (integrated team?).

Depending on answers to each of these questions (yes/no) then eventually the coach will be assigned one of three decision-making styles which is deemed the most appropriate, these styles being either autocratic, consultative or group oriented. *Autocratic* implies that the decision is reached by the coach perhaps after obtaining relevant information from others; *consultative* assumes consultation either with individuals or the team collectively; and a *group* style is one where a joint decision is made by the team as a whole. Subsequent research, while limited, has confirmed the general utility of the model, although it is suggested that two further dimensions ought to be incorporated into the decision tree, namely motivation-time (motivation to minimise time to reach a decision) and motivation-development (motivation to develop team members through participation) (Chelladurai and Doherty, 1998).

Hersey and Blanchard's Situational Leadership Theory – Hersey and Blanchard's (1982) Situational Leadership Theory, otherwise known as Life Cycle Theory, was originally derived from the Ohio State Leadership Studies and focuses on the leader's behaviour in relation to the characteristics of followers and in particular their level of maturity, whether in terms of task experience or socio-emotional concerns. When subordinates are inexperienced it is argued that the leader must be directive (task oriented) but as they become more experienced then the leader must show greater concern for emotional support (socio-emotionally oriented). Later, when the team members have become more mature then the leader must strive to be less directive and more concerned about offering social support.

Although little research has tested the theory in a sporting context, it remains popular among applied sport psychologists and especially for considering changes in coaching styles over the athlete's career. The overriding message which the original theory conveys is that coaches must remain responsive to the changing needs of their athletes, although Chelladurai and Carron (1983) argue that the specifics of the model await adaptation for use in sporting situations. For example, in contrast with paid workers, they suggest that young, immature athletes may need considerable social support early in their sporting careers but this need decreases as time goes by. In addition, according to Case (1987) too much emphasis on skills training may be inappropriate early in a sporting career. Technical advice is most appropriate in mid-career before once more 'backing off' as the mature athlete learns to become self-sufficient. In a field test of this model with basketball players, Case (1987) found general support for these suggestions although he did find that those who went on to elite level then looked for even greater social support from their coaches, presumably as the pressures of high level competition began to take their toll.

Path-Goal Theory – A further contingency model that has enjoyed prominence in the sport psychology literature is that formulated and gradually extended by House and Mitchell (1974), known as Path-Goal Theory. This theory has close ties both with the Ohio State Leadership Studies and more recently with expectancy-value theories of motivation. The theory deals with how leaders can influence motivation and perceptions of work by employing one of four leadership styles (directive; supportive; achievement-oriented; participative). The style should be chosen in response to perceived environmental demands (e.g., the tasks, the organisational structure and interpersonal relationships at work) and followers' characteristics (e.g., their ability, locus of control and authoritarianism). The leader is expected to maximise effort by showing how rewards can be reached, by clearing obstacles to progress and advancement, and by providing positive feedback for a job well done. As with the previous theory, relatively little work has been carried out in sporting contexts (Chelladurai and Saleh, 1978; Vos Strache, 1979) but it is nevertheless seen once more as a potentially useful heuristic tool in applied settings.

Transactional Leadership – Based in principles of social exchange (Homans, 1961), various transactional leadership models approaches regard leadership primarily as a transaction between the leader and his/her followers. For example, followers will only allow themselves to be 'led' if they can see that they will benefit from the exchange or transaction, and the approach has significant implications for the style of leadership that is likely to be most successful in the early meetings of a team. According to Hollander (1985), it is risky simply to impose a style on a team without first assessing what the team values, and then acting in a manner that coincides with their existing expectations, thereby accumulating 'idiosyncrasy credits' that eventually allow more freedom to act individually (Bass, 1990), a lesson that the late Brian Clough should perhaps have borne in mind during his infamous 44 days in charge at Leeds United, as immortalised in the book and film, *The Damned United*.

Transformational Leadership – Over recent years, transformational leadership has grown dramatically in popularity within occupational psychology, although it has yet to enjoy a similar level of popularity within the sport psychology literature (Hoption, Phelan and Barling, 2007). In some respects the theory stands as a counterpoint to the majority of contingency models that focus on situational demands by instead arguing that leaders can transform situations through personal style and will. The theory posits that five leader behaviours in particular will come to exert an influence on followers' values, needs, awareness and finally, performance. The five behaviours are charisma, idealised influence, inspirational motivation, intellectual stimulation and individualised consideration (Bass and Riggio, 2006). While research in the sport domain is not extensive, there is growing evidence to suggest that the framework can be usefully applied to sport, and including, for example, how great West Indian cricket captains have been able to transform the fortunes of teams through their leadership skills (Corbin, 2005), or how levels of aggression exhibited by children's teams can be influenced by the coach's transformational leadership (Tucker *et al.*, 2010).

Chelladurai's Multidimensional Model of Leadership – From the late 1970s onwards Packianathan Chelladurai and his colleagues have sought to develop sport-specific theories and models of leadership by accommodating ideas and concepts from a great many sources and especially occupational psychology. This drive was squarely behind Chelladurai's Multidimensional Model of Leadership (Chelladurai, 1993; Riemer, 2007), a model which considers the relationship between athlete's perceptions and expectations in the determination of appropriate coaching styles in sport. The effectiveness of the leader is measured in terms of two principal outcomes – how well athlete's perform and how satisfied they are with the process. The three interacting aspects of the leader's behaviour which produce these outcomes are first, the behaviour which is required of a leader in these circumstances, second, the actual behaviour displayed by the leader, and third the behaviour which is preferred by the athletes themselves. According to the model, the behaviour required of the coach in any situation will depend on the sport itself, the goals of the organisation and the environment within which the sport exists. His or her actual behaviour as leader will depend on ability, knowledge and interpersonal skills, while his or her preferred behaviour reflects both characteristics of the members and the situation. In recent years the model has been adapted to take on board both the influences of transactional and transformational leadership (Chelladurai, 2001; Bass and Riggio, 2006).

The model remains untested in its entirety but indications from available research are encouraging (Riemer, 2007). For example, both Chelladurai (1984b) and Horne and Carron (1985) found that concordance between players' coaching preferences and actual behaviour of the coach correlated with satisfaction. More recent studies have suggested that congruence between the three dimensions of leader behaviour (required, actual and preferred) does relate to heightened satisfaction and in turn better performance from athletes (Riemer and Chelladurai, 1995; Vealey *et al.*, 1998).

Mediational Model of Leadership Behaviour – Since the 1970s, Ron Smith and Frank Smoll (Smith and Smoll, 2007) have been actively developing techniques both for measuring coach's behaviour and for understanding how coaches can coach more effectively. Their original Mediational Model, and later expanded variations (Kenow and Williams, 1992; Smith and Smoll, 2007; Smoll and Smith, 1989), consider the relationship between the coach's behaviours, player's perceptions and finally, player's responses or evaluations, along the way identifying significant mediating variables which may impact on these relationships. For example, individual differences (referring to both coaches and players) can include gender, age, perceptions, motivations, attributions, anxiety and self-confidence. Situational variables can include the type of sport, level of competition, team success and team cohesion.

The model indicates in general how different communication styles and styles of feedback may be more or less effective with particular individuals, for example, those with low self-esteem or high trait anxiety may have particular needs in terms of the coach's interpersonal style. While the model was developed with youth coaches primarily in mind its underlying principles can be extended to almost any coaching situation (Smith and Smoll, 2002), although primary research using the model, with few exceptions (e.g., Kenow and Williams, 1999), is scarce.

The '3 + 1 Cs' Conceptual Model – Implicitly drawing on earlier transactional models, Sophia Jowett (2007) has recently developed a conceptual model to help understand the dyad relationship between the sport coach and the athlete. Strictly speaking this is not a leadership model but instead the focus is on the mutual and causal relationship between athlete and coach.

The '3Cs' refer to the psychological constructs of closeness, co-orientation and complementarity, with each reflecting on characteristics associated with a positive and healthy relationship. For example, *closeness* refers to trust, care, support and concern, while *co-orientation* refers to shared knowledge and understanding about roles, aspirations, beliefs and values, and finally *complementarity* embraces all aspects of cooperative and affiliative interactions between the two.

In later formulations of the model a fourth component was added, namely *commitment*, and a growing literature has linked this expanded model to a range of issues associated with both interdependence structures within the relationship itself, and wider team dynamics including cohesion, collective efficacy and self-efficacy, and in turn how these impact on performance and satisfaction (Jowett, 2007).

Role Episode Model in Sport – Turning finally to role conflict and ambiguity within teams, work based originally on Kahn, Wolfe, Quinn, Snoek and Rosenthal's (1964) Role Episode Model suggests that contextual and personal factors may determine the relationship between role ambiguity and performance, and including type of sport, anxiety and playing position. Kahn *et al.* proposed that role ambiguity reflects the dynamic interplay between the role sender (e.g., coach or captain) and the focal person (e.g., player), and that responses to that ambiguity can be more or less dysfunctional and will be mediated by the ongoing interactions between both parties. Within sport settings, work by Beauchamp and colleagues (Beauchamp, 2002) suggests that role ambiguity may be more or less significant depending on playing position, for example, defence or offence, and that the effects of role ambiguity on anxiety may likewise be mediated by playing position along with scope of responsibility and leadership. While this work is still in its infancy (e.g. Beauchamp and Bray, 2001; Beauchamp *et al.*, 2005) it may come to represent a significant advance in our understanding of role behaviour within teams.

METHODS AND MEASURES

Individual performance in teams

Although work on social facilitation and loafing is not new, it continues to provoke controversy. For example, it has been argued that social facilitation represents an experimental artefact that is difficult to replicate in the real world (see Gill, 2000, p. 275). While there may be some truth in this argument, and is a criticism that can equally be levelled against the ecological validity of many traditional methods in social psychology, it should not be forgotten that the earliest research in this field was based not on laboratory studies but on real world observations. Furthermore over the years a considerable number of studies have moved beyond the laboratory to consider the phenomenon in real world settings (Bond and Titus, 1983; Everett, Smith and Williams, 1992).

As the previous section suggests there is still no strong consensus as to why social facilitation and social loafing occur, or the entire range of mediating variables that may influence their effect, and this may be the root cause of the disenchantment. It may be that the research methods themselves are not yet sufficiently sophisticated to capture the complexity of the social phenomena in question but this should not be an excuse for abandoning the quest. This remains a methodological challenge which should not be sidestepped but met head on. For example, it may not be acceptable to describe audience or coactor effects without acknowledging differences between types of audience or coactors. Wann (1997, pp. 306–7) has provided a useful taxonomy including three types of audience with further subtypes. Hence 'spectators' can be characterised as either inactive (passive, quiet) or reactive (responsive, noisy), while both 'coactors' (players) and 'regulators' (officials) can be either interactive or non-interactive. Common sense would dictate that the effects of these different types of significant others on individual performance is likely to be quite different, and clearly continues to present a challenge of methodological ingenuity above all else.

Team dynamics

Within research on team cohesion it has long been acknowledged that the type of sport or the type of task will mediate any relationship between cohesion and performance. For example, the more that the sport requires that team members must rely on each other and are interdependent (i.e., interactive sports) then the more significant cohesion is likely to be (Carron and Brawley, 2008). By contrast, in sports where athletes may represent the same team but individual performance does not depend on teamwork (i.e., coacting sports) then team cohesion is likely to be less significant in determining outcome. Intuitively it may be assumed that these two constructs, coaction and interaction, could occupy opposite extremes along a continuum and hence should be regarded as being inversely related. However instead these two dimensions may be more accurately represented as orthogonal, with some sports being both highly interactive and coactive (e.g., rowing, tug-of-war), whereas some may be highly interactive but involve less identifiable coaction (e.g., volleyball). Others may be low on both dimensions (e.g., marathon running, chess) and yet others may be coactive but not interactive (e.g., archery, bowls). This is an issue which future research should not avoid if it is to capture the complexity of teams operating in the real world of sport.

Within social psychology over the years there have been numerous attempts to measure cohesiveness in groups and including the Group Environment Scale (GES; Moos and Humphrey, 1974), the Group Attitude Scale (GAS; Evans and Jarvis, 1986) and the Perceived Cohesion Scale (PCS; Bollen and Hoyle, 1990). Within sport psychology, early attempts to measure team cohesion in sport included the Sports Cohesiveness Questionnaire (SCQ; Martens, Landers and Loy, 1972), the Team Cohesion Questionnaire (TCQ; Gruber and Gray, 1982) and the Multidimensional Sport Cohesion Instrument (MSCI; Yukelson, Weinberg and Jackson, 1984).

The SCQ is a seven-item scale that measures several dimensions of cohesiveness including interpersonal attraction, personal power, value of membership, sense of belonging, enjoyment, teamwork and closeness. This scale has remained a popular instrument despite never being subjected to a formal validation process. The TCQ is a thirteen-item Likert scale used to derive six scores (team performance satisfaction, self performance satisfaction, value of membership, leadership, task cohesion, desire for recognition and affiliation cohesion), while the MSCI identified four factors (attraction to the group, unity of purpose, quality of teamwork and valued roles) although the original items were specific to basketball and the scale has been little used.

Of the various measures on offer, the Group Environment Questionnaire (GEQ; Widmeyer, Brawley and Carron, 1985) remains the most popular, sophisticated and best validated measure of team cohesion in sport (Carron, Brawley and Widmeyer, 1998). The GEQ is an 18-item, questionnaire which measures the four components of cohesiveness previously described:

- Attraction to the Group (Social): *ATG-Social*: group members' perceptions about personal involvement, acceptance and social interaction.
- Attraction to the Group (Task): *ATG-Task*: group members' perceptions about personal involvement with group tasks, productivity and goals and objectives.
- Group Integration (Social): *GI-Social*: group members' perceptions about similarity, closeness and bonding within the whole group as regards social aspects.
- Group Integration (Task): *GI-Task*: group members' perceptions about similarity, closeness and bonding within the whole group as regards its tasks.

In contrast with earlier scales, the GEQ has been psychometrically validated (Schutz, Eom, Smoll and Smith, 1994), with a confirmatory factor analysis confirming the underlying four factor structure (Li and Harmer, 1996). Use of the scale implicitly acknowledges the multifaceted nature of cohesion and provides an opportunity to consider a range of variables that may mediate the cohesion-performance relationship including the type of sport and the nature of team and individual goals (Estabrooks, 2000; Paskevich *et al.*, 2001; Widmeyer, Carron and Brawley,1993), with a more recent variation, the Physical Activity Environment Questionnaire (PAEQ; Estabrooks and Carron, 2000) being employed to consider cohesion in contexts other than competitive sport.

Teams in context

Of the various areas covered in this chapter, methodologically the work dealing with contextual demands has tended to be labelled as the most straightforward as invariably the research is archival, for example, comparing team performances 'at home' or 'on the road'. While this work appears simple at first glance, it is interesting to witness the slow progression from univariate to multivariate analyses as the complexities of the relationships determining performance have been revealed. This includes the influence of an increasing array of variables such as audience characteristics, venue, type of sport, stage of competition and team quality (Nevill and Holder, 1999). Equally, the outcome measures increasingly move beyond simply winning or losing to the effects of context on facets of performance including assertiveness, aggression, fouling, and sport-specific performance indices (e.g., rebounds, field goals, penalties, free throws).

In the past sport psychology could stand accused of inappropriate use of statistics, not because the procedures themselves were flawed but because the scope of the analysis was too narrow (Schutz and Gessaroli, 1993). With greater reliance on multivariate techniques so it is likely that the subtleties of social phenomena such as home advantage will become better understood.

Team roles

Each of the non-sport-specific leadership models outlined earlier has associated measures and a number have adaptations for use in sport settings. One example is the Coaching Decision Style Questionnaire (Chelladurai, Haggerty and Baxter, 1989; Gordon, 1988), which was developed from the decision tree associated with Vroom and Yetton's (1973) Normative Model. The questionnaire includes various sporting situations where choices must be made and problems must be solved. The solutions offered to these problems then reflect in particular decision styles. This questionnaire is designed to be completed either by coaches themselves or by athletes as they perceive (or prefer) their coaches would respond to hypothetical situations.

Given sport psychology's longstanding concern with psychometrics, it will probably come as little surprise to learn that sport psychologists have not been slow to develop a number of sport-specific leadership scales. These measures include the Coach Behavior Description Questionnaire (CBDQ; Danielson, Zelhart and Drake, 1975) and the Leadership Scale for Sports (LSS; Chelladurai and Saleh, 1980). The CBDQ is a twenty item scale which includes eight leadership categories dealing with competitive training, initiation, interpersonal team operations, social behaviour, representation behaviour, organised communication, recognition and general excitement. The CBDQ has not generated a great deal of research since the 1970s, but the same cannot be said of the LSS.

The LSS is a forty-item scale, made up of five subscales – training and instruction, autocratic behaviour, democratic behaviour, social support and positive feedback. The LSS has attracted attention over the years (Chelladurai, 2001), albeit with reservations as to the general applicability of results and the capacity of the LSS subscales to address all salient dimensions of coaching behaviour.

The LSS can be administered in one of two forms. The first considers the way in which the athlete perceives his or her coach ('My coach ....'), the second deals not with athlete's experience of the coach but with preferred behaviour ('I prefer my coach to ....'). Differences between scores derived from both question types (known as the discrepancy score) have been used to quantify the mismatch between experience and preference, and beyond this to relate discrepancy to satisfaction (e.g., Schliesman, 1987). On several occasions, levels of satisfaction with the coach have been found to correlate negatively with discrepancy scores, and particularly those derived from two subscales ('positive feedback', and 'training and instruction').

Other research has used the 'preferred' LSS version ('I prefer my coach to ....') to compare coaching preferences in various sports along numerous dimensions, for example, between males and females, Americans and non-Americans, the young and the old, and elite and non-elite athletes (see Horn, 1992, pp. 186–9). Typically (and very much in line with other leadership research), men have been found to have a greater preference for autocratic styles whereas women prefer democratic and participative styles. While the age and maturity of an athlete do not have a clear effect on preference, contextual issues including culture and type of sport have found to be significant (Chelladurai, 1993; Chelladurai *et al.*, 1988). A more recent version of the LSS, the Revised Leadership Scale for Sport (RLSS; Zhang, Jensen and Mann, 1997) contains 60 items, and includes an additional dimension, situational consideration, but research using the RLSS is limited to date. Neither the RLSS nor the earlier LSS contain items specifically addressing transformational leadership, although this is now core to the Multidimensional Model of Leadership, and this may limit the usefulness of both scales (Riemer, 2007).

Along with the LSS a sport-specific behavioural measure, the Coaching Behaviour Assessment System (CBAS; Smith, Smoll and Hunt, 1977) was also developed in the 1970s to quantify the behaviour of coaches by structured observation. This system has continued to generate interest along a number of research fronts (e.g., Horn, 1984) and Smoll and Smith (1989) have incorporated it as part of their mediational model (see above) and the Coach Effectiveness Training programme (see below).

The CBAS is made up of 12 categories, divided into two primary classes (Reactive Behaviours [8] and Spontaneous Behaviours [4]). Reactive behaviours are those where the coach responds to the team or player (e.g., player performs well, player makes mistake, player misbehaves) while spontaneous behaviours are those where the coach initiates the action (e.g., game-related technical instruction, general encouragement, general communication).

The same authors have used the CBAS to look at the interaction between children's self-esteem and their responsiveness to different coaching styles. They found that those children with low self-esteem most needed coaches who valued their contribution and provided positive feedback for successful work (Smith and Smoll, 2007). Not surprisingly it has been found that coaches who rely on negative styles of communication develop teams where liking of each other and their coach is not high, and that the degree of insight that coaches have regarding their behavioural style and the preferred style of their players is not impressive (Smoll and Smith, 1999).

Another behavioural measure, the Arizona State University Observation Instrument (ASUOI; Lacy and Goldston, 1990), has also been developed to assess coach's verbal and non-verbal behaviour, this time using thirteen categories. Unfortunately, to date research using this scale is more limited.

With regard to specific measures of the coach-athlete relationship, one of the most extensively validated is the Coach-Athlete Relationship Questionnaire (CART-Q). This was designed to quantify the key constructs of the '3 + 1 Cs' conceptual model as outlined earlier (Jowett, 2007).

PRACTICAL ISSUES AND INTERVENTIONS

To be able to bring all this literature to bear on sensible, practical interventions with teams is not an easy task. On the one hand there is a need to ensure that any intervention will sit easily with the available literature while on the other hand there is a need to package this material in a user friendly way. This is a difficult balance to maintain not least because the literature is not always easy to synthesise in a way that can be translated into workable practice.

Increasingly it is recognised that traditional models of intervention, predicated on the athlete working independently with a sport psychologist, may present difficulties (Kremer and Scully, 1998). Instead, any model of intervention must begin by acknowledging the central role of the coach or manager, and the dynamics that exist between the coach and his or her players (Jowett and Poczwardowski, 2007; Lovell and Collins, 1996; Smith and Johnson, 1990; Terry, 1997). Hence modern interventions will often focus on coach development and empowerment, including the appropriate skills for handling team issues as and when they arise. With this in mind, Syer (1991) maintains that a coach must constantly monitor the development of cliques and potential sources of conflict in order to be able to deal with these effectively should problems arise. During team meetings he recommends that the coach should acquaint each player with his or her responsibilities, establish team goals, create open communication channels and monitor the psychological well-being of both fit and injured team members. Additionally, Yukelson (1998) suggests that the coach must be in tune with the interpersonal grapevine within the sports group, most usefully by maintaining a dialogue with both informal and formal leaders within the team. For many good coaches this will already be second nature but for others it may require adjustment to their traditional methods. Eventually it can be argued that the final goal of a successful intervention should be for the sport psychologist as 'outsider' to become largely redundant as the coach comes to embody the principles associated with the intervention in word and deed (Hardy and Parfitt, 1994; Jowett, 2007; Kremer and Scully, 1998).

As for fellow team members, Huang and Lynch (1994) suggest that they also play a significant role in sustaining an appropriate team environment. For example, by constantly offering positive affirmation statements each member can help the team stay focused on its objectives and develop a common sense of purpose among players.

Coach development

The need for this type of work is confirmed both by anecdotal information and available research, which suggests that coaches may not always practice what sport psychologists preach. For example, Hanson and Gould (1988) considered the ability of coaches to recognise their athletes' anxiety states and found very few were able to predict how their athletes were feeling. Gould *et al.* (1990) considered the training needs of 130 elite coaches in the United States and found that the sport sciences in general had still to make their mark. The coaches still felt that the most significant influence on their coaching styles came not from books, manuals or courses but from hands-on experience and international networking, that is watching other elite coaches in action.

Numerous coach development programmes are now available, ranging from highly structured training schemes to general sources of support available from governing bodies and national sports organisations. In the United Kingdom various governing bodies have established programmes of training that are arranged according to grade of coach. In the United States, there are a number of coach training programmes, primarily designed for youth sport coaches. The most popular continues to be Coach Effectiveness Training (CET; Smith and Smoll, 2002; 2007; Smoll and Smith, 2005; 2006). Typical training lasts approximately three hours, usually delivered over three sessions, and includes a number of interactive exercises designed to reinforce sound coaching principles. These include orientation to winning ('Winning isn't everything nor is it the only thing'; 'Failure is not the same as losing'; 'Success is not equivalent to winning'; 'Success is related to effort'; Smith and Smoll, 2002; Smoll and Smith, 2005), appropriate type of feedback and reinforcement (e.g., the 'positive sandwich approach – compliment; future-oriented instruction; compliment), establishment of social norms (e.g., sharing responsibility for team building), engagement in decision-making, and self-reflection and monitoring of the coach's behaviour. The programme continues to enjoy widespread popularity and available evaluation research is positive (see Smith and Smoll, 2007).

More recently Rhind and Jowett (2010) have developed their COMPASS model specifically to focus on practical strategies that coaches can employ to help maintain and grow the coach-athlete relationship. Based on the '3C + 1' conceptual model (see earlier; Jowett, 2007), the model identifies seven categories of behaviour that are critical to the health of this relationship – conflict management, openness, motivation, positivity, advice, support, and social networks).

One issue which has generated growing interest over recent years is gender and cultural diversity in coaching and leadership within sport (Gill, 2007). Traditionally leadership research across psychology has been androcentric (i.e., based on men) but as women have moved in increasing numbers into the labour market and management roles so gender research has increased dramatically (Eagly and Johnson, 1990). Mirroring this trend, gender has emerged as an important issue in the sport psychology of coaching (LaVoi, 2009) but it is an

---

RESEARCH BOX

The role that coaches can play in the development of a sporting mind is considerable, and within sport psychology there is a growing awareness of how far reaching and pervasive that influence can be. A group of sport psychologists based in Greece recently carried out a series of studies designed to consider the impact that coaches can have on athletes' self-talk following exposure to different coaching styles. In the first study, two groups of wrestlers were asked to reflect on their self-talk during competition, within 30 minutes of competing. In addition they were asked to reflect on their coaches' behaviour, and the coach also rated their own behaviour. Results showed clearly that a positive and supportive coaching style reflected in positive self-talk among the wrestlers and in particular regarding confidence, anxiety control and during 'psyching up' for competition. In contrast, negative self-talk was linked to negativity in coaching styles, which also encouraged thoughts of disengagement, fatigue and worry. A second study involved an experimental design where participants were required to perform a forehand tennis drive under different sets of instruction. Initially all participants performed the exercise with no instruction, with their self talk measured immediately after performance of the trials. Three days later the participants were recalled and placed in one of three test conditions – positive instruction ('Doesn't matter, go for the next shot'; 'Very good, keep on like this'); negative instruction (e.g., 'That was a bad shot'; 'You don't follow my instructions'), and a control. Instructions were provided during performance itself and although there were few differences between the groups in terms of actual performance but that the instruction type did have an impact on positive and negative self-talk, broadly in line with previous predictions. Those with positive instructions tended to worry less about making mistakes while those who were given negative instructions tended to lose confidence over time. The implications of such research are considerable – what coaches say before and during competition really does matter, not just by influencing performance but by impacting on the athlete's mental ability to deal with the ups and downs of competition itself.

---

issue which warrants further attention given traditional stereotypes in sport and the additional burdens placed on women coaches (Hasbrook *et al.*, 1990; Kelley, 1994; Gill, 2007; LaVoi, Becker and Maxwell, 2007). To see the mountain that still has to be climbed for women and for those from minority ethnic backgrounds, it is worthwhile perusing the annual report produced by Richard

Lapchick and colleagues entitled Racial and Gender Report Card: College Sport (for 2008, go to http://www.ncasports.org/Articles/2008_College_Sport_RGRC.pdf). This reveals that white males continue to dominate senior sports administration and coaching positions within US colleges to the exclusion of all other groups, and the gap is widening rather than narrowing.

Team building

A given in many applied sport psychology texts is that team building is 'the way to go', with benefits seen to accrue at both the personal and collective levels (Martin, Carron and Burke, 2009). Syer and Connolly (1984) listed the three main benefits of team building. First, it satisfies players' belonging needs, enhances loyalty to the team and coach, and harnesses support among team members. Second, in times of stress it helps provide buffers and facilitates the provision of clear feedback on personal performance. Third, it enables a team to have the edge over a less together but technically superior team.

The techniques that have been employed to facilitate team building have often been borrowed straight from occupational psychology but with little reflection on the special circumstances attaching to sport teams (Crace and Hardy, 1997; Klein *et al.*, 2009). As a consequence team building events have been supported without question in the past, and despite the obvious drawbacks associated with creating highly cohesive teams (Hardy, Eys and Carron, 2005), manifested most vividly in the phenomenon of groupthink (Janis, 1982; Miranda, 1994; Moorhead and Montanari, 1986). As previous work illustrates, effective teams are not necessarily conflict-free zones but are often characterised by healthy levels of conflict (Burke and Collins, 1996) which support individuality and keep unfettered forces of social influence in check.

In terms of intervention strategies, Yukelson (1998) advocates running interactive team building events that encourage a shared vision, unity of purpose, collaborative teamwork, individual and mutual accountability, team identity, team cohesiveness, open and honest communication, and trust. Following an alternative approach, Carron, Spink and Prapavessis (1997) argue that the coach should be more actively involved in the delivery of a tailored team building programme, typically organised in four stages over several weeks. The introductory and conceptual stages provide the foundation in terms of knowledge of team dynamics and cohesiveness followed by the practical and intervention stages where the theory is put into practice through appropriate team building protocols. Lovell and Collins (1996) likewise propose a staged approach which would involve, for example, brainstorming and negotiation in order to enhance a feeling of ownership. As a part of this process Cripps and Cann (1996) also emphasise the importance of work on team goal setting, encompassing cultural issues associated with the team as a whole, perhaps moving from playing to social and financial matters. Two recent meta-analyses of team building in sport (Klein *et al.*, 2009; Martin, Carron and Burke, 2009), while generally positive, both suggest that caution should be employed before simply rushing off to the latest 'boot camp' (Kremer and Moran, 2008, p. 174–5). In particular, only certain activities appear to help teams, those that are task relevant and those involving either role clarification or goal setting procedures.

From previous discussions it is perhaps appropriate to reiterate a word of caution at this stage. Team building may be appropriate but only in certain circumstances, for example, when used as a 'get to know you' exercise if the team has not been together for long. However, as Forsyth (2009) confirms, in line with the extensive cohesiveness-performance research, more significant benefits are likely to be associated with task related activities and not social dimensions. Furthermore the aim of team building should proceed with an awareness that the prime objective is not to create a team which is necessarily comfortable, 'bonded' or conflict-free but one where the team atmosphere is healthy and vibrant and thus conducive to repeatable good performances.

To conclude, the psychology of sports teams remains a fascinating arena for applied research, providing wonderful opportunities for small group research and for model development with implications well beyond the boundaries of sport and exercise. There is already a sound empirical base from which to build and test integrative models designed to consider team processes in sport, and the future looks bright.

CASE STUDY

A longstanding friend of yours, Jimmy Gregg, has been in contact. He has been elected as coach/manager for his local amateur soccer team for the coming season and he has a number of concerns. Jimmy is an ex-player with the team who has managed the youth team for two years with some success. The club as a whole has enjoyed a very good reputation over the years, winning the championship two seasons ago and losing in the final last year. The nucleus of the team is made up of seasoned campaigners who Jimmy used to play alongside. They have 'been there and done that' several times and Jimmy believes that some may be past their prime. Although there are no very clear signs of major problems, he felt that the league performance tailed off towards the end of the season and the team surrendered a two goal lead in the final to lose 3-2. There are several good young players in the reserve team but the older players do not make them feel particularly welcome and there are rumours that some of the injuries picked up in pre-season training may have been caused maliciously. The captain is one of the established players and formerly played along with Jimmy, although injury sidelined him for most of last season and Jimmy is unsure if he should be reappointed. In training it would seem that there are two camps, and with the team about to head off on an arduous and challenging 'team building' long weekend at a remote army camp, Jimmy wants to meet to discuss how he should handle matters, in both the short and longer term.

1. With reference to the Theories and Models section in the chapter, how would you interpret what is happening in this case study?
2. With reference to Methods and Measures, what techniques would you employ to help understand and quantify the issues?
3. With reference to Practical Issues and Interventions, how would you deal with this situation?

STUDY QUESTIONS

1. How do social loafing and social facilitation, individually and collectively, influence individual behaviour in team sports?
2. Critically evaluate the relationship between cohesion and success in team sports.
3. Home advantage – what, when, where and why?
4. Discuss the contribution of contemporary models of leadership models to our understanding of successful coaching in sport.
5. Assess the effectiveness of team building as an applied technique for enhancing team performance.

FURTHER READING

Carron, A. V. and Brawley, F. R. (2008) 'Group Dynamics in Sport and Physical Activity', in T. S. Horn (ed.), *Advances in Sport Psychology* (Champaign, IL: Human Kinetics), 213–38.

Carron, A. V., Loughhead, T. M. and Bray, S. R. (2005) 'The Home Advantage in Sport Competitions: Courneya and Carron's (1992) Conceptual Framework a Decade Later', *Journal of Sports Sciences*, 23, 395–407.

Chow, G. M. and Feltz, D. L. (2007) 'Exploring New Directions in Collective Efficacy and Sport', in M.R. Beauchamp, and M.A. Eys (eds) *Group Dynamics in Exercise and Sport Psychology: Contemporary Themes* (New York: Routledge), 221–48.

Heuze, J.-P. and Brunel, P. C. (2003) 'Social Loafing in A Competitive Context', *International Journal of Sport and Exercise Psychology*, 1, 246–63.

Martin, L. J., Carron, A. V. and Burke, S. M (2009) 'Team Building Interventions in Sport: A Meta-Analysis', *Sport and Exercise Psychology Review*, 5, 3–18.

Wann, D. L., Melnick, M. J., Russell, G. W. and Pease, D. G. (2001) *Sport Fans: The Psychology and Social Impact of Spectators* (London: Routledge).

10 The Athlete's Career

INTRODUCTION, HISTORY AND DEVELOPMENT

As the demands associated with competitive sport have increased over the years, so has the academic interest regarding the athlete's career. While McPherson reported in 1980 that an extensive literature search generated 20 references pertaining to this area, over 500 references have recently identified relating to the career of the athlete (Lavallee, 2010). An international special interest group established in 1999 has helped to take forward this area and exchange information on applied and investigative work (Wylleman, Lavallee and Aflermann, 1999) and European (European Federation of Sport Psychology, 1999) and International (ISSP; Stambulova *et al.*, 2009) position statements have been put forward. In addition, a number of intervention programmes have been developed by governing bodies and sport institutes around the world to assist athletes in their career development.

Following Bookbinder's (1955) pioneering examination of the careers of professional baseball players in the United States, researchers have established that athletes are confronted with a wide range of psychological, interpersonal and financial issues throughout their career. The earliest research in this area concentrated almost exclusively on the psychological difficulties experienced by retiring athletes, and focused on male professional athletes in specific sports (e.g., Hallden, 1965; Hare, 1971; Weinberg and Arond, 1952). These studies also tended to emphasise dysfunctional issues such as depression and alcoholism that this population are occasionally confronted with after they terminate their careers.

As empirical data began to accumulate in the area, several authors challenged the widespread assumption that sports retirement is inherently stressful. For example, the sport sociologist Jay Coakley (1983) argued that it is naive to assume that athletes are universally overwhelmed by stress during and after their careers. Blinde, Greendorfer and colleagues also conducted a series of surveys in the United States in the 1980s with competitive athletes who competed in various individual and team sports (Blinde and Greendorfer, 1985; Greendorfer and Blinde, 1985; Kleiber *et al.*, 1987). In these separate but comparable studies, which constitute some of the largest in this area to date, it was determined that 90% of those surveyed looked forward to their life after sport. This result, combined with comparable findings in the mid to late 1970s at the high school (e.g., Sands, 1978; basketball and football players in Canada), collegiate (e.g., Snyder and Baber, 1979; athletes from a range of sports in the United States), and professional levels (e.g., Haerle, 1975; professional baseball players in the United States), led sport psychologists to begin to consider that athletes do not tend to experience difficulties at the end of their career. A number of subsequent research studies in the 1980s and 1990s, however, demonstrated that the career termination process could be an inevitable source of adjustment.

Svoboda and Vanek (1982), for example, reported that 83% of their sample of former Czechoslovakian Olympic athletes experienced difficulties following retirement from sport. In addition, Werthner and Orlick (1986) conducted in-depth interviews with a sample of Canada's most successful amateur athletes and found that nearly 80% felt some degree of difficulty in making the transition out of sport. In a survey of former Canadian junior male hockey players, Curtis and Ennis (1988) reported that more than 60% experienced some feelings of loss after disengaging from organised sport. The most detailed support in this area of research, however, comes from a survey conducted by McInally, Cavin-Stice and Knoth (1992) with retired professional football players in the United States. In this study, 88 per cent of the former athletes indicated that they found the overall process of ending their careers extremely problematic. More specifically, moderate to severe problems were reported in regard to financial/occupational (31%), emotional (26%) and social (23%) adjustment to their sports career termination. Considering this evidence of adjustment difficulties experienced by former athletes upon retirement, it is interesting to note that 67 per cent of McInally, Cavin-Stice and Knoth's (1992) sample reported that they would still want professional football careers for their children, and 86% of Curtis and Ennis's (1988) sample would prefer their children to be as heavily involved in competitive hockey as they were.

Research in recent years has extended into other, more specific areas. Researchers, for example, have conducted studies on the career transition experiences within specific sports (e.g., Bennie and O'Connor, 2004 with track and field athletes) and with specific populations (e.g., Munroe-Bruner, Munroe-Chandler and Spink, 2008 with "rookie" athletes). Other studies have examined gender (e.g., Giacobbi *et al.*, 2004; Harrison and Lawrence, 2004) and ethnicity (Harrison and Lawrence, 2003), as well specific topics such as well-being (e.g., Stephan *et al.*, 2003), within-careers transitions (e.g., Pummell, Harwood and Lavallee, 2008) and the effect of athlete retirement on parents (e.g., Lally and Kerr, 2008). Cross-national comparisons have been conducted (e.g., Stambulova, Stephan, and Japhag, 2007) and qualitative methods (e.g., Douglas and Carless, 2009) have been employed in more studies. Lastly, there have been important advances in the measurement of career transitions in sport in recent years which can assist practitioners, including the development of the *Athletes' Retirement Decision Inventory* (Fernandez, Stephen, and Fouquereau,

2006), *Retirement Sports Survey* (Alfermann, Stambulova, and Zemaityte 2004), *British Athletes Lifestyle Assessment Needs in Career and Education* (BALANCE) Scale (Lavallee and Wylleman, 1999), *Athlete Retirement Questionnaire* (Sinclair and Orlick, 1993), *Australian Athletes Career Transition Inventory* (Hawkins and Blann, 1993), and *Professional Athletes Career Transition Inventory* (Blann and Zaichkowsky, 1989). Some of these are outlined in more detailed in the Methods and Measures section of this chapter.

THEORIES AND MODELS

Several theories and models have been outlined in the sport psychology literature in order to conceptualise the career of the athlete. These have predominantly been employed from the mainstream psychological literature, and have been developed and revised following research conducted. Akin to the first studies in the area, the earliest theories focused on sports career termination and utilised theories related to ageing (i.e., gerontology) as well as death and dying (i.e., thanatology). More recently, theoretical frameworks related to transitions have been employed to explain the career f the athlete. This section reviews these and other theories and models. Readers should also consult Chapter 4 for reference to socialisation into sport, participation motivation and attrition.

Gerontology theories

Gerontology, as a field of study, has been defined as 'the systematic analysis of the ageing process' (Atchley, 1991). This academic discipline consists of biological, social and psychological subdivisions, with social gerontology concentrating on the mutual interaction between society and the aged. In its broadest sense, social gerontology attempts to explain the lives and activities of those who appear to age successfully. Several gerontological orientations, therefore, have been utilised to explain the career development of the general population.

Sport psychologists have suggested that several models of social gerontology are applicable in the study of sporting careers. In an attempt to understand the career of the athlete, it has been compared to the following social gerontological perspectives: activity theory, subculture theory, disengagement theory, continuity theory, social breakdown theory and social exchange theory.

Havighurst and Albrecht (1953) were perhaps the first theorists to propose a relationship between social activity and changes to the working career, itself. This pioneering conceptualisation of ageing, known as 'activity theory', suggests that individuals strive to maintain homeostatic levels of activity throughout the lifespan. If the adjustment to retirement process is to be successful, the once active roles that are lost upon retirement from the labour force need to be substituted with new ones. Although this perspective has received some empirical support in the gerontological literature, it has been suggested that activity theory is based on an inadequate theoretical foundation (Longino and Kart, 1982).

In terms of retirement from elite-level sport, some theorists have suggested that there is potential in examining the application of activity theory. McPherson (1980), for example, contends that this perspective has utility for individuals who substitute an activity for the athlete role. Rosenberg (1981) has also suggested that when athletes retire voluntarily, it is usually not because their skills and efforts provide the rewards they once did, but because alternatives to sport look more attractive. Activity theory, however, may not apply universally to the career of athletes because there is usually neither a cessation of work activity nor total retirement from sport. Although activity theory may explain the situation of retiring athletes who successfully adjust by retaining previous activity patterns, Baillie and Danish (1992) believe that the schedules which elite-level athletes adhere to during their playing careers are difficult to duplicate outside sport.

Rose (1965) responded to a need for theory building in the area of social gerontology by theorising that it is possible to successfully adjust to retirement from the workforce with less active roles. This 'subculture theory', which asserts that prolonged social interactions among individuals leads to the development of a group consciousness, assumes that people can be less active and well-adjusted following changes in their career even if the situation is different from overall social norms. Although some investigators have demonstrated an application of this perspective, the gerontological community suggests that subculture theory is most applicable when it is integrated with other social gerontological theories. Since elite athletes have fairly distinguishable sub-cultural characteristics, Rosenberg (1981) contends that subculture theory is of value in explaining the career of the athlete. Although it is questionable as to whether this theory can predict successful sports retirement, it does assist in revealing the sources of potential adjustment problems experienced by athletes in transition. This perspective, however, has received considerable criticism in the sport psychology literature because the athlete is moving out of, not into, the proposed subculture (Gordon and Lavallee, in press).

'Continuity theory' originated with Atchley (1989), who focused on the evolution of individual adaptation to normal ageing. Unlike the aforementioned social gerontological models, this theory allows changes to be integrated into one's prior history without necessarily causing disequilibrium. The importance of a stable pattern of previously established role behaviour is assumed in this model, with an emphasis on maintaining continuity throughout the ageing process. Thus, the best-adjusted individuals experience minimal change and greater continuity following changes in their career. When applied within sport, it has been proposed that continuity theory can predict the level of adjustment to retirement by examining the significance of sport in the lives of athletes. If one's athletic role is seen as more meaningful than other roles, an athlete may experience some difficulties in redistributing them upon retirement (Rosenberg, 1981). On the other hand, if sustaining the sporting role is not a priority for the athlete, the reallocation of time and energy to remaining roles will not create problems. Therefore, the decisive question in the application of continuity theory within sport is whether or not any changes in their career are important enough for individuals to reorganise their hierarchy of personal goals.

The belief that retired individuals are content with less active schedules has been challenged in the sport literature. Utilising continuity as a predictor of adjustment to retirement, Lerch (1981) empirically tested continuity theory with a sample of more than 500 professional baseball players in the United States. In this study, it was hypothesised that optimal adjustment would characterise the individual whose post-athletic career remained connected to sports, income remained relatively stable after retirement and level of subjective and behavioural commitment to sport was maintained. This modification of continuity theory was also supplemented with a number of variables which social gerontologists have found to be related to retirement adjustment (namely education level, pre-retirement attitude and health). Lerch found, however, that no continuity variables were significantly related to adjustment to retirement.

'Disengagement theory' was introduced by Cummings et al. (1960) as an extension of Erik Erikson's model of psychosocial development. This structural–functional theory of ageing, which argues that the elderly and society mutually withdraw from one another, is based on the findings from the Kansas City Study of Adult Life. In this longitudinal investigation of retired individuals, it was suggested that a desired equilibrium is obtained when younger workers enter the labour force and replace the disengaging older population. A system-induced mechanism allows society and the elderly to progressively retract from one another, allowing the ageing population to spend their remaining years in leisure. Retirement, according to disengagement theory, is viewed as a necessary manifestation of the mutual withdrawal of society and the ageing population from one another. Because most athletes do not leave the workforce permanently after career termination, this does not appear to fit the theory of general disengagement. Whereas disengagement theory would assume that athletes and the sport structure mutually withdraw from one another, Lerch (1981) has suggested that athletes try to hang on to their sport long after their skills have begun to deteriorate. Moreover, retiring athletes clearly cannot afford to withdraw from society. It has been accepted, therefore, that disengagement theory offers little to the understanding of the athlete's career (Blinde and Greendorfer, 1985).

'Social breakdown theory' was adapted to gerontology by Kuypers and Bengtson (1973) and details the cycle associated with the process of social reorganisation after retirement. Incorporating elements of activity theory, subculture theory and continuity theory, this conceptualisation proposes that individuals become increasingly susceptible to external labelling following the loss of a retirement-related role. This social evaluation leads them to gradually reduce their involvement in certain activities until the role is completely eliminated from their lives. Some authors in the sporting community believe that social breakdown theory has clear applications. In particular, Rosenberg (1981) has suggested that the withdrawal cycle illustrates how elite athletes are vulnerable to social judgement upon retirement, particularly unfavourable redefinition. Edwards and Meier (1984) have empirically investigated the relationship between adjustment to retirement from sport and several variables proposed as significant in social breakdown theory, including socioeconomic status, pre-retirement planning and health. In this study, the data from former professional ice hockey players in North America yielded significant support for the social breakdown paradigm. In the case of career termination, however, retiring athletes are often aware of their deteriorating sporting skills, as well as a lack of congruence with their peers. According to the social breakdown model, this may lead individuals to withdraw further from their sport and become susceptible to more negative evaluation. To avoid such a decline, Baillie and Danish (1992) suggest that athletes should prepare for the redefinition of social breakdown prior to the actual retirement. This procedure, which has been referred to as 'social reconstruction', assists the athlete in restoring and maintaining a positive self-image and thus reduces the impact of negative external evaluation. In career counselling with athletes, Rosenberg (1981) believes a fitting prelude to a discussion of social breakdown is exchange theory.

'Social exchange theory', as initially developed Thibaut and Kelley (1959), was applied by Homans (1961) to explain how ageing individuals rearrange their activities so that their remaining energy generates maximum return. This paradigm has since been adapted to illustrate how successful ageing can be achieved through the specific rearrangement of social networks and activities. Rosenberg (1981) suggested that this theory is one of the most salient gerontological theories applicable to the career of the athlete. In addition, Johns et al. (1990) have demonstrated in a study with former competitive gymnasts in Canada that the examination of factors which contribute to attrition through a social exchange perspective has some merit. More recently it has been suggested that the processes associated with exchange theory do not stand up because they deny the possibility of the development of a career after sport (Koukouris, 1991). Social exchange theory may, however, be heuristically useful in giving athletes a perspective on what their relationship with sport is, as well as what will happen to that relationship upon career termination. As Gordon and Lavallee (in press) have suggested, resources such as physical talent may be able to be exchanged for meaningful rewards from the sport system, but these resources are finite and their inevitable deterioration will affect the degree of control over the sport relationship.

Despite the intuitive appeal of social gerontological theories, many questions have been raised by contemporary theorists about their applicability to the career of the athlete. For example, the general assumption that retirement is a system-induced mechanism that forces athletes to disengage from their sport has been criticised. The applicability of social theories of ageing to the athlete, who will often continue into a post-sport career, has also been questioned. Indeed, it is difficult to compare retirement from the workforce with the termination of a sports career, which biologically and chronologically occurs at a much younger age (Murphy, 1995b). Perhaps the biggest shortcoming of the analogy between sporting careers and social gerontological models, however, is the presumption that career changes are inherently negative events, requiring considerable adjustment. Although this assumption may be useful in drawing a parallel between successful retirement from sport and occupational retirement from the labour force, it is clear that social gerontological theories are unable to adequately capture the nature and dynamics of the athlete's career.

Thanatology theories

Thanatology is the study of the process of death and dying. This area of research, which was introduced by Park (1912) in an outline of the biomedical causes of death, has since evolved into a multidisciplinary science. Academic disciplines such as anthropology, psychology, sociology and theology have all made significant contributions to the study of thanatology, and a total of 62 different sets of variables have been identified in the extant literature which influence the dying individual (Rando, 1986). In addition, 29 separate sets of psychological, social and physical factors appear to influence a person's response to the death of a significant other (Rando, 1984). As Feifel (1990) has suggested, thanatology is such a diverse area that the very mention of it as a field of study is a limitation.

The sport psychology community has suggested that several thanatological theories have implications for the career of the athlete and, in particular, the areas of sports injuries and retirement from sport. Although a number of analytical frameworks from thanatology have been applied within sport, theorists agree that models of social death, social awareness contexts and the stages of grief have the most relevance.

Of the numerous parallels that have been drawn between retirement from sport and models of thanatology, the majority have been examined from social points of view. For example, Kalish's (1966) concept of 'social death' has frequently been employed as a literary device describing the psychodynamics of athletic retirement. This analogy, which refers to the condition of being treated as if one were dead even though still biologically alive, describes the loss of social functioning, isolation and ostracism which may accompany retirement. Whereas numerous fictitious examples of social death have been used to explain this phenomenon in sport, Lerch (1984) has asserted that the non-fictional works are undoubtedly the most compelling depictions of social death.

It has been proposed that 'social awareness contexts' have application for athletes retiring from sport (Rosenberg, 1984). This perspective refers to the individuals who know about a terminal hospital patient's inevitable death. The research of Glaser and Strauss (1965) suggests that depending upon who knows what during this process, there are observable and predictable patterns of interaction between dying patients, family members and the medical staff. As these individuals interact over time, it is suggested that the following awareness contexts develop: closed awareness, suspected awareness, mutual pretence and open awareness.

In 'closed awareness', terminal patients are not aware of the fact that they are going to die, even though other people do. Various factors may contribute to the closed awareness context, including a doctor's reluctance to tell the patient, the family's decision to not inform the dying individual, and/or the general collusion of hospital staff to avoid discussing patients' illnesses with them specifically (Glaser and Strauss, 1965). Terminal hospital patients who remain in this context until they die have little chance to make future plans. When applied to sport, this context is between the retiring athlete, team mates, coaches and management. Just as hospital staff may prefer this context, in that they do not have to discuss the inevitability of death, this could apply in situations where athletes are unaware of management's plan to cut, release or trade them.

The 'suspected awareness' context exists when the dying patient suspects the inevitable death that others know about and tries to confirm or negate that suspicion. These individuals normally try to obtain realistic information about their situation from family, friends and the hospital staff. Factors that contribute to this awareness context, such as the patient's recognition of changing physical symptoms, may be compared to the experiences of retiring athletes. For example, suspicions of being released from a team may be aroused by the tone of coaches and/or team mates. As in closed awareness, the possible consequences are that terminal hospital patients, as well as athletes, do not have the opportunity to express their feelings and emotions because the later awareness contexts (mutual pretence and open awareness) are never realised.

In the 'mutual pretence' context, the patient, family members and hospital staff all are aware that the patient is dying. What occurs in this context, however, is that all the people involved behave as if the inevitable death is not so. In terms of retirement from sport, the athlete's career termination would not be discussed among coaches and team mates. Although one of the consequences of this context is that patients may have some dignity in dying, it is possible that isolation and loneliness may occur.

The context of 'open awareness' exists when all people openly acknowledge that the patient is dying. This awareness gives everyone involved a chance to discuss their feelings and thus gives patients a greater sense of control. In terms of athletic retirement, many individuals may have difficulty in accepting the knowledge of their impending career termination. On the other hand, athletes can begin to plan their post-athletic career in this context. It is, however, more likely to find relations between athletes and coaches characterised by closed and/or suspected awareness.

The 'stages of grief' experienced when facing death is also quite informative in describing retirement from sport. These psychological reactions, as outlined by Elizabeth Kübler-Ross (1969), grew out of her landmark interview-based study with terminal hospital patients. The stages of grief, as applied to retirement from sport, include the following: denial and isolation, in which athletes initially refuse to acknowledge their inevitable career termination; anger, in which retiring athletes become disturbed at the overall situation; bargaining, in which individuals try to negotiate for a lengthened career in sport; depression, in which athletes experience a distressful reaction to retirement; and acceptance, in which individuals eventually come to accept their athletic career termination.

The application of this theory with regard to sports injuries has also become a topic of interest in recent years. For example, a number of authors have employed this particular model to describe the psychological pattern experienced by athletes following a severe injury. This theoretical perspective has also been supported by research with both injured athletes (e.g., Grove, Stewart and Gordon, 1990) and physiotherapists consulting with injured athletes who have noted that many post-injury behavioural reactions resembled the stages of the grief response (e.g., Ford and Gordon, 1993). Although a number of theorists have utilised stage theories to describe the process of retirement from sport, only Blinde and Stratta (1992) have systematically documented the stages of grief via interviews with retired collegiate athletes in the United States who experienced involuntary and unanticipated career terminations.

The stages of grief represent a descriptive rather than normative look at the stages of the terminally ill and therefore may not be the same as those experienced by athletes. Since not everyone goes through every stage in the exact sequence and at a predictable pace, it has been agreed in the mainstream literature that grief and loss is an individualistic experience. As Kastembaum and Weisman (1972) have demonstrated via the psychological autopsy (i.e., a methodological technique providing insight into why and how a patient died and the psychological state of the patient before death), it is unlikely that any two individuals will progress through the stages of grief in the same manner. Nevertheless, the stages of grief and other thanatological models, if used in a flexible way, can provide a useful guide in understanding the different phases that athletes may go through.

Overall, models related to thanatology have been criticised as being inadequate when applied to the career of the athlete. Although Baillie (1993) suggests that these models can be valuable tools in understanding the overall process of retirement from sport, the clinical utility of thanatological models has been criticised because they were developed from non-sport populations (Greendorfer and Blinde, 1985). A number of authors have also questioned whether thanatological models are a generalisable disposition of what happens to the vast majority of athletes (Taylor and Lavallee, 2010). Indeed, there are enough anecdotal and empirical examples showing that career changes can be very difficult for some athletes. As with social gerontological models, however, sport psychologists established that models of thanatology possessed limitations which indicated the need for further conceptual development, and it is for this reason that theorists started to focus on transition models to explain the athlete's career.

Transition models

Whereas theories based on social gerontology and thanatology view the career of the athlete as a series of singular events, transition models characterise it as a process. A transition has been defined by Nancy Schlossberg and colleagues (1995) as an event or non-event, which results in a change in assumptions about oneself and the world and thus requires a corresponding change in one's behaviour and relationships. As such, a number of transition frameworks have been employed to examine the interactions of athletes and their environment. The most frequently employed transition model that has been outlined in the sport psychology literature has been Schlossberg's (1981) 'model of human adaptation to transition'. In this model, three major sets of factors interact during a transition: the characteristics of the individual experiencing the transition; the perception of the particular transition; and the characteristics of the pre-transition and post-transition environments.

The variables that characterise the individual include psychosocial competence, sex, age, state of health, race/ethnicity, socioeconomic status, value orientation and previous experience with a transition of a similar nature. These variables may show considerable differences across the population of athletes facing a transition in their career, and Coakley (2001) asserts that a diversity of factors influencing the athlete must be acknowledged in order to understand the overall process.

Regarding the perception of a particular transition, Schlossberg and colleagues have suggested that role change, affect, source, onset, duration and degree of stress are all important factors to consider. This aspect of the model emphasises the phenomenological nature of transitions, in that it is not just the transition itself that is of primary importance, but also the individual variables that have different salience depending on the transition. For athletes, Sinclair and Hackfort (2000) have acknowledged this position by suggesting that every transition in the career of the athlete has the potential to be a crisis, relief or combination of both, depending on the individual's perception of the situation.

In consideration of the characteristics of the pre- and post-transition environments, the importance to the evaluation of internal support systems, institutional support and physical settings have been noted. Although several researchers have examined social support networks among injured athletes (Rees et al., 2010), little research has been conducted in this area with other populations. A number of theorists over the years have outlined the obligations of coaches and sport associations in assisting athletes with career transitions (e.g., Sinclair and Hackfort, 2000; Thomas and Ermler, 1988).

In an attempt to understand better the careers of athletes, a number of researchers in the 1990s employed Schlossberg's transition model to examine various aspects of the athlete's career. Swain (1991), for example, employed a multiple case design by interviewing athletes from Canada. In this study, empirical support was shown in terms of the characteristics of the athlete in transition, the perception of the transition and the characteristics of the environments. Further evidence in support of this perspective has been documented in Parker's (1994) qualitative study with collegiate football players in the United States, as well as Baillie's (1993) large questionnaire study of elite amateur and professional athletes in North America. However, although transition models provide a conceptual overview of different elements of the sporting career, it has been suggested that they do not provide a flexible, multidimensional approach that is needed to adequately study the topic (Taylor and Lavallee, 2010). Indeed, Schlossberg's model incorporates a wider range of influence than social gerontological and thanatological models, and has been instrumental in stimulating research in the area. However, the transition models that have been applied within sport have not focused enough on the lifespan development of athletes (Wylleman *et al.*, 2000).

More recently, several sport psychologists (e.g., Stambulova *et al.*, 2009; Wylleman and Lavallee, 2004) have adopted a developmental approach by outlining a series of predictable or 'normative' transitions throughout the career of the athlete. These normative transitions are part of a definite sequence of age-related, biological, social and emotional events or changes and can be said to be generally related to the socialisation process, as well as the organisational nature of the setting in which the individual is involved (e.g., school, family). In the sporting domain normative transitions include, for example, the transition from junior to senior level, from regional to national-level competitions, from amateur to professional status, or from active participation to discontinuation from competitive sport. During this type of transition, the athlete exits one stage and enters another, making these transitions generally predictable and anticipated.

Non-normative transitions, on the other hand, do not occur in a set plan or schedule and are the result of important events that take place in an individual's life and to which she or he responds. For athletes, such transitions may include a season-ending injury, the loss of a personal coach or an unanticipated deselection from the team. As a result, these transitions are generally unpredicted, unanticipated and involuntary (Butt and Molnar, 2009). Non-normative transitions also include those which were expected or hoped for but which did not happen, labelled 'non-events' (Wylleman *et al.*, 2000). Not making the senior team although having made the final pre-selection, or not being able to participate in a major championship after years of preparation, are two examples of non-events.

RESEARCH BOX

Butt and Molnar (2009) examined athletes' involuntary sport career termination experiences. The authors noted differences between athletes who experienced forced retirement after competing at the highest level (professional and Olympic levels) and those who did not attain those levels of competition. The study focused on youth athletes who were in the talent development stages of their sporting career but failed to progress to the next competition level. A total of eight former high school athletes (both gender), representing six different sports took part in-depth individual interview. The participants had competed at the high school level for three of more years and experienced deselection from their team. Data were thematically content analysed, and the results revealed six themes, including anticipating success, warning signs, immediate reactions, expendability explanations, empathic resonance, and displacement.

The results indicated that although participants could not make team selection, while actively competing, they were *anticipating success* prior to perceived failure based on their off-season practice, coaches' premise, and high work rate. The findings represented participants' various perceived false hopes about 'making the team'. However, athletes also discussed feelings of doubt for being selected for their teams and began to notice *warning signs* of deselection based on changes in coaches' attitudes, including, a lack of coaches' attention and exclusion of them from practice sessions and changes in their position in the team. Athletes showed two different kinds of *immediate reactions* for the warning signs, including self-victimization (e.g., expressing disappointment and frustration) and rationalisation (e.g., seeing benefits of leaving sport). *Expendability explanations* included athletes' resentment toward their coaches, unrewarded efforts, and a lack of their ability in sport. The final theme was displacement, which refers to changes in social network, feeling of rejection, and experiences of adjustment to their post-sport lives after their actual leaving from sports. Participants showed a loss of social networks and building new social networks, searching for other interests outside sport, and an identity shift.

The authors discussed several issues, including athletes' unrealised expectations for making team during actively compete, coaches' roles and influences during the retirement process, and nature of competitive sport system which produces only few top-level athletes and more failures. Finding coaches' appropriate roles and attitudes which can contribute to athletes' healthy career transitions and examining ways to develop athletes' realistic perspectives during their team selection were suggested as future research directions.

   Career transitions are determined not only by the athlete's age and the structural/organisational characteristics of the world of sport itself, but also the individual's level of sporting achievement. As the level of achievement increases, an athlete will go from regional, to national and finally to international-level competitions. For example, competing in the Olympic Games was shown to have a long-lasting effect on the participation, personal satisfaction and fulfilment as well as the future Olympic success of athletes (Gould et al., 2002). Moreover, Bussmann and Alfermann's (1994) study on junior female track and field athletes also showed that they, who were among the very best in the world within their age category, also remained more often in elite sports as a senior athlete, than did the other junior athletes who were ranked lower in level of athletic performance. Making a transition successfully is, therefore, also related to the athlete's level of sporting achievements.

   In a classic study, Bloom (1985) identified three stages of talent development (within the fields of science, art and sport) that are delineated by specific transitions. These include the 'initiation stage' where young athletes are introduced to organised sports and are identified as talented athletes; the transition into the 'development stage' during which athletes become more dedicated to their sport and the amount of training and level of specialisation is increased; and the transition into the 'mastery' or 'perfection stage' in which athletes reach their highest level of athletic proficiency. Using retrospective qualitative data, Wylleman et al. (1993) related these stages to the ages at which former Olympic athletes made the relevant transitions: they transited into the initiation stage at the average age of 14 years; into the development stage at age 15; and into the mastery stage at 18 years of age. Although normative in nature, the age at which these transitions occur, as well as the age range in between transitions, may vary. Female gymnasts, for example, have been shown to end their competitive career between 15 and 19 years of age (Kerr and Dacyshyn, 2000), the same age at which male rowers have been found to make the transition from the development into the mastery stage (Wylleman et al., 1993). While the average tenure in professional baseball, football, basketball and ice hockey in the United States is between 4 and 7 years (Leonard, 1996), the mastery stage of Olympic-level athletes in Europe has been found to span on average 10–15 years (Wylleman et al., 1993).

   Based on this research, Wylleman and Lavallee (2004) proposed a transition model that takes a developmental perspective and reflects the concurrent and interactive nature of transitions throughout the career of the athlete at athletic, psychological, psychosocial and academic/vocational levels. As outlined in Figure 10.1, this model consists of four layers, with the top layer representing the stages and transitions athletes face in their athletic development, including the three stages identified by Bloom (1985), and a discontinuation stage. This latter stage was added in line with research reflecting that former elite athletes describe their transition out of competitive sport as a process, which could have a relatively long duration. The ages at which the transitions occur as well as the age range of the four athletic stages are based upon empirical data gathered from former Olympic athletes (Wylleman *et al.*, 1993; Wylleman, De Knop and Sillen, 1998), elite student-athletes (Wylleman and De Knop 1996) and talented young athletes (Wylleman and De Knop, 1997). The athletic transitions include the transition into organised competitive sports, transition into an intensive level of training and competitions, transition into the highest or elite level of competitions and transition out of competitive sports.

The second layer reflects the normative stages and transitions occurring at the psychological level. It consists of the developmental stages of childhood, adolescence and adulthood. Although not represented in the model itself, the developmental task of being psychologically ready for competition is related to childhood, while developing a self-identity is a developmental task during adolescence.

The third layer is representative of the changes that can occur in the athlete's psychosocial development relative to her or his athletic involvement. It is based upon conceptual frameworks related to the development of the athletic family (Hellstedt, 1995) and marital relationships, and was further qualified with empirical data on athletes' interpersonal relationships (e.g., Alfermann and Würth, 2001; Price and Weiss, 2000).

Figure 10.1   *Developmental model of transitions in sport*

AGE	10	15	20	25	30	35
Athletic level	Initiation	Development	Mastery/Perfection		Discontinuation	
Psychological level	Childhood	Adolescence	Adulthood			
Psychosocial level	Parents Siblings Peers	Peers Coach Parents	Partner Coach		Family (Coach)	
Academic/ vocational level	Primar education	Secondary education	Higher education	Vocational training Professional occupation		

Note: The age ranges at which the transitions occur are approximate

The final layer contains the specific stages and transitions at the academic/ vocational level. It reflects the transition into primary education/elementary school, the stage of secondary education/high school (including junior high, middle high and senior high) and the transition into higher education (college/ university). Although the transition into vocational training and/or a professional occupation may occur earlier (e.g., after high school), it was included after the stage of higher education. This reflects not only the 'predictable' sports career in some parts of the world (e.g., North America) where collegiate/university sport often bridges high school and professional sport (Petitpas, Brewer and Van Raalte, 1997), but also mirrors the current developments in Europe where many talented athletes continue their education up to the level of higher education (Wylleman and De Knop, 1996). For elite athletes this professional occupation may also be in the field of professional sports, and thus concurs with the mastery stage at the athletic level.

It should be noted that some normative transitions might not occur, thus becoming non-events. For example, due to a stagnating level of athletic achievement, an athlete may not make the transition to the next athletic developmental stage; or because of a lack of support, an athlete may discontinue his or her academic career and not make the transition into college. Although athletes will also often face non-normative transitions that may impact the quality of their participation in competitive sport, these are not included in the model.

METHODS AND MEASURES

A review of extant literature reveals that the methods and measures associated with the athlete's career have focused on three areas. The first of these areas concentrates on the causes of a career transition, and includes research on voluntary and involuntary reasons for career termination. The second area is related to developmental factors, in particular identity-related issues. The third area considers the various coping strategies that mediate the response to changes throughout an athlete's career.

Causes of career transition

Career transitions in sport have been found to be a function of a variety of involuntary and voluntary reasons (Lavallee, Gordon and Grove, 1997a). Although it has been suggested that the causes for a transition are influenced by the structure of sport, researchers have demonstrated that the most common of these causal factors are injuries, age, deselection and personal choice.

Unexpected and sudden career transitions out of sport often arise from injuries, and research supports the notion that transitions due to injuries are difficult because it is something for which individuals are seldom prepared. Kleiber and Brock's (1992) study of athletes who suffered career-ending injuries demonstrates that an injury need not be severe to force athletes out of continued participation in competitive sport. As Taylor and Lavallee (2010) have suggested, elite athletes perform at such a high level that even small reductions in their physical capabilities may be sufficient to make them no longer competitive at the elite level. Consequently, injuries have the potential to be the most distressful reason for a transition in sport.

Research by Mihovilovic (1968) with former Yugoslavian athletes revealed that retirement from sport is largely a function of the advancement of chronological age. In this descriptive survey of former professional soccer players, the decline in performance accompanying the ageing process was identified as the major cause for ending their careers. Taylor and Ogilvie (1998) maintain that retirement due to age is one of the most significant reasons because psychological motivation, social status and physical capabilities can all complicate an athlete's ability to continue competing at an elite level.

Related to the physiological consequences of chronological age is the structural factor of failing to progress to the next highest level of elite competition. This deselection process is largely a function of a 'survival of the fittest' philosophy that occurs at most levels of competitive sport. McInally *et al.*'s (1992) finding that 27 per cent of their sample were deselected from their teams demonstrates that this involuntary reason is a significant contributor to career termination from sport.

The final predominant factor that describes the career transitions of athletes is that of voluntary choice. Wylleman *et al.*'s (1993) research found that many individuals freely elect to disengage from sport for a combination of personal, social and psychological reasons. Some athletes may decide to retire because of financial complications, ethnic/gender-related issues and/or an overall lack of life satisfaction, whereas many others may simply want to spend more time with their families and friends. Although the voluntary decision to retire from sport is perhaps the most appealing reason, it should not be assumed that ending a career voluntarily eases the process.

As researchers have shown, the nature of each athlete's adjustment to a change in their career depends on a complex interaction of factors. Consistent with findings outside sport, Koukouris (1991, 1994) has demonstrated with surveys and interviews of former Greek athletes that no single factor is primarily responsible for ceasing participation in sport. In addition, qualitative research by Stambulova (1994) with Russian athletes has shown that athletic career termination occurs for a combination of reasons. Nevertheless, there is still a lack of research on the specific reasons for career transition, as well as the impact that voluntary and involuntary reasons have on the process.

Developmental factors

The quality of adjustment to sports career transitions also appears to be determined by a range of developmental factors. The majority of these components have been shown to be psychosocial in nature, with developmental experiences that occur during the athlete's career being particularly significant. The social identification and athletic identification with sport, however, appear to be the most fundamental of these issues related to the career of the athlete.

The way athletes react to any career transition appears to be dependent upon the diversity of their social identification with sport. Brewer (1993) has shown that individuals whose socialisation process occurs in an athletic environment may assume a narrow social identity, characterised as role restricted. Participation in high-level competition can also play an important role in the development of life skills, and many athletes may become severely inhibited in their ability to assume non-athletic roles (Murphy, 1995b). Researchers outside sport have discussed the importance of recognising that close identification with one's job may lead to adjustment difficulties upon retirement. This view has also been indirectly supported by studies in the sociology of sport literature on achievement motivation, in which social identity acts to reinforce athletes' decisions to continue their commitment in sport (Stevenson, 1990). In addition, sport psychologists have suggested that athletes with narrow social identities require greater adjustment during a career transition than those with broad-based identities (Brewer, Van Raalte and Petitpas, 2000; Lavallee, Gordon and Grove, 1997a). Hence, as Gordon and Lavallee (in press) have suggested, a need exists for some athletes to gradually resocialise out of strong and exclusive athletic identities, into non-sport participatory roles.

The influence of athletic participation on lifespan development has become an important issue recently. Although developmental research on career transitions is somewhat scarce, an individual's athletic identity, which has been defined as the degree to which an individual defines herself or himself in terms of the athlete role (Brewer, Van Raalte and Linder, 1993), has been hypothesised to have both positive and negative consequences for participants in sport. For example, several studies have found evidence to suggest that individuals with a strong athletic identity risk experiencing emotional difficulties following an athletic injury (e.g., Brewer, 1993). Research by Hale and Waalkes (1994) has also suggested that athletes high in athletic identity are more likely to utilise performance-enhancing drugs. At the same time, an exclusive identification with the athlete role may have positive effects on participation in sport, exercise adherence and athletic performance (Brewer, Van Raalte and Petitpas, 2000).

By way of interviews with former Greek and French athletes, Chamalidis (1995) has demonstrated that those who ascribe great importance to their involvement in sport are more at risk of experiencing transition-related difficulties than those who place less value on the athletic component of their self-identity. In addition, individuals who strongly commit themselves to the athletic role may be less likely to explore other career, education and lifestyle options during their careers. Along these lines, Murphy, Petitpas and Brewer (1996) have demonstrated, with a sample of intercollegiate athletes in the United States, that both athletic identity and 'identity foreclosure' are inversely related to career maturity. Identity foreclosure, the process by which individuals make commitments to roles without engaging in exploratory behaviour, has the potential to hinder the development of coping strategies that are essential during career transitions. As will be explained in the following section, however, few studies have been conducted on how athletes cope with changes in their career.

Coping resources

Whereas many athletes make successful and satisfying transitions throughout their careers, others may face severe difficulties for a variety of reasons. In the athlete's attempt to manage career changes, authors have suggested that those high in coping resources will tend to experience less stress than athletes with few coping skills (Grove et al., 1998). In the general literature outside sport, contemporary scholars have defined coping as constantly changing cognitive and behavioural efforts to manage specific external and/or internal demands that are appraised as taxing or exceeding the resources of the person (Lazarus and Folkman, 1984). Empirical and theoretical investigations on coping processes initially examined how people cope with stress in their lives from a trait-oriented perspective. This approach adopted a belief that variations in stressful occurrences are of little importance, and thus ignored the specific context in which coping takes place.

More recently, personality and social psychology researchers have challenged this viewpoint by focusing on the actual coping processes that people utilise when stressful episodes occur. In this process-oriented perspective, an emphasis is placed on global coping strategies used under particular circumstances, rather than how one reacts generally to a stressor. For example, Lazarus and Folkman (1984) have suggested that there are two broad coping strategies, 'problem-focused coping' and 'emotion-focused coping'. Endler and Parker (1990) have also proposed avoidance-oriented strategies as a third general class of coping resources. On the other hand, Carver, Scheier and Weintraub (1989) and Costa and McCrae (1989) believe that an examination of specific strategies might be more informative than an examination of global coping strategies. However, all these researchers are in agreement that coping is a complex, dynamic process.

A growing body of research is emerging on sport-related coping processes in order to identify how athletes appraise events during their playing careers. For example, several quantitative studies have assessed the relationship between performance and coping in specific sports. A number of qualitative investigations have also been conducted to examine which specific coping strategies are employed by competitive athletes in stressful situations. With regard to the careers of athletes, a number of theorists have discussed how coping resources influence the overall quality of adjustment to retirement from sport (e.g., Gordon and Lavallee, in press; Taylor and Lavallee, 2010). Sinclair and Orlick (1993) have also made an empirical investigation into this by employing the *Athlete*

Retirement Questionnaire to survey athletes who had represented Canada in international competitions. In this study it was found that keeping busy, training, exercising and having a new focus were the most beneficial coping strategies utilised during the first few months of retirement. These results confirmed the preliminary findings of Werthner and Orlick (1986) and Baillie (1993), who found that having a new focus after retirement predicted better adjustment. These collective results, combined with the available data on social support and pre-retirement planning as described below, have shown the importance of coping resources both during and after the athlete's career.

As previously discussed with regard to Schlossberg's (1981) model of transition, changes throughout an athlete's career depend largely on the availability of social support. Social support has been defined as an exchange of resources between at least two individuals perceived by the provider or the recipient to be intended to enhance the well-being of the recipient (Shumaker and Brownell, 1984). The importance of social support networks among both active and injured athletes has been described in detail in the literature (e.g., Rees *et al.*, 2010), with Reynolds' (1981) study of nearly 600 former professional football players in the United States being perhaps the first to outline the general importance of social support during a career transition. Several other researchers and theorists have documented the importance of social support among friends, family and team mates. Alfermann (2000), for example, reported that coaches were the main social support agent among a sample of former track and field athletes from West Germany. However, Kane's (1995) earlier study of former professional athletes demonstrated that the social support networks of athletes also suffer.

It has been asserted that pre-retirement planning is an effective coping skill for athletes nearing the end of their career (Taylor and Lavallee, 2010). Research outside sport has demonstrated that such planning is significantly related to a more effective adjustment following retirement from the labour force, and that activities such as occupational counselling, continuing education and social networking can all have a positive impact on the adaptation process. Research on participation motivation in sport has also suggested that individuals who plan alternative areas in which to direct their attention are more likely to experience positive transitions. Despite the fact that retirement from sport is one of the only certainties in the career of the athlete, a recurring theme in the literature is the resistance on the part of athletes to plan for their inevitable career end.

Utilising the *Professional Athletes Career Transition Inventory*, Blann and Zaichkowsky (1989) reported that only 37 per cent of professional ice hockey players and 25 per cent of professional baseball players in North America had a post-sport career plan before retirement. Although this career indecision among athletes has also been illustrated in other research projects, it has become clear that a sport structure that requires excessive time and energy commitments leaves athletes with little time for pre-retirement planning during their careers.

The *Australian Athletes Career Transition Inventory* was developed by Hawkins and Blann (1993) to assess the career transition needs and post-athletic career awareness of a large sample of athletes and coaches. In this study, 57 per cent of coaches considered pre-retirement planning to be an essential part of the career transition process, but believed that athletes must take responsibility for the utilisation of available programmes. On the other hand, over 98 per cent of the athletes surveyed indicated that they were primarily responsible for the utilisation of programmes and services offered to them, and that this could have a significant impact on their playing careers. This finding is supported by the results of a survey conducted by Petitpas *et al.* (1990) with athletes in the United States. In this study it was reported that some athletes believed that investing effort in the career development process would detract from their sport performance. Sinclair and Orlick (1993) have also reported how athletes consider that coaches and institutional networks should treat retiring/retired athletes with respect rather than as disposable commodities. Although some coaches around the world may have fears that the promotion of pre-retirement planning programmes will distract athletes from their focus on high-level achievement, several others may envision that such preparation can ultimately contribute to the success of athletic teams. As Murphy (1995b) has suggested, many athletes believe that planning for another career actually decreases their anxiety regarding the transition process because it allows them to concentrate more fully on their sport. Therefore, as Gordon and Lavallee (in press) suggest, the influence of coaches, who are often prone to operate as ideologists focused on winning rather than as educators, in promoting discussions about career transition issues may be the most significant determinant of the effectiveness of available intervention programmes.

PRACTICAL ISSUES AND INTERVENTIONS

In recent years, numerous career intervention programmes for athletes have been developed in countries around the world (see Table 10.1). The existing programmes vary in format and often include workshops, seminars, educational modules and individual counselling. As described in Wylleman *et al.* (1999), the majority of programmes focus on lifestyle management and the development of transferable skills that can assist individuals in making the transition from life in sport into a post-sport career. As such, these programmes provide athletes with an introduction to career planning and development by focusing on values and interest exploration, career awareness and decision making, CV preparation, interview techniques and job search strategies.

Career development programmes for athletes are primarily managed by national sports governing bodies, national Olympic committees, specific sport federations, universities and independent organisations linked to sport settings.

Table 10.1 *Athlete career intervention programmes*

Programme country	Athlete retirement programme Ireland Irish Institute of Sport	Organisation
Athlete Career and Education (ACE) Programme	Australia/UK	Australian Institute of Sport/UK Sports Institute
Olympic Job Opportunities Programme (OJOP)	International	Ernst & Young
Olympic Athlete Career Centre (OACC)	Canada	Canadian Olympic Association
Career Assistance Program for Athletes (CAPA)	US	United States Olympic Committee
Making the Jump Program	US	Advisory Resource Center for Athletes
Women's Sports Foundation Athlete Service	US	Women's Sports Foundation
Career Transition Program	US	National Football League
CHAMPS/Life Skills	US	National Collegiate Athletics Association
Study and Talent Education Programme	Belgium	Free University of Brussels
The Retiring Athlete	The Netherlands	Dutch Olympic Committee

While some programmes address the needs of professional athletes, the majority have been developed for a much wider population. In the following section, an overview of some of the most advanced career intervention programmes for athletes will be described, including the Olympic Job Opportunities Programme (OJOP), Career Assistance Program for Athletes (CAPA), Olympic Athlete Career Centre (OACC) and Athlete Career and Education (ACE) Programme. Practical considerations in the provision of career interventions for athlete will then be described.

The OJOP is an international programme that has been initiated in Australia, South Africa and the United States. Sponsored by the company Ernst & Young, the principal goal of OJOP is to develop and source career opportunities for Olympians and potential Olympians. Eligible athletes are either current or Olympic-calibre athletes who need to be certified as such by their respective national federations. In addition to providing direct employer contacts and identifying job positions, OJOP provides career analysis services, personality aptitude testing and interview skills training (Gordon and Lavallee, in press).

A grant from the US Olympic Foundation was awarded to OJOP in 1988 to create a programme to assist elite athletes in coping with the transition out of active sport competition. Following a survey of approximately 1800 Olympic and other elite-level athletes, the CAPA was established to introduce individuals to the career development process while they were competing. This programme was based on the lifespan development model of Danish and D'Augelli (1983), and focused on increasing athletes' sense of personal competence through understanding and identifying transferable skills. A number of one-day workshops were organised around three main themes: managing the emotional and social impact of transitions; increasing understanding and awareness of personal qualities relevant to coping with transitions and career development; and introducing information about the world of work. Although these workshops were well received by the athletes (Petitpas et al., 1990), funding for the CAPA was terminated in 1993.

One of the first career development programmes to be developed for athletes was the OACC in Canada. The OACC was launched in 1985 as part of the Canadian Olympic Association (COA) following a series of needs-based surveys conducted in 1983–4. The original centre, which was based in Toronto, had a mandate to assist athletes through the transition process to a second career, primarily through career and education planning (Sinclair and Hackfort, 2000). Athletes who had achieved approved rankings by way of their performances at Olympic, Commonwealth and Pan Pacific Games had access to the OACC (Anderson and Morris, 2000).

Sinclair and Hackfort (2000) outlined the following career development services that were initially offered through the OACC:

- Clarification of career planning needs, self-assessment, aptitude/interest assessment to assist in the identification of specific occupations of interest, decision-making and action-planning skills
- Booklets were written and made available to all eligible athletes on the topics of CV preparation, interview preparation, job search techniques and information for interviewing
- Retirement planning focused on what athletes should expect during the adjustment period. Transition workshops and peer support groups were established to help athletes deal effectively with the career transition process
- Reference letters of support were provided by the COA, as well as personalised business cards bearing the COA logo for networking purposes
- A shadow programme was developed in 1990 to provide athletes with the opportunity to explore career options by 'shadowing' professionals in the field of their choice.

In recent years, the COA has initiated a reorganisation process, resulting in an increase in the number of centres operating within Canada, as well as additions to the career development services provided. There currently are Olympic Athlete Career Centres operating in Calgary, Montreal, Ottawa, Toronto and Vancouver, each employing consultants to work with athletes living in or around these locations (Anderson and Morris, 2000). The standardisation of service provision across centres is ongoing, influenced by the need and utility of the services for the athlete population in each region.

The ACE Programme was developed in Australia by the Victorian Institute of Sport in 1990, and was later amalgamated with the Lifeskills for Elite Athletes Program (SportsLEAP) in 1995. SportsLEAP was originally established in 1989 by the Australian Institute of Sport, based on the results of a needs-based survey following the 1988 Seoul Olympics (Fortunato et al., 1995). This programme was highly successful, but the scope and content of each programme varied according to athlete demand in each state institute/academy of sport. Thus, a decision was made to integrate SportsLEAP and the ACE Programme (under the ACE name) to form a national programme in Australia.

The overall objective of the ACE programme is to help athletes to balance the demands of their sporting careers while enhancing their opportunities to develop their educational and vocational skills (Anderson and Morris, 2000). A major component of the programme is to assist individuals in developing a career plan that integrates both sporting and non-sporting components. The philosophy is to create an environment where athletes can be encouraged to be independent, self-reliant and have a capacity to meet the demands associated with elite sport.

As outlined in Anderson and Morris (2000), the following services are provided through the Australian ACE Programme:

- Individual athlete assessments are used to provide a structured process in which to assess individual athletes' educational, vocational, financial and personal development needs
- More than thirty personal development training courses, which are structured to assist athletes in meeting their sporting, educational and career aspirations. Many of these courses provide individuals with nationally accredited, competency-based education programmes
- A nationally consistent career and education planning process is employed to enable athletes to manage their own individual vocational requirements. Career development is provided in the form of direct assistance in finding employment through career advice, training paths and vocational training. Secondary and tertiary education support is provided through networking with individuals in secondary schools, universities who can offer unit or course selection advice, as well as assistance in negotiating appropriate academic and residential arrangements for athletes (e.g., quiet halls of residence,

appropriate and sufficient dietary provisions at appropriate times, distance and online learning opportunities)

■ A transition programme provides career and education guidance for elite athletes who are undergoing a transition to a post-sporting career

■ Training opportunities and supervised practice for ACE staff is provided through a Graduate Certificate in Athlete Career and Education Management that has recently been developed by Victoria University in Australia

■ Direct athlete needs-based assessments provide a structured process to assess athletes' eligibility for support.

ACE services are available to over 3000 elite-level athletes throughout Australia. The United Kingdom Sports Institute has also recently initiated the ACE UK Programme across England, Scotland, Wales and Northern Ireland. To be eligible for assistance in Australia, athletes must be a scholarship holder with the Australian Institute of Sport, state institutes/academies of sport, or Olympic Athlete Program participants. ACE managers and advisors are employed in each state institute/academy of sport in Australia, and a national manager coordinates the programme.

Based the existing career programmes for athletes, a number of practical considerations in the provision of career interventions can be suggested. For example, one general aim could be to assist and guide athletes via multiformats (e.g., 'one-on-one' or group counselling, written information, skills enhancement programmes) to manage and cope with their career development in such a way that they are able to achieve optimal well-being, as well as maximise their potential in their different spheres of daily life (Wylleman *et al.*, 1999). Career development programmes for athletes, therefore, need to be multidimensional and include enhancement, support, and counselling components (Petitpas, Brewer and Van Raalte, 1996).

Career programmes for athletes should also not be solely focused on post-retirement interventions. Although Grove *et al.* (1998) have found evidence to suggest that as many as 20 per cent of elite-level athletes experience distressful reactions to retirement from sport, Gorely *et al.* (2001) found that athletes often do not consider retirement as an issue until its proximity draws near. Intervention programmes, therefore, should focus on functional adjustments in the pre-retirement phase, while the emphasis in the post-retirement period should be on the provision of support with regard to emotional adjustment (Baillie, 1993). If the career transition process of athletes is to be enhanced, it also appears critical to educate athletes of the need for long-term career development planning.

Another point in the development of a career intervention programmes for athletes is related to the organisational context of these programmes. Petitpas and Champagne (2000) underline the need to consider the idiosyncrasies of the targeted sport or sports group (e.g., type of sport, nature of the competitive events in which the athletes participate), and the structural aspects of the programme (e.g., group size, programme format and scheduling, required or voluntary participation). Moreover, the financial aspects of developing and running career intervention programmes may require the backing of the major sport federations.

CASE STUDY

Tony is a 21-year-old elite-level middle-distance runner who was informed earlier in the week that he was not selected for the national team going to the World Championships. These championships were going to be his final opportunity to qualify for the Olympic Games, and he has made an appointment to see a sport psychologist to discuss his non-selection. At the start of the meeting he tells the sport psychologist that he 'does not think it is fair that some people just suddenly decided that he could no longer do what we have trained so long and hard for'. He later expresses concerns about what he is going to do next, and says that his 'coach has always said that he shouldn't concentrate on anything other than athletics if he wanted to retain his place on the squad'.

---

1. With reference to the Theories and Models section in the chapter, how would you interpret what is happening in this case study?
2. With reference to Methods and Measures, what techniques would you employ to help to understand and quantify the issues?
3. With reference to Practical Issues and Interventions, how would you deal with this situation?

STUDY QUESTIONS

1. Contrast social gerontology models with thanatology models with regard to the athlete's career.
2. Outline Schlossberg's (1981) model of human adaptation to transition, and discuss how it has been used to describe the athlete's career.
3. Define athletic identity and explain its importance in the sports career transition process.
4. Compare the Olympic Athlete Career Centre with the Athlete Career and Education Programme with regard to the services provided to athletes.
5. Describe some of the practical considerations in the provision of career interventions for athletes.

FURTHER READING

Lavallee, D. and Wylleman, P. (2000) (eds) *Career Transitions in Sport: International Perspectives* (Morgantown, WV: Fitness Information Technology).

Meeker, D. J., Stankovich, C. E. and Kays, T. M. (2000) *Positive Transitions for Student Athletes* (Scottsdale, AZ: Holcomb Hathaway).

Petitpas, A., Champagne, D., Chartand, J., Danish, S. and Murphy, S. (1997) *Athlete's Guide to Career Planning* (Champaign, IL: Human Kinetics).

Taylor, J. and Lavallee, D. (2010) 'Career Transition among Athletes: Is There Life after Sports?' In J. M. Williams (eds), *Applied Sport Psychology: Personal Growth to Peak Performance,* 6th edn (Columbus, OH: McGraw-Hill), 542–62.

Wylleman, P., Alfermann, D. and Lavallee, D. (2004) 'Career Transitions in Sport: European Perspectives', *Psychology of Sport and Exercise,* 5, 7–20.

11 Exercise and Mental Health

INTRODUCTION, HISTORY AND DEVELOPMENT

'Mens Sana in Corpore Sano', or 'a healthy mind in a healthy body, is a motif that has long been familiar to exercise psychologists, but do the two happily co-exist or is the relationship more complicated? This question lies at the heart of this chapter, and likewise is central to the work of many exercise psychologists, those who consider the psychological 'pros and cons' physical activity (Buckworth and Dishman, 2007). When considering the potential benefits and hazards of exercise, from the start it is important to highlight the distinction between the somatic and the psychological, or the body and the mind. With regard to the body we are constantly reminded that physical activity can play a positive role in the prevention and treatment of a range of medical conditions, and that a physically active lifestyle corresponds with a healthy lifestyle. At the same time all the evidence points to a world population that is becoming increasingly sedentary and overweight. Recent statistics from the World Health Organisation (2010; http://www.who.int/dietphysicalactivity/publications/facts/obesity/en/) estimate that of a world population approaching seven billion there are now over one billion people who are overweight (i.e, with a Body Mass Index (BMI) of over 25 kg/m^2) and of these, around 300 million would be defined as clinically obese (i.e., with a BMI of over 30 kg/m^2). What is more this problem is not only confined to affluent western societies but is becoming endemic across large parts of the globe. Within the United States, according to the Surgeon General, the number of overweight children has doubled and the number of overweight adolescents has trebled since 1980. These statistics present serious problems to many societies, where an increasingly large proportion of health care is devoted to weight-related issues (estimated at around 7% worldwide).

For many, with the growth of technology and mechanisation, exercise is no longer a necessity but has become a lifestyle choice for a small minority (Dishman, 2001), and across each population there are large variations in participation in physical activity (see Trost *et al.*, 2002). Sadly, when given the choice many people choose not to exercise, and as a consequence governments increasingly have endeavoured to find ways of stirring their populations into action or activity.

For example, the UK government launched its multifaceted Healthy Living initiative in 2007, designed to identify the main areas where families with children under 11 need further support to limit the risk of unhealthy weight gain, and to break down barriers to a healthier diet and increased participation in physical activity. In Scotland, the Active Nation programme likewise aims to encourage the Scots to be more active in their everyday lives in the run up to the 2014 Commonwealth Games and beyond.

Recent reviews of physical activity interventions (Foster, Hillsdon and Thorogood, 2008; Owen *et al.*, 2006; Van Sluijs, McMinn and Griffin, 2007) have found that in general they can be successful in increasing physical activity and improving cardio-vascular fitness across various populations in the short to medium term and especially where the intervention involves professional guidance and support along with self-direction. These studies also reveal the vast array of personal and environmental factors that impact on participation rates and the need for ever-more sophisticated modelling of how these variables interact to determine activity rates across any population (Giles-Corti *et al.*, 2005).

On a positive note, there is growing evidence that doctors now look upon physical exercise as offering itself as a valuable prescription for a variety of ailments, both physical and psychological (Faulkner and Taylor, 2005; Stathopoulou *et al.*, 2006; Swain and Leutholtz, 2007).

Alongside these findings, research evidence confirms the long-term protection that regular exercise is able to provide against many somatic complaints and including cardiovascular disease (CVD), hypertension, non-insulin dependent diabetes, diabetes mellitus, obesity, stroke, some cancers, and osteoporosis (Biddle, Fox and Boutcher, 2000). Turning to the long-term psychological effects of exercise, the evidence suggests a rather more complex landscape (Landers and Arent, 2007; Stathopoulou *et al.*, 2006), based on an exercise psychology literature that has grown significantly over recent decades and has brought together those with backgrounds in neuroscience, psychopharmacology, sport science, psychology, psychophysiology and physiology. This diverse literature offers generally positive support for the role that exercise can play in the promotion of mental health (Biddle and Mutrie, 2008; Herring, O'Connor and Dishman, 2010; McAuley, 1994; Stathopoulou *et al.*, 2006). Optimism is founded on a number of studies that have identified the positive relationship between exercise and psychological health, and most especially among clinical populations. While this relationship is well established (Smits and Otto, 2009), unfortunately our understanding of both the direction of causality and the relationship between psychosocial and physiological changes remains best defined as unfinished business (De Moor *et al.*, 2008; Morgan and Dishman, 2001, Van de Vliet, Mutrie and Onghena, 2005). Equally, it is appropriate to proceed with caution as the good news story is not without qualifications, and most especially where motives for engaging in exercise in the first place may be unhealthy, and where continuance moves beyond habit to signs of morbidity, abuse or even addiction (Adams and Kirkby, 2002), more commonly referred to as 'excessive exercise' (Loumidis and Roxborough, 1995).

On a more positive note, over the last 25 years a number of significant position papers (see Biddle and Mutrie, 2007; Grant, 2000; Smits and Otto, 2009) have confirmed that particular psychological dysfunctions, most notably depression, anxiety and stress, can benefit from an involvement in physical activity (Landers and Arent, 2007). The reported evidence is reasonably strong for non-clinical conditions but is more compelling in terms of those with existing mental health problems. Before moving on to consider theoretical and practical considerations, key findings in relation to specific psychological conditions will be reviewed and in particular those most often cited in the exercise psychology literature – depression, anxiety, mood state, schizophrenia, self esteem, stress responsivity, pre-menstrual syndrome and body image.

Depression

Depression is a universal human malaise. It has been estimated that between 13 and 20 per cent of the world's population have experience of clinical or sub-clinical depression (Winokur, 1986) and that in 2001, it is estimated that 121 million people worldwide suffered from depression (World Health Organisation, 2001). Studies from both the United States and Europe indicate a lifetime prevalence of between 5 and 12 per cent for males and 9 and 12 per cent or females (Hirschfield and Cross, 1982). Furthermore the incidence of clinical depression seems to increase with age, with prevalence rates perhaps as high as 10% among people over 65 years of age and up to 20 per cent among those over 80.

Laird and Benefield (1995) categorised the target symptoms of depression, dividing these into the emotional, cognitive, psychotic and physical. Emotionally, individuals may report feelings of worthlessness, guilt and shame; they may discuss thoughts of death and suicide, sadness, chronic pessimism, irritability and an inability to continue to derive pleasure from previously enjoyable activities. In cognitive terms depression can interfere with the ability to concentrate, make decisions and is often associated with poor memory. In its psychotic forms bizarre behaviour can occur, taking the form of delusions and hallucinations. Physically, people may report lethargy, insomnia, tardiness of movement, reduced libido and a disinterest in personal hygiene.

Of a number of thorough reviews of the relationship between depression and exercise (see Ströhle, 2009; Ernst, Rand and Stevenson, 1998; Lawlor and Hopker, 2001; O'Neal, Dunn and Martinson, 2000; Stathopoulou et al., 2006), one of the earliest and yet still most significant was that carried out in the late 1980s by North, McCullagh and Tran (1990). Their synoptic, meta-analytic study was based on 80 studies carried out between 1969 and 1989 with their final analysis referencing over 290 effect sizes. Their analysis demonstrated that physical exercise did have an antidepressant effect both immediately and in the longer term. Exercise was found to be most effective in decreasing depression among those who were most unhealthy to begin with and among older age groups, and the effect was equivalent across the sexes. This is an interesting finding given that women tend to report more symptoms of depression than men and are less inclined to exercise under any circumstances, let alone when feeling depressed (Hays, 1999). All modes of exercise, both aerobic and anaerobic, have been found to be effective and the longer the exercise programme (duration) and the greater the total number of sessions (intensity), the more sizeable the decrease in depression. The greatest effects were found after 17 weeks of exercise although positive effects were noted after as few as four weeks. Finally, exercise was found to be a particularly potent antidepressant in an adjunctive sense, which is when combined with other forms of therapy and in particular psychotherapy. Later reviews confirmed this analysis (e.g., Ernst, Rand and Stevenson, 1998), leading Tkachuk and Martin (1999) to conclude:

> Regular exercise is a viable, cost-effective treatment for mild to moderate depression and may serve as a useful adjunct in the comprehensive treatment of more severe episodes of the disorder. Nonaerobic forms of exercise such as strength training are as effective as aerobic exercise in treating depression. Moreover, less strenuous forms of regular exercise, such as walking, may be sufficient to demonstrate significant treatment effects; however, more research is necessary to confirm initial findings.
>
> (p. 280)

In a more recent review, Ströhle (2009) continued to echo many of the original findings of the North, McCullagh and Tran (1990) work. Specifically, she found evidence to suggest that exercise may impact on severe cases of clinical depression, although the precise 'dose' of exercise still remains to be determined (Dunn, Madhukar and Trivedi, 2005) and further work is also required to see how those who are depressed can be encouraged to take exercise, when the very nature of their illness may act as a deterrent. Of all the mental illnesses, clinical depression is the one that shows the most consistent positive response to exercise, with the most powerful effects being noted among clinical populations (Ströhle, 2009). More limited evidence would suggest that aerobic exercise may be most effective and including activities such as walking, jogging, cycling, light circuit training, and weight training, and that exercise regimes extending over several months appear to yield the most positive effects although positive effects can be derived almost immediately. Hence, there is compelling evidence to suggest that physical exercise can have a positive and lasting impact on clinical depression, with the reported efficacy of exercise as a treatment being comparable to antidepressant medication – and much cheaper! (Blumenthal *et al.*, 2007).

Anxiety

Hays (1999) describes a client, referred to as Gordon, who reported a series of panic attacks, high levels of anxiety, a desire for relaxation and a felt need for higher self-confidence:

> I don't feel in charge of my life. I have a real problem with unknowns. I am physically tense much of the time. I don't enjoy myself enough. I'm easily threatened by things and take criticism the wrong way. I'm way too sensitive.
>
> (p. 87)

This description could apply to an experience that many people will be familiar with but often in an acute, transient sense, perhaps precipitated by a particularly stressful life event. In Gordon's case, the unwanted, maladaptive persistence of these intense feelings came to represent a pathological state, and it is these more persistent forms of anxiety that are increasingly recognised as a significant public health issue. For example, within the United States it is estimated that 7.3% of the population could qualify for treatment for anxiety (Raglin, 1997). The long term effects of this type of recurring anxiety can include chronic tiredness, decreased ability to work and irritability, along with somatic complaints such as headaches, nausea and gastrointestinal disorders (American Psychiatric Association, 1994).

In an early experiment in this field, De Vries (1981) famously examined the effects of a bout of acute walking on muscle tension in elderly participants. A control group received the anxiolytic drug meprobamate. In reporting that the walkers had subsequently lower muscle tension readings than those in the control condition, DeVries concluded that exercise can exert a form of 'tranquiliser effect'. This study, and the term which it spawned, was exciting from many perspectives, suggesting that exercise could reduce anxiety without the chemical dependency and expense which until that time had been associated with traditional pharmaceutical remedies.

Since 1980 there have been over numerous reviews of the effects of exercise on anxiety and an increasingly sophisticated multidisciplinary literature describing the relationship between anxiety and exercise (Raglin, 1997; Herring, O'Connor and Dishman, 2010). Despite this concerted effort, and evidence that exercise does reduce anxiety and especially among those who are sedentary and with chronic illness Herring, O'Connor and Dishman, 2010), there is no consensus as to which forms of exercise have the most positive anxiolytic effects (Scully et al., 1998).

One of the most important reviews in this area was carried out in the late 1980s by Petruzzello et al. (1991). More specifically, they performed three meta-analyses of exercise effects on state anxiety, trait anxiety and psychophysiological correlates of anxiety. With regard to state anxiety, an analysis of 207 studies revealed a mean effect size of 0.24 (SE=0.04), representing a small reduction in state anxiety of around 0.25 standard deviation units. The reviewers also found exercise to be as efficacious as other forms of therapy such as relaxation, quiet rest or meditation. Modes of exercise were then broadly divided into non-aerobic (e.g., weight training) and aerobic, the latter being subdivided into activities including jogging, walking, running and swimming. Among the aerobic forms of exercise no differences were found. However, and in contrast to research on depression, non-aerobic exercise was not associated with reductions in state anxiety. While aerobic exercise yielded an effect size of 0.26, the effect for non-aerobic exercise was negligible (–0.05). In keeping with this finding some have speculated that there is a need for exercise to involve deep abdominal breathing in order to have an effect, in a manner somewhat similar to deep breathing relaxation techniques.

Interesting results emerged in terms of the duration of exercise. In cases where exercise lasted less than 20 minutes the effect size was 0.21, while for exercise lasting between 21 and 30 minutes, or even longer, the effect size rose to 0.41. Tentatively it is tempting to infer that perhaps a dose-dependent relationship exists between anxiolytic properties and exercise duration although this assumption awaits further testing.

In their second meta-analysis the reviewers examined 62 studies involving trait anxiety and exercise, and here they found a stronger overall effect size of 0.34 (SE=0.06). Interestingly there were no differences in terms of different trait anxiety measures, exercise intensity, age, health status or type of comparison group. Not surprisingly the greatest effect sizes were observed in studies that followed experimental designs characterised by a higher degree of methodological rigour. Also, as with state anxiety, the length of the exercise programme was significant, with programmes lasting in excess of nine weeks having much stronger effects than shorter programmes, and those lasting over 16 weeks having the strongest effect. The authors concluded that for reductions in trait anxiety to occur regular exercise needs to be completed for more than 10 weeks, which clearly makes intuitive sense given the relatively stable, dispositional nature of trait anxiety.

Finally, the review highlighted a strong effect size of 0.56 (SE=0.06) for psychophysiological effects of exercise. From a total of 138 studies they examined changes in physiological parameters related to anxiety including systolic and diastolic blood pressure, heart rate, skin measures, EMG (electromyography) and CNS measures such as EEG (electrocephalography) alpha or Hoffman reflex. The weakest effects were observed in those studies that measured heart rate or blood pressure while EMG measures exhibited large though localised effect sizes.

The classic Petruzzello et al. (1991) review illustrates that where studies have been well designed then exercise appears to exert tangible, measurable anxiolytic (i.e. anxiety reducing) effects of both a physiological and psychological nature.

Additionally their conclusions reinforce the necessity for persistence with an exercise regimen, given the 21-minute threshold for state anxiety reductions and the 10-week period before trait anxiety can be expected to improve.

In a later meta-analysis, Long and Stavel (1995) specifically examined studies that had distinguished between those who were coping with stress and those who were not. They concluded that aerobic exercise training programmes were effective in reducing anxiety and particularly among those who were experiencing chronic work stress. Herring, O'Connor and Dishman (2010) carried out a meta-analysis of 40 reported studies between 1995 and 2007 that involved exercise training for sedentary adults with chronic illness. Their analysis revealed that exercise training did reduce anxiety symptoms significantly, and especially where the programme lasted no more than 12 weeks, with sessions running for at least 30 minutes.

Reflecting on this literature, Scully *et al.* (1998) note that there is still uncertainty as to what level of exercise intensity is required for anxiolytic effects to occur. This lack of consensus was also noted by Landers and Petruzzello (1994) who observed that some sources recommend low intensity activity such as walking or jogging at around 40–50 per cent of maximum heart rate, others recommend moderate aerobic exercise at around 50–60 per cent while another school of thought espouses the virtues of high intensity activity at 70 per cent of maximum and above. Given this state of uncertainty, Scully *et al.* (1998) conclude that it may be safest to follow the earlier advice of Franks and Jette (1970) and afford individuals the freedom to exercise at a self-selected level of intensity chosen in collaboration with a physician, a view supported strongly by Szabo (2003). This seems a particularly sensible policy given the goal setting literature which suggests that adherence is greater when personal, relative goals are given preference over absolute, externally prescribed ones.

Research in this area has refuted criticisms of earlier studies that implied that anxiety reduction following exercise represented no more than a methodological artefact (Gauvin and Brawley, 1993). At the same time, explicating the variables that mediate the relationship between exercise and anxiety reduction has proved problematic, a task made doubly difficult because so few studies specify levels of intensity, duration, and/or length of exercise programme (Ströhle, 2009). To date, the majority of research studies have involved aerobic exercise, with the few studies examining non-aerobic activities (e.g., strength/flexibility training) actually revealing slight increases in anxiety. Although further research is obviously needed, it does appear that aerobic activity is more beneficial for anxiety reduction (Merom *et al.*, 2007).

The duration of individual training sessions has been considered across individual studies, with somewhat surprising results. According to recent research, even a single, five minute exercise bout may be sufficient to induce an anxiolytic effect (Long and Stavel, 1995). In terms of the length of training programmes, both clinical and non-clinical studies have revealed that the largest anxiolytic effects are noted when programmes have run from 10 to 15 weeks or even longer, with smaller effects observed for programmes lasting fewer than nine weeks.

In conclusion, the literature supports the positive effects that exercise can have on anxiety (Landers and Arent, 2007; Raglin, 1997), with even short bursts of exercise seemingly sufficient to produce a positive effect. The nature of the exercise does not appear to be crucial although the most positive effects tend to be noted among those who adhere to programmes for a considerable period of time, perhaps months.

Stress responsivity

A related literature has considered how exercise may protect against the negative effects of stress (Landers and Arent, 2007; Salmon, 2001). The available research suggests that increases in physical condition or improved fitness are likely to facilitate the individual's capacity for dealing with stress, and in turn this may protect the individual from other psychological illnesses. In reviewing this work Fillingim and Blumenthal (1993) made an important distinction between research based on either cross-sectional (i.e., categorising participants as 'fit' or 'unfit' before observing differences between the groups) or longitudinal designs (i.e., using training and control groups and comparing performance over time). Results derived from both procedures are best described as equivocal; while the majority do show that physical fitness correlates with a reduction in the physiological response to psychological stress, a smaller number of studies report negligible differences in stress reactivity between the physically fit and the less fit.

True experimental training studies remain rare although more recent contributions are attempting first to manipulate levels of aerobic fitness experimentally and second, to correlate these fitness levels with stress responsivity. In addition, a number of studies have found that aerobic exercise does appear to influence stress responses. In each of these studies, comparisons have been drawn between aerobic exercise and anaerobic strength training, with participants typically exercising at least three times a week at moderate intensity for 12 weeks. While the effect appears robust, other studies that have employed a similar exercise paradigm and have used similar measures have failed to replicate these results (Salmon, 2001; Sothmann, Hart and Horn, 1991).

In conclusion, while it may be that aerobically fit individuals do show a reduced psychosocial stress response (Landers and Arent, 2007), the role that exercise can play is probably best described as preventative rather than corrective, and the stress response itself remains only partially understood (Salmon, 2001). With these caveats in mind, it would appear that a regime of aerobic exercise (continuous exercise of sufficient intensity to elevate heart rate significantly above resting pulse rate for over 21 minutes duration) may significantly enhance stress responsivity, and in particular stress which is related to lifestyle or work.

Mood state

Numerous studies have investigated the mood-enhancing properties of exercise and have demonstrated that exercise can indeed have a positive influence on mood state (e.g., Crabbe, Smith and Dishman, 1999; Landers and Arent, 2007). However, early optimism generated by studies of clinical samples has been tempered by the discovery that the effects may not be as pervasive across non-clinical populations and that methodological problems may well have coloured existing results (Scully *et al.*, 1998). Research also suggests that the relationship may be far more complex than earlier research may have thought. For example, Lennox, Bedell and Stone (1990) found no significant improvements in long-term mood states among non-clinical samples while other studies have found improvements to be gender-specific and dependent on the type of exercise, whether aerobic or anaerobic (Cramer, Nieman and Lee, 1991; Maroulakis and Zervas, 1993). Steinberg, Sykes and LeBoutillier (1997) compared different intensity (low-impact/high-impact) aerobic exercise of 25-minutes duration with a passive control group and found increases in positive moods and decreases in negative moods following exercise. A further study (Head *et al.*, 1996) considered whether a lengthy bout of acute aerobic exercise would attenuate the adverse mood effects induced by prescribed beta-blockers to normal healthy individuals. Results showed that one hour of moderate (50% maximum) treadmill walking was able to produce mood states comparable to those recorded from participants in placebo trials. The authors concluded that exercise prescription should be considered a highly desirable adjuvant therapy in cases where drug therapy is necessary.

Overall such studies suggest that various forms of exercise, both aerobic and anaerobic, can be associated with an elevation of mood state, and in particular for clinical samples, although given the diversity of results it is likely that more than one underlying mechanism may be implicated. The nature of these mechanisms, whether psychosocial, psychological, psychopharmacological or psychophysiological, has yet to be fully understood. The reliance on simplistic, traditional unipolar measures of mood, and especially Profile of Mood States (POMS; McNair, Lorr and Droppleman, 1981), may not have helped this endeavour (Gauvin and Spence, 1998), and certainly recent moves toward more sophisticated measures of affective state is a welcome advance (see Buckworth and Dishman, 2002).

Schizophrenia

In comparison with other conditions, schizophrenia has received relatively little attention but the limited evidence that is available would suggest that those suffering from schizophrenia or related illnesses do benefit from exercise (Gorczynski and Faulkner, 2010). Specifically, it would appear that exercise may help alleviate some of the negative symptoms without necessarily improving positive signs of well-being.

Self-esteem

Sonstroem (1997) notes that reflecting upon oneself is a universally favoured mental pastime and that self-esteem is the one psychological variable that tends to transpose most powerfully onto life adjustment more generally. Duly, psychologists have come to recognise the relevance of self-esteem in relation to one life domain, sport and exercise, both as a predictor of adherence and as a consequence of participation. Most of us carry an implicit sense of what self-esteem is but defining the construct has proved difficult. To complicate matters further a related term, self-concept, has frequently been used almost interchangeably. To help clarify the situation, Horn and Claytor (1993) offered the following definitions:

> [self concept is] an individual's overall awareness of self in regard to physical attributes, personal characteristics, social identities and/or behaviours ... [self-esteem] refers to an individual's evaluation of or affective reaction to these attributes or characteristics ... the value the individual places on those self-perceptions.
>
> (p. 312)

In keeping with the other relationships already examined, a positive link between exercise and self-esteem has been established and in turn this appears to be strongest among those whose self-esteem is relatively low (Fox, 2000). To date, the majority of studies have examined global self-esteem rather than domain-specific esteem and few have explored changes in self-esteem over time, with most focusing on differences between exercisers and non-exercisers at any one time (Sonstroem, 1998).

While the notion that exercise enhances self-esteem makes sound intuitive sense, the history of research has tended to be confounded by an implicit belief that self-esteem is a singular, unitary construct that is sensitive to short term, highly specific interventions. Modern researchers would now argue otherwise, claiming that self-esteem has many components, each of which may be influenced by suitable interventions while others may remain impervious to even the most assiduous initiatives. Johnsgard (1989) highlights the fact that exercise will do little to improve self-esteem if it is deficient primarily in other areas of our lives such as learning difficulties, behavioural problems or a lack of social skills. However, if our low self-esteem has its roots in poor body image or lack of fitness or weight control then exercise could have a positive effect. This multidimensional approach has been championed by Harter (1983) and Marsh (1990), sensibly taking into account the reality that people can have different beliefs about themselves in different areas of their lives.

Early research suggested that self-esteem improved with participation in physical activity regardless of physical activity type. However, a meta-analysis that focused solely on self-esteem in young children found a greater effect size for aerobic activities. Recent work in this area has employed multifaceted measures of self-esteem. For example, Fox (2000) has developed the Physical Self-Perception Profile (PSPP) which distinguishes between global self-esteem and physical self-esteem and which in turn has been related to factors including body image and sports competence. Subsequent work using this scale has found support for the notion that physical activity is associated with higher levels of self-esteem in younger and older adult males and females (Landers and Arent, 2007).

In conclusion, self-esteem studies have provided insight into the manner in which exercise contributes to overall life adjustment and mediates the complex interaction between the individual and the environment. Research has been promising and indicates that exercise could do much to bolster self-esteem in cases where it is fragile or underdeveloped. However, as yet the work has not led to any concrete recommendations regarding the use of exercise to improve self-esteem in either clinical or non-clinical contexts. Johnsgard (1989) makes special efforts to emphasise the following conclusion, which he believes is one of few to emerge lucidly from the self-esteem literature:

> self-esteem is more likely to be elevated when exercise is introduced to special populations. While studies of exercise and self-esteem done on individuals who make up the general population reveal conflicting results, those done on special groups in which individuals are in initially poor psychological or physical health show exercise to have a consistently positive effect on self-esteem or self-concept.
>
> (p. 200)

An emerging viewpoint suggests that the more specific sub-domains of self-esteem, in particular perceived sport competence, physical condition, attractive body and strength, may be associated differentially with behaviour in various sports. While these associations are interesting, the literature provides little guidance as to which forms of exercise may be beneficial to which types of self-esteem.

Pre-menstrual syndrome

Despite anecdotal evidence pointing to a relationship between exercise and premenstrual syndrome (PMS) symptomology, and the fact that negative affect, depression and anxiety, are commonly associated with PMS, only a small number of studies have considered the potential benefits of exercise on PMS (Israel, Sutton and O'Brien, 1985; Timonen and Procope, 1971). The research that is available has tended to confirm that exercise can have a prophylactic effect on a range of symptoms both physiological and psychological (Dudgeon, 2000). Choi and Salmon (1995) monitored the effects of various frequencies of exercise on PMS in a self-selected sample across one menstrual cycle. Low exercise and sedentary groups showed no improvement in symptoms whereas the high exercising group experienced significantly fewer symptoms. Interestingly, competitive exercisers did not show improvements, perhaps indicating that strenuous exercise may be dysfunctional, and confirming earlier speculations relating to the negative effects of competitive exercising on anxiety and mood state. Likewise, Cockerill, Lawson and Nevill (1995) found that those who engaged in exercise more than four times a week reported higher tension, depression and anger, whereas those who exercised two to three times per week had healthier mood state profiles as measured by POMS. As regards the type of exercise which appears most beneficial, it may not be necessary to reach aerobic capacity in order to alleviate negative affect as associated with PMS, and hence increased maximal oxygen consumption (VO^2 max) does not appear to be a causative factor (Steege and Blumenthal, 1993).

In conclusion, available evidence points to the benefits of exercise for those who experience PMS, and in particular less strenuous forms of non-competitive exercise. However, the type of exercise, its duration and length and, even more significantly, the reasons for improvement in symptoms, still await clarification.

Body image

When prescribing physical activity, due caution must be taken to ensure that exercise does not trigger more problems than it solves. There is now considerable evidence of the dangers associated with excessive exercise, and of the type of individual who is more prone to use exercise inappropriately (Adams and Kirkby, 2002; Bamber, Cockerill and Carroll, 2000; Cockerill and Riddington, 1996; Iannos and Tiggemann, 1997; Johnston, 2001). The gendered nature of physical activity should not be disregarded in this debate (Scully, Reilly and Clarke, 1998), for despite significant gains in public acceptance and participation, women are still more likely to engage in non-competitive activities such as aerobics and keep-fit, which in turn may serve to reinforce the cult of thinness and femininity (Hausenblas and Fallon, 2002). Franzoi (1995) has described a tendency among females to focus on their body as an aesthetic statement whereas, traditionally at least, males have been more likely to attend to the dynamic aspects of their bodies, such as coordination, strength and speed. This emphasis on the female form in exercise settings may foster feelings of social-physique anxiety (SPA), constrain enjoyment of the activity itself, and may even be exacerbated by the nature of the clothing required (Frederick and Shaw, 1995; Cockburn and Clarke, 2002). McAuley *et al.* (1995) reported that SPA correlates with self-presentational motives for exercise such as weight control and attractiveness, and is higher among women (Frederick and Morrison, 1996). Women consistently score lower than men on measures of self-confidence regarding their bodies and physical competence. Biddle, Goudas and Page (1997), among others, have emphasised the need for exercise promoters to address this issue of poor self-confidence among women, and to think carefully about sporting venues and other contextual factors (e.g., changing facilities) in order to make women feel more comfortable with their body image during exercise.

Body image itself refers to a multidimensional construct consisting of a set of cognitions and feelings about one's physique. Research shows that body image tends to be less positive among women (Koff and Bauman, 1997), and is more closely linked to women's overall self-esteem than men's (Furnham and Greaves, 1994). For example, in a national survey of 803 US women, over half reported globally negative evaluations of their body parts and a preoccupation with losing weight (Cash and Deagle, 1997). The implications of such findings are considerable given that disturbances in body image have been so strongly implicated in the development of eating disorders and clinical depression. Without doubt, physicians who advocate the adoption of exercise regimes must remain alert to these body-related concerns when prescribing forms of physical activity.

When training and diet regimes are overly stringent then women in particular are susceptible to three disorders collectively referred to as the female athlete triad (FAT). Referring to disordered eating, amenorrhea and osteoporosis, FAT is the physical manifestation of a pathological adherence to exercise, often coupled with inappropriate diet (Arena, 1997). In its position paper, the American College of Sports Medicine (1990) maintains that the syndrome can cause morbidity and mortality, and notes in particular that women involved in sports which emphasise low body weight for performance or appearance (e.g., gymnastics and dance) are most at risk. Nattiv (1995) has characterised the typical sufferer as someone driven to excel, who equates leanness with improved performance and who feels pressured to maintain a low body weight.

Furthermore, not only may exercise be associated with body dissatisfaction, once undertaken it may play a sinister role in the perpetuation of eating disorders and weight control. Davis (1999) has described how exercise can sustain the cyclical, repetitive nature of eating disorders, and she has also outlined the manner in which exercise and self-starvation may interact as mutual catalysts (Davis, 1997). Disordered eating practices and a drive for thinness or leanness are often accompanied by psychopathological consequences observable in depressive symptoms such as low energy and poor self-esteem. With these thoughts in mind, caution is required when recommending exercise practices which may provide a link in the chain of disordered eating or which may present itself as a dysfunctional response to body dissatisfaction.

Traditionally discussion of such issues has tended to focus on women but there is increasing evidence to suggest that eating disorders themselves are not the preserve of women (Andersen, 1990; Phillips and Diaz, 1997), and that increasingly young men are at risk of exercise-related disorders including muscle dysmorphia or the pursuit of greater bulk and in particular muscular definition (Olivardia and Pope, 2000).

There is still considerable debate as to the nature of excessive exercise and its relationship with other clinical conditions including anorexia nervosa and bulimia (Yates, 1991). For example, does excessive exercise best warrant description as an addiction (Hausenblas and Downs, 2002), and if there are signs of dependency is this a primary dependence on the physical activity itself or a secondary dependence on the perceived effects of exercise (e.g., body shape)? Bamber, Cockerill and Carroll (2000) found that men and women who exercised to excess but whose exercise was best characterised as 'primary' (i.e., exercise for its own sake) did not show greater signs of morbidity in comparison with a control group, while those whose exercise was seen as motivated by secondary factors exhibited a number of psychological problems often associated with low self-esteem, body dissatisfaction and eating disorders.

THEORIES AND MODELS

As should now be readily apparent, there is no shortage of research into the effects of exercise on psychological health. Although the scientific rigour of some of this research has been challenged, the effort that has gone into this endeavour cannot be questioned. Considerable attention has focused on the 'what, how and where' questions – but what about the 'why'? Are we any closer to understanding why physical exercise may improve general cognitive functioning or specific clinical conditions such as depression? The answer would have to be a qualified 'yes' but with a recognition that there are no simple answers. As more and more time is devoted to understanding the neurological, psychological, psychopharmacological and physiological mechanisms there is a growing acceptance that the phenomenon under investigation may not lend itself to any simple and sovereign explanation but to a multidimensional model.

By way of example, why should physical exercise ameliorate the effects of PMS? Several explanations have been advanced over the years, including the effect that exercise may have on the oestrogen-progesterone ratio. On the one hand some research has indicated that sportswomen have lower levels of oestrogen than non-exercising women, while on the other hand studies have found no differences (Scully *et al.*, 1998). Rather than assuming a direct relationship between exercise and lowered estrogen levels, Wells (1985) has suggested that these levels reflect reduced body fat, since adipose tissue has been identified as a source of oestrogen. An alternative explanation highlights improved glucose tolerance during this stage of the cycle, as the symptoms of poor glucose tolerance are similar to those commonly reported by women who experience PMS and including fatigue, depression, anxiety and increased appetite (Rauramaa, 1984). According to others (Reid and Yen, 1983) the elevation of endorphin levels prior to menstruation may be a significant factor and regular exercise may stabilise or prevent extreme variation in endorphin levels and thus decrease the effects of PMS.

Looking at a further example, why should exercise influence self-esteem? The 'skill development hypothesis' of Marsh (1990) contends that successes and rewarding experiences cause us to feel good about ourselves and develop a sense of competence. Furthermore, the 'self-enhancement hypothesis' notes that we will tend to act in accordance with our conceptions of ourselves in a bid to reinforce the personal image we have developed. In reviewing the relationship between self-esteem and physical fitness, Sonstroem (1984) found that components of self-esteem that were connected to physical potency appeared to rise with great rapidity and in a manner not entirely dependent on actual, tangible developments in fitness. He suggested that the effects were essentially caused by perceptions of physical improvement. Sonstroem and Morgan (1989) then went on to develop a hierarchical model to account for the relationship between self-esteem and physical activity. At the lowest levels of the hierarchy the model describes physical self-efficacies or currently held beliefs about one's physical ability. At the highest level is a global sense of self-esteem, which is directly influenced by intermediate variables involving physical competence and acceptance. Their basic model has been subsequently expanded on by Sonstroem, Harlow and Josephs (1994) to include the concepts of sport competence, physical condition, attractiveness of one's body, strength and physical self-efficacies. More recently, Wilson and Rodgers (2002) have suggested that the link is best understood with reference to self-determination theory (see Chapter 4) and the greater feelings of autonomy that come through engagement with exercise programmes. Clearly each of these explanations may have face validity but their scientific utility is still to be fully tested.

Exercise psychology is now characterised by an array of increasingly sophisticated mechanisms and models used to explain a range of psychological phenomenon (Biddle and Mutrie, 2008; Buckworth and Dishman, 2002; Landers and Arent, 2007). Specifically in terms of the effects of exercise on psychological well-being, some perspectives have their origins in psychology, others in psychophysiology, others in physiology, and others in psychopharmacology. Some relate to specific phenomenon while others describe general effects on psychological functioning. While a summary of some of the major explanations or hypotheses that continue to dominate the extant literature are presented below, readers are directed to Chapter 4 for explanations of exercise behaviour more generally.

The catecholamine hypothesis

The catecholamines, which include adrenaline, noradrenaline and dopamine, function as transmitters in the central nervous system and are strongly implicated in the control of movement, mood, attention and endocrine, cardiovascular and stress responses. Catecholamines act quickly by sending messages directly through the nervous system to specific sites. The catecholamine hypothesis, as originally proposed by Kety (1966), suggests that exercise activates the release of catecholamines, which in turn are associated with euphoria and positive mood states.

Exercise is known to bring about a significant alteration in levels of plasma catecholamines (those carried in the bloodstream), although the actual level is thought to depend on the intensity, type and duration of the exercise as well as individual factors. Although there is no direct proof that levels of catecholamines in the brain itself increase with exercise in humans, analysis of levels of the metabolites (i.e., chemicals remaining when a compound is broken down) excreted by the body following exercise supports the proposal that brain catecholamines (and in particular noradrenaline) also increase with exercise. However whether this increase causes an alteration in mood is still unknown and in general, methodological difficulties continue to bedevil research in this area and place restrictions on interpretation (see Buckworth and Dishman, 2002).

The endorphin hypothesis

In the 1980s, the popular exercise literature seized on the phrase 'endorphin high' or 'runner's high' to describe the effect that endorphins (otherwise known as endogenous morphines or more commonly 'pleasure peptides') may have on feelings of well-being following exercise (Battista, 2004). Endorphins are naturally occurring opiate-like transmitters that appear to bind with specific receptor sites in discrete parts of the central nervous system associated with pain information and affect. Exercise has been shown to cause a significant phasic increase in the release of endorphins into the bloodstream from the pituitary gland.

The evidence suggests that since (i) exercise is associated with positive mood state, (ii) that endorphins have been shown to cause an elevation in mood and (iii) that exercise elevates plasma endorphins then *ergo* there is an endorphin mediated exercise effect on mood. To date the elevation of endorphins during exercise has been noted only in blood plasma rather than in the cerebrospinal fluid or in the brain itself, where it is supposed that the endorphins actually have their effect. As endorphins are unable to cross the blood-brain barrier it is very unlikely that blood plasma endorphin levels can have a direct effect on an individual's psychological state, and this continues to cause theoretical difficulties in explaining endorphin effects associated with exercise (Hoffman, 1997).

The hypothalamic-pituitary-adrenal (HPA) axis hypothesis

Hypercortisolism, or the excessive production of cotrisol by the body because of a dysfunction of the HPA axis, has been associated with depression and other anxiety-related disorders (Holsboer, 2001). Furthermore, animal studies have demonstrated that exercise may delay the production of cortisol in response to stress, and hence may mediate the relationship between cortisol production and depression, although the precise nature of this relationship has yet to be fully understood.

The thermogenic hypothesis

The thermogenic hypothesis or effect (Morgan and O'Connor 1988; Youngstedt *et al.*, 1993) suggests that the increase in body temperature brought about by exercise reduces tonic muscle activity, in turn reducing somatic anxiety and thereby inducing a positive psychological effect. In support of this argument, Raglin and Morgan (1985) noted decreased state anxiety after a hot shower (at a temperature of 38.5°C, lasting five minutes). It has been suggested that the increase in temperature may alter the levels of brain monoamines (including neurotransmitters such as noradrenaline, adrenaline, serotonin and dopamine; see 'catecholamine hypothesis' above), although research is not plentiful (Youngstedt *et al.*, 1993).

The distraction or time-out hypothesis

As the name suggests, this hypothesis leans towards a psychosocial explanation of the positive effects of exercise (Bahrke and Morgan, 1978). It suggests that through the act of engaging in exercise, a psychological release is provided from the primary source of worry or depression (Alfermann and Stoll, 2000). Breus and O'Connor (1998) provided an examination of this theory by measuring state anxiety before and after exercise of moderate intensity and comparing changes in anxiety levels with three other conditions (quiet rest, studying and studying while exercising). State anxiety was reduced in the exercise-only condition but not in the other three, strongly suggesting that 'time-out' may be a significant factor in an exercise effect, although other authors remain sceptical (Landers and Arent, 2001).

The mastery hypothesis

Reiterating the earlier literature on self-esteem, and also bearing in mind the extensive literature in Chapter 4 on participation motivation and in particular self-efficacy, exercise that involves the mastery of particular skills and that is task or goal-oriented rather than ego-oriented is likely to have a positive effect on self-efficacy which will in turn will reflect in heightened self-esteem and a positive affective state (Casper, 1993; Landers and Arent, 2001). The critical variable here is likely to be perceived success or achievement that is associated with the physical activity rather than the activity per se.

The cognitive appraisal hypothesis

Accumulated evidence which suggests that the type, duration or intensity of exercise may not always accurately account for the positive psychological benefits that accrue from physical activity has led some authors to suggest that psychophysiological perspectives alone can only ever hope to offer a partial explanation. Instead, it is argued that the cognitive appraisal of the activity is equally significant. In other words, if the physical activity is interpreted as pleasant it is then likely to trigger positive mood states and this will then have associated psychological benefits (Szabo, 2003). This explanation has not attracted a great deal of support to date but seems to hold promise as a way of integrating both psychophysiological and psychological perspectives.

To summarise this section, as to which theories, models or hypotheses provide the best explanations of psychological effects of exercise, as should be clear by now there is no consensus. Furthermore, it is not sensible to force a consensus given the wide diversity of psychological and physiological processes which intertwine in determining the bi-causal relationship between physical activity and psychological well-being. The sophistication of research and theoretical argument is commendable but the goal of these endeavours is still not well defined. Psychology in general is now more comfortable with the notion of multiple perspectives operating at different levels of analysis, with each providing some insight into the topic in question, and this approach would seem to be the most appropriate in this context.

METHODS AND MEASURES

The exercise psychology literature is awash with measures of psychological and physiological variables, a number of which have been described already. These range from the psychometric to the psychophysiological or increasingly, a combination of both (e.g. Van de Vliet, Mutrie and Onghena, 2005; Woo *et al.*, 2009).

Rather than provide an exhaustive catalogue of all potential psychometric and psychophyiological measures, if carrying out research in any particular field it is recommended that one of the specialist reviews is consulted before deciding which measure to employ (see Landers and Arent, 2001; 2007), always aware that more recent reviews tend to be increasingly critical of more traditional and popular psychometric measures.

Considering methodology more generally, the relationship between exercise and mental health continues to attract considerable popular as well as academic attention (Biddle and Mutrie, 2008). For this reason, if no other, there is a need to be aware of biases that may unintentionally influence the research process

RESEARCH BOX

Although the 'feel good' effect of exercise has received considerable attention, we are still some way from understanding why exercise is good for us psychologically. Minjung Woo and her colleagues set about trying to explore this relationship by using a methodology that involved not only standard psychometric measures of mood (in this case, the Profile of Mood States or POMS) but also measuring activity in the brain, or specifically changes in electroencephalographic (EEG) activity across a range of bands (alpha, beta, delta and theta) in frontal brain processes, the area of the brain most often associated with affective responses including mood state. 16 female undergraduate students were assessed for frontal EEG and self-reported mood state following rest and after three different durations of exercise – 15, 30 and 45 minutes. The exercise was performed at a standard intensity which was set at just below each individual's ventilator threshold (VT), or level that could be sustained at a steady state over time. The results showed clearly that the duration of exercise was critical in determining both a self-report of positive mood state and cortical activation, with the greatest and most positive effects after 30 minutes. Beyond this time the effects diminished, presumably as fatigue took over, while at 15 minutes the brief exercise period had failed to generate a significant increase. Analysis of EEG suggested that the enhanced vigour experienced after 30 minutes of exercise was associated with both a reduction in withdrawal-oriented activity in the brain and an increase in approach-oriented processes. The study provides strong support for an inverted-U relationship between exercise duration and affect, and implicates frontal EEG asymmetry in this process.

and in turn distort the academic literature and accepted wisdom. For example, it seems improbable that many within the exercise psychology community will read empirical articles harbouring hope that established paradigms will be challenged by contrary data. It is entirely possible that such sentimentality can confound judgments about the quality and value of innovatory research. Similarly, it is tempting for researchers to manipulate conditions to provide support for their hypotheses. For this reason it may be useful to focus attention on aspects of research, perhaps not unique to this field, which may distort the production and dissemination of results.

Volunteerism

It goes without saying that research in this field will normally require participants to exercise and therefore it is almost unavoidable that those who volunteer for this type of research will already be inclined to exercise. At a very
general level, Dollinger and Leong (1993), referring to the big-5 model of personality, conclude that volunteers tend to exhibit higher levels of agreeableness
and openness to experience. Furthermore, those who are more extrovert are
more prepared to engage in long term, follow-up studies. Perhaps the extant
literature merely serves to suggest that exercise will hold the greatest benefits
for open, agreeable extroverts? Given the tenacity with which some individuals adhere to their exercise programmes (Adams and Kirkby, 2001; 2002) it
is a plausible hypothesis that exercise psychology may present a skewed perspective on physical activity, based on the reports of some of its more zeal-
ous disciples resident in the vicinity of university campuses. This imbalance
calls into question the 'ecological validity' of the research, which is the degree
to which findings can be generalised beyond the laboratory. It is necessary
that researchers engage in the sincere and honest task of contextualising their
research findings, and indeed, those of other researchers (e.g., Zimmerman,
Bisanz and Bisanz, 1998), and demonstrate a degree of prudence which has, on
occasions, been absent in exercise psychology in the past (Biddle and Fuchs,
2009).

Control comparisons

Isaac and Michael (1995) note that individuals participating as members of a
control group ought to experience all things in common with the treatment
group, except the critical factor. Establishing control groups who experience
'exercise', 'less exercise' or 'no exercise' across a constant, comparable background noise of social and environmental variables is no simple task in the real
world.

Experimental design

In a review of the literature concerning the acute effects of exercise on mood
state, Yeung (1996) developed a classification system and hierarchy to assess
the empirical robustness of almost 100 studies between 1976 and 1995. The
literature was classified according to three prominent methodological types,
which form a hierarchy reflecting their relative empirical merit and potential
for drawing strong inferences.

Experimental:	Random allocation to condition.
	Control condition equivalent.
Quasi-experimental:	Lack of equivalent control groups e.g. a lecture / meal
	Participants allowed to self-select condition
Pre-experimental:	Absence of control group.

Suffice it to say a great many studies in the history of exercise psychology have fallen short of the requisite criteria for classification as 'experimental' (Landers and Arent, 2007). With this in mind, it is unsurprising that reviewers remain critical of the methodological limitations of much of the exercise psychology literature (see Biddle and Mutrie, 2008). At the same time there are encouraging signs of procedural rigour in the more recent literature and this trend is encouraging (Biddle and Fuchs, 2009).

Experimenter's expectancy effects

Morgan (1997) has described three sources of experimenter expectancy effects. The first is termed the 'halo effect' (Thorndike 1920) and describes a process by which the experimenter will ascribe certain characteristics to the participant based on knowledge of that individual, especially regarding his or her placement in a control or experimental group. Within the context of exercise it is easily recognised that elements of personality and physical appearance may interact with the objectivity and impartiality of raters interested in physical performance or psychological variables. Other variables, especially ethnicity (e.g., Sinclair and Kunda, 1999), and body composition (e.g., Pingitore *et al.*, 1994) may hold influence over the ratings of researchers, given the importance and salience of the physical form in this field of research.

A second source of error is what is known as the 'Rosenthal effect' (Rosenthal, 1966) and describes the manner in which the expectancies of the researcher may impact on the outcomes, whether they are communicated intentionally or otherwise. It is not difficult to imagine that improvements in psychological health may occur under circumstances when the experimenter is anticipative of such changes. This differs from the halo effect in that, while ratings may be accurate, the true scores are themselves influenced by the beliefs about the treatment imparted by the researchers. Researchers may also hold the opposite belief about particular individuals in a cohort for whom they feel exercise is of less value and the effect constitutes a significant barrier to a meaningful understanding of people's experience of physical activity.

'Demand characteristics' (Orne 1962) may be leaked unintentionally or deliberately sought and identified by the participants. Within exercise research, especially its more clinical forms, the initiation of the physical activity stems from the presentation of a psychological disturbance itself. Identification of the hypothesis in such circumstances is not necessary but self-evident.

Finally, the 'Hawthorne effect' manifests itself as improved well-being based upon the attention afforded to participants during a treatment rather than the independent variable *per se*. Morgan (1997) notes that observing exercise effects on mental health over and above those observed for an untreated group does not constitute meaningful science but merely reflects the superiority of 'something' over 'nothing'. Sport and exercise psychologists must consider the manner in which control groups are formed with particular attention to both the volume and quality of contact shared by participants and researchers.

Placebo effects

In 1952 Hans Eysenck famously dropped his proverbial bombshell on the psycho-therapy community suggesting that its trade was ineffective (Phares and Trull, 1997). Eysenck claimed that, from a sample of 7000 individuals, 72 per cent of patients receiving ordinary medical care made psychological improvements while only 44 per cent improved with psychoanalytic treatment and 66 per cent who received eclectic therapies. The mechanics of his data collection and statis-tics have subsequently been criticised severely but the legacy of his contention remains and is appealing to a great many who remain sceptical as to the efficacy of any behavioural, cognitive or psychoanalytic 'therapies' devised to improve mental health. Additionally the scepticism is fuelled by studies demonstrating the remarkable placebo rates evident in some drug tests. Frank (1973) proposed that non-specific factors such as motivation for change, positive expectations of improvement, feelings of being understood and being similar to others are prime sources of this placebo effect. The problem is evidently an issue for exer-cise research and Folkins and Sime (1984) concluded that it is nearly impossible, for example, to administer an exercise programme so that it is either single-blind or double blind.

Ojanen (1994) is one of few researchers who have tackled this unpopular issue in a direct fashion and is content to admit that the 'real' effects of exercise on mental health cannot truly be studied. Ojanen proposes a hierarchical structure beginning at the most fundamental level with 'expectations' about the utility of exercise. These in turn give rise to levels of 'involvement' that vary on a contin-uum. Finally, the involvement leads to a natural process of evaluation in which participants assess the efficacy of the activity and form opinions on its 'subjective utility'. Other sources from which 'placeboism' may arise have also been specu-lated upon. In considering the influence of societal, cultural factors he proposes that exercise may not constitute the exclusive, novel behavioural therapy that exercise psychologists like to believe is the case. Ojanen goes on to postulate that the magnitude of the treatment effects derived from any intervention are largely contingent upon two factors - first, that of a need for intervention and help; and second, the social acceptability or appropriateness of that intervention.

Analogue research

In discussing this voluminous slice of exercise psychology Morgan (1997) refers to the clinically oriented work of O'Leary and Borkovec (1978) who distinguish between genuine psychotherapy and analogue therapy:

> 'Psychotherapy refers to psychological treatment of a clinical problem, that is, a problem that represents a real problem, in living for the client – for example, debilitating ... depression ... [Analogue therapy represents] psy-chological treatment of a problem that seldom or never causes concern to

a client in his or her life and may or may not be relevant to a client's daily concerns, such as snake or rat phobias.'

(p. 822)

Analogue research may attempt to mirror or mimic real life concerns and demonstrate the effects of types of intervention, including exercise, but interpretation of these findings must always proceed cautiously as the ego-involvement in these analogous experiences will be less intense and hence the capacity for change will be much greater.

In conclusion, the methods and measures employed in exercise psychology continue to be defined with reference to traditional scientific methods. For example, tried and trusted psychological self-report scales are often used to quantify aspects of psychological health (the dependent variable) and exercise is then introduced as the independent variable. While such studies have been revealing of a number of relationships between exercise and well-being, there is a need to move forwards to more imaginative methodologies in order to explore the intricacies of the relationship more completely (Dishman and Buckworth, 2006; Giles-Corti *et al.*, 2005).

PRACTICAL ISSUES AND INTERVENTIONS

While the existing literature supports the general benefits of exercise (Faulkner and Taylor, 2005), as yet it falls short of suggesting practical guidelines as to how exercise may be used to alleviate particular symptoms and the forms of exercise that are likely to be most beneficial in particular circumstances (Biddle and Fuchs, 2009). For example, should exercise be non-aerobic, aerobic or anaerobic, of short, medium or long-term duration, intensive or non-intensive, competitive or non-competitive, team or individual, single or multi session (Szabo, 2003)? In addition, establishing the direction of causality has proved difficult. Did psychological well-being precede, follow or operate independently from a particular exercise regimen? Unless such issues are resolved then the development of effective intervention programmes will remain problematic.

These problems aside, there are a number of practical difficulties associated with delivering an intervention programme. For example, no matter how beneficial an exercise regimen may be, without a willingness to exercise voluntarily then the practical utility of exercise is worthless. Nowhere is this problem more acute than in relation to the treatment of clinical depression as one of the classic symptoms is lethargy and lack of 'get up and go' (Laird and Benefield, 1995, Ströhle, 2009).

At a more general level, McGeorge *et al.* (1994) maintained that only 10 per cent of the population are committed to physical activity; 20 per cent will start but not adhere to exercise; 40 per cent only ever promise to start an exercise programme; 20 per cent need to be convinced to participate in exercise;

and 10 per cent positively are not interested in any form of organised or recommended activity. Such research highlights the deep-rooted resistance to taking exercise among large sections of the population, a problem that is exacerbated among those with psychological problems and most notably depression.

We next encounter the thorny problem as to who is best placed to promote an exercise programme. There is an emerging consensus that doctors or general practitioners (GPs) are best placed to intervene, and simultaneously, 'exercise by prescription' schemes are gaining in popularity (Faulkner and Taylor, 2005; Smith, Gould, See Tai and Iliffe, 1996; Swain and Leutholtz, 2007). Surveys also suggest a generally favourable reception from GPs to this type of initiative although their role is not unproblematic, particularly in relation to the referral system, their lack of knowledge of exercise recommendations, and difficulties in evaluating community health promotion schemes (Iliffe, See Tai and Gould, 1994; Taylor and Faulkner, 2005).

To ensure effective interventions, it is important that researchers, physicians and exercise practitioners continue to work together to develop sound guidelines. This will be of practical benefit to the patient and will also help advance our understanding of the interplay between exercise and well being. General recommendations are now commonly accepted as to the somatic benefits which accrue from exercise and the relationship between exercise, fitness and general cognitive functioning is now also receiving closer scrutiny (Etnier *et al.*, 1997; Landers and Arent, 2007).

Alongside this research activity, now is the time to develop more specific guidelines relating to psychological benefits of exercise, taking due cognisance of psychosocial variables including gender, age, previous mental health, context and disability.

Prior to the 1990s relatively few articles were published considering exercise in the context of illness. Both the popular and medical worlds appeared fairly ambivalent and disagreed as to the manner in which people with disabilities could be active, expend energy and use their muscles. Perhaps carried by the growth of the disability sport movement practitioners are now becoming more aware of the physical and psychological value of activity within the context of illness and recuperation.

Rimmer, Braddock and Pitetti (1996) wrote an impassioned article advocating increased research and service provision exploring the utility of exercise for people with disabilities. In describing the issue as a national priority they made the point that in this day and age physical activity has received universal, positive attention and yet, perhaps predictably, this focus has not extended to those with disabilities. Similarly, the large scale promotion of physical activity in the United States, called 'Healthy People 2000' (National Center for Health Statistics, 2001), states that,

> ... a clear opportunity exists for health promotion and disease prevention efforts to improve the health prospects and functional independence of people with disabilities.

> (p. 41)

The rationale, from the perspective of physical health, for enhancing exercise for people with disabilities is compelling (Graham, Kremer and Wheeler, 2008). Firstly, there is the self-evident fact that habitual physical activity is often a missing element in the lives of people who have a disability (e.g., Coyle and Santiago, 1995; Painter and Blackburn, 1988; Ponichtera-Mulcare, 1993). Secondly, the knock on effect of this decreased participation is evidenced through lower levels of cardiovascular fitness and yet, even in cases of severe disablement such as paraplegia, improvements in physical fitness are realisable (Cowell, Squires and Raven, 1996). In their review of the literature on disability and exercise, Heath and Fentem (1997) note that even small incremental improvements in fitness can have a profound influence on functional ability, psychological well-being and quality of life. These fitness gains do not depend on radical, heavy exercise programmes but can occur through modest physical activity, even in cases where walking or standing is not possible.

Studies involving young people have observed that children with disabilities tend to spend more of their time engaged in quiet activity and exhibit a lower work capacity than those without disabilities (Brown and Gordon, 1987). Subsequently, many of those with disabilities, either mental or physical, tend to be classified as obese (Alley and Chang, 2007; Rimmer, Braddock and Fujiura, 1993). Obesity exacerbates the effects of other conditions and greatly increases the risk of death before the age of 65 (Bouchard, Depres and Trembley, 1993). The area of secondary complaints is of particular relevance for those with disabilities and their carers, as these often represent the preventable component of the condition. It is noteworthy that exercise may provide a potent brake on the spiralling, multiplication of symptoms that the primary impairment initiates, and that tailored interventions can be effective in not only arresting physical deterioration but also improving a range of psychological conditions including depression and mood state (Graham, Kremer and Wheeler, 2008). Marge (1988) makes the point that it is often the secondary conditions, which have a more devastating effect on individuals and cites 'disuse syndrome' resulting from muscle wasting due to excessive sedentariness in a wheelchair as a prime example of this.

Turning to other marginalised groups, until recently few studies had examined physical activity interventions for minority populations, but there is now growing evidence that more marginalised communities are often those that are characterised by lower rates of physical activity (Buckworth and Dishman, 2007; Trost et al., 2002). In particular, evidence would suggest that demographic variables including age, gender, ethnicity, socio-economic status and educational experience all will have a significant impact on physical activity levels, and that the gap between those who take exercise and those who don't may be widening. The work of Taylor, Baranowski and Young (1998) was fuelled by the observation that people with low income, belonging to a racial minority or with a physical disability were more likely to be sedentary than the general population. Reviewing articles from 1983 to 1997 they identified only 14 studies that had examined these populations, the majority of which used quasi-experimental designs and many of which lacked theory in guiding the intervention. They also concluded that interventions need to embrace a more collaborative, community approach in which participants are given more influence in designing the intervention. In conclusion, there is growing evidence that while the message of *mens sana in corpore sano* (i.e., a healthy mind in a healthy body) is striking home to large section so the community, there remain those who either do not hear or choose not to hear how physical activity can improve their well-being, and this remains a significant challenge for those engaged with health promotion.

CASE STUDY

Joanne is a 21-year-old student who has always tried to stay reasonably fit and healthy but who has not played sport competitively since leaving school. In her first year at university, Joanne put on a considerable amount of weight and especially in the lead up to her exams. She was quite shocked at the reaction of her family and friends when she returned home at the end of the year, and determined to try to do something about it. She went on a strict diet and also joined a local gym. She began to attend regularly and by the end of the summer was working out at least twice a day. While her body weight fell considerably during this period she was reluctant to take advice on diet and began to spend more time alone in her room. On return to college after the summer, Joanne joined the sports centre and also took up running. Her body weight would suggest that she may not be maintaining an adequate diet and indeed she had to curtail her running on several occasions because of injuries brought on by overtraining. On one occasion she saw a student counsellor who began to discuss her eating habits and exercise regime, although Joanna emphatically denied there was a problem and refused to see the counsellor again. Her parents feel that Joanne is currently depressed and would be keen for her to take a complete break from exercise and even to return home.

1. With reference to the Theories and Models section in the chapter, how would you interpret what is happening in this case study?
2. With reference to Methods and Measures, what techniques would you employ to help understand and quantify the issues?
3. With reference to Practical Issues and Interventions, how would you deal with this situation?

STUDY QUESTIONS

1. Review key findings in relation to the specific psychological conditions that have been most often cited in the exercise psychology literature (i.e., depression, anxiety, mood state, self esteem, stress responsivity, pre-menstrual syndrome and body image).
2. Compare and contrast various theories that have been used to explain the relationship between physical exercise and psychological well-being.
3. Discuss the results from meta-analyses conducted on the effects of exercise on anxiety.
4. Critically review some of the methodologies employed in exercise psychology.
5. Consider some of practical difficulties associated with delivering an exercise intervention programme with either a clinical or non-clinical population.

FURTHER READING

Adams, J. and Kirkby, R. (2002) 'Excessive Exercise as an Addiction: A Review', *Addiction Research and Theory*, 10, 415–37.

Berger, B. G., Pargman, D. and Weinberg, R. S. (2002) *Foundations of Exercise Psychology* (Morgantown, WV: Fitness Information Technology).

Biddle, S. J. H. and Mutrie, N. (2008) *Psychology of Physical Activity: Determinants, Well-Being and Interventions* (London: Routledge).

Buckworth, J. and Dishman, R. K. (2002) *Exercise Psychology* (Champaign, IL: Human Kinetics).

Faulkner, G. and Taylor, A. H. (eds) (2005) *Exercise, Health and Mental Health: Emerging Relationships* (London: Routledge).

Smits, J. A. J. and Otto, M. W. (2009) *Exercise for Mood and Anxiety Disorders* (New York: Oxford University Press).

Bibliography

Abernethy, B. (1990) 'Anticipation in Squash: Differences in Advance Cue Utilization between Expert and Novice Players', *Journal of Sport Sciences*, 8, 17–34.

Abernethy, B., Maxwell, J. P., Masters, R. S. W., Van der Kamp, J. and Jackson, R. C. (2007) 'Attentional Processes in Skill Learning and Expert Performance', in G. Tenenbaum and R. C. Eklund (eds), *Handbook of Sport Psychology*, 3rd edn (New York: John Wiley), 245–63.

Abernethy, B. and Russell, D. G. (1987) 'Expert–Novice Differences in an Applied Selective Attention Task', *Journal of Sport Psychology*, 9, 326–45.

Abernethy, B., Farrow, D. and Berry, J. (2003) 'Constraints and Issues in the Development of a General Theory of Expert Perceptual-Motor Performance: A Critique of the Deliberate Practice Framework', in J. ÓL. Starkes and K. A. Ericsson (eds), *Expert Performance in Sports: Advances in Research on Sport Expertise* (Champaign, IL: Human Kinetics).

Abernethy, B., Summers, J. J. and Ford, S. (1998) 'Issues in the Measurement of Attention', in J. L. Duda (ed.), *Advances in Sport and Exercise Psychology Measurement* (Morgantown, WV: Fitness Information Technology), 173–93.

Abernethy, B., Thomas, K. T. and Thomas, J. T. (1993) 'Strategies for Improving Understanding of Motor Expertise (or Mistakes We Have Made and Things We Have Learned!!)', in J. L. Starkes and F. Allard (eds), *Cognitive Issues in Motor Expertise* (Amsterdam: North-Holland), 317–56.

Abernethy, B., Gill, D. P., Parks, S. L. and Packer, S. T. (2001) 'Expertise and the Perception of Kinematic and Situational Probability Information', *Perception*, 30, 233–52.

Abernethy, B., Zawi, K. and Jackson, R. (2008) 'Expertise and Attunement to Kinematic Constraints', *Perception*, 37, 931–48.

Abma, C. L., Fry, M. D., Li, Y. and Relyea, G. (2002) 'Differences in Imagery Content and Imagery Ability between High and Low Confident Track and Field Athletes', *Journal of Applied Sport Psychology*, 14, 67–75.

Abrams, M. and Reber, A. S. (1988) 'Implicit Learning: Robustness in the Face of Psychiatric Disorder', *Journal of Psycholinguistic Research*, 17, 425–39.

Adams, J. A. (1971) 'A Closed-Loop Theory of Motor Learning', *Journal of Motor Behavior*, 3, 111–50.

Adams, J. A. (1987) 'Historical Review and Appraisal of Research on the Learning, Retention, and Transfer of Human Motor Skills', *Psychological Bulletin*, 101, 41–74.

Adams, J. S. (1965) 'Inequity in Social Exchange', in L. Berkowitz (ed.), *Advances in Experimental Social Psychology* (New York: Academic Press), 267–99.

Adams, J. and Kirkby, R. (2001) 'Exercise Dependence and Overtraining: The Physiological and Psychological Consequences of Excessive Exercise', *Research in Sports Medicine*, 10, 199–222.

Adams, J. and Kirkby, R. (2002) 'Excessive Exercise as an Addiction: A Review', *Addiction Research and Theory*, 10, 415–37.

Aglioti, S. M., Cesari, P., Romani, M. and Urgesi, C. (2008) 'Action Anticipation and Motor Resonance in Elite Basketball Players', *Nature Neuroscience*, 11, 1109–16.

Agnew, G. A. and Carron, A. V. (1994) 'Crowd Effects and the Home Advantage', *International Journal of Sport Psychology*, 25, 53–62.

Aiello, J. R. and Douthill, E. A. (2001) 'Social Facilitation from Triplett to Electronic Performance Monitoring', *Group Dynamics*, 5, 163–80.

Ajzen, I. and Fishbein, M. (1970) 'The Prediction if Behavior from Attitudinal to Normative Beliefs', *Journal of Personality and Social Psychology*, 6, 466–87.

Ajzen, I. and Madden, T. J. (1986) 'Prediction of Goal-Directed Behaviour: Attitudes, Intentions, and Perceived Behavioural Control', *Journal of Experimental Social Psychology*, 22, 453–74.

Alain, C. and Proteau, L. (1980) 'Decision Making in Sport', in C. H. Nadeau, W. R. Halliwell, K. M. Newell and G. C. Roberts (eds), *Psychology of Motor Behavior and Sport* (Champaign, IL: Human Kinetics), 465–77.

Alain, C. and Sarrazin, C. (1990) 'Study of Decision-Making in Squash Competition: A Computer Simulation Approach', *Canadian Journal of Sport Science*, 15, 193–200.

Alain, C., Sarrazin, C. and Lacombe, D. (1986) 'The Use of Subjective Expected Values in Decision Making in Sport', in D. M. Landers (ed.), *Sport and Elite Performers* (Champaign, IL: Human Kinetics), 1–6.

Alfermann, D., Stambulova, N. and Zemaityte, A. (2004) 'Reactions to Sport Career Termination: A Cross-National Comparison of German, Lithuanian, and Russian Athletes', *Psychology of Sport and Exercise*, 5, 61–75.

Alfermann, D. (2000) 'Causes and Consequences of Sport Career Termination', in D. Lavallee and P. Wylleman (eds), *Career Transitions in Sport: International Perspectives* (Morgantown, WV: Fitness Information Technology), 49–58.

Alfermann, D. and Stoll, O. (2000) 'Effects of Physical Exercise on Self-Concept and Well Being', *International Journal of Sport Psychology*, 30, 47–65.

Alfermann, D. and Würth, S. (2001) 'Coach–Athlete Interaction in Youth Sport', in A. Papaioannou, M. Goudas and Y. Theodorakis (eds), *In the Dawn of the New Millennium: Proceedings of International Society of Sport Psychology* (Thessaloniki, Greece: Christodoulidis Publications), 165–6.

Allard, F. and Starkes, J. L. (1980) 'Perception in Sport: Volleyball', *Journal of Sport Psychology*, 2, 22–3.

Allard, F., Graham, S. and Paarsalu, M. L. (1980) 'Perception in Sport: Basketball', *Journal of Sport Psychology*, 2, 14–21.

Allen, J. B. and Howe, B. L. (1998) 'Player Ability, Coach Feedback, and Female Adolescent Athletes' Perceived Competence and Satisfaction', *Journal of Sport and Exercise Psychology*, 20, 280–99.

Allen, R. and Reber, A. S. (1980) 'Very Long Term Memory for Tacit Knowledge', *Cognition*, 8, 175–85.

Alley, D. E. and Chang, V. W. (2007) 'The Changing Relationship of Obesity and Disability, 1988–2004', *Journal of the American Medical Association*, 298, 2066–7.

Allison, K. R., Dwyer, J. J. M. and Makin, S. (1999a) 'Self-Efficacy and Participation in Vigorous Physical Activity by High School Students', *Health Education and Behavior*, 26, 12–24.

Allison, K. R., Dwyer, J. J. M. and Makin, S. (1999b) 'Perceived Barriers to Physical Activity Among High School Students', *Preventive Medicine*, 28, 608–15.

American College of Sports Medicine (1990) 'The Recommended Quantity and Quality of Exercise for Developing and Maintaining Fitness in Healthy Adults', *Medical Science and Sports Exercise*, 22, 265–74.

American College of Sports Medicine (1997) *Exercise Management for Persons with Chronic Diseases and Disabilities* (Champaign, IL: Human Kinetics).

American Psychiatric Association (1994) *Diagnostic and Statistical Manual of Mental Disorders*, 4th edn (Washington, DC: American Psychological Association).

Ames, C. (1992) 'Achievement Goals, Motivational Climate and Motivational Processes', in G. C. Roberts (ed.), *Motivation in Sport and Exercise* (Champaign, IL: Human Kinetics), 161–76.

Ammons, R. B. (1950) 'Acquisition of Motor Skills III: Effects of Initially Distributed Practice on Rotary Pursuit Performance', *Journal of Experimental Psychology*, 40, 777–87.

Amorose, A. J. (2007) 'Coaching Effectiveness: Exploring the Relationship between Coaching Behaviour and Self-determined Motivation', in M. S. Hagger and N. L. D. Chatzisarantis (eds), *Intrinsic Motivation and Self-determination in Sport and Exercise* (Champaign, IL: Human Kinetics), 209–27.

Amorose, A. J. and Horn, H. S. (2000) 'Intrinsic Motivation: Relationships with Collegiate Athletes' Gender, Scholarship Status, and Perceptions of their Coaches' Behavior', *Journal of Sport & Exercise Psychology*, 22, 63–84.

Andersen, A. E. (1990) (ed.) *Males with Eating Disorders* (New York: Brunner/Mazel).

Andersen, M. B. (2000) (ed.) *Doing Sport Psychology* (Champaign, IL: Human Kinetics).

Andersen, M. B. (2005) (ed.) *Sport Psychology in Practice*. (Champaign, IL: Human Kinetics).

Andersen, M. B., Van Raalte, J. L. and Brewer, B. W. (2001) 'Sport Psychology Service Delivery: Staying Ethical While Keeping Loose', *Professional Psychology: Research and Practice*, 32, 12–18.

Anderson, A. and Clarke, P. (2002) 'Afterword', in D. Lavallee and I. M. Cockerill (eds), *Counselling in Sport and Exercise Contexts* (Leicester: British Psychological Society), 69–73.

Anderson, D. and Morris, T. (2000) 'Athlete Lifestyle Programs', in D. Lavallee and P. Wylleman (eds), *Career Transitions in Sport: International Perspectives* (Morgantown, WV: Fitness Information Technology), 59–81.

Anderson, J. R. (1983) *The Architecture of Cognition* (Cambridge, MA: Harvard University Press).

Anderson, J. R. (1992) 'Automaticity and the ACT Theory', *American Journal of Psychology*, 105 (2), 165–80.

Anshel, M. (1995) 'Anxiety', in T. Morris and J. Summers (eds), *Sport Psychology: Theories, Applications and Issues* (Brisbane: John Wiley), 29–62.

Anthony, T. and Mullen, B. (1993) 'The Effect of Group Member Similarity on Cohesiveness – Do Birds of a Feather Really Flock Together?' Unpublished Manuscript, Department of Psychology, Syracuse University.

Araújo, D., Davids, K., Bennett, S. J., Button, C. and Chapman, G. (2004) 'Emergence of Sport Skills Under Constraints', in A. M. Williams and N. J. Hodges (eds), *Skill Acquisition in Sport: Research, Theory and Practice* (London: Routledge), 409–34.

Arena, B. (1997) 'Hormonal Problems in Young Female Athletes', *Sports Exercise and Injuries*, 2, 122–5.

Arora, S., Aggarwal, Sevdalis, N., Moran, A., Sirinanna, P., Kneebone, R. and Darzi, A. (2010). 'Development and Validation of Mental Practice as a Training Strategy for Laparoscopic Surgery', *Surgical Endoscopy*, 24, 179–87.

Arrow, H. (1997) 'Stability, Bistablity and Instability in Small Group Influence Patterns', *Journal of Personality and Social Psychology*, 72, 75–85.

Arrow, H. and McGrath, J. E. (1995) 'Membership Dynamics in Groups at Work: A Theoretical Framework', *Research in Organizational Behavior*, 17, 373–411.

Ash, M. G. (1992) 'Cultural Contexts and Scientific Change in Psychology: Kurt Lewin in Iowa', *American Psychologist*, 47, 198–207.

Ashford, B., Biddle, S. and Goudas, M. (1993) 'Participation in Community Sports Centres: Motives and Predictors of Enjoyment', *Journal of Sports Sciences*, 1, 249–56.

Atchley, R. C. (1989) 'A Continuity Theory of Normal Aging', *The Gerontologist*, 29, 183–90.

Atchley, R. C. (1991) *Social Forces and Aging: An Introduction to Social Gerontology*, 6th edn (Belmont, CA: Wadsworth).

Atkinson, J. W. (1964) *An Introduction to Motivation* (Princeton, NJ: Van Nostrand).

Babkes, M. L. and Weiss, M. R. (1999) 'Parental Influence on Children's Cognitive and Affective Responses to Competitive Soccer Participation', *Pediatric Exercise Science*, 11, 44–62.

Baddeley, A. (1996) 'Exploring the Central Executive', *The Quarterly Journal of Experimental Psychology*, 49A, 5–28.

Bahrke, M. S. and Morgan, W. P. (1978) 'Anxiety Reduction following Exercise and Meditation', *Cognitive Therapy and Research*, 2, 323–33.

Baillie, P. H. F. (1993) 'Understanding Retirement from Sports: Therapeutic Ideas for Helping Athletes in Transition', *The Counseling Psychologist*, 21, 399–410.

Baillie, P. H. F. and Danish, S. J. (1992) 'Understanding the Career Transition of Athletes', *The Sport Psychologist*, 6, 77–98.

Bakker, F. C., Boschker, M. S. J. and Chung, T. (1996) 'Changes in Muscular Activity while Imagining Weight Lifting Using Stimulus or Response Propositions', *Journal of Sport and Exercise Psychology*, 18, 313–24.

Bales, R. F. (1965) 'The Equilibrium Problem in Small Groups', in A. P. Hare, E. F. Borgatta and R. F. Bales (eds) *Small Groups: Studies in Social Interaction* (New York: Knopf).

Bamber, D., Cockerill, I. and Carroll, D. (2000) 'The Pathological Status of Exercise Dependence', *British Journal of Sports Medicine*, 34, 125–32.

Bandura, A. (1977a) 'Self-efficacy: Toward a Unifying Theory of Behavioral Change', *Psychological Review*, 84, 191–212.

Bandura, A. (1977b) *Social Learning Theory* (Englewood Cliffs, NJ: Prentice Hall).

Bandura, A. (1986) *Social Foundations of Thought and Action: A Social Cognitive View* (Englewood Cliffs, NJ: Prentice Hall).

Bandura, A. (1997) *Self-efficacy: The Exercise of Control* (New York: W.H. Freeman).

Bannister, R. (2004). 'Fear of Failure Haunted Me Right to the Last Second', *The Guardian* (Sport), 1 May, pp. 12–13.

Bard, C. and Fleury, M. (1976) 'Analysis of Visual Search Activity during Sport Problem Situations', *Journal of Human Movement Studies*, 3, 214–22.

Bard, C. and Fleury, M. (1981) 'Considering Eye Movements as a Predictor of Attainment', in I. M. Cockerill and W. W. McGillivary (eds), *Vision and Sport* (Cheltenham: Stanley Thornes), 28–41.

Barnes, S. (1999) 'Awesome Ace Sinks the Marketing Gurus', *Irish Independent*, 5 July, p. 14.

Bartlett, K. (1994) 'For Many Athletes, Fear is the Opponent', *Providence Journal*, 13, February, 9–10.

Bass, B. M. (1990) *Handbook of Leadership: Theory, Research and Managerial Applications*, 3rd edn (New York: The Free Press).

Bass, B. M. and Riggio, R. E. (2006) *Transformational Leadership*, 2nd edn (Mahwah, NJ: Lawrence Erlbaum Associates).

Battig, W. F. (1979) 'The Flexibility of Human Memory', in L. S. Cermak and F. I. M. Craik (eds), *Levels of Processing in Human Memory* (Hillsdale, NJ: Erlbaum), 23–44.

Battista, G. (ed.) (2004) *The Runner's High: Illuminations and Ecstasy in Motion* (Halcottsville, NY: Breakaway Books).

Baumeister, R. F. (1995) 'Disputing the Effects of Championship Pressures and Home Audiences', *Journal of Personality and Social Psychology*, 68, 644–8.

Baumeister, R. F. and Steinhilber, A. (1984) 'Paradoxical Effects of Supportive Audiences on Performance under Pressure: The Home Field Disadvantage in Sport Championships', *Journal of Personality and Social Psychology*, 47, 85–93.

Beauchamp, M. R. (2002) 'Role Ambiguity: Multidimensional and Multilevel Investigations in Sport'. Unpublished PhD Dissertation, University of Birmingham.

Beauchamp, M. R. and Bray, S. R. (2001) 'Role Ambiguity and Role Conflict within Interdependent Teams', *Small Group Research*, 32, 133–57.

Beauchamp, M. R., Bray, S. R. and Albinson, J. G. (2002) 'Pre-Competition Imagery, Self-Efficacy and Performance in Collegiate Golfers', *Journal of Sports Sciences*, 20, 697–705.

Beauchamp, M. R., Bray, S. R., Eys, M. A. and Carron, A. V. (2002) 'Role Ambiguity, Role Efficacy, and Role Performance: Multidimensional and Mediational Relationships within Interdependent Sport Teams', *Group Dynamics: Theory, Research, and Practice*, 6, 229–42.

Beauchamp, M., Bray, S., Fielding, A. and Eys, A. (2005) 'A Multilevel Investigation of the Relationship between Role Ambiguity and Role Efficacy in Sport', *Psychology of Sport and Exercise*, 6, 289–302.

Beauchamp, M. R. (2007) 'Efficacy Beliefs within Relational and Group Contexts in Sport', in S. Jowett and D. Lavallee (eds), *Social Psychology in Sport* (Champaign, IL: Human Kinetics), 181–94.

Beauchamp, M. R., Bray, S. R., Eys, M. A. and Carron, A. V. (2005) 'Leadership Behaviors and Multidimensional Role Ambiguity Perceptions in Team Sports', *Small Group Research*, 36, 5–20.

Beauchamp, M. R. and Eys, M. A. (eds) (2007) *Group Dynamics in Exercise and Sport Psychology: Contemporary Themes* (London: Routledge).

Becker, M. H., Haefner, D. P., Kasl, S. V., Kirscht, J. P., Maiman, L. A. and Rosenstock, I. M. (1977) 'Selected Psychosocial Models and Correlates of Individual Health-Related Behaviors', *Medical Care*, 15, 27–46.

Beedie, C. J., Terry, P. C. and Lane, A. M. (2000) 'The Profile of Mood States and Athletic Performance: Two Meta-Analyses', *Journal of Applied Sport Psychology*, 12, 49–68.

Beek, P. J. (2000) 'Toward a Theory of Implicit Learning in the Perceptual-Motor Domain', *International Journal of Sport Psychology*, 31, 547–54.

Beek, P. J., Jacobs, D., Daffertshofer, A. and Huys, R. (2003) 'Views on Expert Performance in Sport from the Joint Perspectives of Ecological Psychology and Dynamical Systems Theory', in J. L. Starkes and K. A. Ericsson (eds), *Expert Performance in Sports: Advances in Research on Sport Expertise* (Champaign, IL: Human Kinetics).

Behrmann, M. (2000) 'The Mind's Eye Mapped onto the Brain's Matter', *Current Directions in Psychological Science*, 9, 50–4.

Beilock, S. (2010) *Choke* (New York: Free Press).

Beilock, S. L. and Carr, T. H. (2001). 'On the Fragility of Skilled Performance: What Governs Choking Under Pressure?', *Journal of Experimental Psychology: General*, 130, 701–25.

Benjafield, J., Liddell, W. W. and Benjafield, I. (1989) 'Is There a Homefield Advantage in Professional Sports Championships?', *Social Behavior and Personality: An International Journal*, 17, 45–50.

Bennett, S. J., Davids, K. and Woodcock, J. (1999) 'The Structural Organisation of Practice: The Effects of Practicing under Different Informational Constraints on the Acquisition of One-Handed Catching Skill', *Journal of Motor Behavior*, 31, 3–9.

Bennett, S. J., Button, C., Kingsbury, D. and Davids, K. (1999) 'Manipulating Visual Informational Constraints during Practice Enhances the Acquisition of Catching Skill in Children', *Research Quarterly for Exercise and Sport*, 70, 220–32.

Bennie, A., and O'Connor, D. (2004). 'Running into Transition: A Study of Elite Track and Field Athletes', *Modern Athlete and Coach*, 2–6.

Bernstein, N. A. (1967) *The Co-ordination and Regulation of Movements* (Oxford: Pergamon Press).

Bezjak, J. E. and Lee, J. W. (1990) 'Relationship of Self-Efficacy and Locus of Control Constructs in Predicting College Students' Physical Fitness Behaviors', *Perceptual and Motor Skills*, 71, 499–508.

Biddle, S. (1993) 'Attribution Research and Sport Psychology', in R. N. Singer, N. Murphey, L. K. Tennant (eds), *Handbook of Research on Sport Psychology* (New York: Macmillan), 437–64.

Biddle, S. (1998) 'Sport and Exercise Motivation: A Brief Review of Antecedent Factors and Psychological Outcomes of Participation', in K. Green and K. Hardman (eds), *Physical Education: A Reader* (Aachen, Germany: Meyer and Meyer), 154–83.

Biddle S., Atkin, A. and Pearson N. (2007) *Physical Activity and Children Review 2: Correlates of Physical Activity in Children: A Review of Quantitative Systematic Reviews* (London: NICE Public Health Collaborating Centre – Physical Activity).

Biddle, S. and Nigg, C. (2000) 'Theories of Exercise Behavior', *International Journal of Sport Psychology*, 31, 290–304.

Biddle, S., Bull, S. and Seheult, C. (1992) 'Ethical and Professional Issues in Contemporary British Sport Psychology', *The Sport Psychologist*, 6, 66–76.

Biddle, S. J. H. and Fuchs, R. (2009) 'Exercise Psychology: A View from Europe', *Psychology of Sport and Exercise*, 10, 410–19.

Biddle, S. J. and Mutrie, N. (2008) *Psychology of Physical Activity: Determinants, Well-Being and Interventions*, 2nd edn (London: Routledge).

Biddle, S., Goudas, M. and Page, A. (1994) 'Social-Psychological Predictors of Self-Reported Actual and Intended Physical Activity in a University Workforce Sample', *British Journal of Sports Medicine*, 28, 160–3.

Biddle, S. J. H. and Mutrie, N. (2001) *Psychology of Physical Activity: Determinants, Well-Being and Interventions* (London: Routledge).

Biddle, S. J. H., Fox, K. R. and Boutcher, S. H. (2000) (eds) *Physical Activity and Psychological Well-Being* (London: Routledge).

Bilodeau, E. A. and Bilodeau, I. M. (1958) 'Variable Frequency of Knowledge of Results and the Learning of a Simple Skill', *Journal of Experimental Psychology*, 55, 379–83.

Blann, F. W. and Zaichkowsky, L. (1989) 'National Hockey League and Major League Baseball Players' Post-Sport Career Transition Surveys'. Final report prepared for the National Hockey League Players' Association, USA.

Blinde, E. and Stratta, T. (1992) 'The Sport Career Death of College Athletes: Involuntary and Unanticipated Sports Exits', *Journal of Sport Behavior*, 15, 3–20.

Blinde, E. M. and Greendorfer, S. L. (1985) 'A Reconceptualization of the Process of Leaving the Role of Competitive Athlete', *International Review for the Sociology of Sport*, 20, 87–94.

Bloom, B. S. (1985) (ed.) *Developing Talent in Young People* (New York: Ballantine).

Blumenthal, J. A., Michael, A., Babyak, A. *et al.* (2007) 'Exercise and Pharmacotherapy in the Treatment of Major Depressive Disorder', *Psychosomatic Medicine*, 69, 587–96.

Boiché, J.C.S. and Sarrazin, P.G. (2008) 'Proximal and Distal Factors Associated with Dropout Versus Maintained Participation in Organized Sport', *Journal of Sports Science and Medicine*, 8, 9–16.

Bollen, K. A. and Hoyle, R. H. (1990) 'Perceived Cohesion: A Conceptual and Empirical Examination', *Social Forces*, 69, 479–504.

Bond, C. F. Jr. and Titus, L. J. (1983) 'Social Facilitation: A Meta-Analysis of 241 Studies', *Psychological Bulletin*, 94, 265–92.

Bond, J. and Sargent, G. (1995) 'Concentration Skills in Sport: An Applied Perspective', in T. Morris and J. Summers (eds), *Sport Psychology: Theory, Applications and Issues* (Brisbane: Wiley), 386–419.

Bookbinder, H. (1955) 'Work Histories of Men Leaving a Short Life Span Occupation', *Personnel and Guidance Journal*, 34, 164–7.

Bortoli, L., Robazza, C., Durigon, V. and Carra, C. (1992) 'Effects of Contextual Interference on Learning Technical Sports Skills', *Perceptual and Motor Skills*, 75, 555–62.

Bouchard C., Depres, J. P. and Trembley, A. (1993) 'Exercise and Obesity', *Obesity Research*, 1, 133–47.

Boutcher, S. H. (2008) 'Attentional Processes and Sport Performance', in T. S. Horn (Ed.), *Advances in Sport Psychology*, 3rd edn (Champaign, IL: Human Kinetics), 325–38.

Boutcher, S. H. and Rotella, R. J. (1987) 'A Psychological Skills Educational Program for Closed-skill Performance Enhancement', *The Sport Psychologist*, 1, 127–37.

Boyd, M. and Callaghan, J. (1994) 'Task and Ego Goals in Organized Youth Sport', *International Journal of Sport Psychology*, 25, 411–24.

Boyd, M. P. and Yin, Z. (1996) 'Cognitive-Affective Sources of Sport Enjoyment in Adolescent Sport Participants', *Adolescence*, 31, 383–95.

Brady, F. (1998) 'A Theoretical and Empirical Review of the Contextual Interference Effect and the Learning of Motor Skills', *Quest*, 50, 266–93.

Braithwaite, R. L., Murphy, F., Lythcott, N. and Blumenthal, D.S. (1989) 'Community Organization and Development for Health Promotion within an Urban Black Community: A Conceptual Model', *Health Education*, 20, 56–60.

Braun, S, M., Beurskens, A. J., Borm, P. J., Schack, T., and Wade, D. (2006). 'The Effects of Mental Practice in Stroke Rehabilitation: A Systematic Review'. *Archives of Physical Medicine and Rerhabilitation*, 87, 842–52.

Bray, C. D. and Whaley, D. E. (2001) 'Team Cohesion, Effort, and Objective Individual Performance of High School Basketball Players', *The Sport Psychologist*, 15, 260–75.

Bray, S. R. (2004) 'Collective Efficacy, Group Goals, and Group Performance of a Muscular Endurance Task', *Small Group Research*, 35, 230–8.

Bray, S. R. (1999) 'The Home Advantage from an Individual Team Perspective', *Journal of Applied Sport Psychology*, 11, 116–25.

Bray, S. R. and Widmeyer, W. N. (2000) 'Athletes' Perceptions of the Home Advantage: An Investigation of Perceived Causal Factors', *Journal of Sport Behavior*, 23, 1–10.

Brehm, S. S. and Kassin, S. M. (1996) *Social Psychology*, 3rd edn (Boston, MA: Houghton-Mifflin).

Breslin, G., Hodges, N. J., Kennedy, R., Hanlon, M. and Williams, A. M. (2010) 'An Especial Skill: Further Support for a Learned Parameters Hypothesis', *Acta Psychologica*, 134, 55–60.

Breus, M. J. and O'Connor, P. J. (1998) 'Exercise Induced Anxiolysis: A Test of the "Time-out" Hypothesis in High Anxious Females', *Medicine and Science in Sports and Exercise*, 30, 1107–12.

Brewer, B. W. (1993) 'Self-Identity and Specific Vulnerability to Depressed Mood', *Journal of Personality*, 61, 343–63.

Brewer, B. W., Van Raalte, J. L. and Linder, D. E. (1993) 'Athletic Identity: Hercules' Muscles or Achilles' Heel?', *International Journal of Sport Psychology*, 24, 237–54.

Brewer, B. W., Van Raalte, J. L. and Petitpas, A. J. (2000) 'Self-Identity Issues in Sport Career Transitions', in D. Lavallee and P. Wylleman (eds), *Career Transitions in Sport: International Perspectives* (Morgantown, WV: Fitness Information Technology), 29–43.

Brewer, B. W., Van Raalte, J. L., Petitpas, A. J., Bachman, A. D. and Weinhold, R. A. (1998) 'Newspaper Portrayals of Sport Psychology in the United States, 1985–1993', *The Sport Psychologist*, 12, 89–94.

British Psychological Society (2009) *Code of Ethics and Conduct* (Leicester: British Psychological Society).

Broadbent, D. E. (1958) *Perception and Communication* (New York: Pergamon).

Brown, M. and Gordon, W. A. (1987) 'Impact of Impairment on Activity Patterns of Children', *Archives of Physical Medicine and Rehabilitation*, 68, 828–32.

Bruce, V., Green, P. R. and Georgeson, M. A. (1996) *Visual Perception: Physiology, Psychology and Ecology*, 3rd edn (Hillsdale, NJ: Lawrence Erlbaum).

Bruner, M. W., Munroe-Chandler, K. J. and Spink, K. S. (2008). 'Entry into Elite Sport: A Preliminary Investigation into the Transition Experiences of Rookie Athletes', *Journal of Applied Sport Psychology*, 20, 236–52.

Brustad, R. J. (1996) 'Attraction to Physical Activity in Urban School Children: Parental Socialization and Gender Influences', *Research Quarterly for Exercise and Sport*, 67, 418–24.

Bryan, W. L. and Harter, N. (1897) 'Studies in the Physiology and Psychology of the Telegraphic Language', *Psychological Review*, 4, 27–53.

Bryan, W. L. and Harter, N. (1899) 'Studies on the Telegraphic Language: The Acquisition of a Hierarchy of Habits', *Psychological Review*, 6, 345–75.

Buckworth, J. and Dishman, R. K. (2002) *Exercise Psychology* (Champaign, IL: Human Kinetics).

Buckworth, J. and Dishman, R. K. (2007) 'Exercise Adherence', in G. Tenenbaum and R. C. Eklund (eds), *Handbook of Sport Psychology,* 3rd edn (Hoboken, NJ: John Wiley and Sons), 509–36.

Bull, S. J. (1991) *Sport Psychology: A Self-Help Guide* (Wiltshire: The Crowood Press).

Buonamano, R., Cei, A. and Mussino, A. (1995) 'Participation Motivation in Italian Youth Sport', *The Sport Psychologist*, 9, 265–81.

Burhans, R.S., Richman, C.L. and Bergey, D.B. (1988) 'Mental Imagery Training: Effects on Running Speed Performance', *International Journal of Sport Psychology*, 19, 26–37.

Burke, K. L., Sachs, M. L., Fry, S. J. and Schweighardt, S. L. (2008) (eds) *Directory of Graduate Programs in Applied Sport Psychology*, 9th edn (Morgantown, WV: Fitness Information Technology).

Burke, V. and Collins, D. (1996) 'Physical Challenge and the Development of Conflict Management Skills', in J. Annett and H. Steinberg (eds), *How Teams Work in Sport and Exercise Psychology* (Leicester: British Psychological Society), 49–56.

Burton, D. (1992) 'The Jekyll/Hyde Nature of Goals: Reconceptualising Goal Setting in Sport', in T. S. Horn (ed.), *Advances in Sport Psychology* (Champaign, IL: Human Kinetics), 267–97.

Burton, D. (1998) 'Measuring Competitive State Anxiety', in J.L. Duda (ed), *Advances in Sport and Exercise Psychology Measurement* (Morgantown, WV: Fitness Information Technology), 129–48.

Burton, D., Naylor, S. and Holliday, B. (2001) 'Goal Setting in Sport: Investigating the Goal Effectiveness Paradox', in R. N. Singer, H. A. Hausenblas and C. Janelle (eds), *Handbook of Sport Psychology* (New York: Wiley), 497–528.

Burton, D. and Weiss, C. (2008) 'The Fundamental Goal Concept: The Path to Process and Performance Success', in T. Horn (ed.), *Advances in Sport Psychology*, 3rd edn (Leeds, UK: Human Kinetics), 339–75.

Busby, G. J. (1997) 'Modelling Participation Motivation in Sport', in J. Kremer, K. Trew, and S. Ogle (eds), *Young People's Involvement in Sport* (London: Routledge), 178–210.

Busby, G. J. (1999) 'Participation Motivation, Physical Exercise and Psychological Well-Being among a Long-Term Prison Population'. Unpublished Doctoral Thesis, School of Psychology, The Queen's University of Belfast.

Busby, G. J. and Kremer, J. (1997) 'A Process Model of Participation Motivation in Sport and Exercise', in R. Lidor and M. Bar-Eli (eds), *Innovations in Sport Psychology: Linking Theory and Practice* (Netanya, Israel: International Society of Sports Psychology), 166–8.

Bussmann, G. and Alfermann, D. (1994) 'Drop-Out and the Female Athlete: A Study with Track-and-Field Athletes', in D. Hackforth (ed.), *Psycho-Social Issues and Interventions in Elite Sport* (Frankfurt: Lang), 89–128.

Butcher, J., Lindner, K. J. and Johns, D. P. (2002) 'Withdrawal from Competitive Youth Sport: A Retrospective Ten-Year Study', *Journal of Sport Behavior*, 24, 145–61.

Butt, J. and Molnar, G. (2009) 'Involuntary Career Termination in Sport: A Case Study of the Process of Structurally Induced Failure', *Sport in Society*, 12, 2, 240–57.

Cacioppo, J. T., Berntson, G. G. and Nusbaum, H. C. (2008). 'Neurimaging as A New Tool in the Toolbox of Psychologicak Science', *Current Directions in Psychological Science*, 17, 62–7.

Cañal-Bruland, R. and Williams, A. M. (2010) 'Movement Recognition and Prediction of Movement Effects in Biological Motion Perception', *Experimental Psychology*, 57, 320–6.

Cardinal, B. J. (1997) 'Predicting Exercise Behavior Using Components of the Transtheoretical Model of Behavior Change', *Journal of Sport Behavior*, 20, 272–83.

Callow, N., and Hardy, L. (2004). 'The Relationship Between the Use of Kinaesthetic Imagery and Different Visual Imagery Perspectives', *Journal of Sports Sciences*, 22, 167–77.

Callow, N. and Waters, A. (2005). 'The Effect of Kinaesthetic Imagery on the Sport Confidence of Flat-Race Horse Jockeys', *Psychology of Sport and Exercise*, 6, 443–59.

Cardinal, B. J. (1999) 'Extended Stage Model of Physical Activity Behavior', *Journal of Human Movement Studies*, 37, 37–54.

Carpenter, P. J. (1995) 'Modification of the Sport Commitment Model', *Journal of Sport and Exercise Psychology*, 17, S37.

Carpenter, P. J. and Morgan, K. (1999) 'Motivational Climate, Personal Goal Perspectives, and Cognitive and Affective Responses in Physical Education Classes', *European Journal of Physical Education*, 4, 31–44.

Carpenter, P. J. and Scanlan, T. K. (1998) 'Changes Over Time in the Determinants of Sport Commitment', *Pediatric Exercise Science*, 10, 356–65.

Carpenter, P. J., Scanlan, T. K., Simons, J. P. and Lobel, M. (1993) 'A Test of the Sport Commitment Model Using Structural Equation Modelling', *Journal of Sport and Exercise Psychology*, 15, 119–33.

Carpenter, W. B. (1894) *Principles of Mental Physiology* (New York: Appleton-Century-Crofts).

Carron, A. V. (1982) 'Cohesiveness in Sport Groups: Interpretations and Considerations', *Journal of Sport Psychology*, 4, 123–38.

Carron, A. V. (1988) *Group Dynamics in Sport* (London, Ontario: Spodym).

Carron, A. V. and Brawley, L. R. (2000) 'Cohesion: Conceptual and Measurement Issues', *Small Group Research*, 31, 89–106.

Carron, A. V. and Brawley, F. R. (2008) 'Group Dynamics in Sport and Physical Activity', in T. S. Horn (ed.), *Advances in Sport Psychology* (Champaign, IL: Human Kinetics), 213–38.

Carron, A. V., Colman, M. M., Wheeler, J. and Stevens, D. (2002) 'Cohesion and Performance in Sport: A Meta Analysis', *Journal of Sport and Exercise Psychology*, 24, 168–88.

Carron, A. V., Eys, M. A. and Burke, S. M. (2007) 'Team Cohesion: Nature, Correlates and Development', in S. Jowell and D. Lavallee (eds.), *Social Psychology in Sport* (Champaign, IL: Human Kinetics), 91–102.

Carron, A. V., Hausenblas, H. and Eys, M. A. (2005) *Group Dynamics in Sport*, 3rd edn (Champaign, IL: Human Kinetics).

Carron, A. V., Loughhead, T. M. and Bray, S. R. (2005) 'The Home Advantage in Sport Competitions: Courneya and Carron's (1992) *Conceptual Framework A Decade Later*', *Journal of Sports Sciences*, 23, 395–407.

Carron, A. V. and Chelladurai, P. (1981a) 'Cohesion as a Factor in Sport Performance', *International Review of Sport Sociology*, 16, 2–41.

Carron, A. V. and Chelladurai, P. (1981b) 'The Dynamics of Group Cohesion in Sport', *Journal of Sport Psychology*, 3, 123–39.

Carron, A. V. and Hausenblas, H. A. (1998) *Group Dynamics in Sport*, 2nd edn (Morgantown, WV: Fitness Information Technology).

Carron, A. V., Brawley, L. R. and Widmeyer, W.N. (1998) 'Measurement of Cohesion in Sport and Exercise', in J. L. Duda (ed.) *Advances in Sport and Exercise Psychology Measurement* (Morgantown, WV: Fitness Information Technology), 213–26.

Carron, A. V., Bray, S. R. and Eys, M. A. (2002) 'Team Cohesion and Team Success in Sport', *Journal of Sports Sciences*, 20, 119–28.

Carron, A. V., Hausenblas, H. A. and Mack, D. (1996) 'Social Influence and Exercise: A Meta-Analysis', *Journal of Sport and Exercise Psychology*, 18, 1–16.

Carron, A. V., Spink, K. S. and Prapavessis, H. (1997) 'Team Building and Cohesiveness in the Sport and Exercise Setting: Use of Indirect Interventions', *Journal of Applied Sport Psychology*, 9, 61–72.

Carron, A. V., Widmeyer, W. N. and Brawley, L. R. (1985) 'The Development of an Instrument to Assess Cohesion in Sport Teams: The Group Environment Questionnaire', *Journal of Sport Psychology*, 7, 244–66.

Carver, C. S., Scheier, M. F. and Weintraub, J. K. (1989) 'Assessing Coping Strategies: A Theoretically Based Approach', *Journal of Personality and Social Psychology*, 56, 267–83.

Case, R. W. (1987) 'Leadership Behavior in Sport: A Field Test of the Situational Leadership Theory', *International Journal of Sport Psychology*, 18, 256–68.

Cash, T. F. and Deagle, E. A. (1997) 'The Nature and Extent of Body-Image Disturbances in Anorexia Nervosa and Bulimia Nervosa: A Meta-Analysis', *International Journal of Eating Disorders*, 22, 107–25.

Cashmore, E. (2008) *Sport Psychology: The Key Concepts*, 2nd edn (London: Routledge).

Casper, J. Gray, D. and Babkes Stellino, M. (2007) 'A Sport Commitment Model Perspective on Adult Tennis Players' Participation Frequency and Purchase Intentions', *Sport Management Review*, 10 (3), 253–78.

Casper, R. C. (1993) 'Exercise and Mood', *World Review of Nutrition and Dietetics*, 71, 115–43.

Cassidy, T., Jones, R. L. and Potrac, P. (2004) *Understanding Sports Coaching* (London: Routledge).

Castaneda, B., and Gray, R. (2007) 'Effects of Focus of Attention on Baseball Batting Performance in Players of Differing Skill Levels', *Journal of Sport and Exercise Psychology*, 29, 60–7.

Causer, J., Bennett S. J., Holmes, P. S., Janelle, C. M. and Williams, A. M. (2010) 'Quiet Eye Duration and Gun Motion in Elite Shotgun Shooting', *Medicine and Science in Sport Exercise*, 42, 8, 1599–608.

Causer, J., Holmes, P. S., Smith, N. C. and Williams, A. M. (in press). 'Anxiety, Movement Kinematics and Visual Attention in Elite-Level Performers', *Emotion*.

Cave, K. R. and Bichot, N. P. (1999) 'Visuospatial Attention: Beyond a Spotlight Model', *Psychonomic Bulletin*, 6, 204–23.

Cavill, N., Biddle, S. and Sallis, J.F. (2001) 'Health Enhancing Physical Activity for Young People: Statement of the United Kingdom Expert Consensus Conference', *Pediatric Exercise Science*, 13, 12–25.

Chamalidis, P. (1995) 'Career Transitions of Male Champions', in R. Vanfraechem-Raway and Y. Vanden Auweele (eds), *Proceedings of the 9th European Congress on Sport Psychology* (Brussels: European Federation of Sports Psychology), 841–8.

Charlesworth, R. (1994) 'Designer Games', *Sport Coach*, 17, 30–3.

Chase, M. (1998) 'Sources of Self-Efficacy in Physical Education and Sport', *Journal of Teaching in Physical Education*, 18, 76–89.

Chase, W. G. and Simon, H. A. (1973a) 'The Mind's Eye in Chess', in W. G. Chase (ed.), *Visual Information Processing* (New York: Academic Press), 404–27.

Chase, W. G. and Simon, H. A. (1973b) 'Perception in Chess', *Cognitive Psychology*, 4, 55–81.

Chatzisarantis, N. L. D., Hagger, M. S., Biddle, S. J. H., Smith, B. and Wang, J. C. K. (2003) 'A Meta-Analysis of Perceived Locus of Causality in Exercise, Sport, and Physical Education Contexts', *Journal of Sport & Exercise Psychology*, 25, 284–306.

Chelladurai, P. (1984a) 'Leadership in Sports,' in J. M. Silva and R. S. Weinberg (eds), *Psychological Foundations of Sport* (Champaign, IL: Human Kinetics), 329–39.

Chelladurai, P. (1984b) 'Discrepancy between Preferences and Perceptions of Leadership Behavior and Satisfaction of Athletes in Varying Sports', *Journal of Sport Psychology*, 6, 27–41.

Chelladurai, P. (1990) 'Leadership in Sports: A Review', *International Journal of Sport Psychology*, 21, 328–54.

Chelladurai, P. (2001) *Managing Organizations for Sport and Physical Activity: A Systems Perspective* (Scottsdale: Holcomb Hathaway).

Chelladurai, P. (1993) 'Leadership', in Singer, R. N., Murphey, M. and Tennant, L. K. (eds) *Handbook of Research on Sport Psychology* (New York: Macmillan), 647–71.

Chelladurai, P. and Carron, A. (1983) 'Athletic Maturity and Preferred Leadership', *Journal of Sport Psychology*, 5, 371–80.

Chelladurai, P. and Doherty, A. J. (1998) 'Styles of Decision-Making in Coaching', in J. M. Williams (ed.) *Applied Sport Psychology: Personal Growth to Peak Performance*, 3rd edn (Mountain View, CA: Mayfield), 115–26.

Chelladurai, P. and Haggerty, T. R. (1978) 'A Normative Model of Decision-making Styles in Coaching', *Athletic Administration*, 13, 6–9.

Chelladurai, P. and Saleh, S. D. (1978) 'Preferred Leadership in Sport', *Canadian Journal of Applied Sport Sciences*, 3, 85–92.

Chelladurai, P. and Saleh, S. D. (1980) 'Dimensions of Leader Behavior in Sport: Development of a Leadership Scale', *Journal of Sport Psychology*, 2, 34–45.

Chelladurai, P., Haggerty, T. and Baxter, P. (1989) 'Decision Style Choices of University Basketball Coaches and Players', *Journal of Sport & Exercise Psychology*, 11, 201–15.

Chelladurai, P., Imamura, H., Yamaguchi, Y., Oinuma, Y. and Miyauchi, T. (1988) 'Sport Leadership in a Cross-National Setting: The Case of Japanese and Canadian University Athletes', *Journal of Sport & Exercise Psychology*, 10, 374–89.

Cherry, C. (1953) 'Some Experiments on the Recognition of Speech with One and with Two Ears', *Journal of the Acoustical Society of America*, 25, 975–9.

Chi, L. and Duda, J. L. (1995) 'Multi-Sample Confirmatory Factor Analysis of the Task and Ego Orientation in Sport Questionnaire', *Research Quarterly for Exercise and Sport*, 66, 91–8.

Choi, P. Y. L. and Salmon, P. (1995) 'Symptom Changes across the Menstrual Cycle in Competitive Sportswomen, Exercisers and Sedentary Women', *British Journal of Clinical Psychology*, 34, 447–60.

Chow, G. M. and Feltz, D. L. (2007) 'Exploring New Directions in Collective Efficacy and Sport', in M. R. Beauchamp, and M. A. Eys (eds), *Group Dynamics in Exercise and Sport Psychology: Contemporary Themes* (New York: Routledge), 221–48.

Clarke, D. (with Karl Morris, 2005) *Golf – The Mind Factor* (London: Hodder and Stoughton).

Clews, G. J. and Gross, J. B. (1995) 'Individual and Social Motivation in Australian Sport', in T. Morris and J. Summers (eds), *Sport Psychology: Theory, Applications and Issues* (Brisbane: John Wiley), 90–121.

Coakley, J. J. (1983) 'Leaving Competitive Sport: Retirement or Rebirth?', *Quest*, 35, 1–11.

Coakley, J. J. (2001) *Sport and Society: Issues and Controversies*, 7th edn (Boston: McGraw-Hill).

Coakley, J. J. and White, A. (1992) 'Making Decisions: Gender and Sport Participation among British Adolescents', *Sociology of Sport Journal*, 9, 20–35.

Cockburn, C. and Clarke, G. (2002) '"Everybody's Looking at You!": Girls Negotiating the "Femininity Deficit" They Incur in Physical Education', *Women's Studies International Forum*, 25, 651–65.

Cockerill, I. M. and Riddington, M. E. (1996) 'Exercise Dependence and Associated Disorders: A Review', *Counselling Psychology Quarterly*, 9, 119–29.

Cockerill, I. M., Lawson, S. L. and Nevill, A. M. (1995) 'Mood States, Menstrual Cycle and Exercise-to-Music', in J. Annett, B. Cripps and H. Steinberg (eds), *Exercise Addiction* (Leicester: British Psychological Society), 61–9.

Cohen, J. (1992) 'A Power Primer', *Psychological Bulletin*, 112, 155–9.

Corbin, E. (2005) 'Leadership Issues in West Indies Cricket: A Theoretical Analysis of the Leadership Styles of a Purposive Group of Captains', *Journal of Eastern Caribbean Studies*, 30, 31–53.

Corbetta, M. and Shulman, G. L. (2002) 'Control of Goal-Directed and Stimulus-Driven Attention in the Braain', *Nature Reviews Neuroscience*, 3, 200–15.

Collet, C., Guillot, A., Lebon, F., MacIntyre, T. and Moran, A. (2011) 'Measuring Mental Imagery: Combining Psychometric, Qualitative, Chronometriic and Psychophysiological Techniques', under revision for *Exercise and Sport Sciences Reviews*, 39, 85–92.

Corry, M. (2007) 'Broccoli, Foul Focus Drinks and Hip-Hop: How We Will Prepare for the Big Kick-Off', *The Guardian* (Sport), 13 October, p. 3.

Costa, P. T. and McCrae, R. R. (1989) 'Personality, Stress, and Coping: Some Lessons from a Decade of Research', in K. S. Markides and C. L. Cooper (eds), *Aging, Stress and Health* (New York: Wiley), 269–85.

Cota, A. A., Evans, C. R., Dion, K. L., Kilik, L. and Longman, R. S. (1995) 'The Structure of Group Cohesion', *Personality and Social Psychology Bulletin*, 21, 572–80.

Côté, J., Baker, J. and Abernethy, B. (2001) 'Stages of Sport Participation of Expert Decision-Makers in Team Ball Sports', in A. Papaioannou, M. Goudas and Y. Theodorakis (eds), *In the Dawn of the New Millennium: Proceedings of International Society of Sport Psychology*, 3 (Thessaloniki, Greece: Christodoulidis Publications), 150–2.

Cotterill, S. (2010) 'Pre-Perfomance Routines in Sport: Current Understanding and Future Directions', *International Review of Sport and Exercise Psychology*, 3, in press.

Cotterill, S., Sanders, R. and Collins, D. (2010). 'Developing Effective Pre-Performance Routines in Golf: Why Don't We Ask the Golfer?', *Journal of Applied Sport Psychology*, 22, 51–64.

Courneya, K. S. and Carron, A. V. (1991) 'Effects of Travel and Length of Home Stand/Road Trip on the Home Advantage', *Journal of Sport & Exercise Psychology*, 13, 42–9.

Courneya, K. S. and Carron, A. V. (1992) 'The Home Advantage in Sports Competitions: A Literature Review', *Journal of Sport & Exercise Psychology*, 14, 13–27.

Cowell, L. L., Squires, W. G. and Raven, P. B. (1996) 'Benefits of Aerobic Exercise for the Paraplegic: A Brief Review', *Medicine and Science in Sports and Exercise*, 18, 501–8.

Cox, R. H. (2002) *Sport Psychology: Concepts and Application*, 5th edn (Boston: McGraw-Hill).

Cox, R. H., Martens, M. P. and Russell, W. D. (2003). 'Measuring Anxiety in Athletes: The Revised Competitive State Anxiety Inventory-2', *Journal of Sport & Exercise Psychology*, 25, 519–33.

Coyle, C. P. and Santiago, M. C. (1995) 'Aerobic Exercise and Depressive Symptomatology in Adults with Physical Disabilities', *Archives of Physical Medicine Rehabilitation*, 76, 647–52.

Crabbe, J. B., Smith, J. C. and Dishman, R. K. (1999) 'EEG and Emotional Response after Cycling Exercise', *Medicine and Science in Sports and Exercise*, 31 (suppl.), S173.

Crace, R. K. and Hardy, C. J. (1997) 'Individual Values and the Team Building Process', *Journal of Applied Sport Psychology*, 9, 41–60.

Craik, K. J. W. (1948) 'The Theory of the Human Operator in Control Systems: II. Man as an Element in a Control System', *British Journal of Psychology*, 38, 142–8.

Cramer, S. R., Nieman, D. C. and Lee, J. W. (1991) 'The Effects of Moderate Exercise Training on Psychological Well-Being and Mood State in Women', *Journal of Psychosomatic Research*, 35, 437–49.

Cratty, B. J. (1968) *Psychology and Physical Activity* (Englewood Cliffs, NJ: Prentice Hall).

Cripps, B. and Cann, G. (1996) 'Team Goal Setting in Rugby Union Football: A Nominal Group Technique', in J. Annett and H. Steinberg (eds), *How Teams Work in Sport and Exercise Psychology* (Leicester: British Psychological Society), 31–9.

Crocker, P. R. E. (1997) 'A Confirmatory Factor Analysis of the Positive Affect Negative Affect Schedule (PANAS) with a Youth Sport Sample', *Journal of Sport and Exercise Psychology*, 19, 91–7.

Crognier, L. and Féry, Y. (2005). 'Effect of Tactical Initiative on Predicting Passing Shots in Tennis', *Applied Cognitive Psychology*, 19, 1–13.

Csikszentmihalyi, M. (1990) *Flow: The Psychology of Optimal Experience* (New York: Harper and Row).

Culp, R. H. (1998) 'Adolescent Girls and Outdoor Recreation: A Case Study Examining Constraints and Effective Programming', *Journal of Leisure Research*, 30, 356–79.

Cumming, J. and Hall, C. (2002a) 'Athletes' Use of Imagery in the Off-Season', *The Sport Psychologist*, 16, 160–72.

Cumming, J. and Hall, C. (2002b) 'Deliberate Imagery Practice: The Development of Imagery Skills in Competitive Athletes', *Journal of Sports Sciences*, 20, 137–45.

Cumming, J. and Ramsey, R. (2009). 'Imagery Interventions in Sport', in S. D. Mellalieu and S. Hanton (eds), *Advances in Applied Sport Psychology: A Review* (Abingdon, Oxford: Routledge), 5–36.

Cummings, E., Dean, L. R., Newell, D. S. and McCaffrey, I. (1960) 'Disengagement: A Tentative Theory of Aging', *Sociometry*, 23, 23–35.

Curtis, J. and Ennis, R. (1988) 'Negative Consequences of Leaving Competitive Sport? Comparision Findings for Former Elite-level Hockey Players', *Sociology of Sport Journal*, 5, 87–106.

Curtis, R. (2000) 'Sydney 2000', *Mirror*, 2 October, p. 29.

Danielson, R. R., Zelhart, P. F. and Drake, C. J. (1975) 'Multidimensional Scaling and Factor Analysis of Coaching Behavior as Perceived by High School Hockey Players', *Research Quarterly for Exercise and Sport*, 46, 323–34.

Danish, S. and D'Augelli, A. R. (1983) *Helping Skills II: Life Development Intervention* (New York: Human Sciences).

Danish, S. J., Petitpas, A. J. and Hale, B. D. (1995) 'Psychological Interventions: A Life Developmental Model', in S. Murphy (ed.), *Sport Psychology Interventions* (Champaign, IL: Human Kinetics), 19–38.

Davids, K., Button, C. and Bennett, S. J. (2008) *Dynamics of Skill Acquisition* (Champaign, IL: Human Kinetics).

Davids, K., Williams, A. M., Button, C. and Court, M. L. J. (2001) 'An Integrative Modeling Approach to the Study of Intentional Movement Behaviour', in R. N. Singer, H. A. Hausenblas and C. M. Janelle (eds), *Handbook of Sport Psychology*, 2nd edn (John Wiley & Sons: New York), 144–73.

Davis, C. (1997) 'Eating Disorders and Hyperactivity: A Psychobiological Perspective', *Canadian Journal of Psychiatry*, 42, 168–75.

Davis, C. (1999) 'Excessive Exercise and Anorexia Nervosa: Addictive and Compulsive Behaviors', *Psychiatric Annals*, 29, 221–4.

Davis, H. (1991) 'Criterion Validity of the Athletic Motivation Inventory: Issues in Professional Sport', *Journal of Applied Sport Psychology*, 3, 176–82.

Davis, S. F., Huss, M. T., and Becker, A. H. (2009) 'Norman Triplett: Recognizing the Importance of Competition', in C. D. Green and L. T. Benjamin Jr. (eds), *Psychology Gets in the Game: Sport, Mind and Behaviour, 1880–1960* (Lincoln, NB: University of Nebraska Press), 98–115.

Davison K. and Lawson C. (2006) 'Do Attributes in the Physical Environment Influence Children's Physical Activity? A Review of the Literature', *International Journal of Behavioral Nutrition and Physical Activity*, 3, 3–19.

de Groot, A. D. (1965) 'Perception and Memory Versus Thought', in B. Kleinmuntz (ed.), *Problem Solving Research, Methods, and Theory* (New York: Wiley), 19–50.

De Knop, P., Wylleman, P., Theeboom, M., De Martelaer, K., Van Hoecke, J. and Van Heddegem, L. (1999) 'The Role of Contextual Factors in Youth Participation in Organized Sport', *European Physical Education Review*, 5, 153–68.

De Moor, M. H. M, Boomsma, D. I., Stubbe, J. H., Willemsen, G. and de Geus, E. J. C. (2008) 'Testing Causality in the Association between Regular Exercise and Symptoms of Anxiety and Depression',*Archives of General Psychiatry*, 65, 897–905.

Decety, J. and Ingvar, D.H. (1990) 'Brain Structures Participating in Mental Simulation of Motor Behavior: A Neuropsychological Interpretation', *Acta Psychologica*, 73, 13–34.

Decety, J. and Michel, F. (1989). 'Comparative Analysis of Actual and Mental Movement Times in Two Graphic Tasks', *Brain and Cognition*, 11, 87–97.

Decety, J., Jeannerod, M. and Prablanc, C. (1989) 'The Timing of Mentally Represented Actions', *Behavioral and Brain Research*, 34, 35–42.

Decety, J., Jeannerod, M., Durozard, M. and Baverel, G. (1993) 'Central Activation of Autonomic Effectors during Mental Simulation of Motor Actions', *Journal of Physiology*, 461, 549–63.

Deci, E. L. (1971) 'Effects of Externally Mediated Rewards on Intrinsic Motivation', *Journal of Personality and Social Psychology*, 18, 105–15.

Deci, E. L. (1975) *Intrinsic Motivation* (New York: Plenum Press).

Deci, E. L., Koestner, R., and Ryan, R. M. (1999) 'A Meta-Analytic Review of Experiments Examining the Effects of Extrinsic Rewards on Intrinsic Motivation', *Psychological Bulletin*, 125, 627–68.

Deci, E. L. and Ryan, R. M. (1985) *Intrinsic Motivation and Self-Determination in Human Behavior* (New York: Plenum Press).

Deci, E. L. and Ryan, R. M. (2002) (eds) *Handbook of Self-Determination Research* (Rochester, NY: University of Rochester Press).

Denis, M. (1985) 'Visual Imagery and the Use of Mental Practice in the Development of Motor Skills', *Canadian Journal of Applied Sport Sciences*, 10, 4s–16s.

Derakshan, N., and Eysenck, M. W. (2009). 'Anxiety, Processing Efficiency, and Cognitive Performance: New Developments from Attentional Control Theory', *European Psychologist*, 14, 168–76.

Deutsch, J. A. and Deutsch, D. (1963) 'Attention: Some Theoretical Considerations', *Psychological Review*, 70, 80–90.

De Vries, H. A. (1981) 'Tranquiliser Effects of Exercise: A Critical Review', *The Physician and Sports Medicine*, 9, 46–55.

Dishman, R. K. (2001) 'The Problem of Exercise Adherence: Fighting Sloth in Nations with Market Economies', *Quest*, 53, 279–94.

Dishman, R. K. and Buckworth, J. (2006) 'Exercise Psychology', in J. M. Williams (ed.), *Applied Sport Psychology*, 5th edn (New York: McGraw-Hill).

Dittrich, W. H. (1999). 'Seeing Biological Motion: Is There a Role for Cognitive Strategies?', in A. Braffort, R. Gherbi, S. Gibet, J. Richardson and D. Teil (eds), *Gesture-Based Communication in Human-Computer Interaction* (Berlin, Germany: Springer-Verlag), 3–22.

Doane, S. M. and Sohn, Y. W. (2000). 'ADAPT: A Predictive Cognitive Model of User Visual Attention and Action Planning', *User Modeling and User-Adapted Interaction*, 10 (1), 1–45.

Dobson, R. (1998) 'In the Grip of the Yips', *Guardian* (Sport), 31 March, p. 16.

Dollinger, S. J. and Leong, F. T. (1993) 'Volunteer Bias and the Five-Factor Model', *Journal of Psychology*, 127, 29–36.

Domingue, J. A. and Maraj, B. K. (1998) 'Effects of Model Skill Level in Observational Learning of the Flying Disk Forehand', *Journal of Sport & Exercise Psychology*, 20, s119.

Douglas, K. and Carless, D., (2009) 'Abandoning the Performance Narrative: Two Women's Stories of Transition from Professional Sport', *Journal of Applied Psychology*, 21, 213–30.

Driediger, M., Hall, C. and Callow, N. (2006) 'Imagery Use by Inured Athletes: A Qualitative Analysis', *Journal of Sports Sciences*, 24, 261–71.

Driskell, J. E., Copper, C. and Moran, A. (1994) 'Does Mental Practice Enhance Performance?', *Journal of Applied Psychology*, 79, 481–92.

Duda, J. L. (1989) 'Relationship Between Task and Ego Orientation and the Perceived Purpose of Sport among High School Athletes', *Journal of Sport & Exercise Psychology*, 11, 318–35.

Duda, J. L. (1993) 'Goals: A Social Cognitive Approach to the Study of Achievement Motivation in Sport', in R. N. Singer, M. Murphey and L. K. Tennant (eds), *Handbook of Research in Sport Psychology* (New York: Macmillan), 421–36.

Duda, J. L. (1996) 'Maximizing Motivation in Sport and Physical Education among Children and Adolescents: The Case for Greater Task Involvement', *Quest*, 48, 290–302.

Duda, J. L. (1997) 'What I Like in a Theory of Motivation: Building on the Present with a Look into the Future', in R. Lidor and M. Bar-Eli (eds), *Innovations in Sport Psychology: Linking Theory and Practice* (Netanya, Israel: International Society of Sports Psychology), 248–9.

Duda, J. L. (1998) (ed.) *Advances in Sport and Exercise Psychology Measurement* (Morgantown, WV: Fitness Information Technology).

Duda, J. L. (2001) 'Achievement Goal Research in Sport: Pushing the Boundaries and Clarifying Some Misunderstandings', in G. C. Roberts (ed.), *Advances in Motivation in Sport in Exercise* (Champaign, IL: Human Kinetics), 129–82.

Duda, J. L. (2005) 'Motivation in Sport: The Relevance of Competence and Achievement Goals', in A. J. Elliot and C. S. Dweck (eds), *Handbook of Competence and Motivation* (New York: Guildford Publications), 318–35.

Duda, J. L., Chi, L., Newton, M. L., Walling, M. D. and Catley, D. (1995) 'Task and Ego Orientation and Intrinsic Motivation in Sport', *International Journal of Sport Psychology*, 26, 40–63.

Duda, J. L. and Hom, H. L. (1993) 'Interdependencies between the Perceived and Self-reported Goal Orientations of Young Athletes and Their Parents', *Pediatric Exercise Science*, 5, 234–42.

Duda, J. L. and Hall, H. K. (2000) 'Achievement Goal Theory in Sport: Recent Extensions and Future Directions', in R. N. Singer, H. A. Hausenblas and C. M. Janelle (eds), *Handbook of Sport Psychology*, 2nd edn (New York: Wiley), 417–43.

Duda, J. L. and White, S. A. (1992) 'Goal Orientations and Beliefs about the Causes of Sport Success among Elite Skiers', *The Sport Psychologist*, 6, 334–43.

Duda, J. L. and Whitehead, J. (1998) 'Measurement of Goal Perspectives in the Physical Domain', in J. L. Duda (ed.) *Advances in Sport and Exercise Psychology Measurement* (Morgantown, WV: Fitness Information Technology), 21–48.

Dudgeon, K. (2000) 'Physical Exercise and the Menstrual Cycle: A Psychological Perspective'. Unpublished Doctoral Dissertation, School of Psychology, The Queen's University of Belfast.

Dugdale, J. C., Eklund, R. C. and Gordon, S. (2002) 'Expected and Unexpected Stressors in Major International Competition: Appraisal, Coping, and Performance', *The Sport Psychologist*, 16, 20–33.

Duncan, S. C. (1993) 'The Role of Cognitive Appraisal and Friendship Provisions in a Adolescents' Affect and Motivation Toward Activity in Physical Education', *Research Quarterly for Exercise and Sport*, 64, 314–23.

Dunn, A. L., Madhukar, H., Trivedi, M. D. *et al.* (2005) 'Exercise Treatment for Depression: Efficacy and Dose Response', *American Journal of Preventitive Medicine*, 28, 1–8.

Dunn, J. G. H. (1999) 'A Theoretical Framework for Structuring the Content of Competitive Worry in Ice Hockey', *Journal of Sport & Exercise Psychology*, 21, &259–79.

Dunn, J. G. H., Causgrove Dunn, J., Wilson, P. and Syrotuik, D. G. (2000) 'Re-examining the Factorial Composition and Factor Structure of the Sport Anxiety Scale', *Journal of Sport & Exercise Psychology*, 22, 183–93.

Durand-Bush, N., Salmela, J. and Green-Demers, I. (2001) 'The Ottawa Mental Skills Assessment Tool (OMSAT-3*)', *The Sport Psychologist*, 1–19.

Eagly, A. H. and Johnson, B. T. (1990) 'Gender and Leadership Style: A Meta-analysis', *Psychological Bulletin*, 108, 233–56.

Edwards, J. (1979) 'The Home Field Advantage', in J. H. Goldstein (ed.), *Sports, Games and Play: Social and Psychological Viewpoints* (Hillsdale, NJ: Lawrence Erlbaum).

Edwards, J. and Meier, K. (1984, July) 'Social Breakdown/Reconstruction and Athletic Retirement: An Investigation of Retirement and Retirement Adjustment in National Hockey League Players'. Paper presented at the Annual Meeting of the Olympic Scientific Congress, Eugene, OR, USA.

Edwards, T., Kingston, K., Hardy, L. and Gould, D. (2002) 'A Qualitative Analysis of Catastrophic Performances and the Associated Thoughts, Feelings, and Emotions', *The Sport Psychologist*, 16, 1–19.

English, A. (2006) *Munster: Our Road to Glory* (Dublin: Penguin).

Eitzen, D. S. (1975) 'Group Structure and Group Performance', in D. M. Landers, D. V. Harris, and R. W. Christina (eds), *Psychology of Sport and Motor Behavior* (University Park, PA: Pennsylvania State University Press).

Ellemers, N., Spears, R. and Doosje, B. (1999) (eds) *Social Identity* (Oxford: Blackwell).

Elliot, A. J. and Conroy, D. E. (2005) 'Beyond the Dichotomous Model of Achievement Goals in Sport and Exercise Psychology', *Sport and Exercise Psychology Review*, 1, 17–25.

Endler, N. S. and Parker, J. D. A. (1990) 'Multidimensional Assessment of Coping: A Critical Evaluation', *Journal of Personality and Social Psychology*, 58, 844–54.

Ericsson, K. A. (1996) 'The Acquisition of Expert Performance: An Introduction to Some of the Issues', in K.A. Ericsson (ed.), *The Road to Excellence: The Acquisition of Expert Performance in the Arts and Sciences, Sports and Games* (Hillsdale, NJ: Lawrence Erlbaum), 1–50.

Ericsson, K. A. and Charness, N. (1994) 'Expert Performance: Its Structure and Acquisition', *American Psychologist*, 49, 725–47.

Ericsson, K. A. and Delaney, P. F. (1999) 'Long-term Working Memory as an Alternative to Capacity Models of Working Memory in Everyday Skilled Performance', in A. Miyake and P. Shah (eds), *Models of Working Memory: Mechanisms of Active Maintenance and Executive Control* (Cambridge: Cambridge University Press), 257–97.

Ericsson, K. A. and Kintsch, W. (1995) 'Long-term Working Memory', *Psychological Review*, 102, 211–45.

Ericsson, K. A. and Kintsch, W. (2000) 'Shortcomings of Generic Retrieval Structures with Slots of the Type that Gobet (1993) Proposed and Modeled', *British Journal of Psychology*, 91, 571–90.

Ericsson, K. A. and Smith, J. (1991) 'Prospects and Limits of the Empirical Study of Expertise: An Introduction', in K. A. Ericsson and J. Smith (eds), *Toward a General Theory of Expertise* (Cambridge: Cambridge University Press), 1–38.

Ericsson, K. A., Krampe, R. T. and Tesch-Römer, C. (1993) 'The Role of Deliberate Practice in the Acquisition of Expert Performance', *Psychological Review*, 100, 363–406.

Ericsson, K. A. and Williams, A. M. (2007) 'Capturing Naturally Occurring Superior Performabce in the Laboratory: Translational Research on Expert Performance', *Journal of Experimental Psychology: Applied*, 13, 115–23.

Ericsson, K. A., Nandagopal, K. and Roring, R. W. (2009). 'Toward a Science of Exceptional Achievement: Attaining Superior Performance through Deliberate Practice', *Annals of New York Academy of Science*, 1172, 199–217.

Ericsson, K. A., Hoffman, P., Charness., N., and Feltovich, P. (2006) (eds) *The Cambridge Handbook of Expertise and Expert Performance* (Cambridge, UK: Cambridge University Press).

Eriksen, C. W. and St James, J. D. (1986) 'Visual Attention Within and Around the Field of Focal Attention: A Zoom Lens Model', *Perception and Psychophysics*, 40, 225–40.

Ernst, E., Rand, J. I. and Stevenson, C. (1998) 'Complementary Therapies for Depression: An Overview', *Archives of General Psychiatry*, 55, 1026–32.

Estabrooks, P. A. (2000) 'Sustaining Exercise Participation through Group Cohesion', *Exercise and Sport Sciences Review*, 28, 63–7.

Estabrooks, P. A. and Carron, A. V. (2000) 'The Physical Activity Environment Questionnaire: An Instrument for the Assessment of Cohesion in Exercise Classes for Older Adults', *Group Dynamics*, 4, 230–43.

Etnier, J. L., Salazar, W., Landers, D. M., Petruzzello, S. J., Han, M. and Nowell, P. (1997) 'The Influence of Physical Fitness and Exercise upon Cognitive Functioning: A Meta-analysis', *Journal of Sport & Exercise Psychology*, 9, 249–77.

Etzel, E. F., Watson, J. C. and Zizzi, S. (2003). 'A Web-based Survey of AAASP Members' Ethical Beliefs and Behaviors in the New Millennium', *Journal of Applied Sport Psychology*, 16, 236–50.

European Federation of Sport Psychology (1999). *Position Statement 5: Sports Career Termination* (Biel, Switzerland: European Federation of Sports Psychology).

Evans, N. J. and Jarvis, P. A. (1986) 'The Group Attitude Scale: A Measure of Attraction to Group', *Small Group Behavior*, 17, 203–16.

Everett, J. J., Smith, R. E. and Williams, K. D. (1992) 'Effects of Team Cohesion and Identifiability on Social Loafing in Relay Swimming Performance', *International Journal of Sport Psychology*, 23, 311–24.

Eys, M. A., Beauchamp, M. R. and Bray, S. R. (2006) 'A Review of Team Roles in Sport', in S. Hanton and S.D. Mellalieu (eds), *Literature Reviews in Sport Psychology* (Hauppauge, NY: Nova Science Publishers, Inc), 227–56.

Eysenck, M. and Calvo, M. (1992) 'Anxiety and Performance: The Processing Efficiency Theory', *Cognition and Emotion*, 6, 409–34.

Eysenck, M. W., and Keane, M. T. (2010) *Cognitive Psychology: A Student's Handbook*, 6th edn (Hove, East Sussex: Psychology Press).

Eysenck, M., W., Derakshan, N., Santos, R. and Calvo, M. G. (2007). 'Anxiety and Cognitive Performance: Attentional Control Theory', *Emotion*, 7, 336–53.

Fanning, D. (2002) 'Coping with a Stress Factor', *Sunday Independent* (Sport), 6 October, p. 6.

Farrow, D., Baker, J. and MacMahon, C. (2008) (eds) *Developing Sport Expertise: Researchers and Coaches Put Theory into Practice* (London: Routledge).

Faulkner, G. and Taylor, A. H. (eds) (2005) *Exercise, Health and Mental Health: Emerging Relationships* (London: Routledge).

Feifel, H. (1990) 'Psychology and Death: Meaningful Rediscovery', *American Psychologist*, 45, 537–43.

Feltz, D. and Landers, D. M. (1983) 'The Effects of Mental Practice on Motor Skill Learning and Performance: A Meta-analysis', *Journal of Sport Psychology*, 5, 25–57.

Feltz, D. L. (1987) 'Advancing Knowledge in Sport Psychology: Strategies for Expanding our Conceptual Frameworks', *Quest*, 39, 243–54.

Feltz, D. L. and Mungo, D. (1983) 'A Replication of Path Analysis of the Causal Elements in Bandura's Theory of Self-Efficacy and the Influence of Automatic Perception', *Journal of Sport Psychology*, 5, 263–77.

Feltz, D. L. and Petlichkoff, L. (1983) 'Perceived Competence among Interscholastics Sport Participants and Dropouts', *Canadian Journal of Applied Sport Science*, 8, 231–35.

Feltz, D. L., Short, S. E. and Sullivan, P. J. (2008) *Self-Efficacy in Sport: Research and Strategies for Working with Athletes, Teams and Coaches* (Champaign, IL: Human Kinetics).

Fernandez, A., Stephan, Y. and Fouqereau, E. (2006) 'Assessing Reasons for Sports Career Termination: Development of the Athletes' Retirement Decision Inventory', *Psychology of Sport and Exercise*, 7, 407–21.

Fernandez-Duque, D. and Johnson, M. L. (1999) 'Attention Metaphors: How Metaphors Guide the Cognitive Psychology of Attention', *Cognitive Science*, 23, 83–116.

Ferrer-Caja, E. and Weiss, M. R. (2000) 'Predictors of Intrinsic Motivation among Adolescent Students in Physical Education', *Research Quarterly for Exercise and Sport*, 71, 276–9.

Fiedler, F. E. (1967) *A Theory of Leadership Effectiveness* (New York: McGraw-Hill).

Fiedler, F. E. and Chemers, M. M. (1984) *Improving Leadership Effectiveness: The Leader Match Concept*, 2nd edn (New York: John Wiley and Sons).

Fillingim, R. B. and Blumenthal, J. A. (1993) 'The Use of Aerobic Exercise as a Method of Stress Management', in P. M. Lehrer and R. L. Woolfolk (eds), *Principles and Practice of Stress Management* (London: Guilford), 443–62.

Fishbein, M. and Ajzen, I. (1975) *Belief, Attitude, Intention, and Behavior: An Introduction to Theory and Research* (Reading, MA: Addison-Wesley).

Fitts, P. M. and Posner, M. I. (1967) *Human Performance* (Belmont, CA: Brooks/Cole).

Fleishman, E. A. (1956) 'Psychomotor Selection Tests: Research and Application in the United States Air Force', *Personnel Psychology*, 9, 449–67.

Fleishman, E. A. and Rich, S. (1963) 'Role of Kinesthetic and Spatial-visual Abilities in Perceptual-Motor Learning', *Journal of Experimental Psychology*, 66, 6–11.

Fletcher, D., Hanton, S. and Mellalieu, S. D. (2006). 'An Organizational Stress Review: Conceptual and Theoretical Issues in Competiitve Sport', in S. Hanton and S. D. Mellalieu (eds), *Literature Reviews in Sport Psychology* (New York: Nova Science), 321–73.

Flett, G. L. and Hewitt, P. L. (2005). 'The Perils of Perfectionism in Sports and Exercise', *Current Directions in Psychological Science*, 14, 14–18.

Folkins, C. H. and Sime, W. E. (1984) 'Physical Fitness Training and Mental Health', *American Psychologist*, 36, 373–89.

Folkman, S. (1991). 'Coping Across the Life Span: Theoretical Issues', in E. H. Cummings and K. H. Karraker (eds), *Life-Span Developmental Psychology: Perspectives on Stress and Coping* (Hillsdale, NJ: Erlbaum), 3–19.

Fontaine, K. R. and Shaw, D. F. (1995) 'Effects of Self-efficacy and Dispositional Optimism on Adherence to Step Aerobic Exercise Classes', *Perceptual and Motor Skills*, 81, 251–5.

Ford, I. W. and Gordon, S. (1993) 'Social Support and Athletic Injury: The Perspective of Sport Physiotherapists', *Australian Journal of Science and Medicine in Sport*, 25, 17–25.

Ford, I. W. and Gordon, S. (1998) 'Coping with Sport Injury: Resource Loss and the Role of Social Support', *Journal of Personal and Interpersonal Loss*, 4, 243–56.

Ford, P., Ward, P. and Williams, A. M. (2009) 'Antecedents of Selection to Professional Sport: The Role of Play and Practice in Progression and Regression', *High Ability Studies*, 20, 1, 65–75.

Ford, P, Yates, I. and Williams (2010) 'An Analysis of Activities and Instructional Behaviours Used By Coaches During Practice in English Youth Soccer: Exploring the Link between Theory and Practice', *Journal of Sport Sciences*, 28, 483–95.

Forsyth, D. R. (2009) *Group Dynamics*, 5th edn (Belmont, CA: Wadsworth Cengage Learning).

Fortunato, V., Anderson, D., Morris, T. and Seedsman, T. (1995) 'Career Transition Research at Victoria University', in R. Vanfraechem-Raway and Y. Vanden Auweele (eds), *Proceedings of the 9th European Congress on Sport Psychology* (Brussels: European Federation of Sports Psychology), 533–43.

Foster, C., Cowburn, G., Allender, S. and Pearce-Smith, N. (2007) *Physical Activity and Children Review 3: The Views of Children on the Barriers and Facilitators to Participation in Physical Activity: A Review of Qualitative Studies* (London: NICE Public Health Collaborating Centre – Physical Activity).

Foster, C., Hillsdon, M. and Thorogood, M. (2008) *Interventions for Promoting Physical Activity (Review): The Cochrane Library, Issue 4* (The Cochrane Collaboration: John Wiley and Sons).

Fox, K. R. (1998) 'Advances in the Measurement of the Physical Self', in J. L. Duda (ed.), *Advances in Sport and Exercise Psychology Measurement* (Morgantown, WV: Fitness Information Technology), 295–310.

Fox, K. R. (2000) 'The Influence of Exercise on Self-perceptions and Self-esteem', in S. J. H. Biddle, K. R. Fox and S. H. Boutcher (eds), *Physical Activity and Mental Well-being* (London: Routledg), 78–111.

Fox, K. R. and Corbin, C. B. (1989) 'The Physical Self-perception Profile: Development and Preliminary Validation', *Journal of Sport & Exercise Psychology*, 11, 408–30.

Fox, K. R., Goudas, M., Biddle, S., Duda, J. and Armstrong, N. (1994) 'Children's Task and Ego Goal Profiles in Sport', *British Journal of Educational Psychology*, 64, 253–61.

Frank, J. D. (1973) *Persuasion and Healing. A Comparative Study of Psychotherapy* (Baltimore: John Hopkins University Press).

Franken, R. E. (2007) *Human Motivation*, 6th edn (Belmont, CA: Wadsworth).

Franks, B. D. and Jette, M. (1970) 'Manifest Anxiety and Physical Fitness', *National College of Physical Education Association for Men: Annual Proceedings*, 71 (Chicago: NCPEAM).

Franzoi, S. L. (1995) 'The Body-as-Object Versus the Body-as-Process: Gender Differences and Gender Considerations', *Sex Roles*, 33, 417–37.

Frederick, C. J. and Shaw, S. M. (1995) 'Body Image as a Leisure Constraint: Examining the Experience of Aerobic Exercise Classes for Young Women', *Leisure Science*, 17, 57–73.

Frederick, C. M. and Morrison, C. S. (1996) 'Social Physique Anxiety: Personality Constructs, Motivations, Exercise Attitudes and Behaviour', *Perceptual and Motor Skills*, 82, 963–72.

Frederick, C. M. and Ryan, R. M. (1993) 'Differences in Motivation for Sport and Exercise and the Relationships with Participation and Mental Health', *Journal of Sport Behavior*, 16, 125–45.

Frederick, C. M. and Ryan, R. M. (1995) 'Self-determination in Sport: A Review using Cognitive Evaluation Theory', *International Journal of Sport Psychology*, 26, 5–23.

Frederick, C. M., Morrison, C. and Manning, T. (1996) 'Motivation to Participate, Exercise Affect, and Outcome Behaviors Toward Physical Activity', *Perceptual and Motor Skills*, 82, 691–701.

Furlong, W. B. (1976) 'Psychology of the Playing Fields', *Psychology Today*, July.

Furnham, A. and Greaves, N. (1994) 'Gender and Locus of Control Correlates of Body Image Dissatisfaction', *European Journal of Personality*, 8, 183–200.

Gabbett, T., Wake, M. and Abernethy, B. (2011). 'Use of Dual-Task Methodology for Skill Assessment and Development: Example from Rugby League', *Journal of Sports Sciences*, 29, 7–18.

Gardiner, E. N. (1930) *Athletics of the Ancient World* (Oxford: Oxford University Press).

Gardner, F. and Moore, Z. (2006) *Clinical Sport Psychology* (Champaign, IL: Human Kinetics).

Garfield, C. A. and Bennett, H. Z. (1984) *Peak Performance* (Los Angeles, CA: Tarcher).

Garland, D. J. and Barry, J. R. (1991) 'Cognitive Advantage in Sport: The Nature of Perceptual Structures', *The American Journal of Psychology*, 104, 211–28.

Garavan, H. (1998). 'Serial Attention in Working Memory', *Memory and Cognition*, 26, 263–76.

Gauvin, L. and Brawley, L. R. (1993) 'Alternative Psychological Models and Methodologies for the Study of Exercise and Affect', in P. Seraganian (ed.), *Exercise Psychology: The Influence of Physical Exercise on Psychological Processes* (New York: Wiley), 146–71.

Gauvin, L. and Spence, J. C. (1998) 'Measurement of Exercise-induced Changes in Feeling States, Affect, Mood and Emotions', in J. L. Duda (ed.), *Advances in Sport and Exercise Psychology Measurement* (Morganstown, WV: Fitness Information Technology), 325–36.

Gebhardt, W. A., Van Der Doef, M. P. and Maes, S. (1999) 'Conflicting Activities for Exercise', *Perceptual and Motor Skills*, 89, 1159–60.

Gecas, V. (1989) 'The Social Psychology of Self-efficacy', *Annual Review of Sociology*, 15, 141–51.

Gentile, A. M. (1998) 'Implicit and Explicit Processes during Acquisition of Functional Skills', *Scandinavian Journal of Occupational Therapy*, 5, 7–16.

George, T. R. and Feltz, D. L. (1995) 'Motivation in Sport from a Collective Efficacy Perspective', *International Journal of Sport Psychology*, 26, 98–116.

Giacobbi, P. R., Lynn, T. K., Wetherington, J. M., Jenkins, J., Bodendorf, M. and Langley, B. (2004) 'Stress and Coping during the Transition to University for First-year Female Athletes', *The Sport Psychologist*, 18, 1–20.

Gibson, J. J. (1979) *The Ecological Approach to Visual Perception* (Boston: Houghton-Mifflin).

Giles-Corti, B., Timperio, A., Bull, F. and Pikora T. (2005), 'Understanding Physical Activity Environmental Correlates: Increased Specificity for Ecological Models', *Exercise and Sport Science Reviews*, 33, 175–81.

Gill, D. L. (1979) 'The Prediction of Group Motor Performance from Individual Member Abilities', *Journal of Motor Behavior*, 11, 113–22.

Gill, D. L. (1986) *Psychological Dynamics of Sport* (Champaign, IL: Human Kinetics).

Gill, D. L. (1993) 'Competitiveness and Competitive Orientation in Sport', in R. N. Singer, M. Murphey and K. Tennant (eds), *Handbook of Research on Sport Psychology* (New York: Macmillan), 314–27.

Gill, D. L. (1997) 'Sport and Exercise Psychology', in J. Massengale and R. Swanson (eds), *History of Exercise and Sport Science* (Champaign, IL: Human Kinetics), 293–320.

Gill, D. L. (2000) *Psychological Dynamics of Sport and Exercise,* 2nd edn (Champaign, IL: Human Kinetics).

Gill, D. (2007) 'Gender and Cultural Diversity', in G. Tenenbaum and R. C. Eklund. (eds), *Handbook of Sport Psychology,* 3rd edn (Hoboken, NJ: John Wiley and Sons), 823–44.

Gill, D. L. (2008) *Psychological Dynamics of Sport and Exercise*, 3rd edn (Champaign, IL: Human Kinetics).

Gill, D. L. and Deeter, T. E. (1988) 'Development of the Sport Orientation Questionnaire', *Research Quarterly for Exercise and Sport*, 59, 191–202.

Gillet, N. and Rosnet, E. (2008). 'Basic Need Satisfaction and Motivation in Sport', *Athletic Insight*, 10.

Glamser, F. D. (1990) 'Contest Location, Player Misconduct and Race: A Case from English Soccer', *Journal of Sport Behavior*, 13, 41–9.

Glaser, B. G. and Strauss, A. L. (1965*) Awareness of Dying* (Chicago: Aldine).

Gobet, F. (1998) 'Expert Memory: A Comparison of Four Theories', *Cognition*, 66, 115–52.

Gobet, F. and Simon, H.A. (1996) 'Templates in Chess Memory: A Mechanism for Recalling Several Boards', *Cognitive Psychology*, 31, 1–40.

Godin, G. (1994) 'Theories of Reasoned Action and Planned Behavior: Usefulness for Exercise Promotion', *Medicine and Science in Sports and Exercise*, 26, 1391–4.

Goldstein, E. B. (2008). Cognitive Psychology: Connecting Mind, Research, and Everyday Experience (2nd ed). Belmont, CA: Thompson/Wadsworth.

Goodbody, J. and Nichols, P. (2004).'Marathon Marred By Invader's Attack On Race Leader'. The Times (Sport), 30 August, p. 1.

Goode, S. and Magill, R. A. (1986) 'Contextual Interference Effects in Learning Three Badminton Serves', *Research Quarterly for Exercise and Sport*, 57, 308–14.

Gorczynski, P. and Faulkner, G. (2010) 'Exercise Therapy for Schizophrenia', *Cochrane Database of Sysetmatic Reviews, 5, CD004412* (New York: John Wiley and Sons).

Gordon, S. (1988) 'Decision Styles and Effectiveness in University Soccer', *Canadian Journal of Sport Sciences*, 13, 56–65.

Gordon, S. and Lavallee, D. (in press). 'Career Transitions in Competitive Sport', in T. Morris and J. Summer (eds), *Sport Psychology: The Cutting Edge* (Morgantown, WV: Fitness Information Technology).

Gorely, T., Lavallee, D., Bruce, D., Teale, B. and Lavallee, R. M. (2001) 'An Evaluation of the Athlete Career and Education Program', *Athletic Academic Journal*, 15, 11–21.

Gould, D. (1987) 'Understanding Attrition in Children's Sport', in D. Gould and M. R. Weiss (eds), Advances *in Paediatric Sciences: Volume 2, Behavioral Issues* (Champaign, IL: Human Kinetics), 61–85.

Gould, D. (2009). 'Mental Preparation for Training and Competition', in B. W. Brewer (ed.), *Sport Psychology* (Handbook of Sports Medicine and Science) (Oxford: Wiley-Blackwell), 53–63.

Gould, D. and Horn, T. (1984) 'Participation Motivation in Young Athletes', in J. M. Silva and R. S. Weinberg (eds), *Psychological Foundations of Sport* (Champaign, IL: Human Kinetics), 359–70.

Gould, D. and Petlichkoff, L. (1988) 'Participation Motivation and Attrition in Young Athletes', in F. L. Smoll, R. A. Magill and M. J. Ash (eds), *Children in Sport* (Champaign, IL: Human Kinetics), 161–78.

Gould, D., Damarjian, N. and Greenleaf, C. (2002) 'Imagery Training for Peak Performance', in J. L. Van Raalte and B. W. Brewer (eds), *Exploring Sport and Exercise Psychology*, 2nd edn (Washington DC: American Psychological Association), 49–74.

Gould, D., Dieffenbach, K. and Moffett, A. (2002) 'Psychological Characteristics and Their Development in Olympic Champions', *Journal of Applied Sport Psychology*, 14, 172–204.

Gould, D., Finch, L. M. and Jackson, S. A. (1993) 'Coping Strategies Used by National Champion Figure Skaters', *Research Quarterly for Exercise and Sport*, 64, 453–68.

Gould, D., Greenleaf, C. and Krane, V. (2002) 'Arousal-Anxiety and Sport', in T. Horn (ed.), *Advances in Sport Psychology*, 2nd edn (Champaign, IL: Human Kinetics), 207–41.

Gould, D., Giannini, J., Krane, V. and Hodge, K. (1990) 'Educational Needs of Elite U.S. National Team, Pan American, and Olympic Coaches', *Journal of Teaching in Physical Education*, 9, 332–44.

Graham R., Kremer J. and Wheeler G. (2008) 'Physical Exercise and Psychological Well-Being among People with Chronic Illness and Disability: A Grounded Approach', *Journal of Health Psychology*, 13, 447–58.

Graham, R. (2000) 'Physical Activity and Psychological Well-Being among People with Chronic Illness'. Unpublished Doctoral Thesis, School of Psychology, The Queen's University of Belfast.

Granleese, J., Trew, K. and Turner, I. (1988) 'Sex Differences in Perceived Competence', *British Journal of Social Psychology*, 27, 181–4.

Grant, T. (2000) (ed.) *Physical Activity and Mental Health: National Consensus Statements and Guidelines for Practice* (London: Health Education Authority).

Gray, J. A. and Wedderburn, A. A. (1960) 'Grouping Strategies with Simultaneous Stimuli', *Quarterly Journal of Experimental Psychology*, 12, 180–4.

Green, C. D. (2009) 'Coleman Roberts Griffith: "Father" of Sport Psychology', in C. D. Green and L. T. Benjamin Jr. (eds), *Psychology Gets in the Game: Sport, Mind and Behaviour, 1880–1960* (Lincoln, NB: University of Nebraska Press), 202–29.

Greendorfer, S. L. and Blinde, E. M. (1985) 'Retirement from Intercollegiate Sport: Theoretical and Empirical Considerations', *Sociology of Sport Journal*, 2, 101–10.

Greer, D. L. (1983) 'Spectator Booing and the Home Advantage: A Study of Social Influence in the Basketball Arena', *Social Psychology Quarterly*, 46, 252–61.

Grieve, F. G., Whelan, J. P. and Meyers, A. W. (2000) 'An Experimental Examination of the Cohesion-Performance Relationship in an Interactive Team Sport', *Journal of Applied Sport Psychology*, 12, 219–35.

Griffith, C. R. (1926) *The Psychology of Coaching* (New York: Charles Scribners).

Griffith, C. R. (1928) *Psychology and Athletics* (New York: Charles Scribners).

Griffith, C. R. (1941) *An Introduction to Applied Psychology* (New York: Macmillan).

Grouios, G. (1992) 'Mental Practice: A Review', *Journal of Sport Behavior*, 15, 42–59.

Grove, J. R., Stewart, R. M. L. and Gordon, S. (1990) 'Emotional Reactions of Athletes to Knee Rehabilitation'. Paper presented at the Annual Meeting of the Australian Sports Medicine Federation, Alice Springs, NT.

Grove, J. R., Lavallee, D., Gordon, S. and Harvey, J. H. (1998) 'Account-making: A Model for Understanding and Resolving Distressful Reactions to Retirement from Sport', *The Sport Psychologist*, 12, 52–67.

Gruber, J. J. and Gray, G. R. (1982) 'Responses to Forces Influencing Cohesion as a Function of Player Status and Level of Male Varsity Basketball Competition', *Research Quarterly for Exercise and Sport*, 53, 27–36.

Guadignoli, M. A., Dornier, L. A. and Tandy, R. D. (1996) 'Optimal Length for Summary Knowledge of Results: The Influence of Task-related Experience and Complexity', *Research Quarterly for Exercise and Sport*, 67, 239–48.

Guardian, The (2009) 'The Guardian and Observer Guides to Keeping Fit with Britain's Medal Winners', January, p. 35.

Gucciardii, D. F. and Dimmock, J. A. (2008) 'Choking Under Pressure in Sensorimotor Skills: Conscious Processing or Depleted Attentional Resources?', *Psychology of Sport and Exercise*, 3, 24–39.

Guillot, A. and Collet, C. (2005) 'Duration of Mentally Simulated Movement: A Review', *Journal of Motor Behavior*, 37, 10–20.

Guillot, A. and Collet, C. (eds) (2010) *The Neurophysiological Foundatons of Mental and Motor Imagery* (Oxford: Oxford University Press).

Guillot, A. Collet, C., Nguyen, V. A., Malouin, F., Richards, C. and Doyon, J. (2009) 'Brain Activity During Visual Versus Kinaesthetic Imagery: An fMRI Study', *Human Brain Mapping*, 30, 2157–72.

Guillot, A., Nadrowska, E. and Collet, C. (2009). 'Using Motor Imagery to Learn Tactical Movements in Basketball', *Journal of Sport Behavior*, 32, 189–206.

Guillet, E., Sarrazin, P., Carpenter, P., Trouilloud, D. and Cury, F. (2002) 'Predicting Persistence or Withdrawal in Female Handballers with Social Exchange Theory', *International Journal of Sport Psychology*, 37, 92–104.

Guszkowska, M. (2004) 'Effects of Exercise on Anxiety, Depression and Mood', *Psychiatria Polska*, 38, 611–20.

Haerle, R. K. (1975) 'Career Patterns and Career Contingencies of Professional Baseball Players: An Occupational Analysis', in D. W. Ball and J. W. Loy (eds), *Sport and Social Order* (Reading, MA: Addison-Wesley), 461–519.

Hagger, M. and Chatzisarantis, N. (2005) *The Social Psychology of Sport and Exercise* (New York: Open University Press).

Hagger, M. S. and Chatzisarantis, N. L. D. (2007) (eds.) *Intrinsic Motivation and Self-Determination in Exercise and Sport* (Champaign, IL: Human Kinetics).

Hagger, M., Chatzisarantis, N. and Biddle, S. (2002) 'A Meta-Analytic Review of the Theories of Reasoned Action and Planned Behavior in Physical Activity: An Examination of Predictive Validity and the Contribution of Additional Variables', *Journal of Sport & Exercise Psychology*, 24, 3–32.

Hale, B. and Waalkes, D. (1994, June) 'Athletic Identity, Gender, Self-esteem, Academic Importance and Drug Use: A Further Validation of the AIMS'. Paper presented at the Annual Meeting of the North American Society for the Psychology of Sport and Physical Activity, Clearwater Beach, FL, USA.

Hall, C., Mack, D., Paivio, A. and Hausenblas, H.A. (1998) 'Imagery Use by Athletes: Development of the Sport Imagery Questionnaire', *International Journal of Sport Psychology*, 29, 73–89.

Hall, C. R. (2001) 'Imagery in Sport and Behavior', in R. N. Singer, H. A Hausenblas and C. M. Janelle (eds), *Handbook of Sport Psychology*, 2nd edn (New York: John Wiley), 529–49.

Hall, C. R. and Martin, K. A. (1997) 'Measuring Movement Imagery Abilities: A Revision of the Movement Imagery Questionnaire', *Journal of Mental Imagery*, 21, 143–54.

Hall, K. and Kerr, A. W. (2001) 'Goal Setting in Sport and Physical Activity: Tracing Empirical Developments and Establishing Conceptual Direction', in G. C. Roberts (ed.), *Advances in Motivation in Sport and Exercise* (Champaign, IL: Human Kinetics), 183–235.

Hall, K. G., Domingues, D. A. and Cavazos, R. (1994) 'Contextual Interference Effects with Skilled Baseball Players', *Perceptual and Motor Skills*, 78, 835–41.

Hallden, O. (1965) 'The Adjustment of Athletes after Retiring from Sport', in F. Antonelli (ed.), *Proceedings of the 1st International Congress of Sport Psychology* (Rome: International Society of Sport Psychology), 730–3.

Hanin, Y. and Martens, R. (1978) 'Sport psychology in the USSR', NASPSPA Newsletter, 3, 1–3.

Hanrahan, S. J. and Biddle, S. J. H. (2008) 'Attributions and Perceived Control', in T. S. Horn (Ed.), *Advances in Sport Psychology*, 3rd edn (Champaign, IL: Human Kinetics), 99–114.

Hanrahan, S. and Gallois, C. (1993) 'Social Interaction', in R. N. Singer, M. Murphey and K. L. Tennant (eds), *Handbook of Research in Sport Psychology* (New York: Macmillan), 623–46.

Hanrahan, S. J. and Gross, J. (2005) 'Attributions and Goal Orientations in Masters Athletes: Performance versus Outcome', *Revista de Psicologia del Deporte*, 14 43–56.

Hanson, T. W. and Gould, D. (1988) 'Factors Affecting the Ability of Coaches to Estimate Their Athletes' Trait and State Anxiety Levels', *The Sport Psychologist*, 2, 298–313.

Hanton, S. and Jones, G. (1999) 'The Acquisition and Development of Cognitive Skills and Strategies: I. Making the Butterflies in Formation', *The Sport Psychologist*, 13, 1–21.

Hanton, S., Neil, R. and Mellalieu, S. D. (2008). 'Recent Developments in Competitive Anxiety Direction and Competition Stress Research', *International Review of Sport and Exercise Psychology*, 1, 45–57.

Hanton, S., Thomas, O. and Mellalieu, S. D. (2009), in B. W. Brewer (ed), *Sport Psychology* (Handbook of Sports Medicine and Science) (Oxford: Wiley-Blackwell), 30–42.

Hardy, C. J. (1990) 'Social Loafing: Motivational Losses in Collective Performance', *International Journal of Sport Psychology*, 21, 305–27.

Hardy, C. J. and Kelly-Crace, R. (1991) 'The Effects of Task Structure and Treammate Competence on Social Loafing', *Journal of Sport and Exercise Psychology*, 13, 372–81.

Hardy, J., Oliver, E. and Tod, D. (2009). 'A Framework for the Study and Application of Self-Talk within Sport', in S. D. Mellalieu and S. D. Hanton (eds), *Advances in Applied Sport Psychology: A Review* (Abingdon, Oxford: Routledge), 37–74.

Hardy, J., Eys, M. A. and Carron, A. V. (2005) 'Exploring the Potential Disadvantages of High Cohesion in Sports Teams', *Small Group Research*, 36, 166–87.

Hardy, L. (1990) 'A Catastrophe Model of Anxiety and Performance', in G. Jones and L. Hardy (eds), *Stress and Performance in Sport* (Chichester: John Wiley), 81–106.

Hardy, L. (1997) 'The Coleman Roberts Griffith Address: Three Myths about Applied Consultancy Work', *Journal of Applied Sport Psychology*, 9, 277–94.

Hardy, L. and Callow, N. (1999) 'Efficacy of External and Internal Visual Imagery Perspectives for the Enhancement of Performance on Tasks in Which Form is Important', *Journal of Sport & Exercise Psychology*, 21, 95–112.

Hardy, L. and Fazey, J. (1990) *Concentration Training: A Guide for Sports Performers* (Leeds: National Coaching Foundation).

Hardy, L. and Parfitt, C.G. (1991) 'A Catastrophe Model of Anxiety and Performance', *British Journal of Psychology*, 82, 163–78.

Hardy, L. and Parfitt, C. G. (1994) 'The Development of a Model for the Provision of Psychological Support to a National Squad', *The Sport Psychologist*, 8, 126–42.

Hardy, L., Gammage, K. and Hall, C. (2001) 'A Descriptive Study of Athletes' Self-Talk', *The Sport Psychologist*, 15, 306–18.

Hardy, L., Jones, G. and Gould, D. (1996a) *Understanding Psychological Preparation for Sport: Theory and Practice of Elite Performers* (Chichester: John Wiley).

Hardy, L., Mullen, R. and Jones, G. (1996b) 'Knowledge and Conscious Control of Motor Actions under Stress', *British Journal of Psychology*, 87, 621–36.

Hardy, L., Beattie, S. and Woodman, T. (2007) 'Anxiety-Induced Performance Catastrophes: Investigating Effort Required as an Asymmetry Factor', *British Journal of Psychology*, 98, 15–31.

Hare, N. (1971) 'A Study of the Black Fighter', *The Black Scholar*, 3 (3), 2–9.

Harkins, S. G. and Szymanski, K. (1987) 'Social Loafing and Social Facilitation: New Wine in Old bottles', in C. Hendrick (ed.), *Group Processes and Intergroup Relations* (Newbury Park, CA: Sage), 167–88.

Harris, H. A. (1964) *Greek Athletes and Athletics* (Westport, CT: Greenwood Press).

Harrison, C. K. and Lawrence, S. M. (2004) Female and Male Student Athletes' Perceptions of Career Transition in Sport and Higher Education: A Visual Elicitation and Qualitative Assessment', *Journal of Vocational Education and Training*, 56 (4), 485–505.

Harrison, C. K. and Lawrence, S. M. (2003) 'African American Student Athletes' Perceptions of Career Transition in Sport: A Qualitative and Visual Elicitation', *Race Ethnicity and Education*, 6 (4), 373–94.

Harter, S. (1978) 'Effectance Motivation Reconsidered: Towards a Developmental Model', *Human Development*, 21, 34–64.

Harter, S. (1981) 'A Model of Intrinsic Mastery Motivation in Children: Individual Differences and Developmental Change', in W.A. Collins (ed.), *Minnesota Symposium on Child Psychology* (Hillsdale, NJ: Lawrence Erlbaum), 215–55.

Harter, S. (1983) 'Developmental Perspectives on the Self-system', in E.M. Hetherington (ed.), *Handbook of Child Psychology: Social Personality Development* (New York. John Wiley & Sons), 275–385.

Harter, S. (1985) *Manual for the Self-perception Profile for Children* (Denver, CO: University of Denver).

Harter, S. (1988) *Manual for the Self-perception Profile for Adolescents* (Denver, CO: University of Denver).

Harter, S. (1999) *The Construction of Self: A Developmental Perspective* (New York: Guilford Press).

Harwood, C. G. (2002) 'Assessing Achievement Goals in Sport: Caveats for Consultants and a Case for Contextualisation', *Journal of Applied Sport Psychology*, 14, 106–19.

Harwood, C. and Biddle, S. (2002) 'The Application of Achievement Goal Theory in Youth Sport', in I. Cockerill (ed.), *Solutions in Sport Psychology* (London: Thomson), 58–73.

Harwood, C., Hardy, L. and Swain, A. (2000) 'Achievement Goals in Sport: A Critique of Conceptual and Measurement Issues', *Journal of Sport & Exercise Psychology*, 22, 35–55.

Hasbrook, C. A., Hart, B. A., Mathes, S. A. and True, S. (1990) 'Sex Bias and Validity of the Believed Differences between Male and Female Interscholastic Athletic Coaches', *Research Quarterly for Exercise and Sport*, 61, 259–67.

Hastorf, A. H. and Cantril, H. (1954) 'They Saw a Game: A Case Study', *Journal of Abnormal and Social Psychology*, 49, 129–43.

Hatfield, B. M. and Kerick, S. E. (2007). 'The Psychology of Superior Performance: A Cognitive and Affective Neuroscience Perspective', in G. Tenenbaum and R. C. Eklund (eds), *Handbook of Sport Psychology*, 3rd edn (New York: John Wiley), 84–109).

Hatzigeorgiadis, A. and Biddle, S. J. H. (2000) 'Assessing Cognitive Interference in Sport: Development of the Thought Occurrence Questionnaire for Sport', *Anxiety, Stress and Coping*, 13, 65–86.

Hausenblas, H. A. and Downs, S. A. (2002) 'Exercise Dependence: A Systematic Review', *Psychology of Sport and Exercise*, 3, 89–123.

Hausenblas, H. A. and Fallon, E. A. (2002) 'Relationship among Body Image, Exercise Behavior, and Exercise Dependence Symptoms', *International Journal of Eating Disorders*, 32, 179–85.

Hausenblas, H. A., Hall, C. R., Rodgers, W. M. and Munroe, K. J. (1999) 'Exercise Imagery: Its Nature and Measurement', *Journal of Sport & Exercise Psychology*, 11, 171–80.

Havighurst, R. J. and Albrecht, R. (1953) *Older People* (New York: Longmans, Green).

Hawkins, K. and Blann, F. W. (1993) *Athlete/Coach Career Development and Transition* (Canberra: Australian Sports Commission).

Hays, K. F. (1999) *Working it out: Using Exercise in Psychotherapy* (Washington DC: American Psychological Association).

Haywood, K. M. and Getchell, N. (2001) *Life Span Motor Development*, 3rd edn (Champaign, IL: Human Kinetics).

Head, A., Kendall, M. J., Ferner, R. and Eagles C. (1996) 'Acute Effects of Beta Blockade and Exercise on Mood and Anxiety', *British Journal of Sports Medicine*, 30, 238–42.

Health Education Authority (1997) *Guidelines Promoting Physical Activity with People with Disabilities* (London: Health Education Authority).

Heath, G. W. and Fentem, P. H. (1997) 'Physical Activity among People with Disabilities: A Public Health Perspective', *Exercise and Sport Science Reviews*, 25, 195–234.

Hecker, J. E. and Kaczor, L. M. (1988) 'Application of Imagery Theory to Sport Psychology: Some Preliminary Findings', *Journal of Sport and Exercise Psychology*, 10, 363–73.

Hellstedt, J. C. (1995) 'Invisible Players: A Family Systems Model', in S.M. Murphy (ed.), *Sport Psychology Interventions* (Champaign, IL: Human Kinetics), 117–46. .

Helsen, W. F. and Pauwels, J. M. (1993) 'The Relationship between Expertise and Visual Information Processing in Sport', in J. Starkes and F. Allard (eds), *Cognitive Issues in Motor Expertise* (Amsterdam: North Holland), 109–34.

Helsen, W. F., Starkes, J. L. and Hodges, N. J. (1998) 'Team Sports and the Theory of Deliberate Practice', *Journal of Sport & Exercise Psychology*, 20, 12–34.

Helsen, W. F., Hodges, N. J., Van Winckel J. and Starkes, J. L. (2000) 'The Roles of Talent, Physical Precocity and Practice in the Development of Football Expertise', *Journal of Sport Sciences*, 18, 75–90.

Hemmings, B. (2001) 'Group Cohesion in English Professional Football: A Study of Youth trainees', in W. Spinks, T. Reilly and A. Murphy (eds) *Science and Football IV* (London, Routledge), 283–7.

Herlihy, J. and Gandy, J. (2002) 'Causation and Explanation', *The Psychologist*, 15, 248–51.

Herrigel, E. (1953) *Zen in the Art of Archery* (London: Routledge).

Herring, M. P., O'Connor, P. J. and Dishman, R. K. (2010) 'The Effect of Exercise Training on Anxiety Symptoms among Patients: A Systematic Review', *Archives of Internal Medicine*, 170, 321–31.

Hersey, P. and Blanchard, K. H. (1982) *Management of Organizational Behaviour: Utilizing Human Resources*, 4th edn (Englewood Cliffs, NJ: Prentice Hall).

Heuze, J.-P. and Brunel, P. C. (2003) 'Social Loafing in a Competitive Context', *International Journal of Sport and Exercise Psychology*, 1, 246–63.

Heyman, S. R. and Andersen, M. B. (1998) 'When to Refer Athletes for Counseling or Psychotherapy', in J. M. Williams (ed.), *Applied Sport Psychology: Personal Growth to Peak Performance*, 3rd edn (Mountain View, CA: Mayfield), 359–71.

Hill, D., Hanton, S. M., Matthews, N. and Fleming, S. (2010). 'Choking in Sport: A Review', *International Review of Sport and Exercise Psychology*, 3, 24–39.

Hillsdon, M. and Thorogood, M. (1996) 'A Systematic Review of Physical Activity Promotion Strategies', *British Journal of Sports Medicine*, 30, 84–9.

Hirschfield, R. M. A. and Cross, C. K. (1982) 'Epidemiology of Affective Disorders', *Archives of General Psychiatry*, 29, 35.

Hodge, K., Allen, J. and Smellie, L. (2008) 'Motivation in Masters Sport: Achievement and Social Goals', *Psychology of Sport & Exercise*, 9, 157–76.

Hodge, K. and McKenzie, A. (1999) *Thinking Rugby: Training Your Mind for Peak Performance* (Auckland, New Zealand: Reed).

Hodge, K. and Petlichkoff, L. (2000) 'Goal Profiles in Sport Motivation: A Cluster Analysis', *Journal of Sport & Exercise Psychology*, 22, 256–72.

Hodge, T. and Deakin, J. M. (1998) 'Deliberate Practice and Expertise in Martial Arts: The Role of Context in Motor Recall', *Journal of Sport & Exercise Psychology*, 20, 260–79.

Hodges, N. J. and Franks, I. M. (2001) 'Learning a Coordination Skill: Interactive Effects of Instruction and Feedback', *Research Quarterly for Exercise and Sport*, 72, 132–42.

Hodges, N. J. and Lee, T. D. (1999) 'The Role of Augmented Information Prior to Learning a Bimanual Visual-Motor Coordination Task: Do Instructions of the Movement Pattern Facilitate Learning Relative to Discovery Learning?', *British Journal of Psychology*, 90, 389–403.

Hodges, N. J. and Starkes, J. L. (1996) 'Wrestling with the Nature of Expertise: A Sport Specific Test of Ericsson, Krampe and Tesch-Romer's (1993) Theory of "Deliberate Practice"', *International Journal of Sport Psychology*, 27, 400–24.

Hodges, N. J., Huys, R. and Starkes, J. L. (2007) 'Methodological Review and Evaluation of Research in Expert Performance in Sport', in G. Tenenbaum, and R. C. Eklund (eds), *Handbook of Sport Psychology* (Hoboken, NJ: John Wiley and Sons), 161–83.

Hodges, N. J., Williams, A. M., Horn, R. R. and Breslin, G. (2007) 'What is Modeled during Observational Learning?' *Journal of Sports Sciences*, 25, 5, 531–45.

Hoffman, P. (1997) 'The Endorphin Hypothesis', in W.P. Morgan (ed.), *Physical Activity and Mental Health* (Washington DC: Taylor and Francis), 163–77.

Hogg, M. A. (1992) *The Social Psychology of Group Cohesiveness: From Attraction to Social Identity* (London: Harvester Wheatsheaf).

Hollander, E. P. (1985) 'Leadership and Power', in G. Lindsey and E. Aronson (eds.), *The Handbook of Social Psychology*, 3rd edn (New York: Random House), 485–537.

Holsboer, F. (2001) 'Stress, Hypercortisolism and Corticosteroid Receptors in Depression: Implications for Therapy', *Journal of Affective Disorders*, 62, 77–91.

Holmes, P. and Colllins, D. (2001). 'The PETTLEP Approach to Motor Imagery: A Functional Equivalence Model for Sport Psychologists', *Journal of Applied Sport Psychology*, 13, 60–83.

Holmes, P. and Collins, D. (2002) 'Functional Equivalence Solutions for Problems with Motor Imagery', in I. Cockerill (ed.), *Solutions in Sport Psychology* (London: Thomson), 120–40.

Homans, G. (1961) *Social Behavior: Its Elementary Forms* (New York: Harcourt Brace Javanovich).

Hoption, C., Phelan, J. and Barling, J. (2007) 'Transformational Leadership in Sport', in M. R. Beauchamp and M. A. Eys (eds), *Group Dynamics in Exercise and Sport Psychology: Contemporary Themes* (New York: Routledge), 45–60.

Horn, R. and Williams, A. M. (2004) 'Observational Learning: Is it Time to Take Another Look?', in A. M. Williams and N. J. Hodges (eds), *Skill Acquisition in Sport: Research, Theory and Practice* (London: Routledge).

Horn, R., Williams, A. M. and Scott, M. A. (2002) 'Visual Search Strategy, Movement Kinematics and Observational Learning', *Journal of Sports Sciences*, 20, 253–69.

Horn, T. S. (1984) 'Expectancy Effects in the Interscholastic Athletic Setting: Methodological Considerations', *Journal of Sport Psychology*, 6, 60–76.

Horn, T. S. (1992) 'Leadership Effectiveness in the Sport Domain', in T. S. Horn (ed.) *Advances in Sport Psychology* (Champaign, IL: Human Kinetics), 181–99.

Horn, T. S. and Amorose, A. J. (1998) 'Sources of Competence Information', in J. Duda (ed.), *Advances in Sport and Exercise Psychology Measurement* (Morgantown, WV: Fitness Information Technology), 49–63.

Horn, T. S. and Claytor, R. P. (1993) 'Developmental Aspects of Exercise Psychology', in P. Seraganian (ed.), *Exercise Psychology: The Influence of Physical on Psychological Processes* (New York: Wiley), 299–338.

Horn, R. R., Williams, A. M., Scott, M. A. and Hodges, N. J. (2005) 'The Role of Feedback and Demonstrations in Skill Acquisition', *Journal of Motor Behavior*, 37, 4, 265–79.

Horn, R. and Williams, A. M. (2004). 'Observational Learning: Is it Time We Took Another Look?', in A. M. Williams and N. Hodges (eds), *Skill Acquisition in Sport: Research, Theory and Practice* (Routledge: London), 175–206.

Horne, T. and Carron, A. V. (1985) 'Compatability in Coach–Athlete Relationships', *Journal of Sport Psychology*, 7, 137–49.

House, R. J. and Mitchell, T. R. (1974) 'Path-Goal Theory of Leadership', *Journal of Contemporary Business*, 3, 81–97.

Houston, J. M., McIntire, S. A., Kinnie, J. and Terry, C. (2002) 'A Factorial Analysis of Scales Measuring Competitiveness', *Educational and Psychological Measurement*, 62, 284–98.

Howard, G. E. (1912) 'Social Psychology of the Spectator', *American Journal of Sociology*, 8, 33–50.

Huang, C. A. and Lynch, J. (1994) *Thinking Body, Dancing Mind: Taosports for Extraordinary Performance in Athletics, Business and Life* (London: Bantam Books).

Hull, C. (1943) *Principles of Behavior* (New York: Appleton-Century-Crofts).

Hull, C. L. (1951) *Essentials of Behavior* (New Haven, CT: Yale University Press).

Huys, R., Daffertshofer, A., and Beek, P. J. (2004) 'Multiple Time Scales and Multiform Dynamics in Learning to Juggle', *Motor Control*, 8, 188–212.

Huys, R., Smeeton, N. J., Hodges, N. J., Beek, P. and Williams, A. M. (2008) 'The Dynamical Information Underlying Anticipation Skill in Tennis', *Perception and Psychophysics*, 18, 1217–34.

Huys, R., Cañal-Bruland, R., Hagemann, N. and Williams, A. M. (2009) 'The Effects of Occlusion, Neutralization, and Deception of Perceptual Information on Anticipation in Tennis', *Journal of Motor Behavior*, 41, 158–71.

Hyde, M. (2009). 'Obsessive? Compulsive? Order of The Day at SW19', *The Guardian*, 1 July, pp. 2–3.

Iannos, M. and Tiggemann, M. (1997) 'Personality of the Excessive Exerciser', *Personality and Individual Differences*, 22, 775–8.

Iliffe, S., See Tai, S. and Gould, M.M. (1994) 'Prescribing Exercise in General Practice', *British Medical Journal*, 309, 494–5.

Ingham, A., Levinger, G., Graves, J. and Peckham, V. (1974) 'The Ringelmann Effect: Studies of Group Size and Group Performance', *Journal of Experimental Social Psychology*, 10, 371–84.

Isaac, A., Marks, D. and Russell, E. (1986) 'An Instrument for Assessing Imagery of Movement: The Vividness of Movement Imagery Questionnaire', *Journal of Mental Imagery*, 10, 23–30.

Isaac, S. and Michael, W. B. (1995) *Handbook in Research and Evaluation*, 3rd edn (San Diego, CA: EDITS Publishers).

Israel, R. G., Sutton, M. and O'Brien, K. F. (1985) 'Effects of Aerobic Training on Primary Dysmenorrhea Symptomatology in College Females', *Journal of American College Health*, 33, 241–4.

Jackson, J. M. (1988) *Social Psychology, Past and Present: An Integrative Orientation* (Hillsdale, NJ: Lawrence Erlbaum).

Jackson, R. C. and Baker, J. S. (2001) 'Routines, Rituals and Rugby: Case Study of a World Class Kicker', *The Sport Psychologist*, 15, 48–65.

Jackson, R. C., Ashford, K. J. and Norsworthy, G. (2006) 'Attentional Foucs, Dispositional Reinvestment and Skilled Motor Performance Under Pressure', *Journal of Sport & Exercise Psychology*, 28, 49–68.

Jackson, S. A. (1995) 'Factors Influencing the Occurrence of Flow State in Elite Athletes', *Journal of Applied Sport Psychology*, 7, 138–66.

Jackson, S. A. (1996) 'Toward a Conceptual Understanding of the Flow Experience in Elite Athletes', *Research Quarterly for Exercise and Sport*, 67, 76–90.

Jackson, S. A. and Roberts, G. C. (1992) 'Positive Performance States of Athletes: Toward a Conceptual Understanding of Peak Performance', *The Sport Psychologist*, 6, 156–71.

Jackson, S. A. and Kimiecik, J. C. (2008) 'The Flow Perspective of Optimal Experience in Sport and Physical Activity', in T. S. Horn (ed.), *Advances in Sport Psychology*, 3rd edn (Champaign, Illinois: Human Kinetics), 377–99, 474–77.

Jackson, S. A., Thomas, P. R., Marsh, H. W. and Smethurst, C. J. (2001) 'Relationships between Flow, Self-concept, Psychological Skills, and Performance', *Journal of Applied Sport Psychology*, 13, 129–53.

Jacobson, B. (2003) 'The Social Psychology of the Creation of a Sports Fan Identity: A Theoretical Review of the Literature', *Athletic Insight*, 5, 1–14.

Jacobson, E. (1932) 'Electrophysiology of Mental Activities', *American Journal of Psychology*, 44, 677–94.

Jambor, E. A. (1999) 'Parents as Children's Socialising Agents in Youth Soccer', *Journal of Sport Behavior*, 22, 350–9.

James, K. (2000) 'You Can Feel Them Looking at You: The Experiences of Adolescent Girls at Swimming Pools', *Journal of Leisure Research*, 32, 262–80.

James, W. (1890) *Principles of Psychology* (New York: Holt, Rinehart and Winston).

Janelle, C. M. and Hatfield, B. D. (2008) 'Visual Attention and Brain Processes That Underlie Expert Performance: Implications for Sport and Military Psychology', *Military Psychology*, 20 (Supp. 1), S39–S69.

Janelle, C. M., Duley, A. R. and Coombes, S. A. (in press) 'Psychophysiological and Related Indices of Attention During Motor Skill Acquisition', in A. M. Williams and N. J. Hodges (eds), *Skill Acquisition in Sport: Research, Theory and Practice* (London: Routledge).

Janelle, C. M., Duley, A. R. and Coombes, S. (2004) 'Attentional Considerations for Skill Acquisition: Research, Theory and Practice', in A. M. Williams and N. Hodges (eds), *Skill Acquisition in Sport: Research, Theory, and Practice* (London: Taylor & Francis), 282–308.

Janelle, C. M., Singer, R. N. and Williams, A. M. (1999) 'External Distraction and Attentional Narrowing: Visual Search Evidence', *Journal of Sport and Exercise Psychology*, 21, 70–91.

Janis, I. (1982) *Victims of Groupthink* (Boston: Houghton-Mifflin).

Jeannerod, M. (1994). 'The Representing Brain: Neural Correlates of Motor Intention and Imagery', *Behavioral and Brain Scieces*, 17, 187–245.

Johns, D. P., Linder, K. J. and Wolko, K. (1990) 'Understanding Attrition in Female Competitive Gymnastics: Applying Social Exchange Theory', *Sociology of Sport Journal*, 7, 154–71.

Johnsgard, K. W. (1989) *The Exercise Prescription for Depression and Anxiety* (New York: Plenum Press).

Johnson, C. A., Corrigan, S. A., Dubbert, P. M. and Gramling, S. E. (1990) 'Perceived Barriers to Exercise and Weight Control Practices in Community Women', *Women and Health*, 16, 177–91.

Johnston, O. (2001) 'Eating, Exercise and Body Regulation across the Lifespan: A Qualitative Approach'. Unpublished Doctoral Dissertation, School of Psychology, The Queen's University of Belfast.

Jones, C. M. and Miles, T. R. (1978) 'Use of Advance Cues in Predicting the Flight of a Lawn Tennis Ball', *Journal of Human Movement Studies*, 4, 231–5.

Jones, G. (1995) 'More than Just a Game: Research Developments and Issues in Competitive Anxiety in Sport', *British Journal of Psychology*. 86, 449–78.

Jones, M. I., Lavallee, D. and Tod, D. (in press). 'Developing Communication and Organization Skills: The ELITE Life Skills Reflective Practice Program', *The Sport Psychologist*.

Jones, G. and Swain, A. B. J. (1992) 'Intensity and Direction as Dimensions of Competitive State Anxiety and Relationships with Competitiveness', *Perceptual and Motor Skills*, 74, 467–72.

Jones, G. and Swain, A. B. J. (1995) 'Predispositions to Experience Debilitative and Facilitative Anxiety in Elite and Nonelite Performers', *The Sport Psychologist*, 9, 201–11.

Jones, G., Hanton, S. and Swain, A. B. J. (1994) 'Intensity and Interpretation of Anxiety Symptoms in Elite and Non-elite Sports Performers', *Personality and Individual Differences*, 17, 756–63.

Jones, M. B. (1974) 'Regressing Group on Individual Effectiveness', *Organizational and Human Performance*, 11, 426–51.

Jones, M. V., Bray, S. R. and Lavallee, D. (2007) 'All the World's a Stage: Impact of an Audience on Sport Performance', in S. Jowell and D. Lavallee (eds.), *Social Psychology in Sport* (Champaign, IL: Human Kinetics), 104–113.

Jones, R. L. (2006) (ed.) *The Sports Coach as Educator Re-Conceptualising Sports Coaching* (London: Routledge).

Jowett, S. (2007) 'Coach-Athlete Relationships Ignite Sense of Groupness', in M. R. Beauchamp and M. A. Eys (eds), *Group Dynamics in Exercise and Sport Psychology* (New York: Routledge), 63–78.

Jowett, S. and Lavallee, D. (2007) (eds) *Social Psychology in Sport* (Champaign, IL: Human Kinetics).

Jowett, S. and Poczwardowski, A. (2007) 'Understanding the Coach-Athlete relationship', in S. Jowett and D. Lavallee (eds), *Social Psychology in Sport* (Champaign IL: Human Kinetics), 4–14.

Jordet, G. (2009). 'When Superstars Flop: Public Status and Choking under Pressure in International Soccer Penalty Shootouts', *Journal of Applied Sport Psychology*, 21, 125–30.

Kahn, R. L., Wolfe, D. M., Quinn, R. P., Snoek, J. D. and Rosenthal, R. A. (1964) *Occupational Stress: Studies in Role Conflict and Ambiguity* (New York: Wiley).

Kahneman, D. (1973) *Attention and Effort* (Englewood Cliffs, NJ: Prentice Hall).

Kalish, R. (1966) 'A Continuity of Subjectivity Perceived Death', *The Gerontologist*, 6, 73–6.

Kane, M. A. (1995) 'The Transition Out of Sport: A Paradigm from the United States', in R. Vanfraechem-Raway and Y. Vanden Auweele (eds), *Proceedings of the 9th European Congress on Sport Psychology* (Brussles: European Federation of Sports Psychology), 849–56.

Karau, S. J. and Williams, K. D. (1993) 'Social Loafing: A Meta-analytic Review and Theoretical Integration', *Journal of Personality and Social Psychology*, 65, 681–705.

Karau, S. J. and Williams, K. D. (1997) 'The Effects of Group Cohesiveness on Social Loafing and Social Compensation', *Group Dynamics: Theory, Research and Practice*, 1, 56–68.

Karau, S. J. and Williams, K. D. (2001) 'Understanding Individual Motivation in Groups: The Collective Effort Model', in M. E. Turner (ed.), *Groups at Work: Advances in Theory and Research* (Mahwah, NJ: Erlbaum), 113–41.

Kastenbaum, R. and Weisman, A. (1972) 'The Psychological Autopsy as a Research Procedure in Gerontology', in D. Kent, R. Kastembaum and S. Sherwood (eds), *Research, Planning and Action for the Elderly* (New York: Behavioral Publications).

Katzell, R. A. and Thompson, D.E. (1990) 'Work Motivation: Theory and Practice', *American Psychologist*, 45, 114–53.

Keashly, L. (1997) 'Conflict and Conflict Management', in S.W. Savada and D. R. McCready (eds), *Applying Social Psychology* (Upper Saddle River, NJ: Prentice Hall).

Keetch, K. M, Schmidt, R. A., Lee, T. D. and Young, D. E. (2005) 'Especial Skills: Their Emergence with Massive Amounts of Practice', *Journal of Experimental Psychology: Human Perception and Performance*, 31, 970–8.

Keetch, K. M., Lee, T. D. and Schmidt, R. A. (2008) 'Especial Skills: Specificity Embedded Within Generality', *Journal of Sport and Exercise Psychology,* 30 (6), 723–36.

Kelley, B. C. (1994) 'A Model of Stress and Burnout in Collegiate Coaches: Effects of Gender and Time of Season', *Research Quarterly for Exercise and Sport*, 65, 48–58.

Kelley, H. H. (1983) 'Love and commitment', in H. H. Kelley, E. Berscheid, A. Christensen, J. H. Harvey, T. L. Huston, G. Levinger, E. McClintock, L. A. Peplau and D. R. Peterson (Eds), *Close Relationships* (New York: W. H. Freeman), 265–314.

Kelly, R. B., Zyzanski, S. J. and Alemagno, S. A. (1991) 'Prediction of Motivation and Behavior Change Following Health Promotion: Role of Health Beliefs, Social Support and Self-efficacy', *Social Science and Medicine*, 32, 311–20.

Kelso, J. S. (1995) *Dynamic Patterns: The Self-organization of Brain and Behaviour* (Cambridge: MIT).

Kendall, K. A. and Danish, S. J. (1994) 'The Development of Preliminary Validation of a Measure of Parental Influence on Youth Participation in Organized Sports', Paper presented at the Annual Conference of the Association for the Advancement of Applied Sport Psychology, Lake Tahoe, NV.

Kenow, L. J. and Williams, J. M. (1992) 'Relationship between Anxiety, Self-Confidence and Evaluation of Coaching Behaviors', *The Sport Psychologist*, 6, 344–57.

Kenow, L. J. and Williams, J. M. (1999) 'Coach–Athlete Compatibility and Athlete's Perception of Coaching Behaviors', *Journal of Sport Behavior*, 22, 251–9.

Kerr, G. and Dacyshyn, A. (2000) 'The Retirement Experiences of Elite Female Gymnasts', *Journal of Applied Sport Psychology*, 12, 115–33.

Kety, S. S. (1966) 'Catecholamines in Neoropsychiatric States', *Pharmacological Review*, 18, 787–98.

Kimiecik, J. C. and Harris, A. T. (1996) 'What is Enjoyment? A Conceptual/Definitional Analysis with Implications for Sport and Exercise Psychology', *Journal of Sport and Exercise Psychology*, 18, 247–64.

Kimiecik, J. C. and Jackson, S. A. (2002) 'Optimal Experience in Sport: A Flow Perspective', in T. S. Horn (ed.), *Advances in Sport Psychology,* 2nd edn (Champaign, IL: Human Kinetics), 501–27.

Kimmage, P. (1998) 'I Could Almost Tell the Ball Where to Go', *Sunday Independent*, 24 May, p. 29L.

Kingston, K. M. and Hardy, L. (1997) 'Effects of Different Types of Goals on Processes that Support Performance', *The Sport Psychologist*, 11, 277–93.

Kingston, K. M. and Wilson, K. M. (2009) 'The Application of Goal Setting in Sport', in S. D. Mellalieu and S. D. Hanton (eds), *Advances in Applied Sport Psychology: A Review* (Abingdon, Oxford: Routledge), 75–123.

Kinrade, N. P., Jackson, R. C. and Ashford, K. J. (2010) 'Dispositional Reinvestment and Skill Failure in Cognitive and Motor Tasks', *Psychology of Sport and Exercise*, 11, 312–19.

Kintsch, W. (1988) 'The Use of Knowledge in Discourse Processing: A Construction-integration Model', *Psychological Review*, 95, 163–82.

Kirsch, I. and Sapirstein, G. (1998) 'Listening to Prozac but Hearing Placebo: A Meta-analysis of Antidepressant Medication', *Prevention and Treatment* [Online serial], 1. Available HTTP: journals.apa.org/prevention/volume1/toc-jun26-98.html

Klavora, P. (1978) 'An Attempt to Derive Inverted-U Curves Based on the Relationship between Anxiety and Athletic Performance', in D. M. Landers and R. W. Christina (eds), *Psychology of Motor Behavior and Sport* (vols. 1 and 11) (Champaign, IL: Human Kinetics), 369–77.

Kleiber, D. and Brock, S. C. (1992) 'The Effect of Career-ending Injuries on the Subsequent Well-being of Elite College Athletes', *Sociology of Sport Journal*, 9, 70–5.

Kleiber, D., Greendorfer, S., Blinde, E. and Sandall, D. (1987) 'Quality of Exit from University Sports and Subsequent Life Satisfaction', *Journal of Sport Sociology*, 4, 28–36.

Klein, C., DiazGranados, D., Salas, E., Huy Le, C., Burke, S., Lyons R. and Goodwin, G. F. (2009) 'Does Team Building Work?', *Small Group Research*, 40, 181–222.

Klint, K. and Weiss, M. R. (1986) 'Dropping In and Dropping Out: Participation Motives of Current and Former Youth Gymnastics', *Canadian Journal of Applied Sport Sciences*, 11, 106–14.

Koff, E. and Bauman, C. (1997) 'Effects of Wellness, Fitness and Sport Skills Programs on Body Image and Lifestyle Behaviours', *Perceptual Motor Skills*, 84, 55–62.

Kohl, R. M. and Roenker, D. L. (1980) 'Bilateral Transfer as a Function of Mental Imagery', *Journal of Motor Behavior*, 12, 197–206.

Kohl, R. M. and Roenker, D. L. (1983) 'Mechanism Involvement during Skill Imagery', *Journal of Motor Behavior*, 15, 179–90.

Kosslyn, S. M. (1994) *Image and Brain: The Resolution of the Imagery Debate* (Cambridge, MA: MIT Press).

Kosslyn, S. M., Ganis, G. and Thompson, W. L. (2001) 'Neural Foundations of Imagery', *Nature Reviews: Neuroscience*, 2, 635–42.

Kosslyn, S. M., Seger, C., Pani, J. R. and Hillger, L. A. (1990) 'When is Imagery Used in Everyday Life? A Diary Study', *Journal of Mental Imagery*, 14, 131–52.

Koukouris, K. (1991) 'Quantitative Aspects of the Disengagement Process of Advanced and Eiite Greek Male Athletes from Organized Competitive Sport', *Journal of Sport Behavior*, 14, 227–46.

Koukouris, K. (1994) 'Constructed Case Studies: Athletes' Perspectives on Disengaging from Organized Competitive Sport', *Sociology of Sport Journal*, 11, 114–39.

Kowal, J. and Fortier, S. (2000) 'Testing Relationships from the Hierarchical Model of I Intrinsic and Extrinsic Motivation using Flow as a Motivational Consequence', *Research Quarterly for Exercise and Sport*, 71, 171–81.

Kozub, S. A. and Button, C. J. (2000) 'The Influence of a Competitive Outcome on Perceptions of Cohesion in Rugby and Swimming Teams', *International Journal of Sport Psychology*, 31, 82–95.

Krane, V. (1994) 'The Mental Readiness Form as a Measure of Competitive State Anxiety', *The Sport Psychologist*, 8, 189–202.

Krane, V. and Williams, J. M. (2010). 'Psychological Characteristics of Peak Performance', in J. M. Williams (ed.), *Applied Sport Psychology: Personal Growth to Peak Perfomance*, 6th edn (New York: McGraw-Hill), 169–88.

Kremer, J. (2002) 'Ethical Considerations', in D. Lavallee and I. M. Cockerill (eds), *Counselling in Sport and Exercise Contexts* (Leicester: British Psychological Society), 18–26.

Kremer, J. and Busby, G. (1998) 'Towards an Understanding of Participation in Sport and Physical Exercise', *Irish Journal of Psychology*, 4, 447–63.

Kremer, J. and Scully, D. (1994) *Psychology in Sport* (Hove, East Sussex: Psychology Press).

Kremer, J. and Moran, A. (2008) *Pure Sport: Practical Sport Psychology* (London: Routledge).

Kremer, J., Trew, S. and Ogle, S. (1997) (eds) *Young People's Involvement in Sport* (London: Routledge).

Kremer, J. (2007) 'Afterword', in S. Jowell and D. Lavallee (eds), *Social Psychology in Sport* (Champaign, IL: Human Kinetics, 289–92.

Kremer, J., Moran, A., Walker, G. and Craig, C. (in press) *Key Concepts in Sport Psychology* (London: Sage).

Kübler-Ross, E. (1969) *On Death and Dying* (New York: Macmillan).

Kugler, P. N., Kelso, J. A. S. and Turvey, M. T. (1982) 'On the Control and Co-ordination of Naturally Developing Systems', in J. A. S. Kelso and J. E. Clark (eds), *The Development of Movement Control and Co-ordination* (New York: Wiley), 5–78.

Kugler, P. N. and Turvey, M. T. (1987) *Information, Natural Law, and the Self-assembly of Rhythmic Movement* (Hillsdale, NJ: Lawrence Erlbaum).

Kuypers, J. A. and Bengston, V. L. (1973) 'Social Breakdown and Competence: A Model of Normal Aging', *Human Development*, 16, 181–220.

Kyllo, L. B. and Landers, D. M. (1995) 'Goal Setting in Sport and Exercise: A Research Synthesis to Resolve the Controversy', *Journal of Sport and Exercise Psychology*, 17, 117–37.

Lacey, J. J. (1967) 'Somatic Response Patterning and Stress: Some Revision of Activation Theory', in M. H. Appley and R. Trumbull (eds), *Psychological Stress: Issues in Research* (New York: Appleton-Century-Crofts), 170–9.

Lacy, A. C. and Darst, P. W. (1985) 'Systematic Observation of Behaviors of Winning High School Head Football Coaches', *Journal of Teaching in Physical Education*, 4, 4, 256–70.

Lacy, A. C. and Goldston, P. D. (1990) 'Behavior Analysis of Male and Female Coaches in High School Girls' Basketball', *Journal of Sport Behavior*, 13, 29–40.

Lafrenière, M.-A. K., Jowett, S., Vallerand, R. J. and Carbonneau, N. (2011) 'Passion for Coaching and the Quality of the Coach–Athlete Relationship: The Mediating Role of Coaching Behaviors', *Psychology of Sport and Exercise*, 12, 144–52.

Laird, L. K. and Benefield, W. H. (1995) 'Mood Disorders I: Major Depressive Disorders', in L.Y. Young and M.A. Koda-Kimble (eds), *Applied Therapeutics: The Clinical Use of Drugs* (Vancouver: Applied Therapeutics), 1–76.

Lally, P. and Kerr, G. (2008) The Effects of Athlete Retirement on Parents', *Journal of Applied Sport Psychology*, 20, 42–56.

Landers, D. M. (1974) 'Taxonomic Considerations in Measuring Group Performance and the Analysis of Selected Motor Performance Tasks', in M.G. Wade and R. Martens (eds), *Psychology of Motor Behavior and Sport* (Champaign, IL: Human Kinetics).

Landers, D. M. and Arent, S. M. (2001) 'Physical Activity and Mental Health', in R. Singer, H. Hausenblas and C. Janelle (eds), *Handbook of Sport Psychology* 2nd edn (New York: Wiley), 740–65.

Landers, D. M. and Arent, S. M. (2007) 'Physical Activity and Mental Health', in R. N. Singer, H. A. Hausenblas and C. M. Janelle (eds), *Handbook of Sport Psychology* (New York: John Wiley and Sons), 740–65.

Landers, D. M. and Arent, S. M. (2010). 'Arousal-Performance Relationships', in J. M. Williams (ed), *Applied Sport Psychology: Personal Growth to Peak Perfomance* 6th edn (New York: McGraw-Hill), 221–46.

Landers, D. M. and Boutcher, S. H. (1998) 'Arousal-Performance Relationships', in J. M. Williams (ed.), *Applied Sport Psychology: Personal Growth to Peak Performance* (Mountain View, CA: Mayfield), 197–218.

Landers, D. M. and Lueschen, G. (1974) 'Team Performance Outcome and Cohesiveness of Competitive Coacting Groups', *International Review of Sport Sociology*, 9, 57–69.

Landers, D. M. and Petruzzello, S. J. (1994) 'Physical Activity, Fitness and Anxiety', in C. Bouchard, R. J. Shephard and T. Stephens (eds) *Physical Activity, Fitness, and Health* (Champaign, IL: Human Kinetics), 868–82.

Landers, D. M., Wilkinson, M. O., Hatfield, B. D. and Barber, H. (1982) 'Causality and the Cohesion-Performance Relationship', *Journal of Sport Psychology*, 4, 170–83.

Landin, D. and Herbert, E. P. (1999) 'The Influence of Self-talk on the Performance of Skilled Female Tennis Players', *Journal of Applied Sport Psychology*, 11, 263–82.

Lane, A. M., Sewell, D. F., Terry, P. C., Bartram, D. and Nesti, M. S. (1999) 'Confirmatory Factor Analysis of the Competitive State Anxiety Inventory – 2', *Journal of Sports Sciences*, 17, 505–12.

Lang, P. (1977) 'Imagery in Therapy: An Information-Processing Analysis of Fear', *Behavior Therapy*, 8, 862–86.

Lang, P. (1979) 'A Bio-Informational Theory of Emotional Imagery', *Psychophysiology*, 17, 495–512.

Lang, P., Kozak, M., Miller, G. A., Levin, D. N. and McLean, A. (1980) 'Emotional Imagery: Conceptual Structure and Pattern of Somato-Visceral Response', *Psychophysiology*, 17, 179–92.

Lang, P. J. and Davis, M. (2006) 'Emotion, Motivation, and the Brain: Reflex Foundations in Animal and Human Research', *Progress in Brain Research*, 156, 3–34.

Latané, B. (1997) 'Dynamic Social Impact: The Societal Consequences of Human Social Interaction', in C. McGarty and A. Haslam (eds), *The Message of Social Psychology* (Oxford: Blackwell).

Latané, B., Williams, K. and Harkins, S. (1979) 'Many Hands Make Light Work: The Causes and Consequences of Social Loafing', *Journal of Personality and Social Psychology*, 37, 822–32.

Laughlin, P. R. (1996) 'Group Decision-Making and Collective Induction', in E. H. Witte and J. H. Davis (eds), *Understanding Group Behavior: Consensual Action by Small Groups* (1) (Hillsdale, NJ: Erlbaum).

Lavallee, D. (2010, June). *Transitions in sport*. Keynote address presented at Talented Athlete Scholarship Scheme Annual Conference, London, England.

Lavallee, D. and Cockerill, I. M. (2002) (eds) *Counselling in Sport and Exercise Contexts* (Leicester: British Psychological Society).

Lavallee, D., Gordon, S. and Grove, J. R. (1997a) 'Retirement from Sport and the Loss of Athletic Identity', *Journal of Personal and Interpersonal Loss*, 2, 129–47.

Lavallee, D., Grove, J. R. and Gordon, S. (1997b) 'The Causes of Career Termination from Sport and their Relationship to Post-Retirement Adjustment among Elite-Amateur Athletes in Australia', *The Australian Psychologist*, 32, 131–5.

Lavallee, D. and Wylleman, P. (1999) 'Toward an Instrument to Assess the Quality of Adjustment to Career Transitions in Sport: The British Athlete Lifestyle Assessment Needs in Career and Education (BALANCE) Scale', in V. Hosek, P. Tilinger, and L. Bilek (eds.), *Psychology of Sport and Exercise: Enhancing the Quality of Life* (Prague: Charles University), 322–4.

Lavallee, D., Wylleman, P. and Sinclair, D. A. (2000) 'Career Transitions in Sport: An Annotated Bibliography', in D. Lavallee and P. Wylleman (eds), *Career Transitions in Sport: International Perspectives* (Morgantown, WV: Fitness Information Technology), 207–58.

LaVoi, N. M. (2009) 'Occupational Sex Segregation in a Youth Soccer Organization: Females in Positions of Power. *Women in Sport and Physical Activity Journal*, 18, 25–37.

LaVoi, N. M., Becker, E. and Maxwell, H. D. (2007) '"Coaching Girls": A Content Analysis of Best-Selling Popular Press Coaching Books', *Women in Sport and Physical Activity Journal*, 15, 8–20.

Lawler, E. E. (1973) *Motivation in Work Organizations* (Monterey, CA: Brooks/Cole).

Lawlor, D. A. and Hopker, S. W. (2001) 'The Effectiveness of Exercise as an Intervention in the Management of Depression: Systematic Review and Meta-Regression Analysis of Randomised Controlled Trials', *British Medical Journal*, 22, 1–8

Lawther, J. D. (1972) *Sport Psychology* (Englewood Cliffs, NJ: Prentice Hall).

Lawton, M. P. (1983) 'The Dimensions of Well-Being', *Experimental Aging Research*, 9, 65–72.

Lawton, M. P. (1994) 'Personality and Affective Correlates of Leisure Activity Participation by Older People', *Journal of Leisure Research*, 26, 138–57.

Lazarus, R. S. (2000) 'How Emotions Influence Performance in Competitive Sports', *The Sport Psychologist*, 14, 229–52.

Lazarus, R. S. and Folkman, S. (1984) *Stress, Appraisal, and Coping* (New York: Springer).

Lebon, F., Collet, C. and Guillot, C. (2010). 'Benefits of Motor Imagery Training on Muscle Strength', *Journal of Strength and Conditioning Research*, 24, 1680–87.

Lee, T. D. and Magill, R. A. (1985) 'Can Forgetting Facilitate Skill Acquisition?', in D. Goodman, R. B. Wilberg and I. M. Franks (eds), *Differing Perspectives in Motor Learning, Memory, and Control* (Amsterdam: Elsevier), 3–22.

Lee, T. D., Magill, R. A. and Weeks, D. J. (1985) 'Influence of Practice Schedule on Testing Schema Theory Predictions in Adults', *Journal of Motor Behavior*, 17, 283–99.

Lenk, H. (1969) 'Top Performance Despite Internal Conflict: An Antithesis to a Functionalistic Proposition', in J. W. Loy and G. S. Kenyon (eds), *Sport, Culture and Society* (New York: Macmillan), 393–6.

Lennox, S. S., Bedell, J. R. and Stone, A. A. (1990) 'The Effect of Exercise on Normal Mood', *Journal of Psychosomatic Medicine*, 34, 629–36.

Leonard, W. M. (1996) 'The Odds of Transiting from One Level of Sports Participation to Another', *Sociology of Sport Journal*, 13, 288–99.

Lerch, S. (1981) 'The Adjustment to Retirement of Professional Baseball Players', in S. L. Greendorfer and A. Yiannakis (eds), *Sociology of Sport: Diverse Perspectives* (West Point, NY: Leisure Press), 138–48.

Lerch, S. (1984) 'Athlete Retirement as Social Death: An Overview', in N. Theberge and P. Donnelly (eds), *Sport and the Sociological Imagination* (Fort Worth: Texas Christian University Press), 259–72.

Leslie, E., Sparling, P. B. and Owen, N. (2001) 'University Campus Settings and the Promotion of Physical Activity in Young Adults: Lessons from Research in Australia and the USA', *Health Education*, 3, 116–25.

Lesyk, J. (1998) *Developing Sport Psychology within Your Clinical Practice* (London: Wiley).

LeUnes, A. and Burger, J. (1998) 'Bibliography of the Profile of Mood States in Sport and Exercise Research, 1971–1998', *Journal of Sport Behavior*, 21, 53–70.

Lewin, K. (1947) 'Frontiers in Group Dynamics', *Human Relations* 1, 5–42.

Li, F. (1999) 'The Exercise Motivation Scale: Its Multifaceted Structure and Construct Validity', *Journal of Applied Sport Psychology*, 11, 97–115.

Li, F. and Harmer, P. (1996) 'Confirmatory Factor Analysis of the Group Environment Questionnaire with an Intercollegiate Sample', *Journal of Sport and Exercise Psychology*, 18, 49–63.

Liao, C. and Masters, R. S. W. (2001) 'Analogy Learning: A Means to Implicit Motor Learning', *Journal of Sports Sciences*, 19, 307–19.

Lidor, R., Morris, T., Bardaxoglou, N. and Becker, B. (2001) (eds) *The World Sport Psychology Sourcebook* (Morgantown, WV: Fitness Information Technology).

Lirgg, C. D. and Feltz, D. L. (1994) 'Relationship of Individual and Collective Efficacy to Team Performance', *Journal of Sport and Exercise Psychology*, 16, S17.

Liu, J. and Wrisberg, C. A. (1997) 'The Effect of Knowledge of Results Delay and the Subjective Estimation of Movement Form on the Acquisition and Retention of a Motor Skill', *Research Quarterly for Exercise and Sport*, 68, 145–51.

Locke, E. A. (1968) 'Toward a Theory of Task Motivation and Incentives', *Organizational Behaviour and Human Performance*, 3, 157–89.

Locke, E. A. and Latham, G. P. (1994) 'Goal Setting Theory', in H. F. O'Neil and M. Drillings (eds), *Motivation: Theory and Research* (Hillside: Lawrence Erlbaum), 13–29.

Lockette, K. F. and Keyes, A. M. (1994) *Conditioning with Physical Disabilities* (Champaign, IL Human Kinetics).

Logie, R. H. (1999) 'Working Memory', *The Psychologist*, 12, 174–8.

Long, B. C. and Stavel, R. V. (1995) 'Effects of Exercise Training on Anxiety: A Meta-Analysis', *Journal of Applied Sport Psychology*, 7, 167–89.

Longino, C. F. and Kart, C. S. (1982) 'Explicating Activity Theory: A Formal Replication', *Journal of Gerontology*, 37, 713–22.

Loumidis, K. S. and Roxborough, H. (1995) 'A Cognitive-Behavioural Approach to Excessive Exercising', in J. Annett, B. Cripps and H. Steinberg (eds), *Exercise Addiction: Motivation for Participation in Sport and Exercise* (Leicester: British Psychological Society), 45–53.

Lovell, G. and Collins, D. (1996) 'Applied Interventions for Improving Team Effectiveness', in J. Annett and H. Steinberg (eds), *How Teams Work in Sport and Exercise Psychology* (Leicester: British Psychological Society), 57–65.

Lowry, R. (2002) 'Modelling Adolescent Participation in Sport and Exercise: A Multivariate Approach'. Unpublished Doctoral Thesis, School of Psychology, The Queen's University of Belfast.

Loy, J. W., McPherson, B. D. and Kenyon, G. (1978) *Sport and Social Systems: A Guide to the Analysis, Problems and Literature* (Reading, MA: Addison-Wesley).

McAllistair, A., Williams, A. M., Ward, P. and Eccles, D. (submitted) The influence of contextual knowledge on decision-making in a simulated performance environment. *British Journal of Psychology*.

McAuley, E. (1991) 'Efficacy, Attributional and Affective Responses to Exercise Participation', *Journal of Sport & Exercise Psychology*, 13, 382–93.

McAuley, E. (1992) 'Exercise and Motivation: A Self-Efficacy Perspective', in G. C. Roberts (ed.), *Motivation in Sport and Exercise* (Champaign, IL: Human Kinetics), 107–28.

McAuley, E. (1994) 'Physical Activity and Psychosocial Outcomes', in C. Bouchard, R. J. Shephard and T. Stephens (eds), *Physical Activity, Fitness, and Health* (Champaign, IL: Human Kinetics), 551–68.

McAuley, E. and Courneya, K. S. (1992) 'Self-Efficacy Relationships with Affective and Exertion Responses to Exercise', *Journal of Applied Social Psychology*, 22, 131–9.

McAuley, E. and Jacobson, L. (1991) 'Self-Efficacy and Exercise Participation in Sedentary Adult Females', *American Journal of Health Promotion*, 5, 185–91.

McAuley, E., Pena, M. and Jerome, G. (2001) 'Self-Efficacy as a Determinant and an Outcome of Exercise', in G. C. Roberts (ed.), *Advances in Motivation in Sport and Exercise* (Champaign, IL: Human Kinetics), 235–62.

McAuley, E., Bane, S. M., Rudolph, D. L. and Lox, C. (1995) 'Physique Anxiety and Exercise in Middle-Aged Adults', *Journal of Gerontology: Psychological Sciences and Social Sciences*, 50, 229–35.

McCarthy, P. J., Jones, M. V. and Clark-Carter, D. (2008). 'Understanding Enjoyment in Youth Sport: A Developmental Perspective', *Psychology of Sport and Exercise*, 9, 142–56.

McClelland, D. (1961) *The Achieving Society* (Princeton: Van Nostrand).

McCracken, H. D. and Stelmach, G. E. (1977) 'A Test of the Schema Theory of Discrete Motor Learning', *Journal of Motor Behavior*, 9, 193–201.

McCullagh, P. and Caird, J. K. (1990) 'Correct Learning Models and Use of Knowledge of Results in the Acquisition and Retention of a Motor Skill', *Journal of Human Movement Studies*, 18, 107–16.

McCullagh, P. and Meyer, K. N. (1997) 'Learning Versus Correct Models: Influence of Model Type on the Learning of a Free-Weight Squat Lift', *Research Quarterly for Exercise and Sport*, 68, 56–61.

McCullagh, P. and Noble, J.M. (1996) 'Education and Training in Sport and Exercise Psychology', in J. L. Van Raalte and B. W. Brewer (eds), *Exploring Sport and Exercise Psychology* (Washington DC: American Psychological Association), 377–94.

McCullagh, P. and Weiss, M. R. (2001) 'Modeling: Considerations for Motor Skill Performance and Psychological Responses', in R. N. Singer, H. A. Hausenblas, and C. M. Janelle (eds), *Handbook of Research in Sport Psychology,* 2nd edn (New York: John Wiley and Sons), 205–38.

McGeorge, S. M., Harris J. P., Clark, F. B., Waring, M. and Almond, L. (1994) *Physical Activity Protocols for Primary Health Care* (Loughborough University: Loughborough).

McInally, L., Cavin-Stice, J. and Knoth, R. L. (1992, August) 'Adjustment Following Retirement from Professional Football'. Poster presented at the 100th Annual Convention of the American Psychological Association, Washington, D.C.

MacIntyre, T. and Moran, A. (1996) 'Imagery Use among Canoeists: A Worldwide Survey of Novice, Intermediate and Elite Slalomists', *Journal of Applied Sport Psychology,* 8, p. S132.

MacIntyre, T., Moran, A. and Jennings, D. J. (2002) 'Is Controllability of Imagery Related to Canoe-Slalom Performance?', *Perceptual and Motor Skills*, 94, 1245–50.

McNair, D. M., Lorr, M. and Droppleman, L. F. (1981) *Manual for the Profile of Mood States* (San Diego, CA: Educational and Industrial Training Services).

McPherson, B. D. (1980) 'Retirement from Professional Sport: The Process and Problems of Occupational and Psychological Adjustment', *Sociological Symposium*, 30, 126–43.

McPhershon, S. L. and MacMahon, C. (2008) How Baseball Batters Prepare to Bat: Tactical Knowledge as a Mediator of Expert Performance in Baseball', *Journal of Sport & Exercise Psychology, 30,* 755–78.

McRae, D. (2008). 'Even Great Players Have Tortured Minds', *The Guardian* (Sport), 15 July, p. 6

McRobert, A, Ward, P., Eccles, D. and Williams, A. M. (2011) 'The Effect of Manipulating Context-Specific Information on Perceptual Cognitive Processes during a Simulated Anticipation Task', *British Journal of Psychology,* in press.

MacRury, D. (1997) *Golfers on Golf* (London: Virgin Books).

Maddux, J. (1995) 'Self-Efficacy Theory: An Introduction', in J. Maddux (ed.), *Self-Efficacy, Adaptation, and Adjustment: Theory, Research, and Application* (New York: Plenum Press), 3–27.

Maddux, J. E. and Volkmann, J. R. (2010) 'Self-efficacy and Self-regulation', in R. Hoyle, (ed.), *Handbook of Personality and Self-Regulation* (New York: Wiley-Blackwell), 210–45.

Madrigal, R. and James, J. (1999) 'Team Quality and the Home Advantage', *Journal of Sport Behavior,* 22, 381–98.

Magill, R. A. (2007) *Motor Learning: Concepts and Applications,* 8th edn (New York: McGraw-Hill).

Magill, R. A. (2001) 'Augmented Feedback and Skill Acquisition', in R. N. Singer, H. A. Hausenblas and C. Jannelle (eds), *Handbook of Research in Sport Psychology,* 2nd edn (New York: John Wiley and Sons), 86–114.

Magill, R. A. and Schoenfelder-Zohdi, B. (1996) 'A Visual Model and Knowledge of Performance as Sources of Information for Learning a Rhythmic Gymnastics Skill', *International Journal of Sport Psychology,* 27, 7–22.

Magill, R. A. and Wood, C. A. (1986) 'Knowledge of Results Precision as a Learning Variable in Motor Skill Acquisition', *Research Quarterly for Exercise and Sport,* 57, 170–3.

Mahoney, M. J. and Avener, M. (1977) 'Psychology of the Elite Athlete: An Exploratory Study', *Cognitive Therapy and Research,* 1, 135–41.

Mann, D. T. Y., Williams, A. M., Ward, P. and Janelle, C. M. (2007). Perceptual-Cognitive Expertise in Sport: A Meta Analysis', *Journal of Sport and Exercise Psychology,* 29, 4, 457–78.

Marcus, B. H. and Simkin. L. R. (1993) 'The Stages of Exercise Behavior', *Journal of Sports Medicine and Physical Fitness,* 33, 83–8.

Marge, M. (1988) 'Health Promotion for Persons with Disabilities: Moving Beyond Rehabilitation', *American Journal of Health Promotion,* 2, 29–44.

Markland, D. (1999) 'Self-determination Moderates the Effects of Perceived Competence on Intrinsic Motivation in an Exercise Setting', *Journal of Sport and Exercise Psychology,* 21, 351–61.

Maroulakis, M. and Zervas, Y. (1993) 'Effects of Aerobic Exercise on Mood of Adult Women', *Perceptual and Motor Skills,* 76, 795–801.

Marsh, H. (1990) 'A Multidimensional Self-Concept: A Social Psychological Perspective', *Annual Review of Psychology,* 38, 299–337.

Marsh, H. (1997) 'The Measurement of Self-Concept: A Construct Validation Approach', in K. R. Fox (ed.), *The Physical Self: From Motivation to Well-Being* (Champaign, IL: Human Kinetics), 27–58.

Martens, R. (1975) *Social Psychology and Physical Activity* (New York: Harper and Row).

Martens, R. (1977) *Sport Competition Anxiety Test* (Champaign, IL: Human Kinetics).

Martens, R. (1979a) 'Science, Knowledge and Sport Psychology', *The Sport Psychologist,* 1, 29–55.

Martens, R. (1979b) 'From Smocks to Jocks', *Journal of Sport Psychology,* 1, 94–9.

Martens, R. (1987) *Coaches Guide to Sport Psychology* (Champaign, IL: Human Kinetics).

Martens, R., Landers, D. M. and Loy, J. W. (1972) 'Sport Cohesiveness Questionnaire'. Unpublished Manuscript, University of Illinois, Champaign, IL.

Martens, R., Burton, D., Vealey, R. S., Bump, L. A. and Smith, D. E. (1990) 'Development and Validation of the Competitive State Anxiety Inventory-2 (CSAI-2)', In R. Martens, R. S. Vealey and D. Burton (eds), *Competitive Anxiety in Sport* (Champaign, IL: Human Kinetics), 117–90.

Martin, L. J., Carron, A. V. and Burke, S. M (2009) 'Team Building Interventions in Sport: A Meta-Analysis', *Sport and Exercise Psychology Review*, 5, 3–18.

Martin, J. J. and Gill, D. L. (1991) 'The Relationships among Competitive Orientation, Sport-Confidence, Self-Efficacy, Anxiety and Performance', *Journal of Sport & Exercise Psychology*, 13, 149–59.

Martin, K. A., Moritz, S. E. and Hall, C. (1999) 'Imagery Use in Sport: A Literature Review and Applied Model', *The Sport Psychologist*, 13, 245–68.

Martin, S. B., Jackson, A. W., Richardson, P. A. and Weiller, K. H. (1999) 'Coaching Preferences of Adolescent Youths and Their Parents', *Journal of Applied Sport Psychology*, 11, 247–62.

Martinent, G. and Ferand, C. (2007). 'A Cluster Analysis of Precompetitive Anxiety: Relationship with Perfectionism and Trait Anxiety', *Personality and Individual Differences*, 43, 1676–86.

Martinsen, E. W. (1994) 'Physical Activity and Depression: Clinical Experience', *Acta Psychiatrica Scandinavica*, 89 (377 suppl.), 23–7.

Martinsen, E. W. (1995) 'Effects of Exercise on Mental Health in Clinical Populations', in S. J. H. Biddle (ed.), *European Perspectives on Exercise and Sport Psychology* (Champaign, IL: Human Kinetics), 71–90.

Maslovat, D., Hayes, S., Horn, R. R. and Hodges, N. J. (2010). Motor Learning through Observation', in D. Elliott and M. Khan (eds), *Vision and Goal-Directed Movement* (Champaign, Illiinois: Human Kinetics), 315–37.

Masters, R. S. W. (1992) 'Knowledge, Knerves and Know-How: The Role of Explicit Versus Implicit Knowledge in the Breakdown of Complex Motor Skill Under Pressure', *British Journal of Psychology*, 83, 343–58.

Masters, R. S. W. (2000) 'Theoretical Aspects of Implicit Learning in Sport', *International Journal of Sport Psychology*, 31, 530–41.

Masters, R. (2008) 'The Theory of Reinvestment', *International Review of Sport and Exercise Psychology*, 1, 2, 161–80.

Masters, R. S. W. and Maxwell, J. P. (2004) 'Implicit Motor Learning, Reinvestment and Movement Disruption: What You Don't Know Won't Hurt You?', in A. M. Williams and N. J. Hodges (eds), *Skill Acquisition in Sport: Research, Theory and Practice* (London: Routledge), 207–28.

Masters, R. S. W. and Maxwell, J. P. (2008). 'The Theory of Reinvestment', *International Review of Sport and Exercise Psychology*, 2, 160–83.

Masters, R. S. W., Polman, R. C. J. and Hammond, N. V. (1993) 'Reinvestment: A Dimension of Personality Implicated in Skill Breakdown Under Pressure', *Personality and Individual Differences*, 14, 655–66.

Masters, R. S. W., Law, J. and Maxwell, J. P. (2002) 'Implicit and Explicit Learning in Interceptive Actions', in K. Davids, G. Savelsbergh, S. J. Bennett and J. Van der Kamp (eds), *Interceptive Actions in Sport: Information and Movement* (London: Routledge), 126–43.

Matheson, H., Mathes, S. and Murray, M. (1997) 'The Effect of Winning and Losing on Female Interactive and Coactive Team Cohesion', *Journal of Sport Behavior*, 20, 284–98.

Maxwell, J. P., Masters, R. S. W. and Eves, F. (1999) 'Explicit Versus Implicit Motor Learning: Dissociating Selective and Unselective Modes of Skill Acquisition Via Feedback Manipulation', *Journal of Sport Sciences*, 6, 559.

Maxwell, J. P., Masters, R. S. W., Kerr, E. and Weedon, E. (2001) 'The Implicit Benefit of Learning Without Errors', *Quarterly Journal of Experimental Psychology*, p. 54A, 1049–68.

Maynard, I. (1998) *Improving Concentration* (Leeds: The National Coaching Foundation).

Meece, J. L. and Holt, K. (1993) 'A Pattern Analysis of Students' Achievement Goals', *Journal of Educational Psychology*, 85, 582–90.

Melnick, M. and Chemers, M. (1974) 'Effects of Group Social Structure on the Success of Basketball Teams', *Research Quarterly for Exercise and Sport*, 45, 1–8.

Merom, D., Phongsavan, P., Wagner, R. *et al.* (2007) 'Promoting Walking as an Adjunct Intervention to Group Cognitive Behavioral Therapy for Anxiety Disorders: A Pilot Group Randomized Trial', *Journal of Anxiety Disorders*, 22 959–68.

Meister, I. G., Krings, T., Foltys, H., Boroojerdi, B., Muller, M., Topper, R. and Thron, A. (2004). 'Playing Piano in the Mind – An fMRI Study on Music Imagery and Performance in Pianists', *Cognitive Brain Research*, 19, 219–28.

Messer, B. and Harter, S. (1986) *Adult Self-Perception Profile* (Denver, CO: University of Denver).

Meumann, E. (1904) '*Haus- und schularbeit: Experimente an kindern der volkschule*', *Die Deutsche Schule*, 8, 278–303, 337–59, 416–31.

Michaels, J. W., Blommel, J. M., Brocato, R. M., Linkous, R. A. and Rowe, J. S. (1982) 'Social Facilitation and Inhibition in a Natural Setting', *Replications in Social Psychology*, 2, 21–4.

Mihovilovic, M. (1968) 'The Status of Former Sportsmen', *International Review of Sport Sociology*, 3, 73–93.

Milavić, B., Guć, D. and Miletić, D. (2010) 'The Relations Between Types of Motivation in Sport and Perceived Sport Competence', *Physical Education and Sport*, 8 (1), 59–69.

Miller, P. D. (1995) *Fitness Programming and Physical Disability* (Champaign, IL: Human Kinetics).

Miranda, S. M. (1994) 'Avoidance of Groupthink: Meeting Management using a Group Support System', *Small Group Research*, 25, 105–36.

Moore, J. C. and Brylinsky, J. (1995) 'Facility Familiarity and the Home Advantage', *Journal of Sport Behavior*, 18, 302–11.

Moorhead, G. and Montanari, J. R. (1986) 'An Empirical Investigation of the Groupthink Phenomena', *Human Relation*, 39, 399–410.

Moos, R. H. and Humphrey, B. (1974) *Group Environment Scale – Form R. Palo Alto* (CA: Consulting Psychologists Press).

Moran, A. P. (1993) 'Conceptual and Methodological Issues in the Measurement of Mental Imagery Skills in Athletes', *Journal of Sport Behavior*, 16, 156–70.

Moran, A. P. (1996) *The Psychology of Concentration in Sport Performers: A Cognitive Analysis* (Hove, East Sussex: Psychology Press).

Moran, A. P. (2000) 'Improving Sporting Abilities: Training Concentration Skills', in J. Hartley (ed.), *The Applied Psychologist,* 2nd edn (Buckingham: Open University Press), 92–110.

Moran, A. P. (2002) 'In the Mind's Eye', *The Psychologist*, 15, 414–15.

Moran, A. P. (2003) 'The State of Concentration Skills Training in Applied Sport Psychology', in I. Greenlees and A. P. Moran (eds), *Concentration Skills Training in Sport* (Leicester: British Psychological Society).

Moran, A. P. (2009a). 'Attention in Sport', in S. D. Mellalieu and S. D. Hanton (eds), *Advances in Applied Sport Psychology: A Review* (Abingdon, Oxford: Routledge), 195–220.

Moran, A. P. (2009b). 'Cognitive Psychology in Sport: Progress and Prospects'. *Psychology of Sport and Exercise*, 10, 420–6.

Moran, A. P. (2009c). 'Attention, Concentration and Thought Management', in B. W. Brewer (ed.), *Sport Psychology* (Handbook of Sports Medicine and Science) (Oxford: Wiley-Blackwell), 18–29.

Moran, A. P. (2010). *Learn to Study For Success at College and University (CD).* (Belfast: MindCool Productions).

Moran, A. P. (2012) *Sport and Exercise Psychology: A Critical Introduction,* 2nd edn (London: Routledge).

Moran, A. P. and MacIntyre, T. (1998) 'There's More to an Image than Meets the Eye': A Qualitative Study of Kinaesthetic Imagery among Elite Canoe-Slalomists', *The Irish Journal of Psychology,* 19, 406–23.

Moran, A. P., Byrne, A. and McGlade, N. (2002) 'The Effects of Anxiety and Strategic Planning on Visual Search Behaviour', *Journal of Sports Sciences,* 20, 225–36.

Morgan, W. P. (1970) *Contemporary Readings in Sport Psychology* (Springfield, IL: Thomas).

Morgan, W. P. (1980) 'Test of the Champions: The Iceberg Profile', *Psychology Today,* 6 July, 92–108.

Morgan, W. P. (1997) 'Methodological Considerations', in W. P. Morgan (ed.), *Physical Activity and Mental Health* (Washington DC: Taylor and Francis), 3–32.

Morgan, W. P. and Dishman, M. L. (2001) 'Adherence to Exercise and Physical Activity: Preface', *Quest,* 53, 277–8.

Morgan, W. P. and O'Connor, P. J. (1988) 'Exercise and Mental Health', in R. K. Dishman (ed.), *Exercise Adherence: Its Impact on Public Health* (Champaign, IL: Human Kinetics), 91–121.

Moritz, S. E., Feltz, D. L., Fahrbach, K. R. and Mack, D. E. (2000) 'The Relation of Self-Efficacy Measures to Sport Performance: A Meta-Analytic Review', *Research Quarterly for Exercise and Sport,* 71, 280–94.

Morris, L., Davis, D. and Hutchings, C. (1981) 'Cognitive and Emotional Components of Anxiety: Literary Review and Revised Worry-Emotionality Scale', *Journal of Educational Psychology,* 73, 541–55.

Morris, T. and Terry, P. (eds) (in press) *The New Sport and Exercise Psychology Companion* (Morgantown, WV: Fitness Information Technology).

Morris, T. and Thomas, P. (1995) 'Approaches to Applied Sport Psychology', in T. Morris and J. Summers (Eds), *Sport Psychology: Theory, Applications and Issues* (Milton, Australia: Wiley), 215–58.

Morris, T., Spittle, M. and Watt, A. P. (2005) *Imagery in Sport* (Champaign, Illinois: Human Kinetics).

Moss, S., Cochrane, K. and Burnton, S. (2008) 'Baffled by Beijing', *The Guardian* (g2), 19 August. Retrieved from http://www.guardian.co.uk/sport/2008/aug/19/britisholympicteam.olympics2008 on 25 October 2010.

Motl, R. W., Dishman, R. K., Saunders, R., Dowda, M., Felton, G., Ward, D. S. and Pate, R. R. (2002) 'Examining Social–Cognitive Determinants of Intention and Physical Activity among Black and White Adolescent Girls Using Structural Equation Modeling', *Health Psychology,* 21, 459–67.

Mudrack, P. E. (1989) 'Defining Group Cohesiveness: A Legacy of Confusion?', *Small Group Behavior,* 20, 37–49.

Mullan, E., Albinson, J. and Markland, D. (1997) 'Children's Perceived Physical Competence at Different Categories of Physical Activity', *Pediatric Exercise Science,* 9, 237–42.

Mullen, B. and Baumeister, R. F. (1987) 'Group Effects on Self-Attention and Performance: Social Loafing, Social Facilitation and Social Impairment', in C. Hendrick (ed.) *Group Processes and Intergroup Relations* (Newbury Park, CA: Sage), 189–206.

Mullen, B. and Copper, C. (1994) 'The Relation between Group Cohesiveness and Performance: An Integration', *Psychological Bulletin,* 115, 210–27.

Mullen, B., Anthony, T., Salas, E. and Driskell, J. E. (1994) 'Group Cohesiveness and Quality of Decision Making: An Integration of Tests of the Groupthink Hypothesis', *Small Group Research*, 25, 189–204.

Mullen, R. and Hardy, L. (2000) 'State Anxiety and Motor Performance: Testing the Conscious Processing Hypothesis', *Journal of Sport Sciences*, 18, 785–99.

Müller, S., Abernethy, B. and Farrow, D. (2006). 'How Do World-Class Cricket Batsmen Anticipate a Bowler's Intention?', *Quarterly Journal of Experimental Psychology*, 59, 2162–86.

Munroe, K., Giaccobi, P. C., Hall, C. and Weinberg, R. (2000). 'The Four Ws of Imagery Use: Where, When, Why, and What', *The Sport Psychologist*, 14, 119–37.

Murphy, G. M., Petitpas, A. J. and Brewer, B. W. (1996) 'Identity Foreclosure, Athletic Identity, and Career Maturity in Intercollegiate Athletes', *The Sport Psychologist*, 10, 239–46.

Murphy, S. M. (1994) 'Imagery Interventions in Sport', *Medicine and Science in Sport and Exercise*, 26, 486–94.

Murphy, S. M. (1995a) (ed.) *Sport Psychology Interventions* (Champaign, IL: Human Kinetics).

Murphy, S. M. (1995b) 'Transition in Competitive Sport: Maximizing Individual Potential', in S. M. Murphy (ed.), *Sport Psychology Interventions* (Champaign, IL: Human Kinetics), 331–46.

Murphy, S. M. and Martin, K. A. (2002) 'The Use of Imagery in Sport', in T. Horn (ed.), *Advances in Sport Psychology*, 2nd edn, (Champaign, IL: Human Kinetics), 405–39.

Murphy, S., Nordin, S. and Cumming, J. (2008). 'Imagery in Sport, Exercise, and Dance', in T. S. Horn (ed.), *Advances in Sport Psychology*, 3rd edn (Champaign, Illinois: Human Kinetics), 297–324, 463–467.

National Center for Health Statistics (2001) *Health People 2000: Final Review* (Hyattsville, MD: Public Health Service).

Nattiv, A. (1995) 'The Female Athlete Triad: Managing Acute Risk to Long-Term Health', *Physician and Sports Medicine*, 22, 60–8.

Navon, D. and Gopher, D. (1979) 'On the Economy of the Human Information Processing System', *Psychological Review*, 86, 214–55.

Neemann, J. and Harter, S. (1986) *Self-Perception Profile for College Students* (Denver, CO: University of Denver).

Neiss, R. (1988) 'Reconceptualizing Arousal: Psychobiological States in Motor Performance', *Psycholological Bulletin*, 103, 345–66.

Neisser, U. (1967) *Cognitive Psychology* (New York: Appelton-Century-Crofts).

Nevill, A. M., Balmer, N. J. and Williams, A. M. (2002) 'The Influence of Crowd Noise and Experience upon Refereeing Decisions in Football', *Psychology of Sport and Exercise*, 3, 261–72.

Nevill, A. M. and Holder, R. (1999) 'Home Advantage in Sport: An Overview of Studies on the Advantage of Playing at Home', *Sports Medicine*, 28, 221–36.

Newell, K. M. (1974) 'Knowledge of Results and Motor Learning', *Journal of Motor Behavior*, 6, 235–44.

Newell, K. M. (1985) 'Coordination, Control and Skill', in D. Goodman, R. B. Wilberg and I. M. Franks (eds), *Differing Perspectives in Motor Learning, Memory, and Control* (Amsterdam: Elsevier Science), 295–317.

Newton, M. and Duda, J. (1999) 'The Interaction of Motivational Climate, Dispositional Goal Orientations, and Perceived Ability in Predicting Indices of Motivation', *International Journal of Sport Psychology*, 30, 63–82.

Nicholls, A. R. and Polman, R. C. (2007) 'Coping in Sport: A Systematic Review', *Journal of Sports Sciences*, 25, 11–31.

Nicholls, J. C. (1978) 'The Development of Concepts of Effort and Ability, Perception of Attainment, and the Understanding that Difficult Tasks Require More Ability', *Child Development*, 49, 800–14.

Nicholls, J. G. (1984) 'Achievement Motivation: Conceptions of Ability, Subjective Experience, Mastery Choice, and Performance', *Psychological Review*, 91, 328–46.

Nichols, P. (2000) 'Ice-Man Faulds Keeps his cool', *The Guardian* (Sport), 21 September, p. 7.

Nideffer, R. M. (1976) 'Test of Attentional and Interpersonal Style', *Journal of Personality and Social Psychology*, 34, 394–404.

Nideffer, R. M. (1981) *The Ethics and Practice of Applied Sport Psychology* (Ithaca: Mouvement).

Nideffer, R. M. (1987) 'Issues in the Use of Psychological Tests in Applied Settings', *The Sport Psychologist*, 1, 18–28.

Nideffer, R. M. and Sagal, M. (2001) *Assessment in Sport Psychology* (Morgantown, WV: Fitness Information Technology).

Nideffer, R. M., Sagal, M. S., Lowry, M. and Bond, J. (2001) 'Identifying and Developing World-Class Performers', in G. Tenenbaum (ed.), *The Practice of Sport Psychology* (Morgantown, WV: Fitness Information Technology), 129–44.

Nisbett, R. E. and Wilson, T. D. (1977) 'Telling More than We Can Know: Verbal Reports on Mental Processes', *Psychological Review*, 84, 231–59.

Norris, J. and Jones, R. L. (1998) 'Towards a Clearer Definition and Application of the Centrality Hypothesis in English Professional Association Football', *Journal of Sport Behavior*, 21, 181–95.

North T. C., McCullagh, P. and Tran, Z. V. (1990) 'Effect of Exercise on Depression', *Exercise and Sport Sciences Reviews*, 18, 379–415.

North, J. S., Williams, A. M., Ward, P., Hodges, N. J. and Ericsson, K. A. (2009). Perceiving Patterns in Dynamic Action Sequences: The Relationship between Anticipation and Pattern Recognition Skill', *Applied Cognitive Psychology*, 23, 1–17.

North, J., Ward, P., Ericsson, A. and Williams, A. M. (2011) 'Mechanisms Underlying Skilled Anticipation and Recognition in a Dynamic and Temporally Constrained Domain', *Memory*, 19, 155–68.

Nougier, V., Stein, J. F. and Bonnel, A. M. (1991) 'Information Processing in Sport and Orienting of Attention', *International Journal of Sport Psychology*, 22, 307–27.

Ntoumanis, N. and Biddle, S. J. H. (1998) 'The Relationship Between Competitive Anxiety, Achievement Goals and Motivational Climate', *Research Quarterly for Exercise and Sport*, 69, 176–87.

Ntoumanis, N. and Biddle, S. J. H. (1999) 'A Review of Motivational Climate in Physical Activity', *Journal of Sport Science*, 17, 643–65.

O'Leary, K. D. and Borkovec, T. D. (1978) 'Conceptual, Methodological, and Ethical Problems of Placebo Groups in Psychotherapy Research', *American Psychologist*, 33, 821–30.

Olympiou, A., Jowett, S. and Duda, J. L. (2008) 'The Psychological Interface of the Coach-Created Motivational Climate and the Coach-Athlete Relationship', *The Sport Psychologist*, 22, 423–38.

O'Neal, H., Dunn, A. L. and Martinsen, E. W. (2000) 'Depression and Exercise', *International Journal of Sport Psychology*, 31, 110–35.

O'Sullivan, J. (2002). 'Captain Steers a Steady Ship', *The Irish Times*, 26 September, p. 19.

Ogilvie, B. C. and Tutko, T. (1966) *Problem Athletes and How to Handle Them* (London: Pelham Books).

Ojanen, M. (1994) 'Can the True Effects of Exercise on Psychological Variables be Separated from Placebo Effects?', *International Journal of Sport Psychology*, 25, 63–80.

Olivardia, R. and Pope, H. G. (2000) 'Muscle Dysmorphia in Male Weightlifters: A Case Control Study', *American Journal of Psychiatry*, 157, 1291–6.

Onions, C. T. (1996) (ed.) *The Oxford Dictionary of English Etymology* (Oxford: Clarendon).

Orlick, T. (1990) *In Pursuit of Excellence* (Champaign, IL: Human Kinetics).

Orne, M. T. (1962) 'On the Social Psychology of the Psychological Experiment: With Particular Reference to Demand Characteristics and their Implications', *American Psychologist*, 17, 776–83.

Ostrow, A. C. (1996) (ed.) *Directory of Psychological Tests in the Sport and Exercise Sciences*, 2nd edn (Morgantown, WV: Fitness Information Technology).

Owen, N., Glanz, K., Sallis, J. F. and Kelder, S. (2006), 'Evidence-Based Approaches to Dissemination and Diffusion of Physical Activity Interventions', *American Journal of Preventive Medicine*, 31, 35–44.

Oxendine, J. B. (1984) *Psychology of Motor Learning* (Englewood Cliffs, NJ: Prentice Hall).

Page, L. and Page, K. (2007) 'The Second Leg Home Advantage: Evidence from European Football Cup Competitions', *Journal of Sports Sciences*, 25, 1547–56.

Painter, P. and Blackburn, G. (1988) 'Exercise for Patients with Chronic Disease', *Postgraduate Medicine*, 83, 185–96.

Paivio, A. (1985) 'Cognitive and Motivational Functions of Imagery in Human Performance', *Canadian Journal of Applied Sport Science*, 10, 22–8.

Panchuck, D. and Vickers, J. N. (2006) 'Gaze Behaviors of Goaltenders under Spatial–Temporal Constraints', *Human Movement Science*, 25, 6, 733–52.

Papaioannou, A. and McDonald, A. I. (1993) 'Goal Perspectives and Purposes of Physical Education as Perceived by Greek Adolescents', *Physical Education Review*, 16, 41–8.

Papaioannou, A. and Theodorakis, Y. (1996) 'A Test of Three Models for the Prediction of Intention for Participation in Physical Education Lessons', *International Journal of Sport Psychology*, 27, 383–99.

Park, R. (1912) 'Thanatology', *Journal of the American Medical Association*, 58, 1243–6.

Parker, K. B. (1994) 'Has-beens and Wanna-bes: Transition Experiences of Former Major College Football Players', *The Sport Psychologist*, 8, 287–304.

Partington, J. T. and Shangi, G. M. (1992) 'Developing an Understanding of Team Psychology', *International Journal of Sport Psychology*, 23, 28–47.

Paskevich, D. M., Estabrooks, P. A., Brawley, L. R. and Carron, A. V. (2001) 'Group Cohesion in Sport and Exercise', in R. N. Singer, H. A. Hausenblas and C. M. Janelle (eds) *Handbook of Sport Psychology*, 2nd edn (New York: Wiley), 472–94.

Patmore, A. (1986) *Sportsmen Under Stress* (London: Stanley Paul).

Patrick, G. T. W. (1903) 'The Psychology of Football', *American Journal of Psychology*, 14, 104–17.

Paulus, P. B., Judd, B. B. and Bernstein, I. H. (1976) 'Social Facilitation in Sports', in R. W. Christina and D. M. Landers (eds), *Psychology of Motor Behavior and Sport (2)* (Champaign, IL: Human Kinetics).

Pelletier, L., Fortier, M., Vallerand, R., Tuson, K., Briere, N. and Blais, M. (1995) 'Towards a New Measure of Intrinsic Motivation, Extrinsic Motivation, and Amotivation in Sports: The Sport Motivation Scale (SMS)', *Journal of Sport & Exercise Psychology*, 17, 35–53.

Perkos, S., Theodorakis, Y. and Chroni, S. (2002) 'Enhancing Performance and Skill Acquisition in Novice Basketball Players with Instructional Self-Talk', *The Sport Psychologist*, 16, 368–83.

Perry, C. and Morris, T. (1995) 'Mental Imagery in Sport', in T. Morris and J. Summers (eds), *Sport Psychology: Theory, Applications and Issues* (Brisbane, Australia: John Wiley), 339–85.

Petitpas, A. and Champagne, D. (2000) 'Practical Considerations in Implementing Sport Career Transition Programs', in D. Lavallee and P. Wylleman (eds), *Career Transitions in Sport: International Perspectives* (Morgantown, WV: Fitness Information Technology), 81–93.

Petitpas, A., Brewer, B. W. and Van Raalte, J. L. (1996) 'Transitions of the Student-Athlete: Theoretical, Empirical, and Practical Perspectives', in E. F. Etzel, A. P. Ferrante and J. W. Pinkney (eds), *Counseling College Student-Athletes: Issues and Interventions,* 2nd edn (Morgantown, WV: Fitness Information Technology), 137–56.

Petitpas, A., Brewer, B. W., Rivera, P. and Van Raalte, J. L. (1993) 'Ethical Beliefs and Behaviors in Applied Sport Psychology: The AAASP Ethics Survey', *Journal of Applied Sport Psychology*, 6, 135–51.

Petitpas, A., Danish, S., McKelvain, R. and Murphy, S. M. (1990) 'A Career Assistance Program for Elite Athletes', *Journal of Counseling and Development*, 70, 383–6.

Petitpas, A., Champagne, D., Chartrand, J., Danish, S. and Murphy, S. (1997) *Athlete's Guide to Career Planning. Keys to Success from the Playing Field to Professional Life* (Champaign, IL: Human Kinetics).

Petruzzello, S. J., Landers, D. M., Hatfield, B. D., Kubitz, K. A. and Salazar, W. (1991) 'A Meta-Analysis on the Anxiety Reducing Effects of Acute and Chronic Exercise: Outcomes and Mechanisms', *Sports Medicine*, 11, 143–82.

Phares, E. J. and Trull, T. J. (1997) *Clinical Psychology: Concepts, Methods and Profession,* 5th edn (Pacific Grove, CA: Brooks/Cole).

Phelps, M. (2008). 'Why Pain and Disorder Led to an Iron Will to Win', *The Guardian* (Sport), 13 December, p. 10.

Phillips, K. A. and Diaz, S. F. (1997) 'Gender Differences in Body Dysmorphic Disorder', *Journal of Nervous and Mental Disease*, 185, 570–77.

Phillips, E., Davids, K., Renshaw, I. and Portus, M. (2010) 'Expert Performance in Sport and the Dynamics of Talent Development', *Sports Medicine*, 40, 4, 271–83.

Pijpers, J. R., Oudejans, R. R. D., Holsheimer, F. and Bakker, F. C. (2003). 'Anxiety-Performance Relationships in Climbing: A Process-Oriented Approach', *Psychology of Sport andf Exercise*, 4, 283–304.

Pinder, C. C. (1991) 'Valence-Instrumentality-Expectancy Theory', in R. M. Steers and L.W. Porter (eds), *Motivation and Work Behavior,* 5th edn (Singapore: McGraw-Hill), 144–64.

Pingitore, R., Dugori, B., Tindale S. and Spring, B. (1994) 'Bias Against Overweight Job Applicants in a Simulated Employee Interview', *Journal of Applied Psychology*, 79, 909–17.

Pitetti, K. H. and Tan, D. (1990) 'Cardiorespiratory Responses of Mentally Retarded Adults to Air-Brake Ergometry and Treadmill Exercise', *Archives of Physical and Medical Rehabilitation*, 71, 318–21.

Poag, K. and McAuley, E. (1992) 'Goal Setting, Self-Efficacy, and Exercise Behavior', *Journal of Sport & Exercise Psychology*, 14, 352–60.

Polich, J. (2007). 'Updating P300: An Integrative Theory of P3a and P3b', *Clincial Neurophysiology*, 118, 2128–2148.

Ponichtera-Mulcare, J. A. Q. (1993) 'Exercise and Multiple Sclerosis', *Medicine and Science in Sports and Exercise*, 25, 451–65.

Porter, L. W. and Lawler, E. E. (1968) *Managerial Attitudes and Performance* (Homewood, IL: Dorsey).

Posner, M. (1980) 'Orienting of Attention: The VIIth Sir Frederic Bartlett Lecture, *Quarterly Journal of Experimental Psychology,* 32A, 3–25.

Posner, M. and Rothbart, M. K. (2007) 'Research on Attention Networks as a Model for the Integration of a Psychological Science', *Annual Review of Psychology*, 58, 1–23.

Pratt, M., Macera, C. and Blanton, C. (1999) 'Levels of Physical Activity and Inactivity in Children and Adults in the United States: Current Evidence and Research Issues', *Medicine and Science in Sports and Exercise*, 31, 526–33.

Preston, A. (2000). 'It's All In The Mind, Touch Wood', The Irish Independent, 23 September (Weekend), 18–19.

Price, M. and Weiss, M. R. (2000) 'Relationships among Coach Burnout, Coach Behaviours, and Athletes' Psychological Responses', *The Sport Psychologist*, 14, 391–409.

Prochaska, J. O. and Di Clemente, C. C. (1983) 'Stages and Processes of Self-Change of Smoking: Toward an Integrative Model of Change', *Journal of Consulting and Clinical Psychology*, 51, 390–5.

Propst, D. and Koesler, R. (1998) 'Bandura Goes Outdoors: Role of Self-Efficacy in the Outdoor Leadership Development Process', *Leisure Sciences*, 20, 319–44.

Pummell, B., Harwood, C. and Lavallee, D. (2008). Jumping to the Next Level: A Qualitative Examination of Within-Career Transition in Adolescent Event Riders', *Psychology of Sport and Exercise*, 9, 427–47.

Pylyshyn, Z. (1973) 'What the Mind's Eye Tells the Mind's Brain', *Psychological Bulletin*, 80, 1–24.

Raedeke, T. D. (1997) 'Is Athlete Burnout More Than Just Stress? A Sport Commitment Perspective', *Journal of Sport & Exercise Psychology*, 19, 396–417.

Raglin, J. S. (1997) 'Anxiolytic Effects of Physical Activity', in W. P. Morgan (ed.), *Physical Activity and Mental Health* (Washington DC: Taylor and Francis), 107–26.

Raglin, J. S. and Morgan, W. P. (1985) 'Influence of Vigorous Exercise on Pain Sensitivity and Mood State', *Behaviour Therapist*, 8, 179–83.

Rando, T. A. (1984) *Grief, Dying, and Death: Clinical Interventions for Caregivers* (Champaign, IL: Research Press).

Rando, T. A. (1986) *Loss and Anticipatory Grief* (Lexington, MA: Lexington Books).

Rauramaa R. (1984) 'Relationship of Physical Activity, Glucose Tolerance and Weight Management', *Preventive Medicine*, 13, 37–46.

Rees, T., Ingledew, D. K. and Hardy, L. (2005) 'Attribution in Sport Psychology: Seeking Congruence between Theory, Research and Practice', *Psychology of Sport and Exercise*, 6, 189–204.

Rees, T., Mitchell, I., Evans, L. E. and Hardy, L. (2010) 'Stressors, Social Support and Psychological Responses to Sport Injury in High- and Low-performance Standard Participants', *Psychology of Sport and Exercise*, 11, 505–12.

Reeve, T. G. and Magill, R. A. (1981) 'Role of Components of Knowledge of Results Information in Error Correction', *Research Quarterly for Exercise and Sport*, 52, 80–5.

Reid, P. (2002) 'Campbell Survives a Bleeding', *The Irish Times* (Sport), 8 July, p. 1.

Reid, R. L. and Yen, S. S. C. (1983) 'The Premenstrual Syndrome', *American Journal of Obstetrics and Gynaecology*, 26, 710–18.

Rejeski, W. J. (1994) Dose-Response Issues from a Psychosocial Perspective', in C. Bouchard, R. J. Shephard and T. Stephens (eds), *Physical activity, Fitness, and Health* (Champaign, IL: Human Kinetics), 1040–55.

Renick, M. J. and Harter, S. (1988) *Self-Perception Profile for Learning Disabled Students* (Denver, CO: University of Denver).

Reynolds, M. J. (1981) 'The Effects of Sports Retirement on the Job Satisfaction of the Former Football Player', in S. L. Greendorfer and A. Yiannakis (eds), *Sociology of Sport: Diverse Perspectives* (West Point, NY: Leisure Press), 127–37.

Rhind, D. J. A. and Jowett, S. (2010) 'Relationship Maintenance Strategies in the Coach-Athlete Relationship: The Development of the COMPASS Model', *Journal of Applied Sport Psychology*, 22, 106–21.

Richardson, A. (1967a) 'Mental Practice: A Review and Discussion, Part I', *Research Quarterly*, 38, 95–107.

Richardson, A. (1967b) 'Mental Practice: A Review and Discussion, Part II', *Research Quarterly*, 38, 263–73.

Richardson, A. (1995) *Individual Differences in Imaging: Their Measurement, Origins and Consequences* (Amityville, NY: Baywood).

Richardson, J. T. E. (1999) *Imagery* (Hove, East Sussex: Psychology Press).

Riemer, H. A. (2007) 'Multidimensional Model of Coach Leadership', in S. Jowett and D. Lavallee (eds), *Social Psychology in Sport* (Champaign IL: Human Kinetics), 57–73.

Riemer, H. A. and Chelladurai, P. (1995) 'Leadership and Satisfaction in Athletics' *Journal of Sport & Exercise Psychology*, 17, 276–93.

Rimmer, J. H., Braddock, D. and Fujiura, G. (1993) 'Prevalence of Obesity in Adults with Mental Retardation: Implications for Health Promotion and Disease Prevention', *Mental Retardation*, 31, 105–10.

Rimmer, J. H., Braddock, D. and Pitetti, K. H. (1996) 'Research on Physical Activity and Disability: An Emerging National Priority', *Medicine and Science in Sports and Exercise*, 28, 1366–72.

Ringelmann, M. (1913) *'Reserches sur les moteurs animés: travail de l'homme'*, Annales de l'Institute National Agronomique, 2, 1–40.

Ripoll, H. (1991) 'The Understanding-Acting Process in Sport: The Relationship between the Semantic and Sensorimotor Visual Function', *International Journal of Sport Psychology*, 22, 221–43.

Roberts, G. C. (1992) 'Motivation in Sport and Exercise: Conceptual Constraints and Convergence', in G. C. Roberts (ed.), *Motivation in Sport and Exercise* (Champaign, IL: Human Kinetics), 3–30.

Roberts, G. C. (1993) 'Motivation in Sport: Understanding and Enhancing the Motivation and Achievement of Children', in R. N. Singer, M. Murphey and L. K. Tennant (eds), *Handbook of Research in Sport Psychology* (New York: Macmillan), 405–20.

Roberts, G. C. (2001) 'Understanding the Dynamics of Motivation in Physical Activity: The Influence of Achievement Goals on Motivational Processes', in G. C. Roberts (ed.) *Advances in Motivation in Sport and Exercise* (Champaign, IL: Human Kinetics), 1–50.

Roberts, G. C. and Kiiecik, J. C. (1989) 'Sport Psychology in the German Democratic Republic: An Interview with Dr. Gerd Kanzag', *The Sport Psychologist*, 3, 72–7.

Roberts, G. C. and Treasure, D. C. (1995) 'Achievement Goals, Motivational Climate and Achievement Strategies and Behaviors in Sport', *International Journal of Sport Psychology*, 26, 64–80.

Roberts, G. C., Treasure, D. C. and Conroy, D. (2007) 'Understanding the Dynamics of Motivation in Sport and Physical Activity: An Achievement Goal Interpretation', in G. Tenenbaum and R. C. Eklund (eds) *Handbook of Sport Psychology* (Hoboken, NJ: John Wiley and Sons), 3–30.

Roberts, G. C., Treasure, D. C. and Hall, H. K. (1994) 'Parental Goal Orientation and Beliefs about the Competitive-Sport Experience of the Child', *Journal of Applied Social Psychology*, 24, 631–45.

Roberts, G. C., Treasure, D. C. and Balague, G. (1998) 'Achievement Goals in Sport: The Development and Validation of the Perception of Success Questionnaire', *Journal of Sports Sciences*, 16, 337–47.

Roberts, G. C., Treasure, D. C. and Kavussnu, M. (1996) 'Orthogonality of Achievement g Goals and its Relationship to Beliefs about Success and Satisfaction in Sport', *The Sport Psychologist*, 10, 398–408.

Roberts, R., Callow, N., Hardy, L., Markland, D. and Bringer, J. (2008). 'Movement Imagery Ability: Development and Assessment of a Revised Version of the Vividness of Movement Imagery Questionnaire', *Journal of Sport and Exercise Psychology*, 30, 200–21.

Rodrigues, S., Vickers, J. and Williams, A. M. (2002) 'Eye, Head and Arm Co-Ordination in Table Tennis', *Journal of Sports Sciences*, 20, 187–200.

Rogerson, L. J. and Hrycaiko, D. W. (2002) 'Enhancing Competitive Performance of Ice Hockey Goaltenders using Centering and Self-Talk', *Journal of Applied Sport Psychology*, 14, 14–26.

Rose, A. M. (1965) 'The Subculture of Ageing: A Framework in Social Gerontology', in A. Rose and I. Peterson (eds), *Older People and their Social World* (Philadelphia: F.A. David Company).

Rosenberg, E. (1981) 'Gerontological Theory and Athletic Retirement', in S. L. Greendorfer and A. Yiannakis (eds), *Sociology of Sport: Diverse Perspectives* (West Point, NY: Leisure Press), 119–26.

Rosenberg, E. (1984) 'Athletic Retirement as Social Death: Concepts and Perpectives', in N. Theberge and P. Donnelly (eds), *Sport and the Sociological Imagination* (Fort Worth: Texas Christian University Press), 245–58.

Rosenstock, I. M., Strecher, V. J. and Becker, M. H. (1988) 'Social Learning Theory and the Health Belief Model', *Health Education Quarterly*, 15, 175–83.

Rosenthal, R. (1966) *Experimenter Effects in Behavioral Research* (New York: Appleton-Century-Crofts).

Rotter, J. B. (1966) 'Generalised Expectancies from Internal Versus External Control of Reinforcement', *Psychological Monographs*, 80 (No. 609).

Rudolph, D. L. and Butki, B. D. (1998) 'Self-Efficacy and Affective Responses to Short Bouts of Exercise', *Journal of Applied Psychology*, 10, 268–80.

Ruffer, W. A. (1976) 'Personality Traits of Athletes', *The Physical Educator*, 33, 211–14.

Ruppel Shell, E. (2002) *The Hungry Gene: The Science of Fat and the Future of Thin* (New York: Atlantic).

Rusbult, C. E. (1983) 'A Longitudinal Test of the Investment Model: The Development (and Deterioration) of Satisfaction and Commitment in Heterosexual Involvements', *Journal of Personality and Social Psychology*, 45, 101–17.

Ryan, R. M. and Deci, E. L. (2000) 'Self-Determination Theory and the Facilitation of Intrinsic Motivation, Social Development, and Well-Being', *American Psychologist*, 55, 68–78.

Ryan, R. M. and Deci, E. L. (2002) 'An Overview of Self-Determination Theory.' In E. L. Deci. and R. M. Ryan (eds), *Handbook of Self-Determination Research* (Rochester, NY: University of Rochester Press), 3–33.

Ryan, R. M., Frederick, C. M., Lepes, D., Rubio, N. and Sheldon, K. M. (1997) 'Intrinsic Motivation and Exercise Adherence', *International Journal of Sport Psychology*, 28, 335–54.

Sachs, M. (1993) 'Professional Ethics in Sport Psychology', in R. Singer, M. Murphey and L. K. Tennant (eds), *Handbook of Research on Sport Psychology* (New York: Macmillan), 921–32.

Sackett, R. S. (1934) 'The Influence of Symbolic Rehearsal upon the Retention of a Maze Habit', *Journal of General Psychology*, 10, 376–95.

Sallis, J. F., Haskell, W. L., Fortmann, S. T., Vranizan, K. M., Taylor, C. B. and Solomon, D. S. (1986) 'Predictors of Adoption and Maintenance of Physical Activity in a Community Sample', *Preventive Medicine*, 15, 331–41.

Sallis, J. F., Hovell, M. F., Hofstetter, C. R., Faucher, P., Elder, J. P., Blanchard, J., Casperson, C. J., Powell, K. E. and Christenson, G. M. (1989) 'A Multivariate Study of Determinants of Vigorous Exercise in a Community Sample', *Preventive Medicine*, 18, 20–34.

Sallis, J. F., Prochaska, J. J. and Taylor, W. C. (2000) 'A Review of Correlates of Physical Activity of Children and Adolescents', *Medicine and Science in Sports and Exercise*, 32, 963–75.

Salmela, J. H. (1981) *The World Sport Psychology Sourcebook* (New York: Mouvement).

Salmon, P. (2001) 'Effects of Physical Exercise on Anxiety, Depression, and Sensitivity to Stress: A Unifying Theory', *Clinical Psychology Review*, 21, 33–61.

Salmoni, A. W., Schmidt, R. A. and Walter, C. B. (1984) 'Knowledge of Results and Motor Learning: A Review and Critical Reappraisal', *Psychological Bulletin*, 95, 55–86.

Savelsbergh, G. J. P., Van der Kamp, J., Oudejans, R. R. D. and Scott, M. A. (2004) 'Perceptual Learning is Mastering Perceptual Degrees of Freedom', in A. M. Williams and N. J. Hodges (ed.,) *Skill Acquisition in Sport: Research, Theory and Practice*, 374–89 (London: Routledge).

Sands, R. (1978) 'A Socio-Psychological Investigation of the Effects of Role Discontinuity on Outstanding High School Athletes', *Journal of Sport Behavior*, 1, 174–85.

Sanna, L. J. (1992) 'Self-Efficacy Theory: Implications for Social Facilitation and Social Loafing', *Journal of Personality and Social Psychology*, 62, 774–86.

Sarrazin, P., Biddle, S., Famose, J. and Cury, F. (1996) 'Goal Orientations and Conceptions of the Nature of Sport Ability in Children: A Social Cognitive Approach', *British Journal of Social Psychology*, 35, 399–414.

Savelsbergh, G. J. P., Williams, A. M., van der Kamp, J. and Ward, P. (2002) 'Visual Search, Anticipation and Expertise in Soccer Goalkeepers', *Journal of Sports Sciences*, 20, 279–87.

Scanlan, T. K. and Lewthwaite, R. (1986) 'Social Psychological Aspects of the Competitive Sport Experience for Male Youth Sport Participants. IV: Predictors of Enjoyment', *Journal of Sport Psychology*, 8, 25–35.

Scanlan, T. K. and Simons, J. P. (1992) 'The Construct of Sport Enjoyment', in G.C. Roberts (ed.), *Motivation in Sport and Exercise* (Champaign, IL: Human Kinetics), 199–216.

Scanlan, T. K., Stein, G. L. and Ravizza, K. (1989) 'An In-depth Study of Former Elite Figure Skaters. II: Sources of enjoyment', *Journal of Sport & Exercise Psychology*, 11, 65–83.

Scanlan, T. K., Carpenter, P. J., Lobel, M. and Simons, J. P. (1993a) 'Sources of Enjoyment for Youth Sport', *Pediatric Exercise Science*, 5, 275–85.

Scanlan, T. K., Carpenter, P. J., Schmidt, G. W., Simons, J. P. and Keeler, B. (1993b) 'An Introduction to the Sport Commitment Model', *Journal of Sport & Exercise Psychology*, 15, 1–15.

Scanlan, T. K., Simons, J. P., Carpenter, P. J., Schmidt, G. W. and Keeler, B. (1993c) 'The Sport Commitment Model: Measurement Development for the Youth-Sport Domain', *Journal of Sport & Exercise Psychology*, 15, 16–38.

Schliesman, E. (1987) 'Relationship between the Congruence of Preferred and Actual Leader Behavior and Subordinate Satisfaction with Leadership', *Journal of Sport Behavior*, 10, 157–74.

Schlossberg, N. K. (1981) 'A Model for Analyzing Human Adaptation to Transition', *The Counseling Psychologist*, 9, 2–18.

Schlossberg, N. K., Waters, E. B. and Goodman, J. (1995) *Counseling Adults in Transition: Linking Practice with Theory,* 2nd edn (New York: Springer).

Schmidt, G. W. and Stein, G. L. (1991) 'Sport Commitment: A Model Integrating Enjoyment, Dropout, and Burnout', *Journal of Sport & Exercise Psychology*, 13, 254–65.

Schmidt, R. A. (1975) 'A Schema Theory of Discrete Motor Skill Learning. *Psychological Review*, 82, 225–60.

Schmidt, R. A. and Lee, T. D. (2011) *Motor Control and Learning: A Behavioral Emphasis*, 3rd edn (Champaign, IL: Human Kinetics).

Schmidt, R. A. and White, J. L. (1972) 'Evidence for an Error Detection Mechanism in Motor Skills: A Test of Adams' Closed-Loop Theory', *Journal of Motor Behavior*, 4, 143–53.

Schmidt, R. A. and Wrisberg, C. A. (2009) *Motor Learning and Performance: From Principles to Practice*, 4th edn (Champaign, IL: Human Kinetics).

Schunk, D. H. (1995) 'Self-Efficacy, Motivation and Performance', *Journal of Applied Sport Psychology*, 7, 112–37.

Schutz, R. W. and Gessaroli, M. C. (1993) 'Use, Misuse and Disuse of Psychometrics in Sport Psychology Research', in R. N. Singer, M. Murphey and L. K. Tennant (eds), *Handbook of Research in Sport Psychology* (New York: Macmillan), 901–17.

Schutz, R. W., Eom, H. J., Smoll, F. L. and Smith, R. E. (1994) 'Examination of the Factorial Validity of the Group Environment Questionnaire', *Research Quarterly for Exercise and Sport*, 65, 226–36.

Schwartz, B. and Barsky, S. F. (1977) 'The Home Advantage', *Social Forces*, 55, 641–61.

Scully, D. (1988) 'Visual Perception of Human Movement: The Use of Demonstrations in Teaching Motor Skills', *British Journal of Physical Education Research Supplement*, 4, 12–14.

Scully, D. and Carnegie, E. (1998) 'Observational Learning in Motor Skills Acquisition: A Look at Demonstrations', *The Irish Journal of Psychology*, 19, 472–85.

Scully, D. and Newell, K. M. (1985) 'Observational Learning and the Acquisition of Motor Skills: Towards a Visual Perception Perspective', *Journal of Human Movement Studies*, 11, 169–86.

Scully, D., Reilly, J. and Clarke, J. (1998) 'Perspectives on Gender in Sport and Exercise', *Irish Journal of Psychology*, 19, 424–38.

Scully, D., Kremer, J., Meade, M., Graham, R. and Dudgeon, K. (1998) 'Exercise and Psychological Well-being: A Critical Review', *British Journal of Sports Medicine*, 32, 111–20.

Seifriz, J. J., Duda, J. L. and Chi, L. (1992) 'The Relationship of Perceived Motivational Climate to Intrinsic Motivation and Beliefs about Success in Basketball', *Journal of Sport & Exercise Psychology*, 14, 375–91.

Selvey, M. (1998) 'Getting Up for the Ashes', *The Guardian* (Sport), 20 November, p. 2.

Sewell, D. (1996) 'Chicken or Egg? In search of the Elusive Cohesion-Performance Relationship', in J. Annett and H. Steinberg (eds), *How Teams Work in Sport and Exercise Psychology* (Leicester: British Psychological Society), 11–18.

Shapiro, D. C. and Schmidt, R. A. (1982) 'The Schema Theory: Recent Evidence and Developmental Implications', in J. A. S. Kelso and J. E. Clarke (eds), *The Development of Movement Control and Coordination* (New York: John Wiley), 113–50.

Shaw, W. A. (1938) 'The Distribution of Muscular Action Potentials during Imaging', *Psychological Record*, 2, 195–216.

Shea, C. H., Kohl, R. and Indermill, C. (1990) 'Contextual Interference: Contributions of Practice', *Acta Psychologica*, 73, 145–57.

Shea, J. B. and Morgan, R. L. (1979) 'Contextual Interference Effects on the Acquisition, Retention, and Transfer of a Motor Skill', *Journal of Experimental Psychology: Human Learning and Memory*, 5, 179–87.

Shepard, R. N. and Metzler, J. (1971) 'Mental Rotation of Three-Dimensional Objects', *Science*, 171, 701–3.

Shumaker, S. A and Brownell, A. (1984) 'Toward a Theory of Social Support: Closing Conceptual Gaps', *Journal of Social Issues*, 40 (4), 11–36.

Simon, D. A. and Bjork, R. A. (2001) 'Metacogntion in Motor Learning', *Journal of Experimental Psychology: Learning, Memory and Cognition*, 27, 907–12.

Sinclair, D. A. and Hackfort, D. (2000) 'The Role of the Sport Organization in the Career Transition Process', in D. Lavallee and P. Wylleman (eds), *Career Transitions in Sport: International Perspectives* (Morgantown, WV: Fitness Information Technology), 131–42.

Sinclair, D. A. and Orlick, T. (1993) 'Positive Transitions from High-Performance Sport', *The Sport Psychologist*, 7, 138–50.

Sinclair, L. and Kunda, Z. (1999) 'Reactions to a Black Professional: Motivated Inhibition and Activation of Conflicting Stereotypes', *Journal of Personality and Social Psychology*, 77, 885–904.

Singer, R. N. (1984) 'What Sport Psychology Can Do for the Athlete and Coach', *International Journal of Sport Psychology*, 15, 52–61.

Singer, R. N., Williams, A. M., Frehlich, S. G., Janelle, C. M., Radlo, S. J., Barba, D. A. and Bouchard, L. J. (1998) 'New Frontiers in Visual Search: An Exploratory Study in Live Tennis Situations', *Research Quarterly for Exercise and Sport*, 69, 290–6.

Slater, M. R. and Sewell, D. F. (1994) 'An Examination of the Cohesion-Performance Relationship in University Hockey Teams', *Journal of Sports Sciences*, 12, 423–31.

Sleap, M. and Wormald, H. (2001) 'Perceptions of Physical Activity among Young Women Aged 16–17 Years', *European Journal of Physical Education*, 6, 26–37.

Smeeton, N. J., Williams, A. M., Hodges, N. J. and Ward, P. (2005) 'The Relative Effectiveness of Explicit Instruction, Guided-Discovery and Discovery Learning Techniques in Enhancing Perceptual Skill in Sport', *Journal of Experimental Psychology: Applied*, 11, 2, 98–110.

Smeeton, N., Ward, P. and Williams, A. M. (2004). 'Transfer of Perceptual Skill in Sport', *Journal of Sports Science*, 19, 3–9.

Smith, A. L. (1999) 'Perceptions of Peer Relationships and Physical Activity Participation in Early Adolescence', *Journal of Sport & Exercise Psychology*, 21, 329–50.

Smith, A. L., Ullrich-French, S., Walker, E. and Hurley, K. S. (2006) 'Peer Relationship Profiles and Motivation in Youth Sport', *Journal of Sport and Exercise Psychology*, 28, 362–82.

Smith, D. Wright, C. J., Allsopp, A. and Westhead, H. (2007). 'It's All in the Mind: PETTLEP-Based Imagery and Sports Performance, *Journal of Applied Sport Psychology*, 19, 80–92.

Smith, M. (2002) 'Practice Makes Perfect', *The Daily Telegraph* (Sport), 15 February, p. S3.

Smith, P., Gould, M. M., See Tai, S. and Iliffe, S. (1996) 'Exercise as Therapy: Results from Group Interviews of Practices in an Inner London Prescription for Exercise Scheme', *Health Education Journal*, 55, 439–46.

Smith, P. J. and Davies, M. (1995) 'Applying Contextual Interference to the Pawlata Roll', *Journal of Sports Sciences*, 13, 455–62.

Smith, R. (1986) 'Toward a Cognitive-Affective Model of Athletic Burnout', *Journal of Sport Psychology*, 8, 36–50.

Smith, R. and Johnson, J. (1990) 'An Organizational Empowerment Approach to Consultation in Professional Baseball', *The Sport Psychologist*, 4, 347–57.

Smith, R. and Smoll, F. (1990) 'Self-Esteem and Children's Reactions to Youth Sport Coaching Behaviors: A Field Study of Self-Enhancement Processes', *Developmental Psychology*, 26, 987–93.

Smith, R. and Smoll, F. (1997) 'Coaching the Coaches: Youth Sports as a Scientific and Applied Behavioral Setting', *Current Directions in Psychological Science*, 6, 16–21.

Smith, S. L. and Smoll, F. (2002) *Way To Go Coach! A Scientifically Proven Approach to Coaching Effectiveness*, 2nd edn (Portola Valley, CA: Warde).

Smith, S. L. and Smoll, F. L. (2007) 'Social-Cognitive Approach to Coaching Behaviors', in S.Jowett and D. Lavallee (eds), *Social Psychology in Sport* (Champaign, IL: Human Kinetics), 75–90.

Smith, R., Smoll, F. and Hunt, E. (1977) 'A System for the Behavioral Assessment of Athletic Coaches', *Research Quarterly for Exercise and Sport*, 48, 401–7.

Smith, R., Smoll, F. and Schutz, R.W. (1990) 'Measurement and Correlates of Sport-Specific Cognitive and Somatic Trait Anxiety: The Sport Anxiety Scale', *Anxiety Research*, 2, 263–80.

Smith, R., Smoll, F. and Smith, N. (1989) *Parents' Complete Guide to Youth Sports* (Costa Mesa, CA: HDL Publishing).

Smith, R., Smoll, F. and Wiechman, S. A. (1998) 'Measurement of Trait Anxiety in Sport', in J. L. Duda (ed.), *Advances in Sport and Exercise Psychology Measurement* (Morgantown, WV: Fitness Information Technology), 105–27.

Smith, R., Smoll, F. L., Cumming, S. P. and Grossbard, J. R. (2006). 'Measurement of Multidimensional Sport Performance Anxiety in Children and Adults: The Sport Anxiety Scale-2', *Journal of Sport & Exercise Psychology*, 28, 479–501.

Smits, J. A. J. and Otto, M. W. (2009) *Exercise for Mood and Anxiety Disorders* (New York: Oxford University Press).

Smoll, F. (1972) 'Effects of Precision of Information Feedback upon Acquisition of a Motor Skill', *Research Quarterly*, 43, 489–93.

Smoll, F. and Smith, R.E. (1989) 'Leadership Behaviors in Sport: A Theoretical Model and Research Paradigm', *Journal of Applied Social Psychology*, 18, 1522–51.

Smoll, F. and Smith, R. E. (2005) *Coaches Who Never Lose: Making Sure Athletes Win, No Matter What the Score*, 2nd edn (Palo Alto, CA: Warde).

Smoll, F. and Smith, R. E. (2006) 'Development and Implementation of a Coach-Training Program: Cognitive-Behavioral Principles and Techniques', in J. M. Williams (ed.), *Applied Sport Psychology: Personal Growth to Peak Performance,* 5th edn (Mountain View, CA: Mayfield), 458–80.

Smoll, F. and Smith, R. E. (1999) 'Coaching Behavior Research in Youth Sport: Sport Psychology Goes to the Ballpark', in G. G. Brannigan (ed.), *The Sport Scientists: Research Adventures* (New York: Longman).

Snyder, E. E. and Baber, L. L. (1979) 'A Profile of Former Collegiate Athletes and Non-Athletes: Leisure Activities, Attitudes toward Work, and Aspects of Satisfaction with Life', *Journal of Sport Behavior*, 2, 211–19.

Solso, R. (1998) *Cognitive Psychology*, 5th edn (Boston: Allyn and Bacon).

Sonstroem, R. J. (1984) 'Exercise and Self-Esteem', *Exercise and Sport Science Reviews*, 12, 123–55.

Sonstroem, R. J. (1988) 'Psychological Models', in R. K. Dishman (ed.), *Exercise a Adherence: Its Impact on Mental Health* (Champaign, IL: Human Kinetics), 85–102.

Sonstroem, R. J. (1997) 'Physical Activity and Self-Esteem', in W. P. Morgan (ed.), *Physical Activity and Mental Health* (Washington DC: Taylor and Francis), 127–43.

Sonstroem, R. J. (1998) 'Physical Self-Concept: Assessment and External Validity', *Exercise and Sport Sciences Reviews*, 26, 133–64.

Sonstroem, R. J. and Morgan, W. P. (1989) 'Exercise and Self-Esteem: Rationale and Model', *Medicine and Science in Sports and Exercise*, 21, 329–37.

Sonstroem, R. J., Harlow, L. L. and Josephs, L. (1994) 'Exercise and Self-Esteem: Validity of Model Expansion and Exercise Associations', *Journal of Sport & Exercise Psychology*, 16, 29–42.

Sothmann, M., Hart, B. and Horn, T. (1991) 'Plasma Catecholamine Response to Acute Psychological Stress in Humans: Relation to Aerobic Fitness and Exercise Training', *Medicine and Science in Sports and Exercise*, 23, 860–7.

Spence, J. T. and Helmreich, R. L. (1983) 'Achievement Related Motives and Behaviors', in J. T. Spence (ed.), *Achievement and Achievement Motives* (San Fransisco, CA: Freeman), 7–74.

Spence, K. W. (1956) *Behavior Theory and Conditioning* (New Haven, CT: Yale University Press).

Spielberger, C. S. (1966) 'Theory and Research on Anxiety', in C. S. Spielberger (ed.), *Anxiety and Behavior* (New York: Academic Press), 3–20.

Spink, K. S. (1990) 'Group Cohesion and Collective Efficacy of Volleyball Teams', *Journal of Sport & Exercise Psychology*, 12, 301–11.

Spink, K. S. (1995) 'Cohesion and Intention to Participate of Female Sport Team Athletes', *Journal of Sport & Exercise Psychology*, 17, 416–27.

Spink, K. S. and Carron, A. V. (1992) 'Group Cohesion and Adherence in Exercise Classes', *Journal of Sport & Exercise Psychology*, 14, 78–86.

Spink, K. S. and Carron, A. V. (1993) 'The Effects of Team Building on the Adherence Patterns of Female Exercise Participants', *Journal of Sport & Exercise Psychology*, 15, 39–49.

Spitz, H. H. (1997) *Non-Conscious Movements: From Mystical Messages to Facilitated Communication* (Mahwah, NJ: Lawrence Erlbaum).

Sport England (2005) *Understanding Participation in Sport: A Systematic Review* (London: Sport England).

Stambulova, N. B. (1994) 'Developmental Sports Career Investigations in Russia: A Post-Perestroika Analysis', *The Sport Psychologist*, 8, 221–37.

Stambulova, N. B., Stephan, Y. and Jäphag, U. (2007) 'Athletic Retirement: A Cross-National Comparison Of Elite French and Swedish Athletes', *Psychology of Sport and Exercise*, 8, 101–18.

Stambulova, N., Alfermann, D., Statler, T. and Côté, J. (2009) 'ISSP Position Stand: Career Development and Transitions of Athletes', *International Journal of Sport and Exercise Psychology, 7*(4), 395–412.

Stathopoulou, G., Powers, M. B., Berry, A. C., Smits, J. A. J. and Otto, M. W. (2006) 'Exercise Interventions for Mental Health: A Quantitative and Qualitative Review', *Clinical Psychology: Science and Practice,* 13, 179–83.

Starkes, J. L. (1987) 'Skill in Field Hockey: The Nature of the Cognitive Advantage', *Journal of Sport Psychology*, 9, 146–60.

Starkes, J. L. and Ericsson, K. A. (2003) *Expert Performance in Sports: Advances in Research on Sport Expertise* (Champaign, IL: Human Kinetics).

Starkes, J. L., Deakin, J. M., Allard, F., Hodges, N. J. and Hayes, A. (1996) 'Deliberate Practice in Sports: What is it Anyway?', in K. A. Ericsson (ed.), *The Road to Excellence: The Acquisition of Expert Performance in the Arts and Sciences, Sports and Games* (Hillsdale, NJ: Lawrence Erlbaum), 81–106.

Steege, J. F. and Blumenthal, J. A. (1993) 'The Effects of Aerobic Exercise on PMS in Middle Aged Women: A Preliminary Study', *Journal of Psychosomatic Research*, 37, 127–33.

Steinberg, H., Sykes, E. A. and LeBoutillier, N. (1997) 'Exercise Addiction: Indirect Measures of Endorphins?', in J. Annett, B. Cripps and H. Steinberg (eds), *Exercise Addiction: Motivation for Participation in Sport and Exercise* (Leicester: British Psychological Society), 6–14.

Steiner, I. D. (1972) *Group Process and Productivity* (New York: Academic Press).

Stephan, Y., Bilard, J., Ninot, G. and Delignieres, D. (2003). Repercussions of Transition Out of Elite Sport on Subjective Well-being: A One-year Study', *Journal of Applied Sport Psychology*, 15, 354–71.

Stets, J. E. and Burke, P. J. (2000) 'Identity Theory and Social Identity Theory', *Social Psychology Quarterly*, 63, 224–37.

Stevenson, C. L. (1990) 'The Early Careers of International Athletes', *Sociology of Sport Journal*, 7, 238–53.

Stewart, D. W. and Latham, D. R. (1986) 'On Some Psychometric Properties of Fiedler's Contingency Model of Leadership', *Small Group Behavior*, 17, 83–94.

Stoeber, J., Stoll, O., Pescheck, E. and Otto, K. (2008) 'Perfectionism and Achievement Goals in Athletes: Relations with Approach and Avoidance Orientations in Mastery and Performance Goals', *Psychology of Sport and Exercise*, 9 (2), 102–21.

Stone, E. J., McKenzie, T. L., Welk, G. J. and Booth, M. (1998) 'Effects of Physical Activity Interventions in Youth: Review and Synthesis', *American Journal of Preventive Medicine*, 15, 98–315.

Strahler, K., Ehrlenspiel, F., Heene, M. and Brand, R. (2010). 'Comptitive Anxiety and Cortisol Awakening Response in the Week Leading Up to a Compettion', *Psychology of Sport and Exercise*, 11, 148–54.

Strauss, B. (2002) 'Social Facilitation in Motor Tasks', *Psychology of Sport and Exercise*, 3, 237–56.

Ströhle, A. (2009) 'Physical Activity, Exercise, Depression and Anxiety Disorders', *Journal of Neural Transmission*, 116, 777–84.

Strube, M. B. (2005) 'What did Triplett Really Find? A Contemporary Analysis of the First Experiment in Social Psychology', *American Journal of Psychology*, 118, 271–86.

Suinn, R. (1980) 'Behavioral Applications of Psychology in USA World Class Competitors', in P. Klavora and J. V. Daniel (eds), *Coach, Athlete and Sport Psychologist*, 2nd edn (Champaign, IL: Human Kinetics), 285–96.

Suinn, R. M. (1994) 'Visualization in Sports', in A. A. Sheikh and E. R. Korn (eds), *Imagery in Sports and Physical Performance* (Amityville, NY: Baywood), 23–42. Sundström, A. (2006) 'Beliefs about Perceived Competence: A Literature Review'. *Educational Measurement Report (EMR) No. 55*, University of Umeå, Sweden.

Summers, J. (2004) 'A Historical Perspective on Skill Acquisition', in A. M. Williams and N. J. Hodges (eds), *Skill Acquisition in Sport: Research, Theory and Practice* (London: Routledge), 1–26.

Summers, J. J. and Ford, S. K. (1990) 'The Test of Attentional and Interpersonal Style: An Evaluation', *International Journal of Sport Psychology*, 21, 102–11.

Summers, J. J. and Moran, A. P. (in press). 'Attention', in T. Morris and P. Terry (eds), *The New Sport and Exercise Psychology Companion* (Morgantown, WV: Fitness Information Technology).

Svoboda, B. and Vanek, M. (1982) 'Retirement from High Level Competition', in T. Orlick, J. T. Partington and J. H. Salmela (eds), *Proceedings of the 5th World Congress of Sport Psychology* (Ottawa, ON: Coaching Association of Canada), 166–75.

Swain, A. B. J. and Jones, G. (1996) 'Explaining Performance Variance: The Relative Contributions of Intensity and Direction Dimensions of Competitive State Anxiety', *Anxiety, Stress and Coping*, 9, 1–18.

Swain, D. A. (1991) 'Withdrawal from Sport and Schlossberg's Model of Transitions', *Sociology of Sport Journal*, 8, 152–60.

Swain, D. P. and Leutholtz, B. C. (2007) *Exercise Prescription: A Case Study Approach to the ACSM Guidelines* (Champaign, IL: Human Kinetics).

Sweet, W. E. (1987) *Sport and Recreation in Ancient Greece: A Sourcebook with Translations* (Oxford: Oxford University Press).

Syer, J. (1991) 'Team Building: The Development of Team Spirit', in S. J. Bull (ed.), *Sport Psychology: A Self-Help Guide* (Marlborough, Wilts: Crowood Press).

Syer, J. and Connolly, C. (1984) *Sporting Body, Sporting Mind: An Athlete's Guide to Mental Training* (Cambridge: Cambridge University Press).

Szczepanik, N. (2005). 'Focused Cech Puts Records Low on His List of Priorities', *The Times*, 30 April, p. 100.

Szabo, A. (2003) 'Acute Psychological Benefits of Exercise Performed at Self-Selected Workloads: Implications for Theory and Practice', *Journal of Sports Science and Medicine*, 2, 77–87.

Tajfel, H. (1982) (ed.) *Social Identity and Intergroup Relations* (Cambridge: Cambridge University Press).

Taylor, A. H. and Faulkner, G. (2005) 'From Emerging Relationships to the Future Role of Physical Activity in Mental Health Promotion', in G. Faulkner and A. H. Taylor (eds), *Exercise, Health and Mental Health: Emerging Relationships* (London: Routledge Press), 210–28.

Taylor, J. and Lavallee, D. (2010). Career transition among athletes: Is there life after sports? In J. M. Williams (eds), *Applied Sport Psychology: Personal Growth to Peak Performance*, 6th edn (Columbus, OH: McGraw-Hill), 542–62.

Taylor, M. K., Gould, D. and Rolo, C. (2008). 'Performance Strategies of US Olympians in Practice and Competition', *High Ability Studies*, 19, 19–36.

Taylor, W. C., Baranowski, T. and Young, D. R. (1998) 'Physical Activity Interventions in Low-Income, Ethnic Minority, and Populations with Disability', *American Journal of Preventive Medicine*, 15, 334–43.

Terry, P. (1997) 'The Application of Mood Profiling with Elite Sports Performers', in R. J. Butler (ed.), *Sports Psychology in Performance* (Oxford: Butterworth Heinemann), 3–32.

Terry, P. C. (2000) 'Perceptions of Group Cohesion and Mood in Sport Teams', *Group Dynamics: Theory, Research, and Practice*, 4, 244–53.

Thatcher, J., Lavallee, D. and Jones, M. V. (eds, in press). *Coping and Emotion in Sport*, 2nd edn (Abingdon, Oxford: Routledg).

Theodorakis, Y., Weinberg, R., Natsis, P., Douma, I. and Kazaka, P. (2000) 'The Effects of Motivational Versus Instructional Self-Talk on Improving Motor Performance', *The Sport Psychologist*, 14, 253–72.

Thibaut, J. W. and Kelley, H. H. (1959) *The Social Psychology of Groups* (New York: Wiley).

Thierry, H. (1998) 'Motivation and Satisfaction', in P. J. D. Drenth, H. Thierry and C. J. De Wolff (eds), *Handbook of Work and Organizational Psychology*, 2nd edn (Hove, East Sussex: Psychology Press), 4, 253–89.

Thomas, C. E. and Ermler, K. L. (1988) 'Institutional Obligations in the Athletic Retirement Process', *Quest*, 40, 137–50.

Thomas, S., Reeves, C. and Bell, A. (2008) 'Home Advantage in the Six Nations Ruby Union Tournament', *Perceptual and Motor Skills*, 106, 113–16.

Thomas, O., Mellalieu, S. D. and Hanton, S. (2009) 'Stress Management in Applied Sport Psychology', in S. D. Mellalieu and S. D. Hanton (eds), *Advances in Applied Sport Psychology: A Review* (London: Routledge), 124–61.

Thorndike, E. L. (1920) 'Intelligence and its Uses', *Harper's Magazine*, 140, 227–35.

Thorndike, E. L. (1927) 'The Law of Effect', *American Journal of Psychology*, 39, 212–22.

Thorpe, R. (1996) 'Telling People How to Do Things Does Not Always Help Them Learn', *Supercoach*, 8, 7–8.

Tienson, J. L. (1990) 'An Introduction to Connectionism', in J. L. Garfield (ed.) *Foundations of Cognitive Science* (New York: Paragon House), 381–97.

Timonen, S. and Procope, B. (1971) 'Premenstrual Syndrome and Physical Exercise', *Acta Obstetrica Gynecologica Scandinavica*, 50, 331–7.

Tkachuk, G. A. and Martin, G. L. (1999) 'Exercise Therapy for Patients with Psychiatric Disorders: Research and Clinical Implications', *Professional Psychology: Research and Practice*, 30, 275–82.

Treasure, D. C. (1997) 'Perceptions of the Motivational Climate and Elementary School Children's Cognitive Affective Response', *Journal of Sport & Exercise Psychology*, 19, 278–90.

Treasure, D. C., Duda, J. L., Hall, H. K., Roberts, G. C., Ames, C. and Maehr, M. L. (2001) 'Clarifying Misconceptions and Misrepresentations in Achievement Goal Research in Sport: A Response to Harwood, Hardy and Swain', *Journal of Sport & Exercise Psychology*, 23, 317–29.

Triplett, N. (1898) 'The Dynamogenic Factors in Pacemaking and Competition', *American Journal of Psychology*, 9, 505–23.

Trost, S. G., Owen, N., Bauman, A., Sallis, J. F. and Brown, W. (2002) 'Correlates of Adults' Participation in Physical Activity: Review and Update', *Medicine and Science in Sports and Exercise*, 33, 1996–2001.

Tucker, S., Turner, N., Barling, J. and McEvoy, M. (2010) 'Transformational Leadership and Childrens' Aggression in Team Settings: A Short-Term Longitudinal Study', *The Leadership Quarterly*, 21, 389–99.

Tuckman, B. W. (1965) 'Developmental Sequences in Small Groups', *Psychological Bulletin*, 63, 384–99.

Tuckman, B. W. and Jensen, M. A. (1977) 'Stages of Small Group Development Revisited', *Group and Organizational Studies*, 2, 419–27.

Ullrich-French, S. and Smith, A.L. (2006) 'Perceptions of Relationships with Parents and Peers in Youth Sport: Independent and Combined Prediction of Motivational Outcomes', *Psychology of Sport and Exercise*, 7, 193–214.

Ungerleider, R. S. and Golding, J. M. (1991) 'Mental Practice among Olympic Athletes', *Perceptual and Motor Skills*, 72, 1007–17.

United States Olympic Committee (1983) 'USOC Establishes Guidelines for Sport Psychology Services', *Journal of Sport Psychology*, 5, 4–7.

Uphill, M. (2008). 'Anxiety in Sport: Should We Be Worried Or Excited?', in A. Lane (ed.), *Sport and Exercise Psychology* (London: Hodder Education), 35–51.

Vaeyens, R., Lenoir, M., Williams, A. M., Mazyn, L. and Philippaerts, R. M. (2007) The Effects of Task Constraints on Visual Search Behavior and Decision-Making Skill in Youth Soccer Players', *Journal of Sport & Exercise Psychology*, 29, 156–75.

Vallerand, R. J. (1997a) 'Intrinsic and Extrinsic Motivation in Sport: Implications from the Hierarchical Model', in R. Lidor and M. Bar-Eli (eds), *Innovations in Sport Psychology: Linking Theory and Practice* (Netanya, Israel: International Society of Sports Psychology), 45–7.

Vallerand, R. J. (1997b) 'Toward a Hierarchical Model of Intrinsic and Extrinsic Motivation', in M. P. Zanna (ed.), *Advances in Experimental Social Psychology* (New York: Academic Press), 29, 271–360.

Vallerand, R. J. (2001) 'A Hierarchical Model of Intrinsic and Extrinsic Motivation in Sport and Exercise', in G. C. Roberts (ed.), *Advances in Motivation in Sport and Exercise* (Champaign, IL: Human Kinetics), 263–319.

Vallerand, R. J. (2008) 'On the Psychology of Passion: In Search of What Makes People's Lives Most Worth Living', *Canadian Psychology*, 49, 1–13.

Vallerand, R. J. (2007) 'Intrinsic and Extrinsic Motivation in Sport and Physical Activity: A Review and a Look at the Future', in G. Tenenbaum and E. Eklund (eds), *Handbook of Sport Psychology*, 3rd edn (New York: John Wiley), 49–83.

Vallerand, R. J. and Bissonnette, R. (1992) 'Intrinsic, Extrinsic and Amotivational Styles as Predictors of Behavior: A Prospective Study', *Journal of Personality*, 60, 599–620.

Vallerand, R. J. and Fortier, M. S. (1998) 'Measures of Intrinsic and Extrinsic Motivation in Sport and Physical Activity: A Review and Critique', in J. L. Duda (ed.), *Advances in Sport and Exercise Psychology Measurement* (Morgantown, WV: Fitness Information Technology), 81–101.

Vallerand, R. J. and Losier, G. F. (1999) 'An Integrative Analysis of Intrinsic and Extrinsic Motivation in Sport', *Journal of Applied Sport Psychology*, 11, 142–96.

Vallerand, R. J., Fortier, M. S. and Guay, F. (1997) 'Self-Determination and Persistence in a Real-life Setting: Toward a Motivational Model of High-School Dropout', *Journal of Personality and Social Psychology*, 72, 1161–76.

Vallerand, R. J., Pelletier, L. G. and Koestner, R. (2008) 'Reflections on Self-determination Theory', *Canadian Psychology*, 49, 257–62.

Van de Vliet, P., Mutrie, N. and Onghena, P. (2005) 'Alternative Research Strategies in the Exercise – Mental Health Relationship', *Acta Universitatis Palackianae Olomucensis Gymnica*, 35 (1), 61–7.

Van Eerde, W. and Thierry, H. (1996) 'Vroom's Expectancy Models and Work-related Criteria: A Meta-Analysis', *Journal of Applied Psychology*, 81, 575–86.

Van Meer, J. P. and Theunissen, N. C. M. (2009). 'Prospective Educational Applications of Mental Simulation: A Meta-Review'. *Educational Psychology Review*, 21, 93–112.

Van Raalte, J. L. and Brewer, B. W. (1996) (eds) *Exploring Sport and Exercise Psychology* (Washington DC: American Psychological Association).

Van Rossum, J. H. A. (1990) 'Schmidt's Schema Theory: The Empirical Base of the Variability of Practice Hypothesis. A Critical Analysis', *Human Movement Science*, 9, 387–435.

Van Schoyck, S. R. and Grasha, A. F. (1981) 'Attentional Style Variations and Athletic Ability: The Advantages of a Sports-specific Test', *Journal of Sport Psychology*, 3, 149–65.

Van Sluijs E. M. F., McMinn, A. M. and Griffin, S. J. (2007) 'Effectiveness of Interventions to Promote Physical Activity in Children and Adolescents: Systematic Review of Controlled Trials',*British Medical Journal*, 335, 703–7.

Van Wersch, A. (1997) 'Individual Differences and Intrinsic Motivations for Sports Participation', in J. Kremer, K. Trew and S. Ogle (eds), *Young People's Involvement in Sport* (London: Routledge), 57–77.

Vandenberg, S. and Kuse, A. R. (1978) 'Mental Rotations: A Group Test of Three-Dimensional Spatial Visualisation', *Perceptual and Motor Skills*, 47, 599–604.

Vanek, M. and Cratty, B. J. (1970) *Psychology and the Superior Athlete* (New York: Macmillan).

Varca, P. E. (1980) 'An Analysis of Home and Away Game Performance of Male College Basketball Teams', *Journal of Sport Psychology*, 2, 245–57.

Vazou, S., Ntoumanis, N. and Duda, J. L. (2005) 'Peer Motivational Climate in Youth Sport: A Qualitative Inquiry', *Psychology of Sport and Exercise*, 6, 497–516.

Vazou, S., Ntoumanis, N. and Duda, J. L. (2006) 'Predicting Young Athletes Motivational Indices as a Function of Their Perceptions of the Coach- and Peer-Created Climate', *Psychology of Sport and Exercise*, 7, 215–33.

Vealey, R. S. (1986) 'Conceptualization of Sport Confidence and Competitive Orientation: Preliminary Investigation and Instrument Development', *Journal of Sport Psychology*, 8, 221–46.

Vealey, R. S. (1988) 'Future Directions in Psychological Skills Training', *The Sport Psychologist*, 2, 318–36.

Vealey, R. S. and Greenleaf, C. A. (2010). 'Seeing is Believing: Understanding and Using Imagery in Sport', in J. M. Williams (ed.), *Applied Sport Psychology: Peak Performance to Personal Growth,* 6th edn (Mpuntain View, CA: Mayfield), 267–304.

Vealey, R. S., Armstrong, L., Comar, W. and Greenleaf, C. A. (1998) 'Influence of Perceived Coaching Behaviors on Burnout and Competitive Anxiety in Female Collegiate Athletes', *Journal of Applied Sport Psychology*, 10, 297–318.

Verhoef, M. J. and Love, E. J. (1994) 'Women and Exercise Participation: The Mixed Blessings of Motherhood', *Health Care for Women International*, 15, 297–306.

Vickers, J. N. (1996) 'Visual Control When Aiming at a Far Target', *Journal of Experimental Psychology: Human Perception and Performance*, 22, 342–54.

Vickers, J. N. (2007) *Perception, Cognition, and Decision Training: The Quiet Eye in Action* (Champaign, Illinois: Human Kinetics).

Vickers, J. N. and Williams, A. M. (2007) 'Performing Under Pressure: The Effects of Physiological Arousal, Cognitive Anxiety and Gaze Control in Biathlon', *Journal of Motor Behavior*, 39, 381–94.

Vickers, J. N., Williams, A. M., Rodrigues, S. T., Hillis, F. and Coyne, G. (1999) 'Eye Movements of Elite Biathlon Shooters during Rested and Fatigued States', *Journal of Sport & Exercise Psychology*, 21, S116.

Vlachopolos, S. and Biddle, S. J. H. (1997) 'Modeling the Relation of Goal Orientations to Achievement-related Affect', *Journal of Sport and Exercise Psychology*, 19, 169–87.

Vos Strache, C. (1979) 'Players' Perceptions of Leadership Qualities for Coaches', *Research Quarterly for Sport and Exercise*, 50, 679–86.

Voss, M. E., Kramer, A. F., Chandramallika, B., Ruchika, S. P. and Brent, R. (2010) 'Are Expert Athletes 'Expert' in the Cognitive Laboratory? A Meta-Analytic Review of Cognition and Sport Expertise', *Applied Cognitive Psychology*, 24, 812–26.

Vroom, V. H. (1964) *Work and Motivation* (New York: Wiley).

Vroom, V. H. and Yetton, P. W. (1973) *Leadership and Decision Making* (Pittsburgh, PA: University of Pittsburgh Press).

Walker, M. (2008). 'Cloughie Knew the Trick', *The Irish Times* (Sport), 6 December, p. 7.

Wang, C. and Biddle, S. (2000) 'The Conceptions of the Nature of Athletic Ability Questionnaire for Children: Evidence on Psychometric Properties and its Use in Predicting Physical Activity Intentions', *Journal of Sports Sciences*, 18, 61.

Wang, C. and Biddle, S. (2001) 'Young People's Motivational Profiles in Physical Activity: A Cluster Analysis', *Journal of Sport & Exercise Psychology*, 23, 1–22.

Wang, C. K. J. and Biddle, S. J. H. (2007) 'Understanding Young People's Motivation Toward Exercise: An Integration of Sport Ability Beliefs, Achievement Goals Theory, and Self-Determination Theory', in M. Hagger and N. L. D. Chatzisarantis, (eds) *Self-Determination Theory in Exercise and Sport* (Champaign, IL: Human Kinetics), 193–208.

Wankel, L. M. (1993) 'The Importance of Enjoyment to Adherence and Psychological Benefits from Physical Activity', *International Journal of Sport Psychology*, 24, 151–69.

Wann, D. L. (1997) *Social Psychology* (Upper Saddle River, NJ: Prentice Hall).

Wann, D. L., Melnick, M. J., Russell, G. W. and Pease, D. G. (2001) *Sport Fans: The Psychology and Social Impact of Spectators* (London: Routledge).

Wann, D., Royalty, J. and Roberts, A. (2000) 'The Self-Presentation of Sport Fans: Investigating the Importance of Team Identification and Self-Esteem', *Journal of Sport Behavior*, 23, 198–206.

Ward, J. (2010) *The Student's Guide to Cognitive Neuroscience*, 2nd edn (Hove, East Sussex: Psychology Press).

Ward, P. and Williams, A. M. (2003) 'Perceptual and Cognitive Skill Development in Soccer: The Multidimensional Nature of Expert Performance', *Journal of Sport and Exercise Psychology*, 25, 93–111.

Ward, P., Williams, A. M. and Hancock, P. (2006) 'Simulation for Performance and Training', in K. A. Ericsson, P. Hoffman, N. Charness and P. Feltovich (eds), *The Cambridge Handbook of Expertise and Expert Performance* (Cambridge, UK: Cambridge University Press), 243–62.

Ward, P., Hodges, N. J., Starkes, J. and Williams, A. M. (2007) 'The Road to Excellence: Deliberate Practice and the Development of Expertise', *High Ability Studies*, 18, 119–53.

Ward, P., Williams, A. M. and Bennett, S. J. (2002) 'Visual Search and Biological Motion Perception in Tennis', *Research Quarterly for Exercise and Sport*, 73, 107–12.

Ward, P., Hodges, N. J., Williams, A. M. and Starkes, J. (2004) 'The Role of Deliberate Practice in Developing Elite Performers in Sport', in A. M. Williams and N. J. Hodges (eds), *Skill Acquisition in Sport: Research, Theory and Practice* (London: Routledge), 231–58.

Washburn, M. F (1916) *Movement and Mental Imagery* (Boston: Houghton-Mifflin).

Watson, D., Clark, L. and Tellegen, A. (1988) 'Development and Validation of Brief Measures of Positive and Negative Affect: The PANAS Scales', *Journal of Personality and Social Psychology*, 54, 1063–70.

Watson, J. B. (1913) 'Psychology as the Behaviorist Views It', *Psychological Review*, 20, 158–77.

Wegner, D. M. (1994) 'Ironic Processes of Mental Control', *Psychological Review*, 101, 34–52.

Weigelt, C., Williams, A. M. and Wingrove, T. (2001) 'Transfer of Learning in Soccer: Is Practice on a Juggling Task Beneficial for Ball Control?', in J. Mester, G. King, H. Struder, E. Tsolakidis and A. Osterburg (eds), *Perspectives and Profiles: Proceedings of the 6th Annual Congress of the European College of Sport Science* (German Sport University: Cologne), p. 1266.

Weinberg, R. (1988) *The Mental Advantage: Developing your Mental Skills in Tennis* (Champaign, IL: Human Kinetics).

Weinberg, R. (1996) 'Goal Setting in Sport and Exercise: Research to Practice', in J. L. Van Raalte and B. W. Brewer (eds), *Exploring Sport and Exercise Psychology* (Washington DC: American Psychological Association), 3–24.

Weinberg, R. S. (2008). 'Does Imagery Work? Effects on Performance and Mental Skills?', *Journal of Imagery Research in Sport and Physical Activity*, 3, 1–21.

Weinberg, R. S. (2009). 'Motivation', in B. W. Brewer (ed), Sport Psychology (Handbook of Sports Medicine and Science) (7–17). Oxford: Wiley-Blackwell.

Weinberg, R. and Gould, D. (1999) *Foundations of Sport and Exercise Psychology*, 2nd edn (Champaign, IL: Human Kinetics).

Weinberg, R. and Gould, D. (2007). *Foundations of Sport and Exercise Psychology*, 4th edn (Champaign, IL: Human Kinetics).

Weinberg, R. and Weigand, D. (1993) 'Goal Setting in Sport and Exercise: A Reaction to Locke', *Journal of Sport & Exercise Psychology*, 15, 88–96.

Weinberg, R., Burke, K. and Jackson, A. (1997) 'Coaches' and Players' Perceptions of Goal Setting in Junior Tennis: An Exploratory Investigation', *The Sport Psychologist*, 11, 426–39.

Weinberg, R., Tenenbaum, G., McKenzie, A., Jackson, S., Anshel, M., Grove, R. and Fogarty, G. (2000) 'Motivation for Youth Participation in Sport and Physical Activity: Relationships to Culture, Self-Reported Activity Levels and Gender', *International Journal of Sport Psychology*, 31, 321–46.

Weinberg, S. K. and Arond, H. (1952) 'The Occupational Culture of the Boxer', *The American Journal of Sociology*, 57, 460–9.

Weiner, B. (1979) 'A Theory of Motivation for Some Classroom Experiences', *Journal of Educational Psychology*, 71, 3–25.

Weiss, M. R., Amorose, A. J. and Wilko, A. M. (2009) 'Coaching Behaviors, Motivational Climate, and Psychosocial Outcomes among Female Adolescent Athletes', *Journal of Pediatric Exercise Science*, 21, 475–492.

Weiss, M. R. and Chaumeton, N. (1992) 'Motivational Orientations in Sport', in T.S. Horn (ed.), *Advances in Sport Psychology* (Champaign, IL: Human Kinetics), 61–99.

Weiss, M. R. and Frazer, K. M. (1995) 'Initial, Continued, and Sustained Motivation in Adolescent Female Athletes: A Season-Long Analysis', *Pediatric Exercise Science*, 7, 314–29.

Weiss, M. R. and Hayashi, C. T. (1995) 'All in the Family: Parent-Child Influences in Competitive Youth Gymnastics', *Pediatric Exercise Science*, 7, 36–48.

Weiss, M. R. and Petlichkoff, L. M. (1989) 'Children's Motivation for Participation In and Withdrawal from Sport: Identifying the Missing Links', *Pediatric Exercise Science*, 1, 195–211.

Weiss, M. R., Bredemeier, B. J. and Shewchuk, R. M. (1985) 'An Intrinsic/Extrinsic Motivation Scale for the Youth Sport Setting: A Confirmatory Factor Analysis', *Journal of Sport Psychology*, 7, 75–91.

Welk, G. J. (1999) 'The Youth Physical Activity Promotional Model: A Conceptual Bridge Between Theory and Practice', *Quest*, 51, 5–23.

Wells, C. L. (1985) *Women, Sport and Performance: A Physiological Perspective* (Champaign, IL: Human Kinetics).

Werthner, P. and Orlick, T. (1986) 'Retirement Experiences of Successful Olympic Athletes', *International Journal of Sport Psychology*, 17, 337–63.

Weston, N. J. V., Thelwell, R. C., Bond, S. and Hutchings, N. V. (2009). 'Stress and Coping in Single-Handed, Round-the-World Ocean Sailing', *Journal of Applied Sport Psychology*, 21, 468–74.

Whelan, J. P., Meyers, A. M. and Elkin, T. D. (1996) 'Ethics in Sport and Exercise Psychology', in J. L. Van Raalte and B. W. Brewer (eds), *Exploring Sport and Exercise Psychology* (Washington DC: American Psychological Association), 431–47.

White, A. and Hardy, L. (1995) 'Use of Different Imagery Perspectives on the Learning and Performance of Different Motor Skills', *British Journal of Psychology*, 86, 169–80.

White, R. W. (1959) 'Motivation Reconsidered: The Concept of Competence', *Psychological Review*, 66, 297–333.

White, S. A. (1998) 'Adolescent Goal Profiles, Perceptions of the Parent-Initiated Motivational Climate and Competitive Trait Anxiety', *The Sport Psychologist*, 12, 16–28.

White, S. A. (2007) 'Parent-Created Motivational Climate.' in S. Jowett and D. Lavallee (eds) *Social Psychology in Sport* (Champaign, IL: Human Kinetics), 131–44.

White, S. A. and Duda, J. L. (1994) 'The Relationship of Gender, Level of Sport I Involvement and Participation Motivation to Task and Ego Orientation', *International Journal of Sport Psychology*, 25, 4–18.

White, S. A., Duda, J. L. and Keller, M. R. (1998) 'The Relationship between Goal Orientation and Perceived Purposes of Sport among Youth Sport Participants', *Journal of Sport Behavior*, 21, 474–84.

White, S. A., Kavussanu, M. and Guest, S. M. (1998) 'Goal Orientations and Perceptions of the Motivational Climate Created by Significant Others', *European Journal of Physical Education*, 3, 212–28.

Whitehead, J. (1995) 'Multiple Achievement Orientations and Participation in Youth Sport: A Cultural and Developmental Perspective', *International Journal of Sport Psychology*, 26, 431–52.

Whitworth, D. (2008). 'On the Waterfront', *The Times* (magazine), 13 September, pp. 20–5.

Widmeyer, W. N., Brawley, L. R. and Carron, A. V. (1985) *The Measurement of Cohesion in Sport Teams: The Group Environment Questionnaire* (London, Ontario: Sports Dynamics).

Widmeyer, W. N., Brawley, L. R. and Carron, A. V. (1992) 'Group Dynamics in Sport', in T. S. Horn (ed.), *Advances in Sport Psychology* (Champaign, IL: Human Kinetics), 163–80.

Widmeyer, W. N., Carron, A. V. and Brawley, L. R. (1988) 'Group Cohesion and Individual Adherence to Physical Activity', *Journal of Sport & Exercise Psychology*, 15, 50–62.

Widmeyer, W. N., Carron, A. V. and Brawley, L. R. (1993) 'Group Cohesion in Sport and Exercise', in R. N. Singer, M. Murphey and K. L. Tennant (eds) *Handbook of Research on Sport Psychology* (New York: Macmillan), 672–92.

Wiggins, D. K. (1984) 'The History of Sport Psychology in North America', in J. M. Silva and R. S. Weinberg (eds), *Psychological Foundations of Sport* (Champaign, IL: Human Kinetics).

Wilkinson, J. (2006) *My World* (London: Headline Book Publishing).

Williams, A. M. (2009) Perceiving the Intentions of Others: How Do Skilled Performers Make Anticipation Judgements?', in M. Raab, J. G. Johnson and H. R. Heekeren (eds), *Progress in Brain Research, Vol 174, Mind and Motion: The Bidirectional Link between Thought and Action* (The Netherlands: Elsevier), 73–83.

Williams, A. M. and Abernethy, B. (in press) 'Anticipation and Decision-making: Skills, Methods and Measures', in G.Tenenbaum and R. Ecklund (Ed.), *Handbook of Measurement in Sport and Exercise Psychology* (Human Kinetics: Champaign, Illinois).

Williams, A. M. and Ericsson, K. A. (2005) 'Some Considerations when Applying the Expert Performance Approach in Sport', *Human Movement Science*, 24, 283–307.

Williams, A. M. and Ericsson, K.A. (2008) 'How do Experts Learn?', *Journal of Sport and Exercise Psychology*, 30, 1–11.

Williams, A. M. and Ericsson, K. A. (2007) 'Perception, Cognition, Action and Skilled Performance', *Journal of Motor Behavior*, 39, 5, 338–40.

Williams, A. M. and Hodges, N. J. (2004) (eds) *Skill Acquisition in Sport: Research, Theory and Practice* (London: Routledge).

Williams, A. M. and Hodges, N. J. (2005) 'Practice, Instruction and Skill Acquisition: Challenging Tradition', *Journal of Sports Sciences*, 23, 6, 637–50.

Williams, A. M. and Ward, P. (2007) 'Perceptual-cognitive Expertise in Sport: Exploring New Horizons', in G. Tenenbaum, and R. C. Eklund (eds), *Handbook of Sport Psychology* (New York: John Wiley and Sons), 203–23.

Williams, A. M., Janelle, C. M. and Davids, K. (2004) 'Constraints on the Search for Visual Information in Sport', *International Journal of Sport and Exercise Psychology*, 2, 301–18.

Williams, A. M., Ward, P. and Chapman, C. (2003) 'Training Perceptual Skill in Field Hockey: Is there Transfer from the Laboratory to the Field?', *Research Quarterly for Exercise and Sport*, 74, 98–103.

Williams, A. M., Ward, P. and Smeeton, N. J. (2004) 'Perceptual and Cognitive Expertise in Sport: Implications for Skill Acquisition and Performance Enhancement', in A. M. Williams and N. J. Hodges (eds), *Skill Acquisition in Sport: Research, Theory and Practice* (London: Routledge), 328–48.

Williams, A. M., Ward, P., Allen, D. and Smeeton, N. (2004) 'Training Perceptual Skill Using On-Court Instruction in Tennis: Perception versus Perception and Action', *Journal of Applied Sport Psychology*, 16, 4, 1–11.

Williams, A. M., Ford, P., Eccles, D. W. and Ward, P. (2011) 'Perceptual-Cognitive Expertise in Sport and its Acquisition: Implications for Applied Cognitive Psychology', *Applied Cognitive Psychology*, 25, 432–42.

Williams, A. M., Huys, R., Cañal-Bruland, R. and Hagemann, N. (2009) 'The Dynamical Information Underpinning Deception Effects', *Human Movement Science*, 28, 362–70.

Williams, A. M., Hodges, N. J., North, J. S. and Barton, G. (2006). Perceiving Patterns of Play in Dynamic Sport Tasks: Identifying the Essential Information Underlying Skilled Performance', *Perception*, 35, 317–32

Williams, A. M. (2000) 'Perceptual Skill in Soccer: Implications for Talent Identification and Development', *Journal of Sports Sciences*, 18, 737–40.

Williams, A. M. and Davids, K. (1995) 'Declarative Knowledge in Sport: A Byproduct of Experience or a Characteristic of Expertise?', *Journal of Sport & Exercise Psychology*, 7, 259–75.

Williams, A. M. and Davids, K. (1998) 'Visual Search Strategy, Selective Attention, and Expertise in Soccer', *Research Quarterly for Exercise and Sport*, 69, 111–28.

Williams, A. M. and Elliott, D. (1999) 'Anxiety and Visual Search Strategy in Karate', *Journal of Sport & Exercise Psychology*, 21, 362–75.

Williams, A. M. and Grant, A. (1999) 'Training Perceptual Skill in Sport', *International Journal of Sport Psychology*, 30, 194–220.

Williams, A. M. and Hodges, N. J. (2004) (eds), *Skill Acquisition in Sport: Research, Theory and Practice* (London: Routledge).

Williams, A. M. and Reilly, T. (2000) 'Talent Identification and Development in Soccer', *Journal of Sports Sciences*, 18, 657–67.

Williams, A. M. and Ward, P. (2003) 'Perceptual Expertise; Development', in J.L. Starkes and K.A. Ericsson (eds) *Expert Performance in Sports: Advances in Research on Sport Expertise* (Champaign, IL: Human Kinetics), 220–49.

Williams, A. M., Davids, K. and Williams, J. G. (1999) *Visual Perception and Action in Sport* (London: Routledge).

Williams, A.M., Davids, K., Burwitz, L. and Williams, J.G. (1993) 'Cognitive Knowledge and Soccer Performance', *Perceptual and Motor Skills*, 76, 579–93.

Williams, A. M., Davids, K., Burwitz, L. and Williams, J. G. (1994) 'Visual Search Strategies of Experienced and Inexperienced Soccer Players', *Research Quarterly for Exercise and Sport*, 5, 127–35.

Williams, A. M., Ward, P., Allen, D. and Smeeton, N. J. (in press) 'Training Perceptual Skill using On-Court Instruction in Tennis: Perception Versus Perception and Action', *Journal of Applied Sport Psychology* .

Williams, A. M., Ward, P., Knowles, J. M. and Smeeton, N. J. (2002a) 'Perceptual Skill in a Real-World Task: Training, Instruction, and Transfer in Tennis', *Journal of Experimental Psychology: Applied*, 8, 259–70.

Williams, A. M., Weigelt, C., Harris, M. and Scott, M. A. (2002b) 'Age-Related Differences in Vision and Proprioception During a Lower Limb Interceptive Task: The Effects of Skill and Practice', *Research Quarterly for Exercise and Sport*, 73, 376–85.

Williams, J. M. (1998) (ed.) *Applied Sport Psychology: Personal Growth to Peak Performance*, 3rd edn (Mountain View, CA: Mayfield).

Williams, J. M. (2010) 'Relaxation and Energizing Techniques for Regulation of Arousal', in J. M. Williams (ed), *Applied Sport Psychology: From Personal Growth to Peak Performance*, 6th edn (New York: McGraw-Hill), 247–66.

Williams, J. M., Nideffer, R. M., Willson, V. E., Sagal, M.-S. and Peper, E. (2010) 'Concentration and Strategies for Controlling It', in J. M. Williams (ed), *Applied Sport Psychology*, 6th edn (New York: McGraw-Hill), 336–58.

Williams, J. M. and Widmeyer, W. N. (1991) 'The Cohesion-Performance Outcome Relationship in a Coacting Sport', *Journal of Sport & Exercise Psychology*, 13, 364–71.

Williams, R. (2002) 'Sublime Serena Celebrates the Crucial Difference', *The Guardian* (Sport), 8 July, p. 6.

Wilson, M., Chattington, M., Marple-Horvart, D. E. and Smith, N. C. (2007). 'A Comparison of Self-Focus Versus Attentional Explanations of Choking', *Journal of Sport & Exercise Psycxhology*, 29, 439–56.

Wilson, M., Wood, G. and Vine, S. J. (2009). 'Anxiety, Attentional Control and Performance Impairment in Penalty Kicks', *Journal of Sport & Exercise Psychology*, 31, 761–75.

Wilson, V., Ainsworth, M. and Bird, E. (1985) 'Assessment of Attentional Abilities in Male Volleyball Players', *International Journal of Sport Psychology*, 16, 296–306.

Wilson, P. M. and Rodgers, W. M. (2002) 'The Relationship between Exercise Motives and Physical Self-Esteem in Female Exercise Participants: An Application of Self-Determination Theory', *Journal of Applied Biobehavioral Research*, 7, 30–43.

Winner, E. (1996) 'The Rage to Master: The Decisive Role of Talent in the Visual Arts', in K. A. Ericsson (ed.), *The Road to Excellence: The Acquisition of Expert Performance in the Arts and Sciences, Sports and Games* (Hillsdale, NJ: Lawrence Erlbaum), 271–302.

Winokur, G. (1986) 'Unipolar Depression', in G. Winokur and P. Clayton (eds), *Medical Basis of Psychiatry* (Philadelphia: WB Saunders), 69–86.

Wolfson, S. (2002) 'Current Professional Issues in Sport and Exercise Psychology', *The Psychologist*, 15, 411.

Woo, M., Kim, S., Kim, J. Petruzzello, S. J. and Hatfield, B. D. (2009) 'Examining the Exercise-Affect Dose–Response Relationship: Does Duration Influence Frontal EEG Asymmetry?', *International Journal of Psychophysiology*, 72, 166–72

Woodman, T. and Davis, P. A. (2008). 'The Role of Repression in the Incidence of Ironic Errors', *The Sport Psychologist*, 22, 183–96.

World Health Organisation (2001) *Mental and Neurological Disorders*, Fact Sheet No. 2657. Geneva: World Health Organization.

Wulf, G. (1991) 'The Effect of Type of Practice on Motor Learning in Children', *Applied Cognitive Psychology*, 5, 123–34.

Wulf, G. (2007). 'Attentional Focus and Moror Learning: A Review of 10 Years of Research', *Bewegung und Training*, 1, 4–14.

Wulf, G. (2007). *Attention and Motor Skill Learning* (Human Kinetics: Champaign, Illinois).

Wulf, G. and Shea, C. H. (2004) 'Understanding the Role of Augmented Feedback: The Good, the Bad, and the Ugly', in A. M. Williams and N. J. Hodges (eds), *Skill Acquisition in Sport: Research, Theory and Practice* (London: Routledge), 121–44.

Wulf, G. and Weigelt, C. (1997) 'Instructions about Physical Principles in Learning a Complex Motor Skill: To Tell or Not To Tell', *Research Quarterly for Exercise and Sport*, 68, 362–7.

Wulf, G., Shea, C. H. and Matschiner, S. (1998) 'Frequent Feedback Enhances Complex Motor Skill Learning', *Journal of Motor Behavior*, 30, 180–92.

Wylleman, P. and De Knop, P. (1996, October) 'Combining Academic and Athletic Excellence: The Case of Elite Student-Athletes'. Paper presented at the International Conference of the European Council for High Ability, Vienna, Austria.

Wylleman, P. and De Knop, P. (1997, June) 'Elite Student-Athletes: Issues Related to Career Development and Social Support'. Paper presented at the 12th Annual Conference on Counseling Athletes, Springfield, MA.

Wylleman, P., De Knop, P., Menkehorst, H., Theeboom, M. and Annerel, J. (1993) 'Career Termination and Social Integration among Elite Athletes', in S. Serpa, J. Alves, V. Ferreira and A. Paula-Brito (eds), *Proceedings of the 8th World Congress of Sport Psychology* (Lisbon: International Society of Sport Psychology), 902–6.

Wylleman, P., De Knop, P. and Sillen, D. (1998) 'Former Olympic Athletes' Perceptions of Retirement from High-Level Sport'. Paper presented at the 28th Congress of the International Association of Applied Psychology, San Francisco, CA.

Wylleman, P., Lavallee, D. and Aflermann, D. (1999) (eds) *Career Transitions in Competitive Sports* (Biel, Switzerland: European Federation of Sport Psychology Monograph Series).

Wylleman, P. and Lavallee, D. (2004) 'A Developmental Perspective on Transitions Faced by Athletes', in M. R. Weiss (Ed.), *Developmental Sport and Exercise Psychology: A Lifespan Perspective* (Morgantown, WV: Fitness Information Technology), 503–24.

Wylleman, P., De Knop, P., Ewing, M. and Cumming, S. (2000) 'Transitions in Youth Sport: A Developmental Perspective on Parental Involvement', in D. Lavallee and P. Wylleman (eds), *Career Transitions in Sport: International Perspectives* (Morgantown, WV: Fitness Information Technology), 143–60.

Yaffé, M. (1975) 'Techniques of Mental Training: Case Studies in Professional Football', in G. J. K. Alderson and D. A. Tyldesley (eds), *FEPSAC Proceedings of Sport Psychology* (Edinburgh; British Society of Sports Psychology), 101–15.

Yan, J. H., Thomas, J. R. and Thomas, K. T. (1998) 'Children's Age Moderates the Effect of Practice Variability: A Quantitative Review', *Research Quarterly for Sport and Exercise*, 69, 210–15.

Yates, A. (1991) *Compulsive Exercise and Eating Disorders: Towards an Integrated Theory of Activity* (New York: Brunner/Mazel).

Yerkes, R. M. and Dodson, J. D. (1908) 'The Relationship of Strength of Stimulus to Rapidity of Habit Formation', *Journal of Comparative Neurology and Psychology*, 18, 459–82.

Yoo, J. (2003) 'Motivational Climate and Perceived Competence in Anxiety and Tennis Performance', *Perceptual and Motor Skills*, 96, 403–13.

Yeung, R. R. (1996) 'The Acute Effects of Exercise on Mood State', *Journal of Psychosomatic Research*, 2, 123–41.

Youngstedt, S. D., Dishman, R. K., Cureton, K. J. and Peacock, L. J. (1993) 'Does Body Temperature Mediate Anxiolytic Effects of Acute Exercise?', *Journal of Applied Physiology*, 74, 825–31.

Yukelson, D. (1998) 'Communicating Effectively', in J. M. Williams (ed.), *Applied Sport Psychology: Personal Growth to Peak Performance*, 3rd edn (Mountain View, CA: Mayfield).

Yukelson, D., Weinberg, R. and Jackson, A. (1984) 'A Multidimensional Group Cohesion Instrument for Intercollegiate Basketball Teams', *Journal of Sport Psychology*, 6, 103–17.

Zaichkowsky, L. and Perna, F. (1996) 'Certification in Sport and Exercise Psychology', in J. L. Van Raalte and B. W. Brewer (eds), *Exploring Sport and Exercise Psychology* (Washington DC: American Psychological Association), 395–411.

Zajonc, R. B. (1965) 'Social Facilitation', *Science*, 149, 269–74.

Zani, A. and Rossi, B. (1991) 'Cognitive Psychophysiology as an Interface Between Cognitive and Sport Psychology', *International Journal of Sport Psychology*, 22, 376–98.

Zhang, J., Jensen, B. E. and Mann, B. L. (1997) 'Modification and Revision of the Leadership for Sport Scale', *Journal of Sport Behavior*, 20, 105–122.

Zimmerman, C., Bisanz, G. L. and Bisanz, J. (1998) 'Everyday Scientific Literacy: Do Students use Information about the Social Contexts and Methods of Research to Evaluate News Briefs about Science?', *Alberta Journal of Educational Research*, 44, 188–207.

Zinsser, N., Bunker, L. and Williams, J. M. (2010) 'Cognitive Techniques for Building Confidence and Enhancing Performance', in J. M. Williams (ed.) *Applied Sport Psychology: Personal Growth to Peak Performance*, 6th edn (New York: McGraw-Hill), 305–35.

Zourbanos, N., Hatzigeorgiadis, A., Chroni, S., Theodorakis, Y. and Papaioannou, A. (2009) 'Automatic Self-talk Questionnaire for Sports (ASTQS): Development and Preliminary Validation of a Measure Identifying the Structure of Athletes' Self-Talk', *The Sport Psychologist*, 23, 233–51.

Zourbanos, N., Hatzigeorgiadis, A., Chroni, S., Theodorakis, Y. and Papaioannou, A. (2010) 'A Multimethod Examination of the Relationship between Coaching Behavior and Athletes' Inherent Self-Talk', *Journal of Sport and Exercise Psychology*, 32, 764–85.

Index

Note: Page numbers followed by *f* and *t* refer to figures and tables, respectively.